"Hewlett-Packard has worked with the authors to ensure technical accuracy and to make sure *LaserJet Unlimited* is one of the best LaserJet printer tools available. This book is a first-rate resource for dealers, users, and trainers alike."

Bill McGlynn
Marketing Manager
Hewlett-Packard
Boise Printer Division

Rave Reviews for LaserJet Unlimited

"Best bet if you're faced with learning to use a LaserJet is to have your department order a copy of *LaserJet Unlimited* from Peachpit Press. Loaded with information about LaserJets and how to use them. I rate it as **one of the six best computer books I've read to date.** I learned more in an hour or so from this book than I had from the LaserJet manuals in several months."

—Ken Fermoyle
Computer Currents columnist

"The book includes an appendix of tips and tricks to make your LaserJet work better and help you fix it when it's out of whack. **HP should consider stealing** this section for the next edition of the LaserJet manual."

—Sharon Fisher
Interact

"Ted Nace and Michael Gardner's *LaserJet Unlimited* is great if you own a Hewlett-Packard LaserJet or LaserJet Plus. It **tells you darned near everything** you can do that HP didn't tell you. It also does much better than HP at warning you of some things you should never do."

—Franklynn Peterson and Judi Turkel
Indianapolis Star

"As people collect cookbooks, so they collect computer books, although the latter are certainly less mouth-watering. They acquire shelves full of titles, some not very useful, others **gold mines of ideas.** Into the latter category falls *LaserJet Unlimited.*"

—Erik Sandberg-Diment
New York Times

"Now that I've read *LaserJet Unlimited*, by Ted Nace and Michael Gardner, I have a much better understanding of how the machine works and how to take advantage of its potential as a publishing tool. The book **demystifies the popular printer** and explains how to take advantage of a wide variety of commercially available type fonts, how to mix text and graphics and how to use the printer with a variety of word processing, database, and spreadsheet programs."

—Lawrence Magid
Los Angeles Times

"If you're interested in digging into the belly of the LaserJet or LaserJet Plus and fooling around with their capabilities, then you should send for a copy of the book *LaserJet Unlimited* by Ted Nace and Michael Gardner. The book not only discusses some of the obscure utilities (many that I had never seen or heard of) but also gives you **real insight into the whole laser scene,** from word processing compatibility to typesetting techniques. It's a big plus for anyone with the HP LaserJet."

—John Dvorak
InfoWorld

"**A fantastic resource** for any laser printer owner."

—Shawn Ralston
PC Publishing

More Raves ...

"A carefully-prepared, well-designed, self-published book **produced by authors with pride in their work**."

—Don Biel
Personal Publishing

"*LaserJet Unlimited* is logical and easy to read. The authors have avoided being too 'techy' yet have included enough information to make the book **useful to anyone who owns a LaserJet printer.**"

—*L.U.G. Letter*

"I have loved my LaserJet printer, but found it hard to use with software other than word processing. Now, **after one hour reading your book, I can *print* my worksheets** from Lotus 123."

—Dotty Whalen
Aerojet General

"A thousand thanks for writing your book *LaserJet Unlimited.* Yours is one of the few books (or manuals) dealing with either hardware or software that is written in simple, easy-to-read English. Each year I produce camera-ready copy for a book of scientific abstracts... This year, it's going to look great (for a change), thanks to some neat ideas I got from you. The $25 or so I spent on it was **the best investment I've made in years**."

—Dr. James V. McConnell
University of Michigan

LaserJet
UNLIMITED

Edition II

Ted Nace and Michael Gardner

CONTRIBUTORS

Joe Beda
Katherine Shelley Pfeiffer, Ph.D.
Daniel Will-Harris

PEACHPIT PRESS
Berkeley, California

LASERJET UNLIMITED, EDITION II
Ted Nace and Michael Gardner

Peachpit Press, Inc.
1085 Keith Avenue
Berkeley, CA 94708
415/527-8555

Portions of this book originally appeared in *Computer Currents, Desktop Publishing, PC World, Personal Publishing,* and *Publish!* magazines.

0 9 8 7 6 5 4 3 2 1
Printed and bound in United States of America
ISBN 0-938151-02-9
HP Part No. 92235U

This book is dedicated to our parents and to the memory of Andrew Fluegelman.

Production Note

THE MANUSCRIPT OF this book was written using Microsoft Word on a PC's Limited 386 computer from Dell Computer (800/426-5150). A monochrome monitor driven by a Hercules-graphics board was used for word processing and for making screen shots, and a Moniterm Viking 1 Portrait Monitor (612/935-4151) was used for page layout. Screen shots were made using Hotshot Graphics from Symsoft (415/962-9500).

The book was laid out using Xerox Ventura Publisher 1.1 (800/822-8221), which was also used to generate tables and charts. The full-page examples of LaserJet applications software were photostated to size and pasted onto the pages using white paper tape.

Master pages were produced on a Hewlett-Packard LaserJet II retrofitted with a JetScript PostScript controller (800/367-4772). The LaserTORQ spooler/accelerator from LaserTools Corp. (415/843-2234) was used to speed up the printing process.

The three-dimensional images were rendered by Angelo Williams, Graphics Production Manager at Enabling Technologies (312/427-0386) using Enabling's Pro 3D software.

At the printer during creation of negatives, the 8.5- by 11-inch master pages were photographically reduced by 18 percent, resulting in the final 7- by 9-inch trim size. The cover was designed with the assistance of Ventura Publisher and produced using traditional graphic arts methods.

Contents

Contributors xxi

Acknowledgements xxii

Foreword by Bill McGlynn xxiii

Preface xxv

PART I – BASICS

1. Getting Acquainted 3

Cables 4, Serial Setup 4, Life Expectancy 6, Care and Feeding 6

2. The LaserJet Family 7

Classic LaserJet 7, LaserJet Plus 7, Features Comparison 8, LaserJet 500 Plus 9, LaserJet series II 9, Memory 13, Looking Ahead 13

3. The LaserJet II Control Panel 15

Two Levels of Commands 15, ON LINE Key 17, CONTINUE Key 17, RESET Key 17, PRINT FONTS Key 17, Control Panel Effects and Procedures 18, TEST Key 21, FORM FEED Key 21, ENTER Key 21, RESET MENU 22, First Menu Level 22, Second Menu Level 22, Auto-Continue 24, Selecting Fonts by Numbers 24, Testing Defaults 26

4. How the LaserJet Thinks 27

Printing with Light 27, Text 28, Bit-Mapped Graphics 29, Object Graphics 30, Characters and Codes 30, Graphics as Text and Text as Graphics 32

5. Using Setup Utilities 33

What You Can Do with a Setup Utility 33, Special Features 34, Downloading Fonts 34, Memory Residency 34, Access Table 35

Profile: E-Z-Set **..39**

Simple Enough to Throw Away the Manual 39, Shortcut 40

Profile: JetSet II **...41**

SetLaser 41, Runoff 41

Profile: LaserControl **....................................43**

Main Menu 43, Setup Options 44, Memory Resident 44, Graphics Printing 44, Screen Shots 45, Operation 45

Profile: Printworks for the PC/Laser **..............47**

Overview 47, Font Management and Page Formatting 48, Merging Images 48, Memo Writer 49, Epson Emulation 49, Power Printing 50, Special Features 50

PART II – WORD PROCESSING

Profile: IBM DisplayWrite **............................53**

DBL Software Drivers 53, DWLaser 53, LaserConnection Driver 53, Polaris RAM-Resident PrintMerge 53, Questions and Answers 54

Profile: Microsoft Word **................................55**

Drawbacks of Word 55, Partial WYSIWYG 56, General Formatting Principle 56, Direct Formatting 56, Using Style Sheets 57, Galley Slave Example 59, Applying Styles to Documents 61, Using Word with LaserJet Fonts 62, DAT File 62, Creating New Drivers 62, Combining Drivers with

MERGEPRD 62, Location of Fonts 62, Table of Word's LaserJet Drivers 63, Downloading with Word 64, Tips 64

Profile: MultiMate Advantage **67**

Older Versions 67, Page Length 67, Printer Action Tables and Character Width Tables 67, Selecting a Font 68, Printing 68, Questions and Answers 68

Profile: WordPerfect **71**

Overview 71, How to Create a Printer File 71, How to Format Fonts within a Document 72, Undoing Font Selections 72, How to Change Leading 72, Adding a Graphic 73, Lines, Boxes, and Tables 75, Previewing the Results 75, Style Sheets 75, Using Fontware 76, Adding Fonts from Other Vendors 76, Questions and Answers 76

Profile: WordStar **79**

LaserJet Support in WordStar 4 79, Assigning Escape Sequences to Print Control Keys 79, WordStar 3.3 80, Utilities 81, Patching WordStar 3.3 81, Margins 83

Profile: WordStar 2000 .... **85**

Familiar but Fast 85, LaserJet Features 86, Precise Spacing 87, Columns 88, Inset 88, Extras 89, Questions and Answers 90

6. Merging Text and Graphics **93**

New Software Options 93

Profile: Inset **95**

Examples 95, Graphic Manipulations 96, Word Processor and Graphics Board Support 96

Profile: PageView **97**

Bugs 98, Lack of Editing Capability 99

***Profile: Polaris RAM-Resident PrintMerge* 101**

Word Processor Compatibility 101, Screen-Capture Utility 101

PART III – GRAPHICS

7. Graphics Fundamentals 105

Paint Versus Draw Programs 105, Memory Requirements 107, The Scanner Connection 108, The PostScript Connection 108

***Profile: AutoSketch* 111**

Unique Capabilities 111, A CAD Not a Draw Program 111, Plotter-Style Characters 113, Sluggish 113

***Profile: GEM Draw Plus* 115**

Runs under GEM 116, Fill Patterns and Shades 116, Six Viewing Sizes 116, Fontware 116, Clip Art 117

***Profile: Halo DPE* 119**

Cryptic Icons 119, Expanded Memory 119, Scanner Support 120

***Profile: PC Paintbrush & Family* 123**

Most Flexible PC Paint Program 123, Windows Version 124, Chart Interpreter 124, Designer Series 124, Publisher's Paintbrush 125

***Profile: SLed* 127**

A Hybrid Program 127, Saving Graphics as Fonts 127, Scanner Support 128, Type Manipulations 128, Reversed Type 128

***Profile: Windows Designer* 129**

Fast Performance 129, Comfortable for Complex Jobs 131, Curve Master 131, Clip Art 132

Profile: Windows Draw **135**

Proportional Resizing 135, Slow 135, Windows Convert 137

8. Clip Art **139**

Paint Versus Draw 139, Access Table 142

Profile: Arts & Letters **145**

Comes with Clip Art 145, Text Manipulation 145, No Freehand 145

Profile: Graphics Gallery **147**

Professional Images and Fancy Capitals 147, Fifteen Fonts 147

9. Graphics Conversion Programs **149**

The Graphics Link 149, HiJaak 149

PART IV – DESKTOP PUBLISHING

10. Desktop Publishing **153**

Magazines 154, Books 154, Newsletters 155, Organizations 156, Bulletin Boards 156, WYSIWYG 157, Preview Mode 157, Style Sheets 157, Ventura or PageMaker? 158, Word Publishing 159, Code-based Programs 159, Selecting a Program 161, Access Table 162

Profile: Xerox Ventura Publisher **169**

What's It Good For? 170, Behind the Magic 170, Frame Job 172, Word Processor Friendly 173, Dressing Up the Type 175, Graphics 175, Drawing Your Own 176, Advanced Pagination and Typography 176, Hardware 177, Using with LaserJet 178, Installing for LaserJet Plus or LaserJet II 179, Using with Upgraded LaserJets 179, Adding New Fonts 180, Changing Printers 181

Profile: PageMaker **..............................183**

Windows: Pro and Con 183, Pasteup Metaphor 183, Importing Text 185, Formatting Text 185, Adding Graphics 185, Special Features 187, LaserJet Notes 187, Soft Font Installer 188

PART V – SPREADSHEETS, DATABASES, AND FORMS

Profile: Lotus 1-2-3 **..............................191**

A Quick Solution 191, Another Quick Solution 192, Strange Gaps 192, Embedded Codes 193, Printing the Last Page 193, How to Build a Setup String 194, Wobbly Spreadsheet Columns 196, Access Box for 1-2-3 Tools 197, JetSet 197, Lotica Font 198, Phoenix Drivers 198, Printing Graphics 198

Profile: dBASE **..............................201**

Installing dBASE IV for the LaserJet 201, LaserJet Escape Sequences 203, A Memory Variable Sample 204, dBASE Output Commands 205, dBASE Reports 206, dBASE and Labels 208, Creating a Label Printing Program 209

11. Form and Tax Preparation Software 215

The Generic Approach 215, Access Table (Forms) 216, On-Screen Entry 218, Merging from a Database 218, Scanning Support 218, WYSIWYG or Coding 220, Tax Software 220, Access Table (Tax) 222, Speedup Techniques 222

Profile: IPrint **..............................225**

Three Modules 225

Profile: Lasersoft/PC **229**

Menu Walk-Through 229

PART VI – FONTS

12. Typographic Background **233**

Font Versus Typeface 233, Classifying Type 233, Serif Versus Sans Serif 234, Families 235, Measurement Units 235, Spacing 235, Monospacing Versus Proportional Spacing 235, Justification 236, Leading 236

13. LaserJet Font Basics **239**

Where Fonts are Stored 239, Resident Fonts 239, Cartridge Fonts 239, Table of Resident Fonts 240, Soft Fonts 241, Character Sets 242, 7-Bit and 8-Bit Sets 242, ASCII 243, Roman-8 Set 243, Roman Extension Set 244, IBM Set 244, Ventura Set 244, Miscellaneous Sets 245, Font Names 245, HP Font Name Format 246, SoftCraft Naming Format 246

14. Font Generators **247**

Fontware 247, Type Director 247, Fonts on the Fly 248

Profile: Fontware **251**

Background 251, Creating a Font 253, Printer 253, Monitor 253, Sizes 256, Character Set 256, Font Storage Requirements 256, Using a Font with Software 258

Profile: Glyphix **259**

Determining Parameters 259, Integrating with Software 261

15. Downloading Fonts and Building Drivers **263**

Which Fonts Must Be Downloaded? 263, Survey of Utilities 264, ID Numbers 266, Permanent/Temporary 267, Batch Files 267, Manual Downloading 267, Access Table 268, Memory Limitations 268

Profile: FontLoad **269**

Automatic Font Listing 270, Batch Files 270

Profile: Laser Fonts **273**

Two Windows 274

16. Screen Fonts **275**

Screen Fonts and DTP 275, Screen Font Software 276

Profile: WYSIfonts! **277**

Generating Screen Fonts 277, Installing Printer Fonts 277

17. Font Editors and Enhancers **279**

All Font Editors Are Not Created Equal 280, Font Enhancers 281, Access Table 282

Profile: Publisher's Type Foundry **283**

Outline Editor 284, Bitmap Editor 284, Gadget Box 285

Profile: Font Effects **287**

Effects Option 287, Modify Option 287, Slow Speed 289

18. Selecting Fonts with PCL **291**

Primary Versus Secondary 291, The Escape Character 292, Two Ways of Selecting 292, The Selection Process 293, The Priority System 293, Building an Escape Code 294, Compressing an Escape Sequence 295, Caution 296

PART VII – SPECIAL TOPICS

19. Programming the LaserJet with PCL 301

Setup Commands and Embedded Commands 301, PCL Categories 303, Job Control 303, Page Control 303, Cursor Positioning 304, Font Selection 305, Font Management 305, Embedding the Escape Character 306, Font Creation 310, Graphics 310, Macros 311, Debugging 311, When in Rome... 312, Telling Your LaserJet Where to Go 313, Graphics: At Play in the Fields of Dots 313, Raster Graphics: Bitmania 316, Two Means to An End 317, Overlay Macros 317

20. Screen Snapshots 321

Text Screens with the LaserJet II 321, Text Screens: LaserJet and LaserJet Plus 322, The Y Cartridge 323, Orbit Font 324, Screen-Capture Software 324, Criteria for Comparing Software 324, Adjusting Parameters 325, Making Screen Shots with WordPerfect 5.0 326, Speed 326, Access Table 327, Memory Requirements 327

***Profile: Hotshot Graphics* 329**

Screen Capture 329, Legalized Graffiti 329, File Conversions 331, Printing Options 331, Hotshot Grab 331

***Profile: GrafPlus* 333**

Display Adapters 333, Adjusting Parameters 334

21. Envelopes 337

Basic Tips 337, Types of Envelopes 337, ASCII File 338, Building the Escape Sequence 338, Printing 339, MultiMate Advantage II 340, Microsoft Word 340, WordPerfect 340, EnvLJ and GrabPlus 341, ERMASoft Laser Envelopes 341, Printworks for Lasers 343, LaserJet Plus 343

22. Label Sheets **345**

Selecting Labels 345, Access Table 346, One at a Time 347, Lower the Tailgate 347, Feeding Sheets Manually 347, The Unprintable Area and Image Position 348, Polaris LabelMaker 349, dBASE 350, VPMail 350

23. Microsoft Windows **351**

Installation 351, Cartridge Fonts 352, Soft Fonts 352

24. Using the LaserJet with the Macintosh **355**

Graphics 355, Text 356, Printworks for the Mac 356, Laserstart 356

25. Using the LaserJet with Other Computers **359**

Convergent Technologies 359, Prime 359, Wang 359, Burroughs 360, Power 360, Z-System 360, CP/M 360, DEC VAX 360, IBM Mainframe 361, NBI 361, IBM DisplayWriter 361, IBM Minicomputer 361

26. LaserJet Shareware Gems **363**

Envelope Printing 364, EnvLJ 364, GrabPlus 364, Text Printing 365, LJBook 365, Pamphlet 365, Access Table 366, 4Print 366

PART VIII – ENHANCEMENTS AND UPGRADES

27. Upgrade Options **371**

PostScript 371, PostScript Clones and Compatibles 372, Non-PostScript Upgrade Boards 372, Access Table 373

Profile: JetScript **375**

Two Printers in One 375, Performance 376, JetSet 377, Fonts 377

Profile: PS Jet Plus 379

Installation 379, Operations 380, Hewlett-Packard Graphics Language 380

Profile: LaserMaster CAPCard 381

Speed Tests 381, Font Generation 383

28. Other Enhancements 385

Paper Feeders 385, Collators 385, Printer-Sharing Devices 386, Buffers and Spoolers 386, Cable Extenders 387, Access Table 388

Profile: LaserTORQ 397

A Spooler with a Twist 398, Help for the Harried 399

PART IX – APPENDICES

A. Answers to Common Questions 403

GENERAL QUESTIONS 403, Emulation 403, Printer Not Printing 404, Creeping Margin 404, Blank Pages 404, Crooked Print Test 405, Manual Feed 405, Paper Sizes 405, Missing Parts Of Document 406, Speed Less Than 8 Pages Per Minute 406, Ordering Supplies 406, Printer Service 406, Feeding Envelopes 406, Benefits of Centronics Parallel Interface 407, Problem with MS-DOS 3.2 Version 407, Switching Interfaces 407, Line Drawing 408, **GRAPHICS** 408, Screen Dump 408, Plotter Emulation 409, Problem With Landscape 409, Image Split Between Pages 409, **FONTS** 409, Cartridge Font Not Working 409, Effect of Continue/Reset 409, Problem Switching to Bold 410, Soft Versus Cartridge Fonts 410, Problem with B Cartridge 410, Compressed Type in Landscape 410, Can't Justify Margin 411, Compressing Courier 411, Maximum Fonts Per Page 411, Envelope Feed 411, **LASERJET 500 PLUS** 412, Accessing Second Paper Tray 412, Job Offset 412, **LASERJET II** 412, Font Selection from Control Panel 412, Resident Fonts 412, Changing Font ID 412, Second Menu Level 413, Changing Default Font 413, Accessing Font by ID 413, **ERROR CODES** 413, Error 40 413, Error 54 413, Error 50 414, **PRINT**

QUALITY 414, Vertical Smear 414, Paper 415, **EP CARTRIDGES** 415, Broken Tape 415, Nothing Printing 415, Extending Toner Life 415, Fading from Left to Right 416, Life Span of Cartridge 416, Shelf Life of Cartridge 416, **SOFTWARE** 416, Languages 417, Inputting Escape Sequence 417, Problem with Escape Sequence 417, Memomaker 417

B. Tips, Tricks, and Troubleshooting 419

COMMON PROBLEMS 419, Nothing Happening 419, Paper Jam 419, Streaks 420, Blanks or Stripes 420, Faint Areas 420, Envelopes Jamming 420, Wrong Page Breaks 420, No First Line 420, Positioning Graphics 421, Mode Commands 421, Blank Pages 421, Word Style Sheets 421, Control Codes Not Working 421, Won't Switch to Bold 422, Printer Freezes 422, Weird Symbols 422, Wrong Line Spacing 422, Landscape 423, Missing Last Page 423, Only a Few Lines Printing 423, Printer Ignores Codes 423, Control Codes Printing 423, **WAYS TO SAVE MONEY AND PRESERVE THE LIFE OF YOUR EQUIPMENT** 423, EP Cartridges 423, Font Cartridges 424, Paper 424, **SIMPLE SOLUTIONS TO COMPLICATED PROBLEMS** 424, Correct Order Output 424, Speed Up Output 425, **CAUTION!** 425, Moving the Printer 425, Font Cartridges 425, Transparencies 425, EP Cartridges 425, Mechanical Switch Boxes 425, **MISCELLANEOUS** 426

C. Font Cartridge Escape Sequences 427

D. Table of PCL Commands 443

Job Control 443, Page Control 443, Cursor Positioning 444, Primary Font Selection 444, Secondary Font Selection 444, Other Font Selection 445, Font Management 445, Font Creation 445, Raster Graphics 445, Rectangle Graphics 445, Macros 446, Programming Aids 446

E. Font Directory 447

F. Product Directory 465

G. Glossary 489

Index 493

Contributors

Joe Beda

A Shareware author himself who spends 8 to 12 hours per week evaluating software made available on bulletin board systems, Joe Beda was the ideal person to write Chapter 26, "LaserJet Shareware." He also compiled Appendix C, "Font Cartridge Escape Sequences." He is the founder of Orbit Enterprises, Inc., which has been working with the HP LaserJet printer family since its introduction in 1985.

Orbit currently publishes two software packages for the HP LaserJet family, E-Z-Set and FormSet, as well as a newsletter (free upon request) on using laser printers. Joe can be contacted at Orbit Enterprises, P.O. Box 2875, Glen Ellyn, IL 60138.

Dr. Katherine Shelly Pfeiffer

An associate professor of art at City College of Los Angeles, Dr. Pfeiffer is also an amateur typographer who last year traded in her letterpress equipment of a LaserJet II and a LaserMaster CAPCard. She quickly made her presence felt in the desktop publishing world, winning First Prize in Xerox Corporation's "Design for Excellence" contest (Miscellaneous Publications category). Currently writing *The LaserJet Font Reference* for Peachpit Press, she used her extensive database of font vendors to prepare Appendix E, "Annotated Font Directory."

Daniel Will-Harris

Daniel Will-Harris wrote "Profile: WordStar 2000" as well as all twelve chapters in Part III, Graphics: Chapter 7, "Graphics Fundamentals" (with Ted Nace); "Profile: AutoSketch"; "Profile: GEM Draw Plus"; "Profile: Halo DPE"; "Profile: PC Paintbrush Family"; "Profile: SLed"; "Profile: Windows Designer"; "Profile: Windows Draw"; Chapter 8, "Clip Art"; "Profile: Diagraph Arts & Letters"; "Profile: HP Graphics Gallery"; and Chapter 9, "Graphics Conversion Programs." A frequent contributor to Personal Publishing and other computer magazines, Daniel is also the author of *Desktop Publishing with Style* (AND Books, 1987). His latest book, *WordPerfect 5: Desktop Publishing in Style*, will be published in September 1988 by Peachpit Press.

Acknowledgements

This book would not have been possible without the assistance of a great many people. While it's not possible to mention everyone who helped, a few people deserve special thanks.

At Hewlett-Packard, Jeri Peterson served as a most capable liaison, and numerous other people encouraged us and shared their technical expertise. We wish to especially thank the staff of the LaserJet Assist Line, who ganged up to check the manuscript for technical accuracy and gave us numerous helpful suggestions.

Also valuable were the letters we received from numerous LaserJet users across the country in response to the first edition, and the articles that appeared in newspapers and magazines. Sometimes readers and reviewers praised the book to the skies, and sometimes they reamed us out for mistakes and omissions. Usually they did both. Thanks in particular to James V. McConnell, Dotty Whalen, John Dvorak, Jim Heid, Robert Wilkins, Don Beil, Larry Magid, Shaun Ralston, Harry Wong, Erik Sandberg-Diment, Ron Mansfield, Luther Sperberg, Franklynn Peterson, Judi Turkel, Ken Fermoyle, Malcolm Rubel, George Haller, Doug Griffith, Fred Cooke, James Hitchcock, and Lana Bryan.

Three LaserJet experts—Joe Beda, Daniel Will-Harris, and Katherine Pfeiffer—agreed to contribute to the book. Although they're credited elsewhere, we want to thank them here simply for being interested in the LaserJet and sharing their enthusiasm. Special thanks to Daniel Will-Harris for writing *Desktop Publishing with Style,* an invaluable resource in preparing this book.

The book was copyedited by Julie Harris. The cover was designed by John Nguyen of Design One. At Peachpit Press, Gregor Clark, Naomi Gardner, and Helen Hampton Nace kept things rolling while we sank out of sight to work on the book.

On a personal note, we also wish to thank Helen Hampton Nace, Naomi Gardner, Ellen Schremp, John Spriggs, Wendy Monroe, Emma Nace, Jasper Patch Nace, and Marian Hampton.

Foreword

by Bill McGlynn
Marketing Manager
Hewlett-Packard Boise Printer Division

The success of any product in the market is dependent upon its acceptance by a public willing to pay a price for its benefits. In 1984, Hewlett-Packard took a gamble and introduced the first desktop laser printer, the HP LaserJet printer. The price was relatively high, the technology new to the market, and laser printer software support virtually nonexistent. Yet the LaserJet printer family has enjoyed unparalleled success.

In many ways, the LaserJet printer's success is a compliment to the early users of the printer, who immediately saw the benefits laser printing brought to the office. People have made the LaserJet printer successful because the LaserJet printer makes them more successful, with better looking reports, memos, spreadsheets, newsletters, correspondence, charts, tables, schematics, manuals, catalogs, forms, tax statements, envelopes, labels, bar codes, overhead presentations, and much, much more. You name it and the LaserJet printer most likely prints it.

But the LaserJet printer doesn't print all these things on its own. A key ingredient in the success of any personal computer product is "third party support." Software and hardware vendors have moved quickly to support the new capabilities of the LaserJet printer and provide easy-to-use solutions for their customers. As a result, the LaserJet printer has become the focal point of a veritable galaxy of software products and hardware accessories.

"HP has worked with the authors to ensure technical accuracy and to make sure LaserJet Unlimited, Edition II is one of the best LaserJet printer tools available."

In this book, Ted Nace and Michael Gardner guide you through that galaxy. They tell you how to select the fonts, utilities, and accessories for your particular needs. In addition, they provide step-by-step instructions on the effective use of the software you currently use with the LaserJet printer. With over 750,000 LaserJet owners, it is extremely important to provide high-quality, thorough, product information. Hewlett-Packard has worked with the authors to ensure technical accuracy and to make sure *LaserJet Unlimited, Edition II* is one of the best LaserJet printer tools available. This book is a first-rate resource for dealers, users, and trainers alike.

"... the last word on the LaserJet printer has yet to be written."

That brings me to a final ingredient in the recipe for the LaserJet's success: education. Everyone involved in the LaserJet phenomenon can benefit from a better understanding of the fundamentals of using type and graphics, in addition to learning the specifics of their particular software. Hewlett-Packard believes that independent guides such as this book complement our own efforts to provide the right educational and technical support tools for LaserJet printer users.

Of course, the last word on the LaserJet printer has yet to be written. In the future, you can expect to see more capabilities in the LaserJet printer family as Hewlett-Packard continues to expand the product line. So, stay tuned for Edition III of *LaserJet Unlimited.*

Preface

The year was 1969, and Gary Starkweather had a thorny assignment. Xerox Corporation, which a decade earlier had introduced the first office copier, wanted to adapt that technology to a new application—printing. The idea was to design a machine that would use a laser beam to "write" a pattern of tiny charged spots on a light-sensitive copier drum, expose this electrostatic image to oppositely charged toner particles, and transfer the image onto paper to produce a printed page.

Such a machine would have many advantages over previous printers. First, it would be extremely fast, since the printed image would be produced by a beam of light rather than by mechanical parts. Second, it would be virtually silent—gone would be the noise of print head striking printing surface. Third, because of the inherent precision of the laser, such a machine could potentially create sharp, high-resolution output.

But to build such a printer, Starkweather and his engineering team had some major hurdles to clear. Lasers had just graduated from the status of laboratory curiosities and were still wildly expensive, as were the other precision components required by the printer. For a laser printer to be feasible—much less, marketable—the cost of modulators, polygonal mirrors, and other components would have to be reduced by a full 98 percent.

By 1977 Starkweather had accomplished this imposing job, and Xerox introduced its 9700 laser printer. Innovative design had lowered costs, and the performance of the 9700 was stunning. The new printer could produce more than 7,000 lines per minute while maintaining the exacting tolerances necessary to create images with 300 dot-per-inch density.

Laser Printing for Personal Computers

The introduction of the Xerox 9700 (priced at a then-reasonable $350,000) fired the starting gun for a new race—mostly among the Japanese electronic giants—to drive the cost of laser printers down and bring laser printing to a mass market.

In 1983, Canon broke ahead of the pack with the debut of the first low-cost laser printer engine. Selling for $1,000 or less in quantity, the Canon LBP-CX engine, built with components adapted from Canon's popular photocopiers, created a market for under-$7,000 laser printers virtually overnight.

The first to take advantage of the new engine was Hewlett-Packard. Recognizing the LBP-CX as a virtuoso piece of engineering, HP added the specifications for the command set that would be built into the LaserJet's controller. Early in 1984 the result of this trans-Pacific alliance—the HP LaserJet—hit the American market.

The introduction of the LaserJet heralded a new era in communications and publishing. For an astonishingly low price, users of personal computers suddenly could produce print with a professional look, without the noisy clatter of pins and daisy wheels.

At first the LaserJet was drafted into service merely as a quieter version of the standard letter-quality printer, but soon resourceful people started recognizing the versatility of laser printing. One of the first groups to spot the special abilities of the LaserJet were users of Lotus 1-2-3. The LaserJet's ability to print small characters in landscape orientation—i.e., sideways down the length of the paper—made it possible to print very wide spreadsheets, and spreadsheet users by the thousands began snapping up LaserJets.

Then came the wordsmiths. Publishers of newsletters, frustrated novelists, technical manual writers, and many others were drawn to the printer's proportional typefaces. The LaserJet offered solutions for many types of users: mathematical symbols for engineers and scientists; logos, forms, and graphics for analysts and others in business; foreign character sets for those writing in languages other than English.

Software

There may be more powerful laser printers than the LaserJet, but no vendor of laser printers can boast anywhere near the user base staked out by HP. By late 1985, market researchers at IMS America reported that 83 of every 100 laser printers sold were LaserJets. Now, many hundreds of thousands of LaserJets later, the LaserJet family is still dominating the market. This benefits not just HP, but everyone who uses the LaserJet. When software developers hear a booming hardware market, they move quickly to supply software products for that hardware, products that generally make the hardware easier to use.

The first wave of LaserJet software comprised small, special-purpose programs known as utilities, which assist other programs with tasks such as switching between fonts. Soon more broadly based utilities were introduced. People learned that there was a control language behind the LaserJet, for example, and so utilities appeared that were sort of pocket-dictionaries of commands.

In the second wave, software companies began adapting their existing programs to support the LaserJet. Such support is necessary because no matter what a printer is theoretically capable of, if your software doesn't support it, you can't use the printer. Today, most popular software packages, including a large number of word processors, spreadsheets, and database managers, support the LaserJet.

In the third wave, increasingly sophisticated software applications developed especially for the LaserJet began to appear. That wave has already delivered programs that can turn out high-resolution graphics and text, and even combinations of the two on the same page—traditionally a tough problem for printers.

The next wave of LaserJet support consists of new types of hardware to spice up the "vanilla" LaserJet. Hardware products designed to work with the early LaserJets include digitizers, sheet feeders, accelerator boards, and printer buffers. HP itself contributed to this wave by replacing the original LaserJet with the LaserJet Plus, which can print larger graphic images, use fonts distributed on floppy disks, and store forms and letterheads within the printer. In 1987 HP upgraded the LaserJet Plus to the LaserJet series II, offering even more hardware enhancements, including a feeder for envelopes in quantity and a much better control panel.

Meanwhile, new users by the tens of thousands keep flocking to laser printing. Many of them aren't ready for the latest integrated desktop publishing package. Just like the people who first hooked up personal computers to LaserJets, most newcomers start with modest objectives—like printing a wide spreadsheet or a nice-looking memo—and only later begin exploring the LaserJet's other capabilities.

LaserJet Unlimited—A Helping Hand

This book is intended to help all of you: the experts, the beginning LaserJet users, and curious onlookers thinking about buying a laser printer. Since everyone's interests and needs are different, we organized it cookbook fashion, so that you can find the information you need and skip the rest.

Part 1, "Basics," deals with the fundamentals of the LaserJet—the machine itself, its various incarnations, its basic operation, and an introduction to using the LaserJet II. Part 2, "Word Processing," focuses on document processing. Part 3, "Graphics," is about software that lets you create business graphics and commercial illustrations. Part 4, "Desktop Publishing," covers perhaps the most well known of a laser printer's uses: as a kind of all-in-one graphic arts center. Part 5, "Spreadsheets, Databases, and Forms," provides tips on using the LaserJet with dBASE, Lotus 1-2-3, form generation programs, and tax preparation software. Part 6, "Fonts," offers an introduction to the various kinds of fonts, tells you how to use and manage them, and even discusses how to design your own fonts. Part 7, "Special Topics," covers many diverse subjects, including how to talk to the LaserJet in its own language; how to print screen shots, envelopes, or labels; how to use the LaserJet with a Macintosh. Part 8, "Enhancements and Upgrades," provides information on several avenues for increasing the speed of the LaserJet or equipping it with the PostScript page description language. The appendices include information on common problems encountered by LaserJet users with tips and troubleshooting suggestions, a product directory, a list of escape sequences for font cartridges, a directory of fonts, and a glossary.

A Disclaimer

Although this book includes instructions on using the LaserJet with numerous programs, we cannot guarantee that any of the software products discussed here will perform as their vendors claim. Moreover, due to the complexity of the information contained here and because of the continuing evolution of software and hardware products, we must caution you that errors may exist in this book. We expressly disclaim any liability in connection with any of the products or techniques mentioned in this book and in connection with the instructions we provide for using those products or techniques. It is your responsibility to determine whether a product is suitable for your needs and to verify with the vendor the accuracy of all product information, including that provided in this book, before making a purchase.

New Applications

We practice what we preach, and the first edition of *LaserJet Unlimited*, issued in 1986, was one of the first desktop published books ever. Now, a few years later, there are more LaserJet-compatible hardware and software products than ever. We've done the best we can to make sure the second edition covers all these thoroughly. Fonts, for example, have gone through a major transformation, and you'll find a good deal of this book devoted to them. We are also proud to be able to cover new releases of almost all the major software products. Our look is different too; not only are there more pages (544 instead of 212), but we've improved the design as well, incorporating some of the latest ideas in desktop layout.

Creating the masters for a book with a laser printer is obviously faster, cheaper, and more convenient than using traditional typesetting. And it has one additional advantage: flexibility. With the tools we've assembled, we can put together new revisions literally in a matter of weeks.

We intend to take advantage of this flexibility to keep the book up to date, and for that reason we're asking for your help. LaserJet user groups are not common, but they should be, because the LaserJet is only as useful as our knowledge of how to put it to use. We hope this book will be a catalyst for more exchange of information among LaserJet users.

Ted Nace and Michael Gardner
Berkeley, California
July 1988

1

BASICS

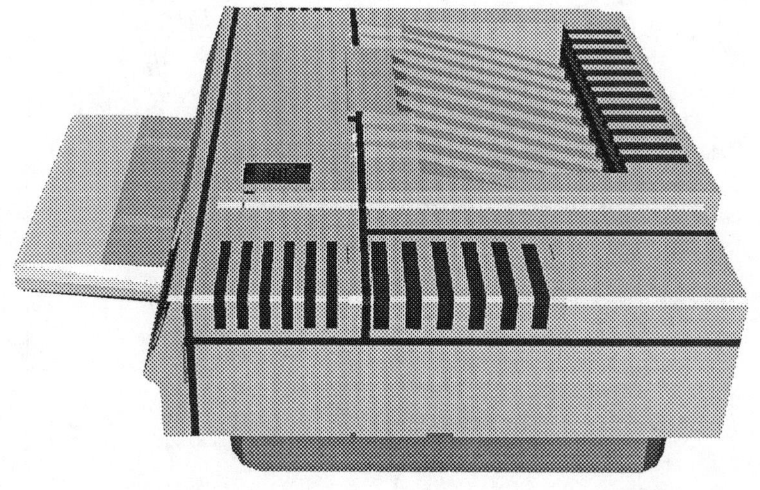

Section Focus

Hewlett-Packard's introduction of the LaserJet in 1984 was a breakthrough that has led to a transformation in the way people and businesses create their documents. This section starts with an overview of that transformation: the history, the technology, the machines, and the capabilities.

Next, it moves into some important hands-on information for getting started with your laser: how to operate the LaserJet II Control Panel and how to make use of "setup utilities," programs specifically designed to configure your printer for other software products.

CHAPTER ONE

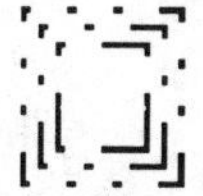

Getting Acquainted

THIS BOOK IS about the possibilities that arise out of a new combination of technologies: the personal computer and the 300-dot-per-inch laser printer. Although most people still use the LaserJet merely as a faster and quieter substitute for a daisy wheel or dot matrix printer, our thesis is that laser printing technology is capable of much more. With the right software, a LaserJet can produce typesetter-style fonts, crisp graphics, decorative type, foreign language characters, bar codes, mathematical symbols, forms, logos, digitized pictures, even musical notation. But to extract the full potential of the LaserJet, you need to become aware of the diversity of products being made available by software and hardware developers and to understand the LaserJet itself well enough to use them effectively.

First Steps

Let's begin by surveying the items you need for laser printing. First, there's the LaserJet itself, which can be described in a nutshell as a modified photocopying machine plus a built-in laser and an on-board computer to guide the laser.

Before we get involved any further with this bundle of rollers, lasers, and circuitry, we'd like to briefly pay some respects to another piece of finely engineered machinery: YOUR BACK. The LaserJet makes a nice armful, but if you're not paying attention it can also leave you with a nifty injury. At 50 pounds, the LaserJet II is a nice improvement over the 71-pound LaserJet Plus, but it's still advisable to be careful when you move the printer. Take some time to think before you just lean over a table and try to snatch it up. Better yet, go find somebody and lift it together.

This printer is sturdy and asks for little in the way of physical amenities: just a level surface, a few inches of clear space on each side to keep it ventilated, and reasonable levels of temperature and humidity.

Besides the printer itself, you need a cable to attach printer to computer, a supply of paper, and an EP cartridge. In addition, you may want extras such as font cartridges, soft fonts, a printer sharing device, additional memory, a paper feeder, a print spooler, etc.

A manual is essential for properly setting up and using the printer, as this book is not intended to replace HP's manuals. If you've lost your manual or want to replace your old one with the new versions, you should be able to obtain them through any HP dealer. For the LaserJet series II there are two volumes, the *LaserJet series II User's Manual* (part number 33440-90901), and *Getting Started with the LaserJet series II* (part number 33440-90908). Another excellent reference is the *LaserJet series II Technical Reference Manual*, intended for the more technically inclined among us (Part Number 33440-90905). If you own an earlier model LaserJet, such as the LaserJet Plus, you'll want the earlier manuals, the *Laser Printer Operator's Manual* (part number 02686-90914), and the *Technical Reference Manual* (Part Number 02686-90915).

Cabling Up

To be able to send information from the computer to the LaserJet, you need to set up the proper avenue of communication. With the LaserJet Plus or LaserJet II, you have the option of using a serial (RS-232C or RS-422) or a parallel (also known as a Centronics) cable. Go with parallel unless you have a special reason to use serial communications. Parallel transmission is much faster as well as easier to set up. You merely connect up one end of the parallel cable to one of the LPT ports on your computer and the other end to the printer, and change the configuration (with the LaserJet or LaserJet Plus, this requires changing dip switches; with the LaserJet II you can do it from the Control Panel). The parallel cable sold by HP for the LaserJet II is HP part number 24542D.

Serial Setup

All in all, it's much easier connecting your computer to your LaserJet using a parallel cable. But the original LaserJet (sometimes now called the "classic" LaserJet) supported only a serial interface. If you plan to use a serial cable with your LaserJet for this or any other reason, your computer must have a serial port, also known as an asynchronous communications adapter.

The most commonly used serial cable is a male-to-female "special"

RS232C, sold by Hewlett-Packard under part number 24542G. Note that some serial cables have a female connector at the printer end and a male connector at the computer end. When you attempt to connect the cable, you may find that your serial port is also a male connector or has a different number of pins than the cable. To remedy such mismatches you need a female-to-male converter and/or a 25-to-9 pin converter. Both types of converters are available at most computer stores.

Some computers have two serial ports. On an IBM PC these are generally assigned the names COM1: and COM2:. If the computer is unable to communicate with the printer, it may be that the cable is attached to the wrong serial port of the computer.

In addition to connecting the cable to the serial port, the computer port itself must be properly configured so that data moves through the cable at 9,600 baud, with no parity, 8 data bits, and 1 stop bit. In English, that means you want data transferred to your printer at the rate of 9,600 bits (approximately equal to 1,200 characters) per second. You can tell this to your PC using the MODE command of DOS. From the DOS prompt, type

MODE COM1:9600,n,8,1,p

Most MS-DOS computers do not as a default print via the serial port, so you must also redirect printer output to there from the normal printer port. You can accomplish this by typing the following command from the DOS prompt:

MODE LPT1:=COM1:

It's easiest to embed both these commands in a batch file so that you don't have to type them each time. You can use your word processor if it can produce unformatted ASCII files, or you can use the COPY CON: command of DOS to type them in from your keyboard. From the DOS prompt, type

COPY CON: LASER.BAT *Enter*

Once you've pressed the Enter key, you will be in the primitive built-in text editor of DOS, and any characters you type will be written to a file called LASER.BAT. The only hitch is that you can't move back up in the file to edit a prior line. You can, however, move back along the line you're on, so don't press Enter at the end of a line to move to the next until you've checked it for accuracy. Now type

MODE COM1:9600,0,8,1 *Enter*

MODE LPT1:=COM1: *Enter*

Ctrl-Z

Ctrl-Z means to hold the control key down while simultaneously pressing the Z. DOS will then save your new file. You can proofread it by entering the command:

```
TYPE LASER.BAT
```

Now when you need to configure your computer for serial communications with the LaserJet, you need only type the following command from the DOS prompt:

```
LASER.BAT
```

If you want to get really lazy, you'll put these two MODE commands into your AUTOEXEC.BAT file, so that they will be automatically executed whenever your computer boots. Since COPY CON: cannot edit an existing file, but instead overwrites any existing file with the same name as the one you give it, don't use COPY CON: to put the commands into the AUTOEXEC.BAT unless you are prepared to type in all the old commands from your previous AUTOEXEC.BAT.

Life Expectancy

The Canon LBP-CX engine used in the original LaserJet and the LaserJet Plus is a sturdy, reliable piece of machinery. So is the LBP-SX engine used in the LaserJet II. It's too early to draw any definite conclusions about the ultimate life expectancy of printers with the LBP-SX engine, but the repair record of printers with the LBP-CX engine is excellent. That engine was rated at 100,000 copies or 5 years, whichever comes first. That rating didn't mean it was expected to be useless after that point, but merely that it might no longer meet other specifications, such as the expected failure rate (defined as a breakdown that requires a service call) of once per 30,000 copies.

One reason the LaserJet is such a reliable machine is the design of the Canon engine. The parts that tend to run out or wear out—toner, developer, drum, and light receptor—are all contained in the EP cartridge, rated at 3,000 copies for the LaserJet and LaserJet Plus, and at 4,0000 copies for the LaserJet II. When you put a new cartridge into the machine, you're in effect overhauling the printer.

Care and Feeding

The most important thing you can do to maximize the life of your LaserJet is to keep it clean. According to repair technicians, complete breakdowns of LaserJets are rare. But when a printer is brought in for service, it's generally the result of an accumulation of dust or toner.

To avoid a toner spill, remove the toner cartridge when you move the printer. While you're moving the printer, keep the toner in a box so that it's not exposed to light.

One more tip: avoid leaving the printer in your car for a long time. The fumes can damage the surface of the drum inside the EP cartridge.

CHAPTER TWO

The LaserJet Family

AS OF THIS writing, there are five printers in the LaserJet family: the original LaserJet (sometimes called the "classic LaserJet") the LaserJet Plus, the LaserJet 500 Plus, the LaserJet series II, and the LaserJet 2000. Throughout this book, when we speak generically about the LaserJet, you can presume we mean the LaserJet family, and that we are describing a feature common to all the printers. When we describe a feature that may be found only in one or more models, we will make it obvious and will state which models support the feature.

Classic LaserJet

The first "personal" laser printer (and the child prodigy that started the whole laser printer revolution) was the original LaserJet, which Hewlett-Packard introduced in 1984. Characterized by ROM-based font cartridges, a serial interface, and 128K bytes of RAM, the basic LaserJet gave many people their first taste of what desktop publishing was all about. However, users soon clamored for improvements in data transfer speed, for more and larger fonts, and for more RAM. These and other requests were addressed by the LaserJet Plus, in 1985.

LaserJet Plus

On the outside, the Plus looked almost identical to the LaserJet, except for a new reset switch and light. Under the cover, however, was a beefed-up controller board featuring 512K of memory (expandable with an optional kit to 2 megabytes), a big improvement over the LaserJet's 128K.

The Plus also boasted a new parallel port that made setup somewhat easier and allowed faster data transfer. Unlike the LaserJet, which had to be

Features Comparison

Feature	LaserJet	LaserJet Plus	LaserJet II
Engine	Canon LBP-CX	Canon LBP-CX	Canon LBP-SX
Weight	71 lbs	71 lbs	50 lbs
Basic memory	128K	512K	512K
Memory upgrades	None	2MB - $2500	1MB - $495
			2MB - $995
			4MB $1995
Correct order output	no	no	yes
Quality of solid areas	dark grey	dark grey	black
Adjustable toner intensity	yes	yes	yes
Envelope feed	manual	manual	manual or automatic
Manual feed	from back	from back	from front
Font cartridge bays	1	1	2
Input paper tray	100 sheets	100 sheets	200 sheets
Output paper tray	20 sheets	20 sheets	100 sheets
Ports	serial	serial & parallel	serial & parallel
Status panel	2-character LED	2-character LED	15-character LED
EP cartridge rating	3,000 pages	3,000 pages	4,000 pages

Figure 1: Features comparison of the successive stages in the evolution of the LaserJet family of printers.

shut off to reset, the Plus could be reset by holding down a button on its front panel.

With its heftier memory, the Plus was able to print 300-by-300 dot-per-inch (dpi) graphics on a third of a standard letter-size page, versus the meager 5.4 square-inch image possible with the LaserJet. An entire page of graphics at 150-by-150 dpi was standard for the Plus, twice the full-page resolution of the LaserJet. Not only could the Plus print larger images at 300 dpi, it also supported several new commands for creating patterns, shades of gray, and solid rectangular shapes.

In addition to being useful for graphics, the printer's fortified memory gave it the muscle to handle "soft fonts," fonts from floppy disks. With soft fonts, users had much greater flexibility in font selection than was possible with the LaserJet's plug-in cartridges.

Finally, with the release of the LaserJet Plus, a new feature called macro capability was added to Printer Command Language. Macros allow you to save long sequences of printer codes under a single abbreviated command. A typical application of the macro capability might be to store a letterhead or a form as a macro and then print it out with a brief command. (For more information on macros, see Chapter 19, "Programming the LaserJet with PCL.")

In general, the LaserJet Plus proved to be a flexible machine with plenty of power, but there was still room for improvement in the areas of paper handling, memory expandability, and font sizes (the Plus was limited to 30-point type).

LaserJet 500 Plus

One of the main shortcomings of the LaserJet and the LaserJet Plus was the size of the paper bin and the fact that only one type of paper could be automatically fed into the printer at a time. To correct that deficiency, HP followed the LaserJet Plus with the LaserJet 500 Plus, which was virtually identical except that it had two paper trays.

One tray might be used for legal-size paper and the other for letter-size paper. Alternatively, one tray might hold company letterhead and the other tray plain paper. Accessing the two trays required using software that incorporated the correct tray selection commands.

LaserJet series II

Although the classic LaserJet, the LaserJet Plus, and the LaserJet 500 Plus had all been well received, other laser printer manufacturers had begun to offer increased competition by the end of 1986. HP's response was the LaserJet series II, introduced in early 1987. (At the same time, HP also in-

Figure 2: The LaserJet series II printer.

troduced the LaserJet 2000, which, although it is technically a LaserJet and supports the LaserJet's Printer Command Language, is actually a large departmental laser printer and as such is not covered in detail in this book.) Not only was the LaserJet II a dramatic improvement over the LaserJet Plus in features and print quality, it was also priced at about $1,000 less than the Plus.

The response to the LaserJet II was nothing short of phenomenal. Not only did the success of the new model quickly eclipse that of the previous versions of the LaserJet, it also wiped out any serious competition to HP's dominance in the office laser printer market. Henceforth, HP's Printer Command Language would be generally accepted as a de facto standard for laser printing, and any company attempting to sell laser printers in the corporate market would have to do so on HP's terms, conforming to the PCL standard.

Canon LBP-SX engine: While earlier members of the LaserJet family used the Canon LBP-CX engine, the LaserJet II uses the newer LBP-SX engine, which is faster and slightly quieter than the LBP-CX, features higher print quality, has improved paper handling, and is more compact.

Smaller size: The superiority of the LBP-SX is noticeable from the moment you lift the printer out of the box. Because it is a more compact engine, the LBP-SX allows the LaserJet II to be smaller than earlier models: about 3 inches shorter and 20 pounds lighter than the original LaserJet.

Longer-lasting toner: As with the previous model, the LBP-SX's replaceable EP cartridge houses the toner, developer, and photosensitive drum in one unit. Due to a new minimum life span of 4,000 rather than 3,000 pages, you'll have to replace that cartridge 25 percent less often.

Speedup: When you turn on the LaserJet II, you'll notice another improvement: faster warmup speed. Self-test and warmup take slightly under 30 seconds, compared with about 75 seconds for the LaserJet Plus.

Blacker blacks: Next on the list of improvements is print quality. As with previous models, letters are crisp but now solid areas of black are really black—a nice improvement over the streaks, patches, and lackluster grays sometimes produced by previous models.

Paper handling: Error-free printing is more likely, thanks to the Series II's improved paper handling. Previous LaserJets couldn't hold more than about 30 printed sheets without threatening to jam the printer or spill sheets onto the floor, forcing you to hover nearby during long jobs. The Series II's output tray capacity is rated at 100 sheets, but it actually accepts about 180 sheets of 16- to 35-pound stock, which approximates the rated capacity of the input tray. And if you've ever had to collate a stack of LaserJet output by hand, you'll be happy to learn that the LaserJet II ejects pages face down, so the pages of documents end up in the right order.

Paper feeding is nearly as convenient as paper delivery. Switching from manual to automatic feed used to require a special command; now, when printing a multipage business letter, you can feed a sheet of letterhead manually and let the subsequent pages feed automatically from the input tray.

In addition, a new alternate paper delivery tray on the back of the machine is specially designed to receive bond exceeding the primary tray's 35-pound maximum rating. Envelope feeding is also much easier. A new adjustable slot atop the input tray replaces old LaserJets' envelope feeding mechanism, which was inconveniently located at the rear of the machine. Another limitation on older models was that you could feed only one envelope at a time; the LaserJet II offers a new optional stacked feeder for printing envelopes in quantity.

Fonts: The improvements in the LaserJet II's font-handling capabilities start with an increase in the number of resident fonts. Now 12-point Courier, 12-point Courier Bold, and 8.5-point Line Printer Condensed are all built into the printer in both portrait and landscape orientations and in 23 different symbol sets, including IBM, Roman-8, and many international sets. The IBM character sets are particularly useful because they make screen shots from an IBM-compatible PC very simple.

As for font cartridges, two slots are now provided, and selection of fonts can be done from the Control Panel.

A final improvement in the font department is that there is no longer any limitation to the size of a downloadable font. This feature beats both the original LaserJet, which had a maximum font size of 14.4 points, and the Laserjet Plus, which was limited to fonts that were 30 points or smaller.

Since you can use two cartridges simultaneously and select fonts from built-in or software sources via the keypad, you can create a medley of typefaces on each page.

Memory: Like the LaserJet Plus, the Series II comes with only 512K of RAM, but HP has made the upgrade path much less painful. For less than $500 you can upgrade the LaserJet II to 1.5MB. That's enough memory to accommodate a full page of 300-dpi graphics and a few soft fonts besides. Alternative expansion packs to of 2MB and 4MB are available. A major drawback of these memory boards, however, is that none of them can be expanded. Thus, if you originally upgraded to 1.5MB and then decide you'd rather have 2.5MB, you have to replace the entire board rather than just adding more chips.

Subtle improvements: There are many small but noticeable improvements that give evidence of the LaserJet II's superior design. For example, when you use the LaserJet II for extended periods, you will hear it vent a brief whirring noise every 30 minutes or so. This is the sound of the main motor rotating an inner part, the fuser roller, so that the heat on it is distributed evenly over time, and it lasts longer.

Control Panel: Improved paper handling meshes well with another major improvement: a functional keypad and display on the printer's front panel. The basic LaserJet and LaserJet Plus's hardware command facilities were rudimentary, offering a two-character display and a few simple controls for executing a form feed, taking the printer on and off line, and so on. When using a program that didn't fully support the LaserJet, you had to send command codes to the printer to select fonts or the default page size.

The LaserJet II features a 16-character light emitting diode (LED) display and three extremely useful keys. The Menu key, along with the new plus and minus keys, enables you to cycle through menu selections in the display. You can toggle manual feed on and off, set the number of copies to be printed, choose the font source and a font, set the page length, toggle the interface between serial and parallel, choose from the many available symbol sets, and perform other common tasks.

Of course, you can still use software commands to control the printer, as well. But the Control Panel is much simpler.

Compatibility: The real power of the LaserJet family lies in the more than 500 third-party products that support it, from soft font packages to desktop publishing programs. It was thus mandatory that the Series II be compatible with previous models. Our tests on dozens of software products have convinced us that virtually any program, driver, or font that worked with the LaserJet Plus will function equally well on the LaserJet II.

Memory

Users of all models should be aware of some general rules of thumb about memory requirements. If you're doing general word processing, reports, or spreadsheets using the internal fonts or a few fonts accessed from a font cartridge, and no bitmapped graphics, you'll probably find the 512K RAM which is standard on the LaserJet II and LaserJet Plus to be sufficient. If you're printing a medium amount of bit-mapped graphics (up to a full page of 300x300 dot per inch graphics) and using a few downloaded soft fonts, you'll need the 2 MB LaserJet II memory upgrade, or equivalent. If you plan to use every soft font in the book, or you want to print full-page graphics while keeping more than a minimum number of soft fonts or overlay macros in memory, you need the 4MB LaserJet II option. You will probably also want this configuration if you are using the LaserJet with a print spooler on a network.

For more information on adding memory, PostScript capability, or other enhancements, see Chapter 27, "Upgrade Options," and Chapter 28, "Other Enhancements."

Looking Ahead

The best way to think about the LaserJet family is as a platform for the future. You can use it now in all kinds of ways, but the "iron" is there for the future, as well. The LaserJet II in particular was designed for easy upgrading, and several sorts of upgrades are now available. Some examples of recent and upcoming developments:

- Several companies have introduced accelerator boards for the LaserJet, of which the most notable is the LaserMaster CAPCard. (See Chapter 27, "Upgrade Options," and "Profile: LaserMaster CAPCard.")
- When installed with the JetScript board available from Hewlett-Packard, the LaserJet II even now supports PostScript, the industry-standard page description language widely used for intensive graphics and typesetting applications. (See "Profile: JetScript.")
- Alternatives to PostScript are also coming onto the market, such as Imagen's PC Publisher Kit, which provides both the DDL language and PostScript compatibility.
- Hewlett-Packard has licensed Intellifont, a scalable font technology, from Compugraphic Corporation and has announced that it is investigating extensions to the LaserJet's Printer Command Language. Compugraphic has also announced that it is developing a phototypesetting machine that uses Printer Command Language.

CHAPTER THREE

The LaserJet II Control Panel

ALTHOUGH THE LASERJET II is one of the most capable printers around, it hides its sophisticated powers behind a very simple-looking Control Panel and 16-character LED display (see the figure on the next page). Some of the touch-sensitive pads on the Control Panel duplicate functions found on previous LaserJet models; five of the keys are completely new, however. Using them properly, you can print samples of the available fonts, toggle manual feed on and off, set the number of copies to be printed, choose the font source and a font, set the page length, choose from the many available symbol sets, and perform other common tasks.

You can also accomplish all this using PCL software instructions called escape sequences, which were your only choice on previous LaserJet models. (Escape sequences are described in detail in Chapter 19, "Programming the LaserJet with PCL.") Software instructions have their uses, but are sometimes inconvenient. If you are in the middle of your favorite word processor, for example, it may be awkward to send to the LaserJet the particular escape sequences that cause it to switch into Landscape mode. The option to control the printer using a hardware interface is one of the major benefits of the LaserJet II.

Two Levels of Commands

The six keys across the bottom of the Control Panel are a little confusing to use at first, because they represent two levels of operation. The white labels indicate the first level; the yellow keys indicate the second level. Throughout this chapter, we will refer to a two-label key by the one label we're discussing at that time. For example, we'll call the CONTINUE/RESET key CONTINUE when we are discussing the continue operation, and

The Control Panel

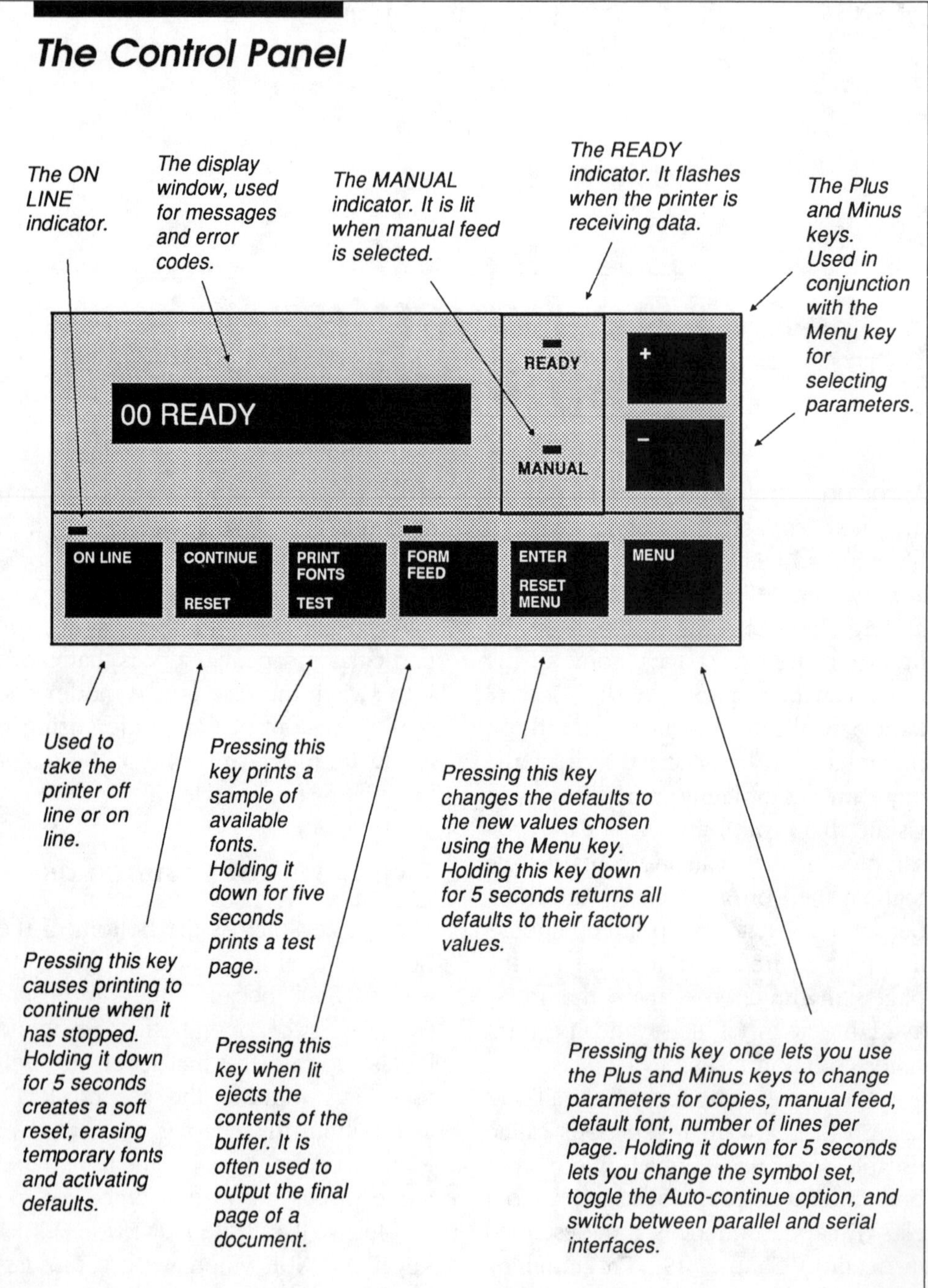

The ON LINE indicator.
The display window, used for messages and error codes.
The MANUAL indicator. It is lit when manual feed is selected.
The READY indicator. It flashes when the printer is receiving data.
The Plus and Minus keys. Used in conjunction with the Menu key for selecting parameters.
READY
+
00 READY
–
MANUAL
ON LINE
CONTINUE
RESET
PRINT
FONTS
TEST
FORM
FEED
ENTER
RESET
MENU
MENU
Used to take the printer off line or on line.
Pressing this key prints a sample of available fonts. Holding it down for five seconds prints a test page.
Pressing this key changes the defaults to the new values chosen using the Menu key. Holding this key down for 5 seconds returns all defaults to their factory values.
Pressing this key causes printing to continue when it has stopped. Holding it down for 5 seconds creates a soft reset, erasing temporary fonts and activating defaults.
Pressing this key when lit ejects the contents of the buffer. It is often used to output the final page of a document.
Pressing this key once lets you use the Plus and Minus keys to change parameters for copies, manual feed, default font, number of lines per page. Holding it down for 5 seconds lets you change the symbol set, toggle the Auto-continue option, and switch between parallel and serial interfaces.

RESET when we're discussing resetting the printer.

ON LINE

The key at the far left of the Control Panel is the ON LINE key; there is also a small amber light above it. When the amber light is on, the printer is "on line," or ready to receive information from the computer. When you press the ON LINE key once, the light goes out; the printer is now "off line," or not ready to accept information from the computer. Pressing the ON LINE key once more will put the LaserJet back on line, and the amber light should go on again. Most hardware control operations require you to take the printer off line using this key, so that the printer knows it does not have to wait for a signal from the computer.

Tip: EEPROMs

The LaserJet uses EEPROMs (Electronically Erasable Programmable Read Only Memory chips) to save default parameter values. Like RAM memory, EEPROMs can be altered. But like ROM memory, the contents of EEPROMs are not erased when the power goes off.

CONTINUE

To the right of the ON LINE key is the CONTINUE key. This key can be used in certain situations to tell the LaserJet that you're ready to go back to printing mode. For example, if you take the LaserJet off line by pressing the ON LINE key so the light goes out, then press CONTINUE, the LaserJet will automatically go back on line.

RESET

Taking the printer off line and then holding down the RESET key for 2 to 5 seconds (until 07 RESET appears on the display), performs a "soft reset." This is similar to what happens on your computer when you press Ctrl-Alt-Del. Alternatively, it can be thought of as roughly equivalent to turning the printer off and on, except that permanent fonts and permanent macros are not wiped out.

PRINT FONTS

Pressing this key causes the LaserJet to print a list of available fonts. The listing includes fonts from any font cartridges you may be using, as well as the internal (also called resident) fonts that every LaserJet II contains. These internal fonts include 12-point Courier, 12-point Courier bold, and 8.5-point Line Printer, each in portrait and landscape orientations and in 4 basic symbol sets and 23 ISO (Inter-

Control Panel Effects and Procedures

Effect	Procedure
Set the printer on line (makes the printer ready to receive data).	If the light above the ON LINE key is not on, press the ON LINE key.
Set the printer off line (stops the printer from receiving data).	If the light above the ON LINE key is on, press the ON LINE key.
Clear away errors and return the printer on line (overrides manual feed and paper size requests).	Press the CONTINUE key.
Soft reset (clears away temporary soft fonts, temporary macros, and stored data, but not permanent soft fonts or permanent macros).	Hold the CONTINUE/RESET key for 2 to 5 seconds.
Print out a font sample (tells what fonts are currently available, including resident, downloaded, and cartridge fonts).	Press the PRINT FONTS key.
Print a test page (shows how many pages the printer has produced in its life, the defaults, the date of the printer's ROM, the amount of installed memory, the current symbol set, the default parameters, and the alignment of the page).	If the light above the ON LINE key is on, press the ON LINE key once. Press the PRINT FONTS / TEST key and and hold just until 05 SELF TEST is displayed.

Effect	Procedure
Print the contents of the page buffer (prints the last partial page remaining in the printer).	If the light above the ON LINE key is on, press the ON LINE key once. Press the FORM FEED key when lit.
Change the number of copies.	If the light above the ON LINE key is on, press the ON LINE key. Press the MENU key to display COPIES=01. Press the Plus key or the Minus key to change the number of copies. Press the ENTER key to save the selection (an asterisk will appear). Hold down the CONTINUE/RESET key until 07 RESET is displayed.
Turn manual feed off or on (turn off to feed envelopes and non-standard-size paper into the printer by hand; turn back on to reactivate automatic paper feed).	If the light above the ON LINE key is on, press the ON LINE key. Press the MENU key twice to display MANUAL FEED=OFF (or MANUAL FEED=ON). Press the Plus key to change to MANUAL FEED=ON (or MANUAL FEED=OFF). Press the ENTER key to save the selection. Hold down the CONTINUE/RESET key until 07 RESET is displayed.
Change the default font.	Before starting this procedure, you'll need to find out the ID number of the font you wish to make the default. You can find this out by printing a font sample page (see elsewhere on this chart). If the light above the ON LINE key is on, press the ON LINE key. Press the MENU key three times to display FONT SOURCE= I, L, R, or S (I is internal, L is left cartridge, R is right cartridge, S is downloaded soft fonts). Press the Plus key to change to the location of the new default font. Press the ENTER key once. Then press the MENU key once again. The display will now read FONT NUMBER=00 (assuming 00 is the ID number of the current default font). Press the Plus key until the new ID number is displayed. Press the ENTER key to save the selection. Hold down the CONTINUE/RESET key until 07 RESET is displayed.

Effect	Procedure
Change the number of lines printed on each page.	If the light above the ON LINE key is on, press the ON LINE key. Press the MENU key five times to display FORM=060 LINES. Press the Plus or the Minus key until the desired number is displayed. Press the ENTER key to save the selection. Hold down the CONTINUE/RESET key until 07 RESET is displayed.
Change the default symbol set.	If the light above the ON LINE key is on, press the ON LINE key. Hold down the MENU key for about 5 seconds until SYM SET= is displayed. Press the Plus key until the desired symbol set is displayed. Press the ENTER key to save the selection.
Turn Auto-Continue off or on. (When Auto-Continue is on, pages will continue to print even if an error is encountered. When Auto-Continue is off, pages will stop printing until you press the CONTINUE key.)	If the light above the ON LINE key is on, press the ON LINE key. Hold down the MENU key for about 5 seconds until SYM SET= is displayed. Press the MENU key once to display AUTOCONT=OFF. Press the Plus key to display AUTOCONT=ON. Press ENTER to save the selection.
Change the interface from serial to parallel or from parallel to serial.	If the light above the ON LINE key is on, press the ON LINE key. Hold down the MENU key for about 5 seconds until SYM SET= is displayed. Press the MENU key twice to display I/O=PARALLEL. Press the Plus key to display I/O=SERIAL. Press ENTER to save the selection.

national Standards Organization) symbol sets for foreign languages. If this choice of fonts isn't enough and you are downloading soft fonts from your computer to the LaserJet, the printed font listing will also show any soft fonts that have been downloaded and designated as "permanent," to reside in memory until the LaserJet's power is switched off.

TEST

If you take the LaserJet off line and then hold down the PRINT FONTS/TEST key for about 5 seconds, the display will read 04 SELF TEST. At this point you can release the key and wait for the LaserJet to perform a test on itself and print out the results. Beware: if you hold down the key too long, you'll get many copies of the test. To stop them from emerging from the printer, press ON LINE.

FORM FEED

Like the ON LINE key, the FORM FEED key has an amber light above it. This light goes on when there is any information in the LaserJet's memory buffer. The LaserJet will not actually print and eject the information until one of the following happens:

- Enough additional information is sent to the printer to compose a full page. Whenever the buffer holds a full page, the LaserJet automatically prints it and clears the buffer.
- The LaserJet is sent a software command to print whatever is held in the buffer.
- You take the printer off line and press the FORM FEED key. This third way of clearing the memory buffer of data can be used to force the LaserJet to print a partial page that's been sent to it. After using the FORM FEED key, be sure to remember to press the ON LINE key again to put the LaserJet back on line, so it is ready to receive more information from your computer.

> ### *Tip: The Asterisk*
>
> *An asterisk (*) next to a selection on the Control Panel indicates that this is the current value for the parameter.*

ENTER

The ENTER key is used in conjunction with the MENU key to change internal LaserJet parameters. The whole procedure is described below under MENU LEVEL 1 and MENU LEVEL 2 below.

RESET MENU

The purpose of this key is to reset all parameters to their factory default settings. It's much easier to accomplish this with one keystroke than it would be by going to every menu option and entering your choices. To use it, get the printer to the READY state, and off line. The quickest way to do this, even from within one of the menus, is to press ON LINE twice. Once 00 READY appears in the console display, press RESET MENU and hold it in for about 5 seconds until 09 MENU RESET appears in the display. When you release the key, the printer will return to the READY state with the factory defaults immediately in effect.

MENU LEVEL 1

The key labeled MENU is actually two keys in one. Pressing the key and then immediately releasing it gives you access to the first set of options, which we'll call MENU LEVEL 1 (HP calls it the Printer Menu). The options are as follows:

- Number of Copies. This allows you to set the LaserJet to print a specified number of any page it outputs.
- Manual Feed. This allows you to turn the manual feed option on or off.
- Font Source. This should be called Default Font Source. It tells the LaserJet the location of your default font (resident in the printer, on the left cartridge, on the right cartridge, or downloaded in memory).
- Font Number. This should be called Default Font Number. It tells the LaserJet the ID number of your default font.
- Form Length. This establishes the number of lines you want printed on each page.

To change one of the parameters, use the following procedure:

- Take the printer off line.
- Press the MENU key.
- If necessary, press the MENU key several times more until you reach the parameter you wish to change.
- Use the Plus and Minus keys to examine the possible settings for that menu item.
- When the setting is as you want it, press the ENTER key to confirm your choice. An asterisk will appear next to the new parameter.
- At this point the new default will be selected, but will not yet be activated. To make it immediately active, hold down the RESET key (not the RESET MENU key) for 2 to 5 seconds until the 07 RESET

appears. Now you can release the key and 00 READY is displayed.

MENU LEVEL 2

If you hold the MENU key down for about 5 seconds, you get access to a different set of parameters, which we call MENU LEVEL 2 (HP calls it the Configuration Menu). This menu lets you control the following default settings:

- Symbol Set. This lets you choose which symbol set to use for your default font. "Symbol set" refers to the collection of characters included in the font and is discussed in more detail in Chapter 13, "LaserJet Font Basics."
- Auto-Continue. If you set this option to off, the LaserJet will stop printing when it encounters a command to print on a size of paper that is not in the printer's paper cassette. If you set Auto-Continue to on, the LaserJet will continue printing.
- I/O. This lets you specify whether you want to use a parallel or a serial cable to connect the computer to the LaserJet.

The procedure for changing one of the parameters is almost identical to the procedure for changing parameters in MENU LEVEL 1:

- Take the printer off line.
- Hold down the MENU key for about 2 to 5 seconds.
- Press the MENU key once or twice more until you reach the parameter you wish to change.
- Use the Plus and Minus keys to examine the possible settings for that menu item.

Tip: Context-Sensitive Menus

Menu choices are context sensitive, so don't be surprised if selections you remember making don't appear. For example, if I/O is set to parallel, there are no further menu options, and if you press Menu again you will return to the 00 READY state. However, if on the I/O selection you choose I/O=Serial, when you next press the Menu key, additional choices will follow to allow you to specify the baud (transmission) rate and protocols. These last two choices have no meaning when a parallel interface is used, so the LaserJet doesn't bother you with them when the parallel interface is selected.

- When the setting is as you want it, press the ENTER key to confirm your choice.

Auto-Continue: Look Ma, No Hands!

Many people have trouble understanding what the Auto-Continue option of the second menu tier accomplishes. The Auto-Continue On setting instructs the LaserJet II that when an error occurs, it should display the error message for 10 seconds, then resume printing. When Auto-Continue is off and an error occurs, you must press the ON LINE key before the LaserJet will resume printing. Having Auto-Continue on is handy in certain situations requiring unattended operation. For example, you may have a communications application requiring that the LaserJet be available to print throughout the night, and you don't want to discover in the cold light of morning that an error occurred on page 2, and the LaserJet has been waiting patiently ever since for you to press the ON LINE key. Auto-Continue can lead to problems though, because certain errors may lead to lost images. When Auto-Continue is off, the user presumably has a better opportunity to discover and rectify any such problems..

> ### *Tip: Activating Defaults*
>
> *Defaults selected in Menu Level 1 do not go into effect as soon as they are selected. To activate the new default, you must either hold down the RESET key for several seconds or else turn the printer off and then back on.*

Fonts by Numbers

You're most likely to use the Control Panel for changing the default font. To do this, you should first use the PRINT FONTS key to print a sample sheet.

Each font on the printed list has a letter and number to the left of it. This is known as the font list ID, and is useful when you are using the Control Panel to select fonts. The first letter will either be I (internal, or resident, fonts), L (left cartridge), R (right cartridge), or S (soft fonts). For example, I00 stands for 12-point Courier font in portrait orientation, which is one of the LaserJet's resident fonts.

You can easily set the LaserJet to print in any of the listed fonts by merely paying attention to the font list IDs and pressing a few keys. For example, here's how to set the LaserJet to print in 8.5-point Line Printer, which is always listed as font I11. Make sure the printer is off line, using the ON LINE key (the amber light above it goes out when the printer is off line). Now press the MENU key three times, until

FONT SOURCE=I *

appears in the display. The asterisk marks the current default selection, and the I stands for "internal," so the LaserJet is set to print from an internal font as its default, rather than from a font cartridge or soft font. If R, L, or S appears as the font source rather than I, someone has already specified a different default font source. Press the – key in the upper right corner of the Control Panel, until the font source is I. Then press the ENTER key once, which should cause the asterisk to appear. If you wanted to choose another available font source at this point, you could do so using these keys in this way, as well. If no other font sources are available (because, for example, there are no font cartridges in the LaserJet), the Plus and Minus keys will have no effect at this point.

> ### *Tip: Font IDs*
>
> *The Font ID numbers listed on the sample sheet produced by the PRINT FONTS key are only relevant for selecting fonts using the Control Panel and have no bearing on selecting fonts using any other method. In particular, you cannot use these numbers when selecting fonts using Printer Command Language codes.*

With the internal font source selected and an asterisk showing, press the MENU key once more. The display should now show FONT NUMBER=00.

Press the Plus key at the top of the pad. Each time you press it, the font number shown in the display should increase by one. Press this key ten more times, until the font number is 11. (If a number other than 00 first appears, it means someone has already selected a different font number. Press the Minus or Plus keys as necessary until the font number is 11.) Now press the ENTER key. You will see an asterisk appear to the right of the font number, showing that 11 has been selected as the new default value.

Once an item has been selected as a default, the LaserJet will use that item whenever it reverts to its default settings (unless your software tells it to use a different font).

Now that we have specified what we want as the default font, you still have to activate the default. This is done in two ways:

- By turning the printer off and then on again.
- By holding the RESET (not the RESET MENU) key for several seconds until 07 RESET is displayed. (This method is preferable because turning the printer off and on again is time consum-

ing as well as a strain on the printer.)

Testing the Defaults

An easy way to check that your new defaults are in effect is to print a file from the DOS command line. For example, let's say we switched our default font to 12-point Courier bold in landscape orientation. To check, enter the following from the DOS prompt:

```
COPY CON: PRN:

I like Swipe!

Ctrl-Z
```

The amber light above the FORM FEED key should now be lit up, showing that the LaserJet has something to print but has not yet received a page eject. Press the ON LINE key to take the printer off line (so the amber ON LINE light winks off), then press the FORM FEED key to manually instruct the LaserJet to eject the page. It should slide out into the delivery tray, and the FORM FEED light should go out. Press the ON LINE key once more to bring the LaserJet back on line.

If the font that printed was not 12-point Courier bold in landscape orientation, you probably made a simple mistake somewhere. Take the printer off line, and use the MENU key to check your menu selections. If the values shown for the font source and the font number are not I (internal) and 16 respectively, repeat the selection procedure.

CHAPTER FOUR

How the LaserJet Thinks

KNOWING WHAT GOES on inside the printer is not essential, but it does help in understanding how applications, fonts, and drivers work together, and why some types of pages print quickly while others print slowly.

In this chapter, we'll follow the stream of data as it leaves the computer and enters the laser printer, and then see how the LaserJet processes that data.

Printing with Light

Laser printing can be summed up as a technology for converting bits of data (zeros and ones) in a computer's memory into spots of toner on paper. The process is not unlike that used by a television, in which a beam of electrons rapidly scans across a video tube, building a coherent image out of tiny dots of light. The term raster, originally used in reference to video technology, is now commonly used to describe any such scanning and imaging technique.

In a laser printer, a rapidly spinning mirror directs the stationary laser beam across the width of the electrostatic drum; then the rollers move the drum ahead and the beam moves across it again. Eventually the drum stores a full-page image made up of electrically charged dots—300 per inch horizontally and vertically. Toner particles, or tiny specks of a special plastic, attach themselves to the charged locations on the drum and are then transferred onto paper.

Anything printed on a laser printer, whether it be a box, a character, or a digitized picture, is constructed as a mosaic of tiny spots. The LaserJet has three fundamentally different ways of creating the mosaic, one used primarily for text, the other two for graphics. Throughout this book we frequently refer to these three methods as text mode, bit-mapped graphics mode, and object graphics mode.

Text

Information is transferred from your computer to your LaserJet as a continual stream of zeros and ones. Each particle of data—each zero or one—is referred to as a bit.

In computer parlance, a grouping of eight bits is called a byte. Since there are 256 possible combinations of zeros and ones in one byte, it is possible to assign a different byte to each member of an entire European character set—including lowercase letters, uppercase letters, numerals, punctuation marks, and special symbols. For example, when the LaserJet receives the stream of bits 01000001, which is the same as the decimal number 65, it prints an uppercase letter A in the currently active font.

In text mode, whenever the LaserJet receives a byte from the computer, it looks into its font memory for a pattern of tiny spots and white spaces assigned to that byte, and then prints the pattern. A typical character pattern is 26 spots wide and 31 spots high, or 806 spots per character shape.

The process is extremely efficient, since it allows a software application to request that a particular character be printed without actually specifying all the thousands of printer spots that make up that character. The process is rather like ordering from a restaurant menu written in an unfamiliar language. If the items are numbered, you can order a meal simply by asking for a particular number on the menu.

Similarly, to get the LaserJet to print the letter G, the computer program you are using doesn't have to know which of the 806 sections of an image grid must have a spot of toner and which must must have a white space. It only has to know that the letter G is number 71 in the character set stored in the printer. The computer then sends this number (in binary format: 01001111). The fact that the computer needs to send only one byte to the printer to call up the pattern for a character accounts for the LaserJet's quickness at printing standard characters.

There is one additional level of complexity, though, because the LaserJet is capable of printing in a variety of fonts. When it receives the sequence 01100011 01100001 01110100 (c-a-t, in English), how does it know which font to use to print the word cat? The answer is that at any given time, one of the fonts stored in the printer's memory is designated as the active font. To change active fonts, the printer must receive a special control code. We'll talk about these in a moment.

Bit-mapped Graphics

In text mode, the LaserJet translates the raw stream of zeros and ones it receives into character data. In bit-mapped graphics mode, data bits are converted directly into printed dots or white spaces.

In bit-mapped graphics mode, you can print virtually anything you can describe—a logo, a picture, or text. Bit-mapped graphics printing is much slower than text printing, though, because it is less efficient.

In bit-mapped graphics mode, the computer must send a bit to the printer for each spot in the fine-grained matrix that makes up the printed image. For example, to print a picture that is one inch wide and one inch high in the highest resolution of which the LaserJet is capable, the computer must send one bit to the printer for each location in a 300-by-300 (one square inch) grid. That's 90,000 bits, or roughly 11,000 bytes. In contrast, in text mode a full page of text can be transmitted to the printer using about 3,000 bytes, one for each character, white space, or line feed.

Bit-mapped graphics printing thus can slow the LaserJet from its normal pace of several pages per minute down to several minutes per page. Graphics printing also gobbles up the LaserJet's internal memory. The 90,000 bits for our one-inch-square image occupy 11,250 bytes of memory. This posed a big problem for the original LaserJet, which could store only 59,000 bytes. The largest image it could print at 300 dpi was slightly larger than 5 square inches. The LaserJet Plus and the base configuration of the LaserJet II provide enough standard memory for a third of a page of graphics, and additional memory, up to a maximum of 4.5MB for the LaserJet II, is readily available.

Using additional memory is only one way of increasing the size of an image you may print. An alternative technique is to drop to a lower resolution. By default, the LaserJet prints in its highest resolution, 300 dots by 300 dots per square inch, or 300 dpi. The LaserJet is also capable of less fine-grained resolution, however, such as 150-by-150 dpi, and even 75-by-75 dpi. If you've ever printed the same image at different resolutions, you've noticed that when you reduce the number of dots per inch, the size of the image increases proportionately. The reason is that at 300 dots per inch, each bit sent from the computer causes one spot to be printed, but at 150 dots per inch, each bit sent to the printer causes a 2-by-2 box of spots to be printed.

Most graphics applications for the LaserJet give you the option of lowering the resolution. When your use permits it, you can also switch to lower resolution yourself, using the appropriate Printer Command Language instructions. Images printed at lower resolutions have a somewhat jagged appearance, but at 75 dpi you can print a large image even on the original LaserJet.

Object Graphics

With the LaserJet Plus and LaserJet II, some simple graphics can be printed using the Printer Command Language built into the printer. You can create lines and boxes filled with either patterns (like horizontal or slanted parallel lines) or shades of gray. This graphics mode doesn't suit every need, but it is much faster than bit-mapped graphics mode because the computer only needs to send the command to create the graphic shape rather than individually specifying each spot to be printed.

Chapter 19, "Programming the LaserJet with PCL," describes how to build and combine printer control commands such as those you might use for object graphics. For most purposes, directly sending such commands to the printer is too awkward to be practical, but fortunately the job is usually taken care of automatically by your software application.

Characters and Codes

Inside the LaserJet is a controller board that is actually as powerful as most personal computers. It includes a Motorola 68000 microprocessor, the same chip that drives the Apple Macintosh.

There are times when your computer needs to send commands—called control codes—to the printer controller. One obvious occasion is when your application wants to tell the LaserJet to merge a graphic image into a page of text. In that case, it will have to send the printer a code that switches the LaserJet from text mode to bit-mapped or object graphics mode.

Other typical uses of control codes are to set the width of the margin or to switch the printer to a different font. To distinguish such control codes from data that needs to be printed, they are always preceded by the byte 00001011, which is the same as the decimal number 27 and is called the escape character. When the LaserJet receives the escape character, it interprets whatever follows (until it receives a capital letter) as a printer command.

Because they always begin with the escape character, you'll frequently see LaserJet control codes referred to as escape sequences. The full set of possible codes makes up Hewlett-Packard's Printer Command Language (PCL).

When the LaserJet first came out in 1984 and before most software directly supported it, LaserJet owners often had to learn the ins and outs of PCL if they wanted their printers to be anything more than expensive letter quality printers. Since most popular software products now include very

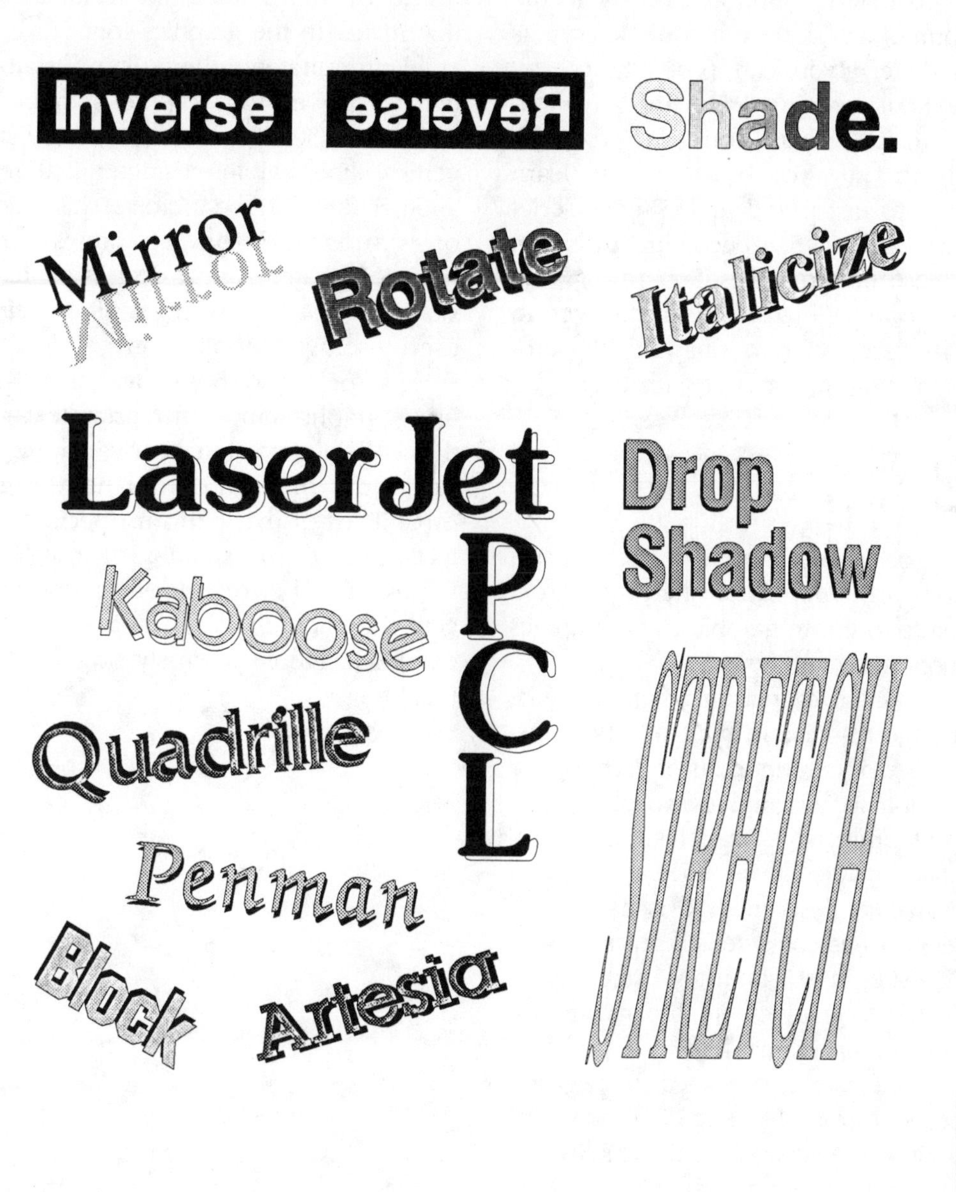

Figure 1: This page, created with Diagraph, is an example of text being printed in graphics mode. The type shown here is printed without using actual soft fonts; rather, each letter is "drawn" as a graphic image.

good LaserJet support (usually in the form of an interface module known as a driver), you can probably get by without learning PCL. For any software packages you plan to use, chances are you'll just have to learn how to install and utilize the LaserJet driver rather than becoming an expert on escape sequences. Some programs, however, still lack a LaserJet driver. In that case, refer to Chapter 19, "Programming the LaserJet with PCL."

Graphics as Text, Text as Graphics

On occasion, you may encounter a software application that uses text mode to create graphics, and graphics mode to create text.

Why? One reason is speed. Since a page of text can generally be transmitted to the printer faster than a page of bit-mapped graphics, some applications print "fake" graphics that are actually made up of special graphics characters. This method is usually referred to as character graphics.

The most common examples of character graphics are the word processing programs that use graphics characters to create lines, boxes, and borders around a page. A more unusual example is VS Software's SLed, a drawing program that converts the parts of a graphic image into a special-purpose font, downloads the font to the printer, and then prints the image by transmitting the characters that make up the graphics font.

Unfortunately, there is no standard alphabet for graphic symbols. Character 230 of one font may be a vertical line, while character 230 in another font may be a cross. This lack of standardization of character graphics creates a great deal of confusion and has tended to inhibit their use by software applications.

As for the opposite technique—using graphics mode to print text—this is used occasionally by graphics programs that lack font-handling capabilities or that perform special effects on text. An example is shown in Figure 1. The result of trying to generate each character as a separate graphic image is extremely slow printing.

CHAPTER FIVE

Using Setup Utilities

THESE DAYS, ALL computer programs can be divided into two categories: LaserJet-Aware and LaserJet-Unaware. Those aren't technical terms, but they do a pretty good job of characterizing two different kinds of software. LaserJet-Aware programs are those whose designers understood the capabilities of the LaserJet and provided drivers for controlling the printer. LaserJet-Unaware programs are those that lack such controls.

If you are using your printer with sophisticated, LaserJet-Aware programs like Microsoft Word 4.0 or WordPerfect 5.0, you'll probably never need a setup utility. These utilities are designed to ease the process of using the LaserJet with LaserJet-Unaware software.

Here are some of the things that setup utilities let you do:

- Emulate another printer: If your software lacks a driver for the LaserJet, some setup utilities cause the LaserJet to emulate a Diablo or an Epson printer. Since practically every program ever written includes either a Diablo or an Epson driver, you'll be able to print. The most popular utility for setting up Diablo or Epson emulation is LaserControl. It's described in "Profile: LaserControl."
- Set printer parameters: With the LaserJet II, there are a number of settings that can be controlled directly via the Control Panel, including number of copies to be printed, paper bin, manual or envelope feed, and serial or parallel interface parameters. However, with a setup utility you can easily change these settings—as well as others not accessible from the Control Panel.
- Set page parameters: Most setup utilities allow you to set margins,

number of lines per page, and other page parameters.

- **Manage fonts:** Setup utilities typically let you select a font from a cartridge, download a set of soft fonts, change symbol sets, choose primary and secondary fonts, and assign font ID numbers.

Special Features

Depending on which setup utility you purchase, you may have access to some features that go well beyond mere printer setup. For example:

- With LaserControl you can print justified text (i.e., text aligned with both margins) in programs such as Symphony and Framework that do not themselves provide for text justification with proportional fonts.
- With Printworks for PC, you can embed a variety of font commands within a document, making it possible to print italics, superscript, international character sets, and multiple fonts using programsu that lack LaserJet drivers.
- Another feature of Printworks for PC is a Memo Writer, which lets you type and print a single page of text—quite handy for generating envelopes and other small jobs.

Downloading Fonts

Some utilities take care of downloading fonts. However, if all you need to do is download soft fonts to your printer, don't buy a setup utility such as LaserControl or Printworks. Instead, you'll get more font downloading features from a utility designed specifically for that purpose. See Chapter 15, "Downloading Fonts and Building Drivers," for a complete discussion.

Memory Residency

Most setup utilities are known as TSR (terminate and stay resident) programs, i.e., software that loads into memory and remains hidden from view until you activate it with a designated key combination. This is useful if you need to change your printer configuration from within an application. However, as most people are aware by now, there are some drawbacks to using memory-resident programs.

One problem is that TSRs occasionally interfere with each other; another is that they eat up scarce memory resources. For these reasons, it's preferable to use a setup utility that gives you the option of making it memory-resident or not. E-Z-Set is not a TSR program. Both LaserControl (which uses 91K) and Printworks for the PC Release 3 (which uses 60K) provide the option of being used in TSR status or not.

Recommendation

Although numerous setup utilities are on the market, most are home-brew programs that don't really make your life much easier. The table below lists the programs that are on the market. Among those, our top choices are LaserControl and E-Z-Set. We also recommend Printer Marshall, Laser Bat, and Printworks for PC. For more information on LaserControl, Printworks for PC, and E-Z-Set, see the profiles on those programs following this chapter.

Access: Setup Utilities

Easy Laser
Acorn Plus, Inc.
4219 W. Olive Ave. #2011
Burbank, CA 91505
213/876-5237
Price: $99.95
Description: A memory-resident utility that works in conjunction with word processing or spreadsheet software. It allows you to format documents using embedded codes.

EZ-Laser
JRM Software, Ltd.
P.O. Box 2847
2035 Lakewinds Dr.
Reston, VA 22091
703/860-3085
Price: $99.95
Description: A memory-resident utility that lets you incorporate PCL commands into files and make screen shots of other applications.

E-Z-Set (Formerly SetHP)
Orbit Enterprises
799 Roosevelt Rd., Bldg. 6, Suite 1
Glen Ellyn, IL 60137
312/469-3405
Price: $49.95
(HIGHLY RECOMMENDED)
Description: A simple, well-designed utility that lets you select fonts, create macros, control page parameters, and control printer parameters including paper bin, paper type, and envelope printing. (For more details, see "Profile: E-Z-Set.")

Fontastic
Koch Software Industries
11 W. College Dr., Bldg G
Arlington Heights, IL 60004
312/398-5440
Price: $120

Description: A memory-resident program that lets you control fonts and issue formatting commands from within another application. Warning: poorly written, confusing documentation.

Jet-Set
Probe Software
23 Rumbrook Rd.
Elmsford, NY 10523
201/285-1500
Price: $129
Description: Although this is not a particularly powerful piece of software (it only supports the A, B, and F cartridges and no soft fonts), its main advantage is that it comes not only in a DOS version but also in CP/M 80 and CP/M 86 versions.

JetSet II
DataMate Company
4135 S. 100th East Ave. #128
Tulsa, OK 74146
800/262-7276
Price: $99
Description: Includes a setup program called SetLaser and a formatting program called Runoff. (For more details, see "Profile: JetSet II.")

Laser Bat
Sumsion Enterprises
P.O. Box 102
Springfield, UT 84663
801/798-8434
Price: $25
(RECOMMENDED)
Description: This is actually two products. One is a menu-driven program for selecting fonts from cartridges. It is well-designed and simple to use. The other is a set of small programs, each of which handles a specific task. For example, ff.com issues a form feed to the printer. These small programs are particularly useful for controlling the LaserJet from within batch files. The programs let you control the number of copies, characters per inch, form feed, horizontal motion index, landscape or portrait mode, margins, lines per inch, page length, primary and secondary font, reset printer to defaults, print test sample, text length, vertical motion index, and wraparound.

LaserControl
Hewlett-Packard Company
Direct Marketing Division
1320 Kifer Rd.
Sunnyvale, CA 94086
415/376-9451
Price: $150
(HIGHLY RECOMMENDED)
Description: This memory-resident utility provides a wide variety of emulations as well as numerous setup options. (For more details, see "Profile: LaserControl.")

Laser Fonts
Keller Software
1825 Westcliffe Dr.
Newport Beach, CA 92660
714/854-8211
Price: $49
Description: Laser Fonts is a memory-resident program that works in conjunction with word processors, spreadsheets, and databases. To use fonts, you embed a three-digit font code into your documents. At print time, the short code is converted into the long escape sequence needed to select a particular font. The program supports all font cartridges and allows multiple fonts to be printed on a page.

Laserific
Computerific, Inc.
316 Fifth Ave.
New York, NY 10001
212/695-2100
Price: $149
Description: This is a memory-resident setup and formatting utility with extensive capabilities, including cartridge font selection, BDT and Ziyad sheet feeder control, and network and switching box support.

Printer Marshall
Client Marketing Systems
2582 N. Santiago Blvd.
Orange, CA 92667
714/921-1768
Price: $19.95
(RECOMMENDED)
Description: This is a memory-resident utility that lets you select fonts from within other programs using pop-up menus. The program can be altered with any ASCII editor.

Printility
Metro Software
2509 N. Campbell #214
Tucson, AZ 85719
800/621-1137
Price: $179
Description: A RAM-resident utility, Printility emulates the IBM ProPrinter, IBM Graphics Printer, and Epson MX-80. It also provides pop-up menus for selecting fonts and merging graphics with text.

Printworks for the PC
Hewlett-Packard Company
Direct Marketing Division
1320 Kifer Rd.
Sunnyvale, CA 94086
415/376-9451
Price: $125
(RECOMMENDED)
Description: A comprehensive utility that provides printer emulations, font support, printer setup, formatting, and other functions. (For more details, see "Profile: Printworks for PC.")

Profile: E-Z-Set

SETUP UTILITIES ARE supposed to make life easier, not harder. After all, if you wanted to wade through manuals and learn complex codes, you could just as well learn the native PCL language of the LaserJet and do the programming yourself. Unfortunately, many utilities with only modest capabilities are surprisingly difficult to use. We've got our own name for this kind of junk: "Utilities from Hell."

E-Z-Set is the opposite. Maybe "Manna from Heaven" is too much of an exaggeration, but you get the idea. The program is ridiculously simple to use, yet it does an amazing number of things. Throw away the manual and just type

```
e-z-set
```

The menu shown below will appear on the screen. From there it's obvious what to do. If you want to select a font from a cartridge, type

```
@
```

You'll then be shown a list of the HP cartridges, A to Z. Type the letter of the cartridge, then select the font. The program will immediately send the appropriate codes to the printer and you're in business.

The same simplicity applies to other functions, such as those that for-

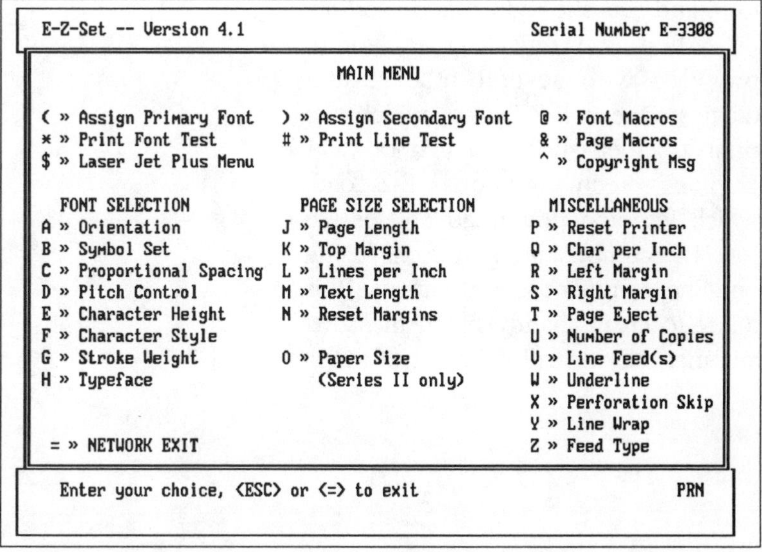

Figure 1: The main menu for E-Z-Set. From this menu, any one-letter selection takes you to a lower-level menu.

mat margins, set text length, eject the page, select number of copies, reset the printer, etc. It's all there on the main menu: just type the right one-letter command.

By-passing the Menus

Since E-Z-Set is not memory-resident, you normally use it to configure the printer with the desired margins, page length, etc., before you start using another program. If you're one of those people who always uses the same settings, there's a shortcut. Simply type

```
e-z-setb
```

(instead of e-z-set) followed by the letters of the commands you wish to execute. For example,

```
e-z-setb p r5 s75
```

resets the printer, sets the left margin to 5, and sets the right margin to 75.

When you buy E-Z-Set, you're provided with several other useful utilities. One is E-Z-Dump, which can print a screen shot of a text or CGA graphics screen. Another is E-Z-Load, which lets you download and assign font ID numbers to soft fonts using one-line commands. You can use this utility to create handy batch files that automatically download a set of fonts.

Access

E-Z-Set
Orbit Enterprises, Inc.
799 Roosevelt Road
Building. 6, Suite 1
Glen Ellyn, IL 60137
312/469-3405
Price: $49.95

Profile: JetSet II

JETSET II CONTAINS two separate programs—SetLaser and Runoff. SetLaser lets you build printer control codes using menu selections. Runoff is a text formatter program; using any text editor, you can embed Runoff commands in your documents. If you print them using Runoff, the finished output will be formatted according to the commands you use.

SetLaser

SetLaser lets you send any escape sequence the LaserJet will respond to, including those that control lines per page, lines per inch, margins, feed mode, print orientation, and font. You simply select a choice off the main menu (for example, the second selection lets you choose portrait mode). Some choices call secondary menus or prompts for additional specifications. For example, if you choose menu number 16 to set the number of lines per inch, SetLaser will prompt you for the number of lines per inch you want to print, from 1 up to 48.

To select a particular font using SetLaser you have to specify its attributes from a menu—orientation, weight, size, etc. This is not as convenient as the selection method some utilities employ, where you merely specify the font cartridge you have and the font number you want to print in. But using SetLaser is still easier than having to create the escape sequences yourself.

Once you have selected all the output characteristics you desire, you simply press Enter. SetLaser sends formats you have selected to the LaserJet. You can also save a format for subsequent use. Once the format has been sent to the LaserJet, it will print using the selected attributes until it gets new instructions that override the old ones.

Runoff

Runoff, the second program of JetSet II, is specifically for printing files. If you are familiar with the NROFF printing module of UNIX or with WordStar, Runoff's commands will seem familiar. The program recognizes two kinds of commands, dot commands (beginning with a period in the first column) and embedded control-characters. One nice feature of Runoff is that you can easily change the commands Runoff will recognize. This eliminates compatibility problems with word processors that use the same codes Runoff recognizes as a default. For example, WordStar also uses dot commands. To avoid confusion between Runoff's commands and WordStar's you can use the .$$ command to reconfigure Runoff so that it hunts for another character in the first column rather than a period.

One limitation is that Runoff can use only ASCII files. Most word processors have the capability to save files in ASCII form (Transfer Save Unformatted in Microsoft Word, or Non-Document Mode in WordStar).

Runoff offers a wide variety of commands. You can format text, select fonts, merge-print files, underline, ask for user input, and define headers and footers.

Access

JetSet II
DataMate Company
4135 S. 100th East Ave. #128
Tulsa, OK 74146
800/262-7276
Price: $99

Profile: LaserControl

OF ANY UTILITY available for the LaserJet, LaserControl offers the best combination of ease of use and usefulness. Its ease of use arises from its main purpose, which is to allow the LaserJet to faithfully emulate printers that your applications are already acquainted with: the Diablo 630; the NEC 3550, 5510, or 7710; the Qume Sprint V; the Epson MX-80 (with GrafTrax Plus) and the Epson FX-80; and the IBM Graphics Printer. In the world of PC software, it would be very hard to find a program that doesn't work with at least one of those printers. Hence the usefulness of LaserControl—allowing tens of thousands of programs, unaltered, to work with the laser printer.

Of course, the immediate question that comes to mind is: Why own a laser printer if all you're going to do is emulate less powerful printers? The answer is threefold. First, many software applications have not yet been upgraded to take advantage of laser printers. Second, by letting the LaserJet emulate both dot matrix and daisy wheel printers, LaserControl lets your single LaserJet function as both a letter-quality printer and as a high resolution graphics printer, in effect giving you two printers in one. Third, if you do want to have access to the more

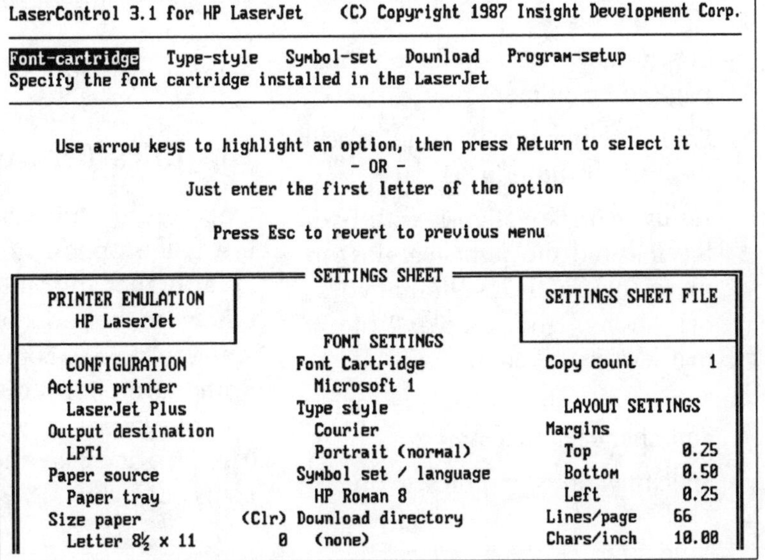

Figure 1: The LaserControl main menu. The top portion of the screen is used for making selections. The bottom half shows what printer is currently being emulated and shows the parameters in the current Settings Sheet.

powerful features of the LaserJet, LaserControl does give you the option of emulating the LaserJet itself and provides a powerful set of laser printer controls.

Setup Options

In addition to providing emulation of common printer standards, LaserControl also provides a number of printer setup controls. These can be stored in a Settings Sheet. Typing

LC *Name of Settings Sheet*

at the beginning of a work session configures the printer. Alternatively, you can place that command in your AUTOEXEC.BAT file to make the setup process automatic.

A Settings Sheet can include the following options:

- Specify a font cartridge, a symbol set, and a font;
- Set number of copies of each page to be printed;
- Shift the horizontal and vertical position of the printed page;
- Justify text (i.e., align it with both the left and the right margins) in programs such as Framework, Symphony, and DisplayWrite 3 that lack justification;
- Specify margins, lines per page, and character spacing;
- Specify various graphics settings.

Access

LaserControl
Hewlett-Packard Company
Direct Marketing Division
1320 Kifer Rd.
Sunnyvale, CA 94086
415/376-9451
Price: $150

Note that you can save different Settings Sheets under different names, and call up each as needed.

Memory Resident

You can install LaserControl as a memory-resident program that takes up 91K. This is called Pop-up mode, because you can activate the program any time using a key combination. Alternatively, you can use the program without making it memory resident.

Graphics Printing

One very useful feature of LaserControl is the option of printing graphics at a higher resolution than would otherwise be possible. The best example of this is Lotus 1-2-3. Both 1-2-3 and Symphony only support printing of graphs at 75 dots per inch (dpi). To increase the resolution with Lotus, use the MX-80 Density 3 setting. The result is a dramatic improvement.

Screen Shots

You can use LaserControl to print any screen in CGA or Hercules graphics modes. Currently, higher-resolution modes such as those used by EGA and VGA boards are not supported.

Operation

From the LaserControl menu, you first select the printer you wish to emulate, then define the page settings appropriate for your application. You can save these settings in a Settings Sheet.

LaserControl is particularly useful with spreadsheet programs such as Lotus 1-2-3. In printing very wide worksheets, you can use the landscape Line Printer font on the B cartridge. With the Chars/inch command in the LaserControl layout menu, you can select 18.5 characters per inch, rather than the default 16.66 characters per inch value.

With word processing programs, LaserControl lets you print with proportional fonts even if you're using an older word processor that does not support such fonts.

Profile: Printworks for the PC/Laser Version

PRINTWORKS IS A memory-resident setup utility. After you load the program into your computer's memory, it lurks there behind the scenes while you use other programs. When you press the Shift-PrtSc key combination, the Printworks menu pops into view. When you have finished entering commands with this menu, pressing Esc sends you back to the previous screen.

As of version 3.0, you can now elect either to make Printworks memory-resident or else to use it as a nonresident application. This allows you to conserve memory if necessary and also avoid conflicts with other memory-resident utilities.

Overview

Printworks lets you perform the following functions:

- **Select a font.** With the original LaserJet, you can use the utility to select internal and cartridge fonts. With the LaserJet Plus or LaserJet II, you can also download soft fonts from a disk into the printer, keep track of the fonts you have downloaded, and select the soft font you wish to use.
- **Set up page and printing specifications.** You can set margins, page length, lines per inch, and number of copies.
- **Save a graphics screen,** alter its dimensions, and then merge it into a different page at a particular line and column position on a page.
- **Print a graphics screen,** either in normal black-on-white mode or in reversed white-on-black mode.
- **Print a text screen.**
- **Create a text file of up to 63 lines**. This feature, referred to by Printworks as the Memo Writer, is especially useful for quickly addressing envelopes.
- Make the LaserJet emulate an Epson MX-80 graphics printer. This automatically provides laser printing for scores of programs

that have Epson graphics drivers but not LaserJet drivers.

- **Create macros.** Using this feature, you could create a letterhead logo combining text and an image, and then have this letterhead appear as an overlay on letters you write with your word processing program.

Font Management and Page Formatting

Figure 1 on the next page shows the Printworks menu. On the left are the options for managing fonts. Printworks allows you to easily select a cartridge font or a downloaded soft font without knowing the LaserJet escape sequences. Thus, it provides you with one of the main functions of HP's PCLPak utility, but with the added advantage of being able to add and delete soft fonts from inside any program. In addition, the utility provides an easy means for downloading fonts from disks into the LaserJet Plus and keeping track of the fonts you have downloaded.

Conveniently, Printworks does not require you to know all the attributes of a font, since most of the cartridge font attributes are already stored in the utilities font file. You can add more fonts to this file (it has room for 100) or delete fonts you don't need.

Access

Printworks for the PC/ Laser Version
Phoenix Technologies (formerly SoftStyle)
7192 Kalanianaole Hwy. #205
Honolulu, HI 96825
800/367-5600
Price: $125
Also available from HP Direct Marketing 800/358-8787
HP Part No. 35184C

Merging Images

The following scenario shows how Printworks' features work well together in letting you combine text and images. Let's say you want to place an image created by PC Paint in a WordStar document. With the PC Paint image on the screen, you press Shift-PrtSc to see the Printworks menu. Selecting SavS (by pressing function key 9 or numeral 9) saves this image with the file name that you designate (for example: B:PICTURE). Now exit Printworks, exit PC Paint, and open the text file in WordStar into which you want to place the image. Print the page, but do not eject it from the printer. Now bring the Printworks menu into view again and set the image size by choosing the P command and selecting option 1, 2, 3, or 4, which represent 66 percent reduction, 33 percent reduction, normal size, and 33 percent enlargement respectively. Depending on the option you select, the size of the image will vary from 2.13 by 1.66 inches, to 8.53 by 5.33 inches. Select the L command, Position and Print Saved Image. The program will ask you for the name of the file with the saved image and for the row and column number for the upper-left corner of the image. When you provide this information, the image will be printed. Type the Page command to eject the merged text and graphics page from the printer.

Memo Writer

The Memo Writer, which supports up to a page of text, is convenient for many purposes. For example, you can put the printer into landscape mode and then use the memo writer to quickly address and print an envelope. Or you can create text to merge with a graphic image.

With the Memo Writer, you still are limited to using one font per page, but you can switch to bold or underlined text. Obviously, the editing capabilities of Memo Writer are not up to those of a word processing program. For example, there are no paragraph formatting commands and no line justification. But for the purpose that it was designed to meet, the editing commands are adequate.

Epson Emulation

By providing Epson MX-80 emulation, Printworks opens the door to producing graphics output at 150 dots per

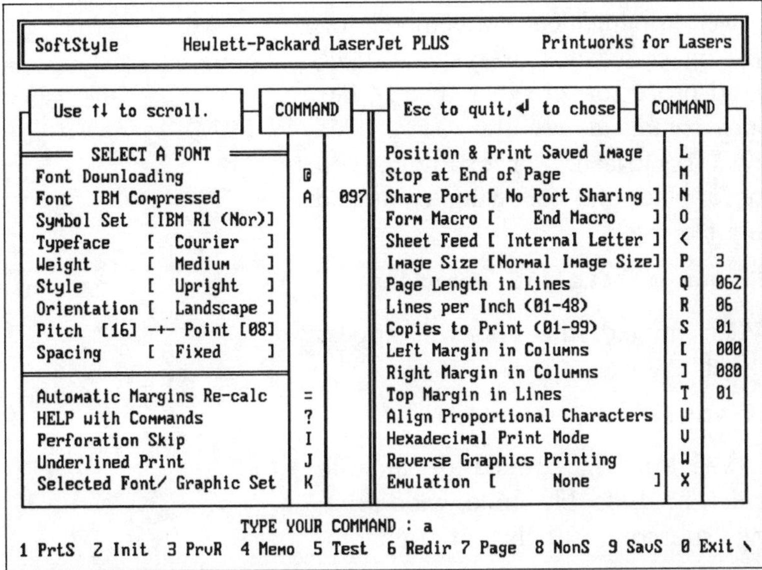

Figure 1: The Printworks main menu. The upper-left portion is used for font selection. The remainder of the screen is devoted to page layout and print control options.

inch with the LaserJet. Without this feature, many graphics programs could not produce laser output. Epson emulation is especially important with Lotus 1-2-3's PrintGraph module. Even with the LaserJet driver available through Lotus dealers for version 1A, and provided as a part of 1-2-3 Release 2.0, the print resolution is a mere 75 dots per inch. Moving from 75 to 150 dpi produces dramatically improved results.

Because Lotus 1-2-3 addresses the screen in a nonstandard way, bypassing the normal procedures supported by DOS, Printworks provides a special feature, Nonstandard Screen, that must be selected before you print a screen snapshot with Lotus 1-2-3.

Power Printing

A new Printworks feature, called Power Printing, lets you embed formatting commands in a spreadsheet, word processor, or other type of file. Such commands are always preceded by a backslash. For example, you might place the following command in a file:

```
It was a \4tall\5 mountain.
```

When printed, the line will appear like this:

It was a *tall* **mountain.**

Power Printing commands include italics, bold, double strike, wide printing, subscript, superscript, underlining, compressed printing, symbol set selection, macros, and font selection.

Special Features

Before concluding, two special features of Printworks deserve note. One is the program's Grafset option, which lets you map the upper 128 characters of a font onto the graphics characters that appear on the IBM screen. This makes it possible to make an accurate screen snapshot from the IBM monochrome display.

Another feature, useful to some programmers, is Hexadecimal Print Mode, which causes characters sent to the printer to be printed in sets of 20 characters, with their corresponding hexadecimal codes on the left side of the page.

2

WORD PROCESSING

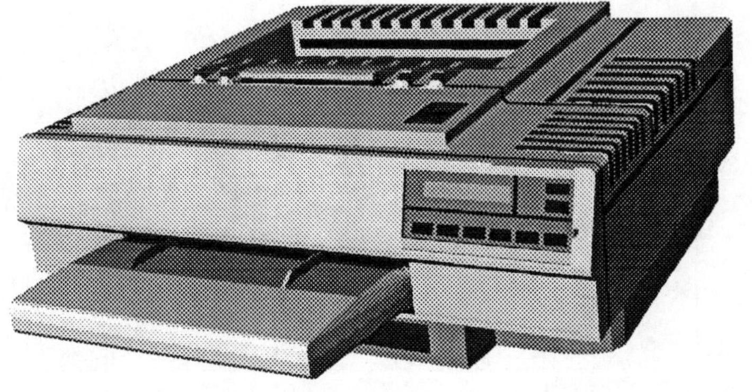

Section Focus

Laser printing differs from dot matrix and daisy wheel technology in many respects. The most important of these is the increasing availability of proportionally spaced fonts in a wide range of sizes. In addition, laser printing offers the potential to incorporate graphics with text.

This section tells how to use the LaserJet with six popular word processing programs: IBM DisplayWrite, Microsoft Word, MultiMate Advantage, WordPerfect, WordStar, and WordStar 2000. It also includes a chapter on merging graphics into word processed documents.

Profile: IBM DisplayWrite

THE FORMATTING AND font selection capabilities of IBM DisplayWrite 4 are not as advanced as WordPerfect, Microsoft Word, or WordStar 2000. However, with the help of several third-party utilities, you can overcome some of the limitations of the program. These utilities generally supply the Printer Driver Tables (PDTs) needed by DisplayWrite 3 and the Printer Function Tables (PFTs) needed by DisplayWrite 4 as well as providing some other capabilities.

DBL Software Drivers

DBL Software provides a set of drivers for DisplayWrite 3 and DisplayWrite 4 ranging in price from $75 to $125. The drivers support the following cartridge fonts for DisplayWrite 3: A, D-H, L-N, Q, and Y. With DisplayWrite 4 they support the following cartridge fonts: A, D-H, J, L-N, P-R, and Y. They also support the DA, AD, and EA soft font sets. Features include centering, overstriking, underlining, superscript, subscript, bold, italics, all paper sizes except legal, and landscape orientation, but not justification of proportional fonts.

DWLaser

This program sells for $195 and supports DisplayWrite 3 and DisplayWrite 4. It allows centering, justification, overstriking, underlining, superscript, subscript, bold, and italics. The program works with all HP cartridges, supports all paper sizes, works in both portrait and landscape orientation, and includes some soft fonts from Koch Software.

LaserConnection ESI-1312

This program supports DisplayWrite 2, DisplayWrite 3, and DisplayWrite 4 with the following cartridges: A-H, J, L-N, and Q-R, and supports the DA and EA soft font sets. It supports centering, superscript, subscript, italics (DisplayWrite 4 only), all paper sizes, and landscape orientation, but not justification, and there are some limits on underlining and overstriking.

Polaris Ram-Resident PrintMerge

This program is described in "Profile: Polaris Ram-Resident PrintMerge." It costs $149 and provides the following

Access: DisplayWrite Utilities

DWLaser
Koch Software Industries
11 W. College Dr., Bldg G
Arlington Heights, IL 60004
Price: $195

Polaris RAM-Resident PrintMerge
Polaris Software
613 West Valley Parkway #323
Escondido, CA 92025
800/338-5943
800/231-3531 California
Price: $149

LaserConnection ESI-1312
Extended Systems
P.O. Box 4937
6062 Morris Hill
Boise, ID 83711
208/322-7163
Price: $895 (site license)

DBL Software Drivers
DBL Software
12808 Woodbend Court
Dallas, TX 75243
214/238-5945
Price: $75 to $125

capabilities: support for DisplayWrite 3 and DisplayWrite 4, support for all HP cartridges and soft fonts, centering, justification, overstriking, underlining, superscript, subscript, bold, italics, landscape orientation, and all paper sizes.

Questions and Answers

Q: I am getting a blank page between pages. How can I prevent this?
A: Change your last typing line or footer line so that it is less than 60.

Q: How do I get extended characters to print in DisplayWrite 4?
A: Change the character set used by the font to Roman Extension symbol set and type in the ASCII character equivalent. It is a good idea to do the entire keyboard when setting type in Roman Extension to see which key corresponds to which extended character.

Profile: Microsoft Word

MICROSOFT WORD WAS introduced earlier than the LaserJet, but its design shows that Microsoft anticipated the increased typographic powers of laser printers and planned the program accordingly. Other word processors, for example, allow you to use multiple fonts in a document, but Word makes it quite easy. There's no need to keep notes on which fonts you have available—Word supplies you with a list accessible with the Format Character command. Nor do you need to exit the program to install a different printer driver; pressing Print Options F1 shows you the list of options available and lets you select one.

A second big plus for Word is that it's easy to get the program to recognize any LaserJet font cartridge or soft font. That's because Word comes with drivers for all the cartridges and soft fonts offered by HP, and companies selling soft fonts almost invariably provide a driver generator.

Drawbacks

Word works in a consistent fashion, but the command terminology and the way of selecting commands is confusing. Some examples:

To change the font for an entire paragraph you use the Format Character command rather than the Format Paragraph command. That's because a font change is considered a change in the character attribute of the paragraph.

- The command to view a style sheet is Gallery, an obscure term that probably derives from some sort of analogy between a collection of style sheets and an art gallery full of paintings.
- To view the hidden codes in a document, you select the Options command. However, to view the hidden styles, you select the Window Options command.
- To automatically change all occurrences of the word *Pig* to *Prig,* you use the Replace command. But to change the style of all occurrences of the word *Prig* from style SP to style QR, you must use the Format Replace command.

Partial WYSIWYG

On the screen, Word gives you some feedback about your fonts, but the program does not go all the way in showing you what font you have selected. If you have a graphics monitor, you'll see whether a word is italic or boldface. If you have a character monitor, italics will show up as underlined characters. Word does not show you the size of a font, true line spacing, or the actual typeface. The line breaks you see on the screen are not the same as those that will be printed, unless you select Options and choose Printer Display: Yes.

General Principle

Despite the obscurity in command names, there's a logical consistency to Word that cuts down the difficulty of formatting even fairly complex documents. Whether you're setting the font of a single character or setting margin widths that apply to the entire document, the same two-step method is always used:

- Select the element you wish to format—character, word, sentence, paragraph, or other block of text. Use the F7 (previous word), F8 (next word), Shift-F7 (previous sentence), Shift-F8 (next sentence), F9 (previous paragraph), Shift-F9 (current line), F10 (next paragraph), or Shift-F10 (whole document) keys to make the selection.
- With the element selected (i.e., highlighted), you can now apply a style to the text element. This can be done directly using Word's Escape Format command or by applying styles from a style sheet. The Escape Format method and the Style Sheet method are described separately below.

Direct Formatting

Although Word is renowned (and sometimes avoided) for its style sheet method of formatting, it's perfectly feasible to do all your formatting without using style sheets. For example, here's the procedure to change the font for a single word to HELV 10 point. (If you don't happen to have that font on one of your cartridges, substitute a different font.) To do this you need to select the word, then apply character attributes. As is frequently the case, the terminology used by Word is a bit confusing. Even though you're formatting an entire word, a font change is considered a change in character attributes.

- Press F7 or F8 to highlight the word.
- Press Esc to get into the Command menu.

- Select Format by pressing F or by moving the cursor to the Format command and pressing Enter.
- Select Character (for character attributes) and then Tab over to Font Name, press F1 to reveal the possibilities, use the cursor keys to select the desired font, and press Enter to complete the sequence.

Using Style Sheets

Specifying how you want a paragraph, a sentence, or even a single word to look means setting a large number of parameters: typeface, type size, alignment, italicization, boldface, indentation, line spacing, and so on. The purpose of style sheets is to allow you execute a large number of formatting decisions with a single two-character keystroke. To apply a collection of parameters to a portion of your document, you merely select that portion and then hold down the Alt key while you type the two-character code.

Once you've labeled all the parts of your document with the appropriate code, it's easy to change them. For example, if you set all your subheads in 12-point bold and want to change them to 14-point bold, you don't have to go through the document changing each one. Instead, you merely change the subhead style and watch all the subheads automatically switch to the new point size.

Because of the ease with which style sheets allow you to fiddle with the parameters of a document until you get them just right, learning style sheet formatting is one of the most important skills to have in making effective use of the LaserJet.

Look at the difference between the documents shown in Figures 1 and 3. Both contain the same information, but one presents it in a more readable form by using a variety of formatting elements. These include varied left margins, centered elements, non-uniform vertical spacing, blocks of text aligned in tables, and different fonts for sub-heads, text, tables, and footnotes.

The purpose of style sheets is to provide standard formats appropriate to different documents. A number of style sheets are provided with Word on the program's utility disk. You can create additional style sheets yourself.

When using style sheets, you enter the text first and format it later. **Begin by typing and saving the document in the form shown in Figure 1.** Do not use any extra tabs, spaces, or lines—the style sheet will take care of those. Any formatting you implement at this point would be incorporated into your document in addition to information from the style sheet.

The next step is creating a style sheet. **From the main editing menu**

```
*  Galley Slave Instruction Manual - 6
*  2.2 Arriving in Port
*  When the ship arrives in port, all galley slaves shall
   remain in their seats until the galley until the galley has
   come to a full stop. You may then file out in an orderly
   fashion. At this time everyone will receive one crust of
   bread as payment for the previous day's work.
*  Table 2.2.1 shows your tasks during stays at port.
*  ____________________________________________
*  Rowing position    Task
*  Starboard aft  Repainting fearsome designs
*  Port fore Carrying food supplies
*  Port aft  Repairing pallets
*  Table 2.2.1: Tasks while in port
*  ____________________________________________
*  2.3 Ramming Phoenician Vessels
*  Upon the sighting of a Phoenician galley, you will increase
   the frequency of strokes to battle pace.12 The battering ram
   must be driven into the enemy galley at top speed. After the
   ship has smashed into the Phoenician vessel, the ship's mate
   will unlock each slave's chains and issue you a weapon so
   that you can fight for your lives. At this point everyone
                                                      GALLEY.DOC
1411 characters
```

Figure 1: The unformatted text for the "Galley Slave Instruction Manual."

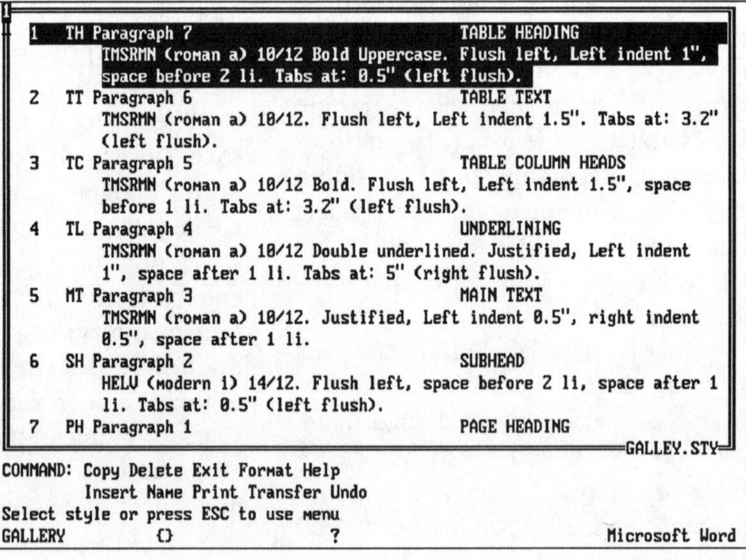

```
1  TH Paragraph 7                                TABLE HEADING
      TMSRMN (roman a) 10/12 Bold Uppercase. Flush left, Left indent 1",
      space before 2 li. Tabs at: 0.5" (left flush).
2  TT Paragraph 6                                TABLE TEXT
      TMSRMN (roman a) 10/12. Flush left, Left indent 1.5". Tabs at: 3.2"
      (left flush).
3  TC Paragraph 5                                TABLE COLUMN HEADS
      TMSRMN (roman a) 10/12 Bold. Flush left, Left indent 1.5", space
      before 1 li. Tabs at: 3.2" (left flush).
4  TL Paragraph 4                                UNDERLINING
      TMSRMN (roman a) 10/12 Double underlined. Justified, Left indent
      1", space after 1 li. Tabs at: 5" (right flush).
5  MT Paragraph 3                                MAIN TEXT
      TMSRMN (roman a) 10/12. Justified, Left indent 0.5", right indent
      0.5", space after 1 li.
6  SH Paragraph 2                                SUBHEAD
      HELV (modern i) 14/12. Flush left, space before 2 li, space after 1
      li. Tabs at: 0.5" (left flush).
7  PH Paragraph 1                                PAGE HEADING
                                                            GALLEY.STY
COMMAND: Copy Delete Exit Format Help
         Insert Name Print Transfer Undo
Select style or press ESC to use menu
GALLERY         {}         ?                           Microsoft Word
```

Figure 2: The style sheet for the "Galley Slave Instruction Manual."

Galley Slave Instruction Manual - 6

2.2 Arriving in Port

When the ship arrives in port, all galley slaves shall remain in their seats until the galley has come to a full stop. You may then file out in an orderly fashion. At this time everyone will receive one crust of bread as payment for the previous day's work.

Table 2.2.1 shows your tasks during stays at port.

Rowing position	**Task**
Starboard fore	Patching holes with pitch
Starboard aft	Repainting fearsome designs
Port fore	Carrying food supplies
Port aft	Repairing pallets

TABLE 2.2.1: TASKS WHILE IN PORT

2.3 Ramming Phoenician Vessels

Upon the sighting of a Phoenician galley, you will increase the frequency of strokes to battle pace.12 The battering ram must be driven into the enemy galley at top speed. After the ship has smashed into the Phoenician vessel, the ship's mate will unlock each slave's chains and issue you a weapon so that you can fight for your lives. At this point everyone shall commence jumping up and down and screaming: "Kill! Kill!"

Galley Slave Tip: Think positive for hand-to-hand combat. Let your pride show!

2.4 Rest Periods

All galley slaves are entitled to two rest periods per day in addition to regular meal breaks. The rest periods are from 6:15 to 6:18 a.m. and from 7:10 to 7:13 p.m.

Battle pace is defined as rowing your buns off.

select Gallery. The screen will clear and a new menu will appear at the bottom. You'll use this menu to create styles for each element of your document.

Select Insert. This command presents four areas for which you supply information: key code, usage, variant, and remark.

The key code is a two-letter code that tells the program what style you want to use for a text element. To create a style for subheads, **type the key code SH. Then tab to the next item on the menu, usage.**

Usage defines the text level the element occupies. Word divides all text elements into three categories: Division, Paragraph, and Character. The Division style controls the entire document, including the placement of headers and footnotes and number of columns to a page. Paragraph styles specify indentation, tabs, margins, justification, and typefaces for text elements such as paragraphs, headlines, footnote text, and tables—any element ending in Enter. Character styles identify the style of single characters when no other formatting information is required, such as an italicized word within a paragraph.

Select Paragraph as the usage for subheads, then tab to the next item, variant.

The variant is the number Word assigns a style to distinguish between different elements that have the same usage, such as page headings and subheads, which are both paragraphs. In Figure 2, the variant is the number following the usage on the first line of each style. For example, Page Heading is variant 6 of the Paragraph usage category. Word will suggest a variant number; to accept the suggested number, just tab to the next item, remark.

The remark is strictly for your use, identifying different styles on the style sheet. It's helpful to capitalize remarks so they'll stand out. **Type SUBHEAD and press Enter.**

After you enter the remark, the style specification will appear on the screen. Note that the second line of the style definition contains default information provided by Word. Your next step is to replace these defaults with a description of how this element should look. **Select the Format option from the Gallery menu.** Word will display a menu of settings that you must complete. For Paragraph usages, Word asks for Character, Paragraph, and Tab settings.

Select Paragraph. You'll use the defaults for the first three lines of options, so simply tab to "space before" and type 2 li. Tab to "space after" and type 1 li. These commands define the space surrounding the element. **Press Enter.**

Now select Format Tabs Set, type 0.5", and press Enter. This defines a half-inch indent for any tabs used in subheads.

To select a typeface for this style, select Format Character.

Then tab to "font name" and use CursorRight to reveal the choices. Use a cursor control key to highlight Helv. Then tab to "font size" and press CursorRight to reveal the one choice, 14 point. Press Enter.

Now the subhead style is complete. Figure 2 shows the style sheet used to format the document illustrated in Figure 3; the style you just created appears as style 6. **Create each style on the sheet the same way. When all the styles are defined, select Transfer Save from the Gallery and give the style sheet a name. To go back to your document and select Exit.**

Applying Styles to Documents

Once you've created the document shown in Figure 1 and the style sheet shown in Figure 2, you can combine the two. The first step is to attach the sheet to the document. **To do this, select Format Style Sheet, press CursorRight to see the names of the various style sheets on your disk, highlight your choice, and press Enter.**

Next you must label each element in the document with the key code of the appropriate style. **Before you do, though, select Window Options and then pick Yes for "style bar" so that key codes will be displayed as you select them.**

There are two ways to assign a style to a text element. The first way is via the menu. **To format a subhead, for instance, you would select Format Style Paragraph, use CursorRight to select variant 1, and press Enter to enter your choice. Alternatively, you can simply put the cursor on the subhead and type Alt-sh.**

Once the subhead is labeled, Word knows to print it in 14-point Helv, flush left, preceded by two blank lines, and followed by one blank line. You can now move through the entire document, labeling each element with the appropriate style from the attached style sheet. The result will look like Figure 3.

Using style sheets may seem laborious at first, but with some practice it becomes second nature. You'll soon find that creating documents is much easier when you separate the work of creating text from the work of formatting it. Most documents pass through several stages. In the first few rounds, you're concerned with editing and proofreading. For this stage you can either use no style or create a very simple style, such as double-spaced Courier for all text elements. When you finally format the document, the formats established in the style sheet will standardize elements within the document, producing a clean and professional piece. If you want to fine-tune certain elements, such as subhead indentation or table tabs, you can alter these details a single time in the style sheet rather than labor over individual elements throughout the document.

Translating the typographic power of the LaserJet and Word into professional-looking output takes some practice and creativity. But in return for your efforts, you'll gain control over the visual factors that are all too often the missing ingredient in written communications.

Using Microsoft Word with LaserJet Fonts

Microsoft Word 4.0 comes with drivers for all LaserJet font cartridges and the soft fonts sold by Hewlett-Packard. You can install more than one of these drivers for Word and then switch between them using the Print Options command. Installing a driver is easy: simply copy the appropriate PRD file and the matching DAT file from one of the Printer disks to the subdirectory on your hard disk that contains Word. The PRD files that come with Microsoft Word 4.0 are listed in Table 1.

The DAT file

Every PRD file is accompanied by a DAT file, which contains information necessary for Word to perform automatic downloading. The name of the DAT file is the same as the matching PRD file except for the different extensions. For example, HPDWNSFP.PRD is matched by HPDWNSFP.DAT. Note that the PRD files for cartridge fonts do not have matching DAT files.

Creating New Drivers

If you have purchased fonts for which Word does not provide PRD files, you can make a new PRD file. Utilities available for that purpose are listed below. They are described in greater detail in Chapter 15, "Downloading Fonts and Building Drivers," and in "Profile: Laser Fonts" and "Profile: FontLoad."

Combining Drivers with MERGEPRD

Once you have created a new driver using one of the utilities mentioned above, you can combine it with an existing driver. This lets you use fonts from two different cartridges simultaneously, or combine soft fonts and cartridge fonts. Copy the MERGEPRD file from Microsoft Word's Utility disk to your hard disk. Then from the DOS prompt type **MERGEPRD** and follow the prompts to combine two or more PRD files or to add or delete fonts.

Location of Fonts

Soft fonts don't have to be stored in the directory that contains Word, but

Microsoft Word 4.0 LaserJet Drivers

Drivers for Cartridge Fonts, Portrait Orientation

HPLASER1.PRD .... A, B, C, D, E, G, H, J, L, W, X
HPLASER2.PRD .... F, K, P, R, U
HPLASER3.PRD .... J, R, Z
HPLASMS.PRD .... Z
HPLASRMN.PRD .... F
HPLASPS.PRD .... B
HPLASTAX.PRD .... T
HPPCCOUR.PRD .... Y
HPLASLAN.PRD .... A, B, C, G, H,

Drivers for Cartridge Fonts, Landscape Orientation

HPLASLAN.PRD .... A, B, C, G, H, Internal, L
HPLASLAN.PRD .... M, N, P, Q, U, V
HPLASMSL.PRD .... Z

Drivers for Soft Fonts, Portrait Orientation

HPDWNCNP.PRD .... SA Portrait
HPDWNGAP.PRD .... RA Portrait
HPDWNHLP.PRD .... UA Portrait
HPDWNLGP.PRD .... DA Portrait
HPDWNPRL.PRD .... EA Portrait
HPDWNSFP.PRD .... AC and AE Portrait
HPDWNR8P.PRD .... AD and AF Portrait
HPDWNZHP.PRD .... TA Portrait

Drivers for Soft Fonts, Landscape Orientation

HPDWNLGL.PRD .... DA Landscape
HPDWNPRL.PRD .... EA Landscape
HPDWNSFP.PRD .... AC and AE Landscape
HPDWNR8L.PRD .... AD and AF Landscape

Table 1: These are the LaserJet drivers provided with Microsoft Word 4.0. To use a driver, copy the PRD file from the Printer disks (or the Utilities disk) to your Word subdirectory. For more information, see Word's "Printer Information" manual.

they must be in the same directory with the PRD and DAT files. When you select the printer driver using the Print Options command, you'll have to type the name of this directory and the PRD file name in the Printer field. For example, if the directory is \Fonts and the driver is HPDWNSFP.PRD, type

```
\FONTS\HPDWNSFP.
```

Downloading with Word

When you are working with soft fonts, Word provides a convenient auto-downloading feature. After you select Print Printer, the program prompts you with "Enter Y to download fonts, press N to skip, Esc to cancel."

If you enter Y, the program then looks for the fonts needed for your document in the directory containing Microsoft Word and downloads them to the printer.

A problem with the way Microsoft implemented the automatic downloading procedure is that at the end of printing the document, the program clears away the downloaded font. The reason is that Word downloads fonts in "temporary" status rather than "permanent" status and then erases them from the LaserJet's memory by sending a soft reset (Escape E) at the end of printing.

There are two ways to correct the problem. The easiest is to use the MAKEPRD program on the Word utility disk to remove the soft reset that Word sends to the printer at the conclusion of printing a file. MAKEPRD is easy to use. Just follow the directions in the "Microsoft Word Printer Information" manual supplied with the program. Use the utility to change the desired PRD file to text form. Then, using Word, find the line near the end of the driver that looks like this:

```
byte:4 mod:0 "^[E"
```

and change it to look like this:

```
byte:4 mod:0
```

Save the file in unformatted form and run the MAKEPRD program again to change the driver file back into compiled form. Make sure to give it the same name as it originally had.

Another way to avoid the problem is to download the fonts you want to use in permanent status before using Word. Utilities for that purpose are described in Chapter 15, "Downloading Fonts and Building Drivers."

Tips

- Always use the Tab key, not the Spacebar, for horizontal alignment when using proportional fonts.
- Sometimes you may wish to remove a style altogether from a text element. To do this, select

the element and type Alt-Spacebar.

- To print any ASCII character with Word, including the high-bit graphic characters and foreign letters in the range 127 to 255, hold down the Alt key while typing the number of the character on the numeric keypad. For example, to print a the pound sterling sign (£), type Alt-176. The character appearing on the screen will not be the same as the character printed out, because the screen uses a different symbol set than any of the cartridges. For more information on symbol sets and special characters.
- To embed the escape character in a document (in order to send control commands to the printer), type Alt-27 on the numeric keypad. To print an overlay macro on a page include the following command anywhere on the page: Ec&f#y2X, where # is the number of the macro. The text in which the command is placed cannot be centered or justified, because then Word will place spacing commands between the elements of the command, thereby disabling it.
- To apply a style to a single character, press the appropriate key combination twice.
- The "Microsoft Word Printer Information" manual supplied with the program has specific information on PRD files, the MERGEPRD program, and the MAKEPRD program.
- With versions of Word earlier than 4.0, it was necessary to set paper length at 10.5 inches. In Word 4.0, paper length should be set at 11 inches. The setting is controlled with the Format Division Margins command.
- Under Print Options, set Feed to Continuous unless you are using the LaserJet 2000 and want to use the third bin. In that case, set the Feed to Bin3.

Profile: MultiMate Advantage

LASERJET SUPPORT IS MUCH improved in MultiMate Advantage II over earlier versions, although the program still does not provide the level of formatting and font selection capabilities of more advanced word processors like WordPerfect, Microsoft Word, or WordStar 2000. With MultiMate Advantage II, you can use fonts from more than one cartridge at a time. Justification and column alignment are also improved over previous versions, and you can download soft fonts from within the program. In addition, you can now generate new drivers for MultiMate Advantage II using the latest release of the Conofonts Manager from Conographic. For access information, see Chapter 15, "Downloading Fonts and Building Drivers."

Older Versions

Versions of MultiMate numbered 3.20 and earlier do not have drivers for the LaserJet. Versions 3.5 and 3.60 offer slightly better support for the LaserJet. They allow one proportional font per document and use of only one font cartridge at a time.

Page Length

When you use MultiMate with the LaserJet, you should set the page length to 60 lines. This is done by selecting Other Utilities from the main menu and then selecting Edit System Defaults.

PATs and CWTs

MultiMate stores font information in Printer Action Tables (PATs) and Character Width Tables (CWTs). To select a PAT and store it as a default, follow these steps:

- Load MultiMate.
- From the main menu, select Printer Control Utilities by typing 4.
- Select Edit Printer Defaults by typing 2.
- Enter the name of the desired PAT.
- Return to the main menu by pressing F10.

Selecting a Font

To change from one font to another within a document, type

Alt-C

Next, enter the font letter of the font. You can now type in the new font.

Printing

If you are printing with a proportional font, you need to carry out the following steps:

- From the Document Print Options screen, select Yes for proportional.
- Leave the CWT name blank unless you are personalizing character widths (for more information, see page 39 of the "MultiMate Advantage II Printer Guide.")
- Type the name of the PAT file.
- Print by pressing F10.

Questions and Answers

Q: I am using MultiMate Advantage II with a LaserJet printer, but I do not have a legal paper tray. How can I produce a document on legal paper?
A: MultiMate Advantage II Printer Action Tables (PATs) do not directly support manual feeding of legal paper with the LaserJet. Manually fed legal documents can be produced in one of two ways:

- The escape sequence, for legal manual feed, which can be embedded in the MultiMate document, is

  Alt-A027&184p2H

  When embedding a command, do not place the command against the left margin on the screen; instead, space over one more column than the width of the left margin. Also, make sure that you type the numbers 027 on the numeric keypad.
- Your PAT can be modified to accommodate legal manual feed, as described in the "MultiMate Advantage II Printer Guide."

Q: I want to print envelopes. How is this done?
A: MultiMate Advantage II has a PAT for printing envelopes. The PAT name is LJETENV. Instructions for use of this PAT are in the "MultiMate Advantage II Printer Guide." Note: The instructions for use of this PAT advise that you insert 35 carriage returns prior to your address. This is correct for all LaserJet printers except the LaserJet II, which requires 24 carriage returns to position your mailing address.

Q: Can I use multiple fonts in a document?
A: Yes. MultiMate Advantage II defines as many as 26 different font selections within a single PAT. Font changes are made using the Alt-C command followed by the appropriate font letter for the desired selection.

Q: I have several font cartridges. How do I choose the correct PAT for the cartridge that I want to use?
A: Many of the PAT selections are documented in the "MultiMate Advantage II Printer Guide," where the PATs are identified for particular font cartridges. More complete documentation is available from Ashton-Tate in a publication titled "Using MultiMate Advantage II with Your LaserJet Printer."

Q: Can I use soft fonts with MultiMate?
A: Direct soft font support is limited and it is suggested that you print out the LJETPLUS.DOC document from the \LJETPLUS subdirectory of the Conversions 2 disk for instructions. The PATs and CWTs for soft font use are also in the same directory and will have to be copied to the \MM directory of your hard disk before they can be accessed. These PATs and CWTs are not copied during program installation. Also, Ashton-Tate is working on supplementary PATs and CWTs for soft fonts.

Q: I have a LaserJet II printer, which has the line and box drawing symbols in resident fonts, but I have been unable to access these characters using MultiMate Advantage II.
A: MultiMate Advantage II does not directly support the symbol set that contains these characters. They can be accessed in one of two ways:

- Use the Control Panel to set the printer's default symbol set to IBM-US. (See Chapter 3, "The Control Panel.").
- Embed the following printer command in your document: Alt-A027(10U. Remember to type the numbers 027 on the numeric keypad.

Profile: WordPerfect

PRIOR TO RELEASE 5.0, the laser printing capabilities of WordPerfect were somewhat limited. The new release, however, represents a quantum leap forward. Whereas it used to be the case that Microsoft Word was unrivaled in its support of the LaserJet, WordPerfect 5.0 is roughly equal to Word in most regards and quite superior to Word in others.

Overview

Here are some of the features of WordPerfect 5.0 that make the program especially amenable to laser printing:

- Without going through any difficult maneuvers, you can use almost any combination of soft fonts and cartridge fonts in a document.
- You can draw lines and boxes on a page.
- You can import graphics generated in other software.
- You can preview the actual appearance of a page.
- You can combine multiple fonts on a line and still have justified text.
- You can create style sheets that make it easy to consistently format and later consistently alter a document.

How to Create a Printer File

Before you can start printing with WordPerfect, you have to set up what's known as a printer file, or PRS file. To create it, do the following:

- Select the following: Print / Select Printer / Additional Printers.
- Scroll down to the model of LaserJet you are using and pick one by pressing Enter.

Now you can specify which font cartridges and which soft fonts you wish to use.

- Select the following: Print / Select Printer / Edit / Cartridges and Fonts.
- Highlight Cartridge Fonts (skip to "Highlight Soft Fonts" if you're only using soft fonts).
- Choose Select Fonts, then mark the cartridge(s) you are using with an asterisk (*).
- Select Exit.
- Highlight Soft Fonts.
- Choose Select Fonts.

- Mark the ones you want WordPerfect to download with a plus sign (+) and the ones you want to download yourself prior to printing with an asterisk (*).
- Select Exit.

As you select fonts for your printer file, notice that WordPerfect keeps track of how much memory they'll take up in the LaserJet. If your printer has 512K of memory (the standard configuration for the LaserJet Plus or LaserJet II), you will be limited to about 350K for fonts. If you've added a 1-megabyte memory board, you can increase the amount of storage available to about 1Mb.

How to Format Fonts within a Document

Once you've created a printer file, you can easily switch from one font to another within a document. First select your Initial Font. This is the default font. To select the Initial font,

- Select Print / Select Printer / Edit / Initial Font.
- Highlight the desired font and press Enter.
- Select Exit.

Once you are inside a document, you can change to a new font with the following sequence:

- Select Font / Base Font.
- Move the highlight to the desired font and press Enter.

At any time, you can change to a new Base Font. Just move the cursor to where you want the new font to start and select the new Base Font.

Let's say you are printing in 10-point HELV and want to switch to 12-point HELV. One option would be to go through the steps for selecting a new Base Font. Alternatively, you can select Size after selecting Font, which gives you the options Fine, Small, Large, Very Large. The problem with using this route is that you won't know for sure if selecting Large will actually give you 12-point.

Similarly, if you are switching to italic or bold in the same size you can select either italic or bold as a new Base Font or select Font and then select Appearance.

Undoing Font Selections

If you change your mind about a font selection, it is simple to undo:

- Select Reveal Codes.
- Delete the code for the font.

Note that this is an improvement in WordPerfect 5.0. Previously, it was not as simple to edit codes directly.

How to Change Leading

Leading is the amount of space between lines. Before the days of laser printers, leading did not need to be adjusted because type was all the same size. Typically, it was six lines to the inch.

With various font sizes in a document, the leading must change so letters on one line don't overlap those on another. WordPerfect takes care of this automatically by adjusting the leading allotted to a line to match the largest font used in that line.

If you wish to override the automatic setting, here's what to do:

- Select Format / Line / Line Height.
- Enter the desired leading. If the measurement shown is in inches, you can still enter a new figure in points. If you type 15p, for example, WordPerfect will automatically convert the 15p to inches. Note that there are 72 points to an inch and WordPerfect measures leading from baseline to baseline. The reason for using points for leading is that they are the standard unit of measure for fonts. For proper leading, you normally add two or three points to the size of the font. However, the appearance of a document can frequently be improved dramatically by increasing the leading. For instance, 16 points of leading for a 12-point font results in a much more readable document than 13 points of leading. Once you realize how much better most text looks with a bit of extra leading, you may use this technique all the time.

If you wish, you can change the units of measurement used throughout a document:

- Select Setup / Units of Measure.
- Select the desired measurement units.

Adding a Graphic

The ability to merge graphics into text is a nice feature that has been available for a while for word processors with utilities like Inset. However, the capabilities of WordPerfect 5.0 go far beyond what you can do with Inset, comparing quite favorably even to the advanced graphics features of high-end desktop publishing programs like PageMaker and Ventura Publisher.

The Graphics command is the starting point for merging graphics into text, creating boxes, creating ruling lines, or creating tables. To merge a graphic into a page of text, you do the following:

- Select Graphics / Figure / Create.
- Specify the name of the file containing the graphic, the location of the graphic, the size, whether you want text to wrap around, and whether you want a caption.

Once you have created the graphic using these steps, you can select the Graphics / Figure / Options command to add more parameters to

Cash in the Real World

Making it Count

■ Time, Money and Computers

(or how to use one to save the other two)

"Time is Money." One of the great cliches of all time. Another popular and pervasive myth, is that if you throw enough money into computers, you somehow create extra time from the ether; sit down in front of a machine and you will instantly work harder and produce more.

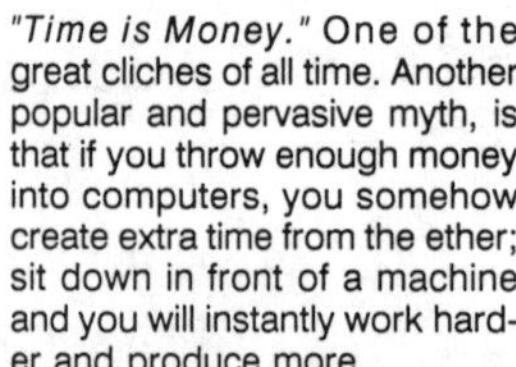

The hype that surrounds computers makes you think if you have enough money you can buy time. This fiction is somehow comforting. The truth is that computers *aren't* inherently efficient and productive.

They *are* inherently frustrating, maddening, and difficult. They require much thought and concentration, something not in vogue this year. They also require effort, a thing that's never popular.

And the results? The results are that you work just as hard, but in different ways. At first it's far harder to do something on a computer than to do it by hand. You try to tell the machine to do something, but it doesn't understand what you mean, so you have to learn its language as well as your own. A real time-saver, huh?

But after enough trial and error, after enough tension and stress, computers start to pay off. They do what you want. If you leave it at that, you will save time from there on in, until the machine breaks, which it inevitably will.

But if you get hooked, if you get reeled in—that's it. You'll spend hours, days, weeks, months, years, learning new things, experimenting, discovering. And it's wonderful. You have fun in ways you never knew existed.

However, if you're not careful, it can hit you. The desire to learn how to do things you have no intention of ever using, just to learn them. You've never been near a spreadsheet, but you find yourself in a store buying a spreadsheet program, learning what statistical formulas are, even though you don't believe statistics.

And then you're lost. You spend all your time in the quest to master software, to know its ins-and-outs, and you forget that you originally got the computer so you'd never have to retype anything ever again.

Therein lies the danger. Not with the fun. Not with the hours that disappear like seconds when you are at the keyboard. But with forgetting what you originally obtained a computer to do. With forgetting everything but the computer.

When it works, you are the master. When it doesn't work, you figure out why, and once again you are the master. When it breaks, you fix it, or throw it out, but still you are in control (or at least you think you are).

But slowly, almost imperceptibly, the unthinkable happens. Before you know it, you've become:

A SLAVE TO TECHNOLOGY.

control the thickness of the box surrounding the graphic (you can have no box if desired), the amount of outside space (between the box and the surrounding wraparound text), the amount of inside space (between the borders of the box and the graphic image), the shading of the box, the position of the caption, etc. Selecting the Graphics / Figure / Edit command lets you rotate the graphic, shift its position within the box, or change its size.

Lines, Boxes, and Tables

WordPerfect uses the same general approach for creating lines, boxes, and tables as it uses for creating graphics. Select the Graphics command, then select Table, Box, or Line. If you're setting up a table, you'll be provided with a special editing screen for typing in the contents. When you go back to working on your main document you won't actually see the contents of the Table but you will be able to check them with preview mode, as explained below.

Boxes can be freely positioned on the page, and ruling lines can be placed either vertically or horizontally along the left margin, between columns, along the right margin, or at another specified location.

Previewing the Results

Provided you have a graphics monitor, you can check the results of your formatting. When you are in the preview mode, you can't actually change anything, but it's easy enough to go in and out of preview mode until the document is adjusted to your liking:

- Select Print / View Document.
- Select how much magnification you want.

Style Sheets

As shown by programs such as Microsoft Word and Ventura Publisher, style sheets are one of the most powerful tools for formatting documents. Each style defines the appearance of a particular type of text, such as a headline. The font, the positioning, the spacing, and other features defining the appearance of the headline are all summarized in the style called "Headline." By labelling all the headlines in your document with the Headline style rather than formatting each one individually, you can more

Figure 1: Here's a sneak preview from Daniel Will-Harris's next book, WordPerfect 5: Desktop Publishing in Style. It was created entirely within WordPerfect 5.0 with no pasteup. The pictures of the coins were scanned and then loaded into WordPerfect as graphics. The illustration is reduced by 41 percent.

easily achieve a consistent appearance. Moreover, if you want to change the appearance of every headline, all you have to do is change the definition of the style and everything labeled with that style changes automatically.

To create a style, select Style / Create. You then specify the name, the type (paired or open), the description, and the codes that make up the style. Paired styles have a definite beginning point and ending point, while open styles do not have an ending point. You can save a set of styles under a file name, which makes it possible to use one set for one type of document, then use another set for a different type of document.

To activate a style, you select Style, then select the name of the style from the list.

Using Fontware

One of the best aspects of WordPerfect 5.0 is that it comes with a free offer for Bitstream's Fontware package. With Fontware, you can generate fonts of any size for the LaserJet Plus or LaserJet II from master typeface outlines, as described in Chapter 14, "Font Generators," and in "Profile: Fontware." Not only does this give you flexibility in sizes of fonts, but the quality of Bitstream's fonts is excellent.

Adding Fonts from Other Vendors

WordPerfect 5.0 supports almost all the cartridge and soft fonts available from Hewlett-Packard, including several not supported in WordPerfect 4.2: the X cartridge and the AD and AF soft fonts.

To add soft fonts from other vendors, you need a utility that can build the appropriate drivers, or PRS files. Currently, most vendors that sell soft fonts have utilities that generate these files for version 4.2. You'll need to check with the soft font vendor to make sure they have added the same capability for WordPerfect 5.0.

If the vendor can't supply you with the drivers you need or a utility to create them, check into SoftCraft's Laser Fonts program (described in "Profile: Laser Fonts.")

Questions and Answers

Q:. Can I use cartridges and soft fonts together on the same page?
A: Yes.

Q: What's the difference between the Initial Font and the Base Font?
A: The Initial Font gives WordPerfect a starting default for any document, but you can change that at any time by selecting a new Base Font. The setting for Base Font applies only to

the document you are working on at the moment.

Q: I do not have the LaserJet II printer driver available on my WordPerfect 4.2 printer diskette. What should I use?

A: If the LaserJet II printer driver is not available, select the LaserJet Reg, +, 500+, A: PC Courier printer definition. This definition is the closest to the LaserJet II internal fonts. You can contact the WordPerfect Corporation and request an updated version of their printer drivers.

Q: When I attempting to print my document in WordPerfect 4.2, why does the printer display PC Load Exec or PC B5?

A: This can occur when:

- You have specified the incorrect page or length. The normal setting for 7 lpi, letter-size paper is a form length of 77 and text length of 54. For legal paper the form length should be set at 84 with the text length set at 72.
- Your LaserJet's default page length (60 lines) has been changed. Reset your printer either by shutting it off or by taking it off line and holding down the HOLD TO RESET (LaserJet Plus) until 07 is displayed, or by holding down the ENTER /RESET MENU key (LaserJet II) until 09 Menu Reset is displayed.

Q: An Error 50 is appearing on the Control Panel—what should I do?

A: To correct this problem, check your baud rate setting in your AUTOEXEC.BAT file to verify that it is set correctly—the LaserJet's default is 9,600 baud. If that is set correctly, make sure that when selecting printers in WordPerfect, you selected a baud rate of 9,600.

Q: I'm using WordPerfect 4.2. The top margin and left margin of my document are much larger than I specified. Why?

A: If you selected #3 Sheet Feeder as the Type of Forms, make sure you specified zero Extra Lines Between Pages as well as a Column Position of Left Edge of Paper equal to zero.

Profile: WordStar

WHILE PREVIOUS VERSIONS of WordStar were notoriously difficult to use with the LaserJet, release 4 does a creditable job of supporting a variety of fonts. The program comes with five LaserJet drivers. These are as follows:

- HPLJET—Supports the F and P cartridges.
- HPLJ:B—Supports the B cartridge.
- HPLJ:U—Supports the U and V cartridges.
- HPLJ:V—Supports the Y cartridge and the AC soft font set.
- HPL:AD—Supports the AD soft font set.

In addition, you can obtain two new drivers (free!) by calling MicroPro (800/227-5609) or by writing to the MicroPro Technical Support, P.O. Box 7079, San Rafael, CA 94901. You need to specify that you are requesting the "WordStar 4 Added Printer Support In-Line Kit."

The new drivers are as follows:

- HPLJ:K—Supports the K and J cartridges.
- HPLJ2—Specially designed for the LaserJet II; supports the F and P cartridges.

Once you have copied the drivers to the WordStar subdirectory, you can select the one you wish to print with by pressing P on the main menu and entering the name of the driver in response to the prompt.

You can assign LaserJet escape sequences to the four print control keys, ^PQ, ^PW, ^PE, and ^PR. To define ^PQ, type .XQ at the top of your document, followed by the escape sequence in hexadecimal. (Sounds like trouble? It is! While this book does include all the font cartridge escape sequences in Appendix C, they are shown in ASCII only because there simply wasn't space to include the hexadecimal equivalents. You'll need to refer to HP's "LaserJet series II Printer Technical Reference Manual," which does have a table of hex equivalents for escape sequences.)

Assuming you've been able to assign the necessary escape sequences to select the fonts you wish to use, the remaining step is to tell WordStar what spacing you wish to use. The command .PS OFF on one line followed by .CW# on the next line, in which # is replaced by the pitch (such as 10 characters per inch), works for monospaced fonts. For proportionally spaced fonts, use the command .PS ON. Make sure the period is in the first column of your document.

C	Printer name	HP LaserJet
D	Initialization	
	Initialization code	1B 28 30 55 1B 28 73 31 70 31 30 76 73 42
	Deinitialization code	1B 28 38 55
G	Protocol	A (handled outside WordStar)
O	User-defined functions	
	^PQ	1B 28 73
	^PW	73 37 42
	^PE	31 30 76
	^PR	1B

Table 1: Changes in the Printer Installation Menu to create "LaserStar."

WordStar 3.3

The remainder of this chapter is aimed at those fanatical diehards (I know you're out there!) who never switched to WordPerfect or Microsoft Word—who never even upgraded to WordStar 2000 or WordStar 4. I'm talking about those of you who are still using good old WordStar 3.3. If you had switched to WordStar 4 at least, you'd find that the program now offered significant LaserJet support. When you install the program, you can select a driver for the B, F, U, V, and Y cartridges and for the AC and AD soft fonts. But here you are, still using WordStar 3.3. What are you going to do with that new LaserJet II that just arrived?

First, you'll be glad to know that you can actually get started printing on the LaserJet with WordStar 3.3, even though the program doesn't have a LaserJet driver, as long as you are content with the printer's default Courier font.

Because the LaserJet does not print in a small margin around the edges of the paper, you need to adjust the number of lines per page using three of WordStar's dot commands: page length (.pl), bottom margin (.mb), and top margin (.mt). WordStar's defaults for these three parameters are 65, 8, and 3 respectively. To achieve the same dimensions on the LaserJet, change the settings by typing the following dot commands at the beginning of each document, making sure that each dot is in the first column:

```
.pl 62
```

S Function keys	Code	Description
F1	^PQ^PEsB	TR10
F2	^PQ8V	TR8
F3	^PQ^PE1S	TR10it
F4	^PQ^PE^PW	TR10bo
F5	^PQ14V	Helv
F6	^PR	Escape

Table 2: Changes in the Menu of WordStar Features to create "LaserStar."

```
.mb 4
.mt 5
```

Alternatively, you might try the single command .pl 60.5

Utilities

To use fonts other than Courier, you have several options. One is to use the Winstall utility to patch WordStar, as explained below. Another is to buy an enhancement utility. The most widely used such utility is Polaris PrintMerge (not to be confused with Polaris RAM-Resident PrintMerge).

A third option is to use WordStar in conjunction with a more powerful page layout program. Both Ventura Publisher and PageMaker can import text directly from WordStar 3.3. This provides an easy solution to WordStar's lack of support for multiple fonts. If you're comfortable with WordStar, you can keep using it for your everyday word processing. Then when it comes time for fancy formatting, leave the jobs to the heavy-duty programs designed for that purpose.

Patching WordStar 3.3

With the following procedure, you modify WordStar 3.3 using the Winstall utility provided on the WordStar disk. After going through the steps described below, you'll have two versions of WordStar you can switch between—an unaltered version to use with a standard printer and a new version for use with the LaserJet's B or F cartridge. Note: The procedure has been tested only on WordStar 3.30 and may not work correctly with WordStar 3.31.

Before you begin, format a system disk (with the /S option of DOS's FORMAT command). Then copy the file MODE.COM from the DOS disk onto the new disk. Next, copy the following files from the WordStar disk onto the new disk:

- WS.COM
- WSOVLY1.OVR
- WINSTALL.OVR
- WINSTALL.COM
- WSMSGS.OVR
- WS.INS.

Use the new disk to make your changes. (We assume you're using a floppy disk system; you can also use the files on a hard disk if you have the original disks as a backup.) After you finish the modification, the new disk will contain two versions of the WS.COM file—a laser printer version named LWS.COM and a regular version, WS.COM.

The laser version of WordStar that you create using Winstall will differ from the regular version in several respects. It will automatically send an initialization code to the LaserJet prior to each printing job, causing the printer to use 10-point Tms Rmn until it receives the code for a different font. After printing ends, the program will send a deinitialization code, which resets the printer to 12-point Courier.

The first five function keys on the computer will be programmed with codes allowing you to switch between the five proportionally spaced fonts on the B or F cartridge: Tms Rmn in 8-point, 10-point, 10-point italic, and 10-point bold; and 14.4-point Helv bold. Using Helv for headlines or titles, 10-point Tms Rmn for body text, and 8-point Tms Rmn for footnotes and tables produces professional-looking, readable documents. If you prefer, you can adapt the codes for use with a different cartridge.

The Winstall utility on the WordStar disk lets you customize the program. Codes and other information that you plug into Winstall to create "LaserStar"—the LaserJet version of WordStar—are summarized in Tables 1 and 2. To use Winstall, type

WINSTALL.WS

Winstall will ask what drive your WordStar files are located on. Type

A:

When Winstall asks the name of the file to install, type

WS.COM

When you're asked for the name of the file for the installed version, type

LWS.COM

From the main Installation menu, select D, Custom Installation of Printers. This takes you to the Printer Installation menu. Select C (Printer Name), and type

HP LaserJet

When Winstall returns you to the Printer Installation Menu, select D, Initialization. When prompted, enter the initialization code shown in Table 1. Since the code is a sequence of hexadecimal numbers, precede each entry by a comma to distinguish it as hexadecimal. After entering last number, type a period and press Enter to finalize the change. Then enter the deinitialization code in the same manner.

Again at the Printer Installation menu, select G to display the Protocol menu and choose option A, Protocols Handled Outside WordStar.

From the Printer Installation Menu select O, User-defined Functions. WordStar allows you to define four printer functions according to your needs. Enter the hexadecimal codes shown in Table 1 for ^PQ, ^PW, ^PE, and ^PR.

After returning to the Printer Installation Menu, select X to return to the main Installation menu. Then select E, Menu of WordStar Features. From this menu select S, Function Keys.

You'll need to enter codes for six function keys and provide the names you want to appear on the menu. Table 2 shows the codes, which can be entered as ASCII characters, and suggests function key labels.

Why insert the user-defined functions (^PQ, ^PW, ^PE, and ^PR) into the function key codes instead of assigning the codes directly to the function keys? This seemingly roundabout method is necessary for two reasons. First, WordStar routinely discards any escape (1B hex) characters it encounters unless they are "hidden" in the user-defined functions. Second, function keys can contain no more than six characters—too few to accommodate the lengthy codes required for switching between fonts.

After coding the function keys, type X once to leave the Installation Menu, and X again to leave Winstall. Finally, at the Exit Options Menu press A to save your changes.

That's it. You now have a version of WordStar that lets you change fonts merely by pressing a single function key. In addition, with the F6 key you can embed the escape character in any document and thus can send any control codes to the printer, including commands to select other fonts.

Margins

Unfortunately, this new flexibility in changing typefaces leads to complications elsewhere, especially in setting margins.

Two types of margin problems can occur. The first is caused by the codes inserted in your text for switching fonts. Although the codes are not printed, they affect your margins because WordStar counts them as text characters.

The best solution to this problem is to make any font changes after the document is formatted. Once you establish the margins, turn off word wrap (Ctrl-OW) and insert the printer codes with the newly programmed function keys. The lines containing code will look too long on the screen but will print out correctly.

If, as you initially type a document, you want to mark the spots where codes should be inserted, you can use symbols such as {, }, @, ~, and |. After completing the document, you can do a search and replace to substitute the function key codes for these symbols.

The other problem is the irregular left margin that may result when you use several typefaces in one document. This happens because font selection affects not only the letters but also the width of spaces and the width of margins. The width of the left margin is determined by the last font used. For example, if most of the text is in 10-point Tms Rmn but one line ends with a word in 8-point Tms Rmn, the next line will have too narrow a left margin since the margin is set for a smaller font. To prevent this problem, make sure that all lines end in the same font. If most of your text is in Tms Rmn 10-point, for example, press F1 at the end of any lines that end in other fonts.

Profile: WordStar 2000

Every word processing program has its partisans. For years, we were fanatical about Microsoft Word, mainly because it was the only program that really made it possible to utilize the advanced font and typographic features of the LaserJet. Lately we've been forced to admit, with the release of WordPerfect 5.0, that Microsoft Word no longer reigns unchallenged as king of the laser hill. Nor is WordPerfect the only viable challenger. In this chapter, contributor Daniel Will-Harris makes the case for a dark horse contender: WordStar 2000 Release 3.

—TN & MG

Microsoft Word and WordPerfect get all the attention. It's as if someone decided those two are the only two word processing programs for bona fide computer users. I hope the recent release of WordPerfect 5.0 will finally put to rest the unfounded rumor that only Word really works with a laser printer.

In the midst of all the hype surrounding the two biggies, people are overlooking a great word processing program. A program with the ability to create its own printer drivers for any downloadable font; to integrate graphics and automatically wrap text around them; to preview the entire page on-screen; and one that doesn't require a Ph.D. to learn.

What is this remarkable program? Why, it's the much ignored, oft maligned WordStar 2000—the Rodney Dangerfield of word processing programs. It has been maligned because it was slow, and ignored because it was maligned. But with release 3 of the program, things have changed, and this is now a program that deserves respect.

Familiar but Fast

WordStar 2000 uses the ubiquitous old WordStar interface and efficient cursor diamond, but with all new, easy to remember, mnemonic commands. ^CB is cursor beginning. ^CE is cursor end. ^BB is block beginning. One guess as to what *B*lock *E*nd is. Or *B*lock *M*ove. If you are familiar with English, you can remember WordStar 2000's commands. Many users find this much easier than trying to remember WordPerfect's Alt F4 for marking a block, or Word's F6.

And what of WordStar 2000's fabled sloth? Gone. WordStar 2000 is now just as fast as either Word or WordPerfect. You can move quickly from beginning to end, or page to page. A special "fast cursor" feature truly makes the cursor move swiftly. It's so much faster, maybe they should have called it *WordStar 3000*. What's more, WordStar 2000's output to a LaserJet II is better than Word's (but more on that later).

A "Page Preview" feature that shows a reduced view of your page on-screen, so you can see what the entire page will look like, also comes standard with WordStar 2000 Release 3. This feature works with numerous graphics cards, including CGA, EGA, VGA, Hercules, and even the full page Genius monitor. Although you cannot edit in this mode, it is a godsend for avoiding so much trial and error reprinting.

LaserJet Features

MicroPro also improved its already exceptional LaserJet support. WordStar 2000's on-screen ruler uses inches instead of spaces as its measurement units—a boon for those using proportional fonts. WordStar 2000 calculates how much text can fit on a line and shows you accordingly. When you change fonts, the lines change to reflect this. Even when you use multiple fonts on a single line, WordStar 2000 shows you exactly where you are on a line, something even Word can't do.

This especially important capability really pays off with proportionally spaced fonts, as they are spaced differently than the monospaced fonts on all PC screens. With the new ruler line, it's much easier to line up numerical columns or figure out how long lines need to be. There's no guessing because you see exactly, to a hundredth of an inch, where you are on a line. And WordStar 2000 never requires repagination. (Do I hear begrudging sighs from Word users?)

WordStar 2000 can work with up to 32 fonts at a time. These fonts can be downloaded, built into the printer, or both. To change fonts, type ^PF (Printer-Fonts), and the program gives you a list of available fonts. After you make your selection, WordStar 2000 inserts a code. The codes are kept hidden unless you type ^OD (Option Display), which leaves them in plain sight and in plain English. "[Dutch 10 point]" is displayed when you're using that font, and all font names are complete and clear.

Headers and footers are simple and automatic. Typing ^OH (Option Headers) puts two header markers into the text, and between them is room for the header. You create them just like typing anything else, and they are easily visible, accessible, even searchable, at any time. You can create different footers for the left and right pages, making facing pages practical. WordStar 2000 is even smart enough to automatically change top and bottom margins when you change the headers and footers. It's the little things like this that save you a lot of time and frustration, and a thoughtful detail Microsoft Word lacks.

Precise Spacing

For LaserJet users, here's the clincher: the precise quality of WordStar 2000's microspaced justification far exceeds even Word's, which means that WordStar 2000 has some of the best printed output from any word processing program. Only WordPerfect gives you more precise control over letter and word spacing. With WordStar 2000 and a LaserJet II, you can turn out truly impressive pages.

Don't believe it? It's true. Microsoft Word relies on the printer to do much of the work, and only varies the size of interword spaces. But WordStar 2000 adjusts the space between every character, which provides much more attractive, readable, and professional-looking text, the kind of feature you pay much more for in complex page composition programs.

Microsoft Word's infinitely variable line-spacing adjustment and the ability to set up a style for every paragraph are big advantages, but style sheets can be extremely hard to figure out. WordStar 2000 offers a simpler alternative, which it calls "format" files. These files contain the basic design of the document: the margins, columns, headers, footers, and other functions of what Word calls "division." With WordStar 2000, when you create a new file, you select a format file and your new file is formatted. The format file also includes printer and font information, so you can design your page specifically for whatever printer you want to use. These files can also include text or graphics, so you might have a format file that contains your company letterhead.

WordStar 2000 includes automatic formats for paragraph indents, hanging indents, left indents, and indents on both sides of paragraphs. One command selects any of these formats, and the format is applied to all text following the command—very easy to understand and implement.

WordStar 2000 also outclasses Microsoft Word with its ability to create printer drivers for whatever laser fonts you might unearth. HPFONT automatically creates perfect LaserJet drivers from any downloadable soft fonts. The entire names of up to eight of them will even appear on the font menu. The same program also gives you the freedom to select the right line spacing for each font you're using. You can choose up to eight different line heights (leading) in points—one for each font family available. HPFONT also creates batch files that quickly and easily download fonts to the printer. The process is easy to understand, and you can even download fonts from within WordStar 2000. As if to prove this point, sections of the WordStar 2000 manual were created and printed with WordStar 2000 and a laser printer.

You can always get excellent context-sensitive on-line help by pressing F1, the standard help key for most PC software. The help system has an index, so while you are presented with help that is relevant to what you're doing at the time, you can get help about any topic at any time. The help is so good that when other commands or possibly unfamiliar words such as "fonts" are mentioned, you can move to that word and get more information about it.

Columns

Columns are another sticky area with word processing programs. With Microsoft Word it's difficult to create multiple columns. WordStar 2000, on the other hand, creates columns with ease, even when they contain graphics. And you can see them on-screen using the Page Preview feature.

Although you can't have columns with different widths, you can change margins while in column mode, and turn columns on and off as much as you like within a page, making it easy to do side-by-side paragraphs. You won't see columns side-by-side on-screen, except in Preview mode, but they do appear offset, so unlike Word, where all columns are along the left edge of the screen, you can see if you're in column 1, 2, or 3.

Inset

WordStar 2000 also includes Inset, a third-party program that allows you to integrate graphics with your text. With this program, you can paste graphics or text into a WordStar 2000 document from WordStar, Lotus 1-2-3, Symphony, Framework, PC Paintbrush, or AutoCAD. You can also capture text or graphics screens and paste them into your document. Inset provides some editing capability for cleaning up or altering images. No matter what the content of the inserted graphic, WordStar 2000 will automatically wrap text around it.

While Inset can be purchased separately (see "Profile: Inset") and works with many other programs, the bundled version has been customized for WordStar 2000. When you choose ^GM (Graphics Merge), a list of graphics files appears on-screen. You select a file, tell the program if you want the graphic on the left, center, or right of the column, whether you want the text to flow around or under it, and what size you want the graphic, and a marker is inserted in your file. This marker leaves the exact amount of space necessary for the graphic, and wraps the text around it. The graphic will always stay with its associated text because the marker moves with the text.

Inset includes a built-in paint program you can access at any time to edit or create a graphic. Inset will put a box around any image, rotate it, and even convert straight text into graphics. While Inset will not read PC Paintbrush or other file formats directly, it does come with a screen capture program to "grab" graphics from any program off almost any screen.

Some Extras

WordStar 2000's excellent hyphenation is completely automatic (it simply inserts "soft hyphens" when necessary, and doesn't bother you at all). It's also much faster than either WordPerfect or Microsoft Word.

WordStar 2000 includes its own thesaurus with 550,000 synonyms—over twice the size of the popular Word Finder thesaurus. It even gives you definitions of words, so you can be sure you're using the right one. The word count feature is wonderful for writers; it not only tells the number of words in a file, but how many paragraphs and sentences as well.

Other important features include the ability to have up to three windows on-screen at a time, a built-in macro function for automating complex commands, sorting, arithmetic (useful to insure accuracy in reports and, once again, the easiest to use), the ability to read 1-2-3 files directly and automatically keep them updated, DOS access from within files, and automatic index and table of contents creation. The only features I couldn't find were flush right tabs and dot-leader tabs, although both these can be kludged using WordStar 2000's versatile columns.

If you've ever forgotten what file contained the information you wanted, and spent time sifting through them all, you'll appreciate a feature called FileLocator. FileLocator indexes every word in every WordStar 2000 file on a disk. When you are looking for a particular word or phrase, you type ^L for "locate" and the program quickly sifts through its index and pulls up the files with the words you want. Then it will jump to the word and display the context. You can search for words linked with "and," "or," "not," and even request to see only files where two words are within a certain number of letters of each other. This is an effective system for finding and retrieving the masses of information stored in a computer.

WordStar 2000 comes with a slew of useful add-on programs for free. MailList is, guess what, a mailing list management program. It's not particularly powerful, but it does come all set up for most uses, and works easily with WordStar 2000's mail-merge function.

TelMerge, the telecommunications program, includes a script language to automate electronic mail, and converts a WordStar 2000 file to ASCII as it sends.

In the personal edition, you get ShowText, a genuinely terrific desktop presentations/word chart program. ShowText creates clean, professional word charts for slides, presentations, and signs. The first-rate, high resolution fonts and pre-designed formats that come with the program turn out impressive visuals—precisely what many organizations need.

Star Exchange is a special version of the popular Software Bridge file conversion program, which converts to and from WordStar, WordPerfect, Word, DisplayWrite, and MultiMate. Fill-a-Form lets you do just that—create a template to match pre-printed forms, and fill them in without using a typewriter.

With these free extra programs, WordStar 2000 is the most complete word-handling package around.

WordStar 2000 does not work directly with either Ventura or PageMaker, and this is unfortunate. Because Ventura writes any changes back to your word processor's files, if you use a program like WordPerfect or Word, you can edit a file you've changed in Ventura. But with WordStar 2000, you'd have to convert the file, re-edit it, then convert it back to the DCA file format, adding many more steps every time you want to edit the file. But when used by itself, WordStar 2000 may be all desktop publishing software you require.

MicroPro has not only cleaned up its act in the technical support department, it now has tech support that even surpasses WordPerfect's. Registered owners have access to a toll-free 800 number—seven days a week. Someone finally realized that people need answers on weekends—hooray!

WordStar 2000 is in a class with WordPerfect and Microsoft Word. It no longer lacks speed, is easier to use than either of them, produces outstanding output on LaserJets, and comes with all the additional software necessary to effectively produce both desktop and presentations. So don't ignore it, because now you'll know what you're missing.

—Daniel Will-Harris

Questions and Answers

Q: How can I print foreign accented characters?

A: The HPPLUS.KEY file contains macros that allow you to use high-bit characters. You won't see the characters onscreen, but they will appear in the printed version of your document.

Q: How do I print envelopes?

A: WordStar 2000 has a new printer driver available for printing envelopes. To embed the escape sequence manually, type the following code:

```
^[&l1o3H
```

(That's caret, left bracket, ampersand, lowercase l, numeral 1, lowercase o, numeral 3, uppercase H.)

Q: How do I switch the LaserJet to legal paper?
A: To feed legal paper manually, use the following escape sequence:

```
^[&l80p2H
```

(That's caret, left bracket, ampersand, lowercase l, numeral 8, zero, lowercase p, numeral 2, uppercase H).

Q: Which printer driver do I install if I don't have a font cartridge?
A: Select the driver "HP LaserJet F and all others."

CHAPTER SIX

Merging Text and Graphics

AT SOME POINT most LaserJet users will be interested in mixing together graphics produced by one program with text produced by another and printing them on a single page. There's a fairly simple way to do this—just leave a blank for the graphic image you want to insert and then run the paper through the printer twice. On the LaserJet II place your page in the bin face up; on earlier LaserJets place it face down.

Of course, this twice-through-the-printer trick won't get you too far—it's time consuming and inexact. What you need is assistance at the software level. Fortunately, there are more options now than any before. Here are your choices:

- First, before you run out and buy a special graphics-merging utility, check to see whether your word processor already has that capability. For example, WordStar 2000 Release 3 comes with Inset, a utility described in one of the following software profiles. Similarly, WordPerfect 5.0 has the built-in ability to "grab" graphics from other programs and merge them into pages.
- Assuming your word processor doesn't have a graphics merge capability, consider buying one of the utilities discussed in the following three profiles. If you're a Microsoft Word user, consider PageView. If you use another word processor, consider Inset or RAM-Resident Polaris PrintMerge. Of the latter two, Inset has our vote because it allows you to actually preview the graphic merged in with text to check positioning. With Polaris RAM-Resident PrintMerge you don't have that capability, and it can take many trial-and-error print-

outs to get a picture positioned correctly.

- If you frequently need to merge graphics into text pages, you're almost certainly better off skipping the utilities altogether and using a full-fledged desktop publishing program instead. Go to Part IV of this book and read about Ventura and PageMaker.

Profile: Inset

THE PURPOSE OF INSET is to let you position and merge text and graphics together on a single page. The utility lets you clip an image that you see on the screen and store it on the disk for later insertion, then mark a spot in a different document where you want to insert the image.

For example, you can create a chart using Lotus 1-2-3, clip and save it, and then insert it into a document created with MultiMate. Or, some more possibilities:

- Without ever leaving your word processing program, you can print the company logo on the top of your stationery
- Print your signature on the bottom of a mail-merged letter (and protect your signature with a password);
- Edit and enhance a graph from within your word processing or spreadsheet program;
- Merge a scanned image into text; read a draw-type program screen, paint on it, and finally insert the finished artwork into your word processing file.

Here's how it works. Whenever you want a picture to appear in your file, you place a "tag" in your text. A tag consists of square brackets with a file name inside them, like this: [C:\wp\inset\summer]. If your program uses brackets for its own commands, as WordStar 2000 does, you can change them to any other symbol you want. I use the braces: {}.

When Inset sees this tag, it inserts the picture of the same name. You place enough blank lines in your word processing file so the graphic doesn't print over your text. Inset shows you exactly what it's going to look like, on-screen, without leaving your word processing program.

To make sure the picture won't print over your text, Inset shows you how large the picture will be and lets you resize it, either proportionally or by stretching.

Enhancing its main features of cut and paste, Inset has some other interesting features, not least of which is a

Access

Inset
Inset Systems
12 Mill Plain Road
Danbury, CT 06811
203/794-0396
Price: $149

complete paint program built in, so you can create graphics with it.

You can manipulate pictures in several ways. One way is to rotate them 90 degrees. In other words, you can print an image either in its normal orientation or sideways. You can also shrink and expand images. And you can print a border around an image.

Inset is a memory-resident program, which means that you load it into the computer's RAM at the beginning of each session. Once you are in your word processor, spreadsheet program, or other piece of software, you can see the Inset menu at any time by pressing the two-key combination Shift-PrintScrn.

Inset can be used with most word processors (WordStar, MultiMate, DisplayWrite, Samna, Microsoft Word, WordPerfect, Volkswriter) as well as with most graphics programs, including 1-2-3, Symphony, the Grafix Partner, Energraphics, Fontrix, PC-Paint, Graphwriter, and AutoCAD.

Most graphics boards are supported, including CGA, EGA, Hercules, and Tecmar graphics adapters. If you have a mouse that emulates a Microsoft or PC Mouse, you can use it with Inset for graphics editing.

—Daniel Will-Harris

Profile: PageView

IF YOUR PROBLEM is a few flies around the house, you need a fly swatter, not a submachine gun. Powerful, feature-loaded page layout programs like PageMaker and Ventura are great for serious laser printer mavens, but suppose you're the type of person who just wants to occasionally spruce up an ordinary memo by inserting a chart or a picture. If that's all you need, aiming a program like Ventura at the task is simply overkill.

Enter PageView. Compared with the heavy hitters of Laserdom, it does relatively little—however, that little bit may be just what you need. The main benefit of PageView is that it lets you preview the pages of your document on-screen and alter the appearance of the pages in several ways. Using the mouse (or keyboard keys), you can adjust the margins of your page, change positions of headers and footers, and push the page number to a desired location. As most Microsoft Word users will agree, these are actions that are quite difficult to perform within Word itself.

The mystery, however, is why it should be necessary to use a separate program just to perform these few additional functions. Why not build a page preview mode into Microsoft Word, as has been done in the most

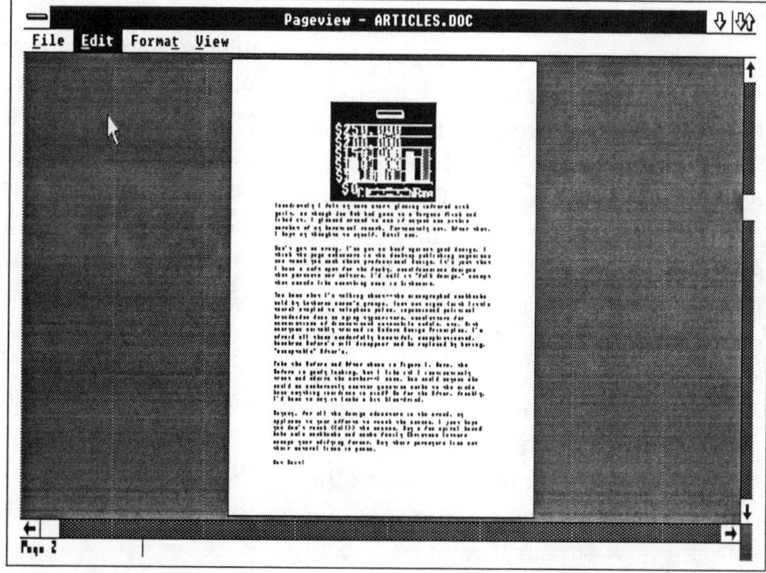

Figure 1: As this screen snapshot shows, you can check the general layout of your page but not read the text in Pageview's full page mode. Note the distortion in the graphic, which was imported from Excel.

recent release of WordPerfect? And why not simplify Word's procedure for setting up headers, formatting page numbers, and adjusting margins?

For whatever reason (perhaps merely because Microsoft wanted a way to tie Word into its Windows interface), PageView is here. The program is a Windows application, but for those users who don't already have Windows, Microsoft has bundled the program with a scaled-down version of Windows called PageView Windows. Unfortunately, when you run PageView under PageView Windows rather than under standard Windows 2.0 or Windows/386, you can't take advantage of PageView's capability to insert pictures saved from other programs into a Microsoft Word document.

Those running PageView under standard Windows will find the cut-and-paste capability simple and powerful, but somewhat buggy. Let's say you want to add a chart from Excel to a memo created in Microsoft Word. First you load Excel from Windows, create the chart, pull the selection box around the chart, hold down the Shift key while selecting the Edit menu, and select the Copy or Cut command to save the chart to the Windows Clipboard. Then you load PageView, load your memo, create a picture frame to hold the chart, and select the Paste command to insert the chart into the frame. That's not all: you can now stretch the frame to any size and crop unwanted portions of the chart. Other utilities on the market do allow graphics to be inserted into word processed documents, but none makes it this easy.

Access

PageView
Microsoft Corporation
16011 N.E. 36th Way
Redmond, WA 98073-9717
206/882-8080
Price: $49.95

We noticed two sorts of bugs in PageView's graphics insertion capability. One was that labels that were correctly positioned in our original Excel graphic seemed to lose their bearings and run over the axes of the chart when it was pasted into a PageView picture frame. Another problem was that graphics correctly copied into the Windows Clipboard could not be pasted into a PageView frame. We did find a workaround for the problem, which involved pasting the picture into Windows Paint and then cutting it from Paint back into the Clipboard. After this intermediate step was carried out, the picture could be pasted.

All in all, PageView is a clumsy, limited program that hardly qualifies as a demonstration of the advantages of Windows. Until Microsoft cleans up the bugs and adds a few more capabilities to the program, it won't really be worth the effort to use it.

For example, it's nice to be able to push and pull the margins of your page as easily as stretching a rubber band. But what if in the process of adjusting margins you notice a missing letter in a word? When you try inserting the letter, you quickly discover that PageView provides no text editing capabilities whatsoever. To fix the word you have to save your document, go back into Microsoft Word, type the missing letter, then go back into PageView to resume formatting.

PageView is a nice start, but until it gets a bit less clunky and a lot more powerful, we'd advise that you hang onto your fifty bucks.

Profile: Polaris RAM-Resident PrintMerge

POLARIS RAM-RESIDENT PrintMerge is designed to supplement the features of word processors. It is a finishing tool, enabling word processors to create boxes, lines, and shaded areas and to insert graphics created with other programs.

RAM-Resident PrintMerge works with all the major word processing programs on the market, including Microsoft Word, WordPerfect, MultiMate, WordStar, WordStar 2000, Volkswriter, IBM DisplayWrite 3 and 4, and XyWrite. Once PrintMerge has been loaded into RAM, the program automatically intercepts a document on the way to the printer, executing PrintMerge commands that have been embedded in the text.

For example, the command

```
&BX 2,3,10,0&
```

creates a 2-by-3-inch box made of solid black lines that are 10 printer dots wide. Using the horizontal and vertical positioning commands, you can place the box anywhere on the page, regardless of where you embedded the box command itself.

PrintMerge supports all the LaserJet's gray shades and patterns, and it can use fonts from third-party vendors. You can set horizontal and vertical rules of any weight and length anywhere on the page.

For merging graphics into text, PrintMerge has a "graph-grabber" screen capture utility. To crop the image you have to use a separate utility, Polaris Crunch. You cannot see the graphic while you're cropping it, but by compressing the data that makes up the picture, Crunch makes it possible to print larger images on the

Access

RAM-Resident PrintMerge
Polaris Software
613 West Valley Parkway #323
Escondido, CA 92025
800/338-5943
800/231-3531 in California
Price: $149

basic LaserJet than would otherwise be possible.

The beauty of the PrintMerge approach is its lack of ambition. Rather than attempting to start from scratch, the designers of the program realized that other products were already handling text quite well, and that what PC users needed was not to start over with new software but to equip their familiar word processing programs with some missing parts.

3

GRAPHICS

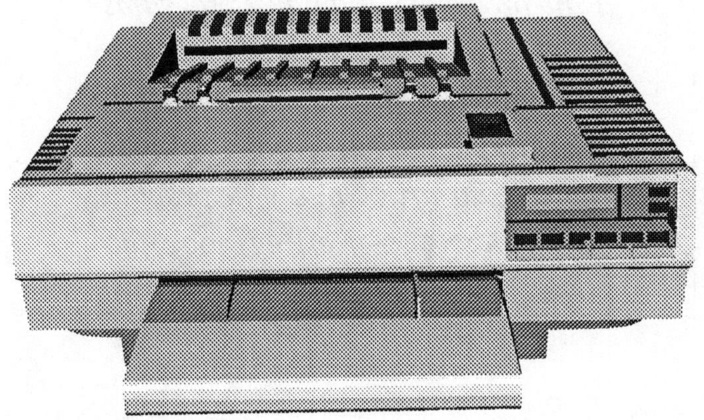

Section Focus

One of the advantages of laser printers over previous dot matrix and daisy wheel printers is that they can easily switch from producing high-quality text to producing high-quality graphics—even on the same page. With its expandable memory, the LaserJet II has even more graphics potential than previous versions of the LaserJet.

This section introduces the two major types of graphics software, draw programs and paint programs. In addition, it tells how you can take advantage of commercially available collections of images, called "clip art." Finally, it provides advice about converting your pictures among formats.

CHAPTER SEVEN

Graphics Fundamentals

HAVE YOU HEARD the one about the PC that walked into a bar full of Macs? I hope so, because I forgot the punchline. But it had something to do with the Mac myth that IBM PCs and compatibles are artless. They point to the graphic-packed little Mac and say, how can a PC possibly compete? The point they seem to miss is that the PC, being an open machine, can have graphics capabilities on a par with, or even surpassing, the Mac's. More and more programs are showing that PCs aren't just for word processing and spreadsheets anymore—they can be full-fledged, full-powered graphics workstations.

While almost everyone has a favorite word processing program for text, fewer people know about the graphics half of this duo. Graphics programs are significant because in desktop publishing, text without graphics is like Lucy without Ricky, Rocky without Bullwinkle...you get the picture.

Paint Programs Versus Draw Programs

First, let's consider the difference between a "paint" program and a "draw" program. A paint program allows for the same feeling you have when freehand drawing. You paint on the screen as if you had a canvas. You use the cursor, or mouse, to draw lines, boxes, and circles and to fill them in with different patterns.

Everything is part of a single "painting." If you want to change something, such as the pattern you've used to fill in a box, you usually have to erase the box and start over. The finished painting is made up of tiny little dots, so if you try to make the entire picture bigger or smaller, the quality deteriorates, and solid grays can turn into unwanted tartan plaids.

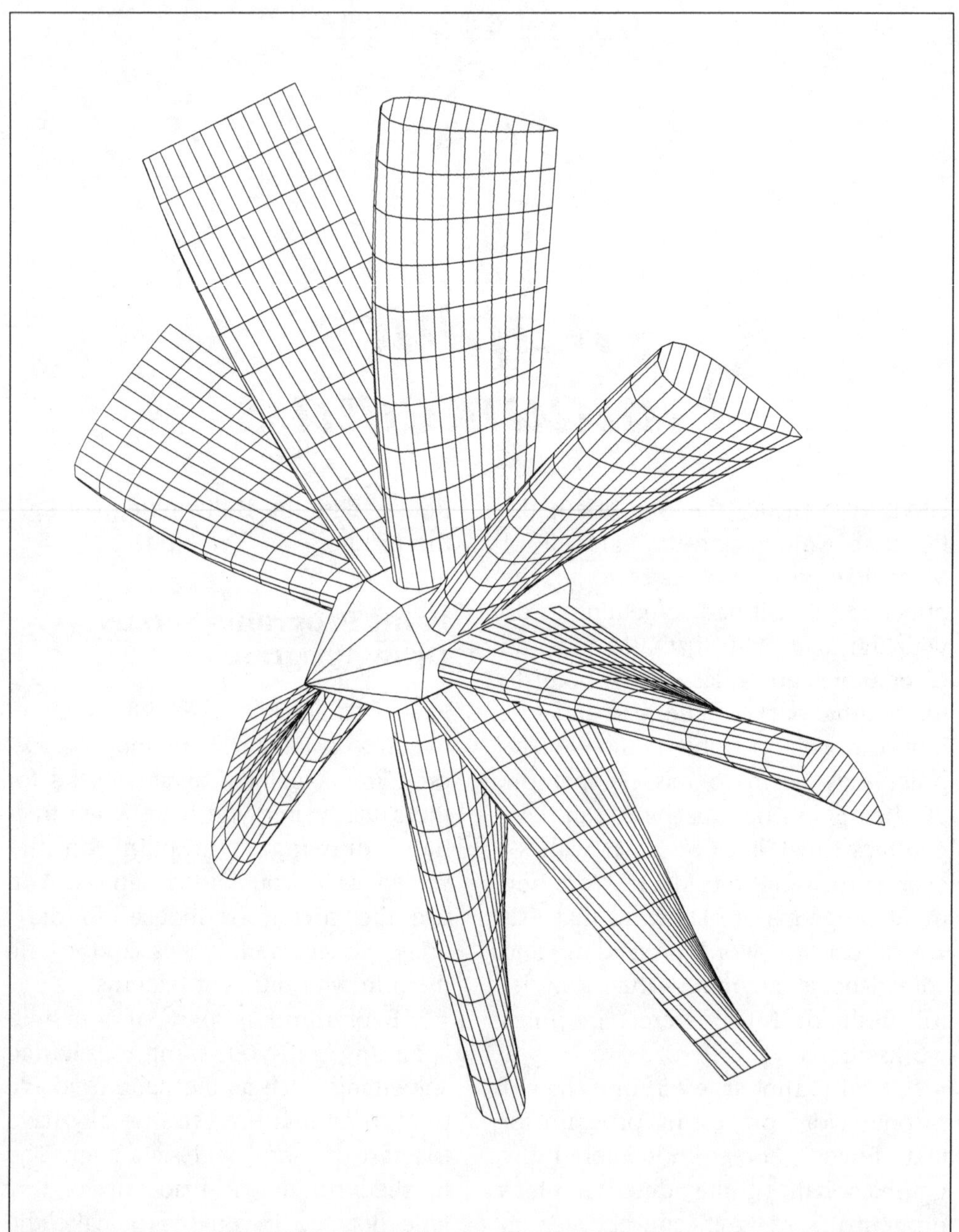

Figure 1: AutoCAD, which was used to create the illustration shown here, is a prime example of a "draw" program.

Draw programs use the same basic idea of drawing on screen, but they treat what you draw in a totally different way. In a draw program, everything you draw is a separate entity. If you draw a circle, then place a box halfway inside it, you still have two separate graphic items. You can fill the box with one pattern and the circle with another, and change the patterns later on if you want. You can move the box independently of the circle, put one on top of the other, then change which one is on top. This makes creating (and revising) complex graphics easier than with a paint program.

Pictures created with a draw program are not made up of little dots, like those created with a paint program, but of geometric shapes—lines, circles, ovals, squares, etc. When a drawing is made smaller or larger, its quality is unaffected because the shapes themselves are being rescaled. The technical term for the pictures made with a draw program is "object-oriented" graphics, or simply "object graphics." The term for the pictures made by paint programs is "bitmap graphics."

Draw programs are best for creating technical, structured, or geometric-based graphics, such as floor plans, architectural drawings, technical illustrations, and presentation graphics. Computer Aided Design (CAD) programs, such as AutoCAD, all use the draw approach to graphics. A new development is for draw programs to also allow the use of curves, which means that draw programs are becoming increasingly useful in artistic drawing as well.

Memory Requirements

A picture created with a paint program is stored within the computer as a pattern of dots. This turns out to be a storage-intensive method, since every dot must be associated with one bit in the computer's RAM or on a disk. The implications are threefold:

- When you work with large paint images, you'll need a good deal of RAM in your computer to handle the bitmaps. For example, with Publisher's Paintbrush, a paint program from ZSoft, you'll need 2Mb of enhanced memory in your computer to fully take advantage of the software.
- When you store your masterpiece on your hard disk, you'll find that a single paint image can take up an immense amount of storage space. For example, a full-page picture at 300 dpi requires a full megabyte of storage.
- When you go to print your picture, you may run up against the memory limitations of the LaserJet. A LaserJet Plus or a LaserJet II with no memory upgrade has 512K of memory, of which about

395K is usable for storing fonts and graphics. That's enough memory to handle a 300-dpi picture that takes up about a third of a page, assuming that no soft fonts have been downloaded in the printer. To print very large bitmapped images, you'll need a memory upgrade.

The Scanner Connection

So far, we've made it sound like draw programs have everything going for them and paint programs are nothing but trouble. The fact is, however, that paint programs turn out to be extremely valuable in conjunction with another tool—the digital scanner.

There's not much in this book about scanners such as the HP ScanJet (the book's fat enough already). In a nutshell, what a scanner does is translate a real-world image such as a photograph into a pattern of dots, i.e., a bitmap. You can then load that bitmap into a paint program and touch it up with the editing tools provided by the software.

At this point, draw programs are not capable of automatically disassembling a scanned image into a collection of shapes. So you can't load a scanned image into a draw program the way you can load it into a paint program. However, with some of the newer draw programs, such as Micrografx Designer, you can load the scanned image into a draw program and then use the mouse to trace the image.

The PostScript Connection

Paint programs have one other advantage over draw programs: they're more closely adapted to the capabilities of the LaserJet. Unfortunately, perhaps the biggest shortcoming of Printer Command Language (PCL), the set of instructions that software applications use to communicate with the LaserJet, is that the language contains no words for geometric shapes such as "curve," "circle," or even "diagonal line." In fact, the only words for shapes in PCL are "line" and "filled rectangle."

Because of this deficiency in PCL, draw programs have to describe shapes like ovals to the LaserJet in terms of the dots that make up the shape, partially defeating the purpose of using a draw program in the first place.

Here's where PostScript comes in. Like PCL, PostScript is a language for describing what should be printed on a page. It's slower than PCL, but has an immense graphics vocabulary. Shapes like ovals and Bezier curves are easy stuff for PostScript, which can handle the most complex descriptions (though it may take a long time to spit out the page).

In the past, if you wanted to take advantage of the capabilities of PostScript, you had to scrap your LaserJet and—God forbid—buy a laser printer from another company. But these days you can have your cake and eat it to by getting a PostScript upgrade unit and attaching it to your LaserJet. For details, see Chapter 27, "Upgrade Options."

—Daniel Will-Harris and Ted Nace

Profile: AutoSketch

AUTOSKETCH LETS ANYONE with $79 try their hand at computer aided design (CAD). As well as being a swell CAD program, AutoSketch is also a swell little draw-type graphics program, and less expensive than any other draw program I know of.

AutoSketch is from the same people who make AutoCAD, a $2,500 super-duper CAD program. AutoSketch isn't a stripped-down version of AutoCAD, but a new approach to CAD programs, using the familiar "drop-down" menus. AutoSketch can create the same kind of SLD and DXF files AutoCAD can, which means you can import illustrations made with the program into Ventura and PageMaker.

Because of its drop-down menus, AutoSketch works in a more familiar way than the older CAD programs with menus along the side. You can draw circles, arcs, curves, lines, boxes, dots, polygons, or text. You can undo, erase, group, ungroup, rotate, move, stretch, or copy, just as with other draw programs.

AutoSketch does several things the plain draw programs don't. It will automatically create on-screen measurements of items. These measurements change whenever you change the object. You can create curves from a series of dots, which allows you precise control over curves. You can work with layers, making your drawings much more intricate, yet easier to work with. These features are all vital to creating correct mechanical and architectural drawings, and can be valuable even when all you want to do is draw a simple illustration.

AutoSketch can rotate objects or groups of objects, including text, at any angle—something most other draw programs can't do. The choice of viewing distances is unlimited, from extremely close up to extremely far back. AutoSketch also includes a game, to take your mind off all that hard work.

But because AutoSketch is really a CAD program and not a draw program, it does differ in several ways. First, you can't fill an object with a pattern. All objects are hollow, and filling one with black requires you to place innumerable individual lines right next to each other. This is impractical. Because most CAD programs don't need to fill objects, it's not a problem with the program, it's just something most CAD programs don't do.

AutoSketch has several specific hardware requirements: you must have either the Microsoft mouse (most

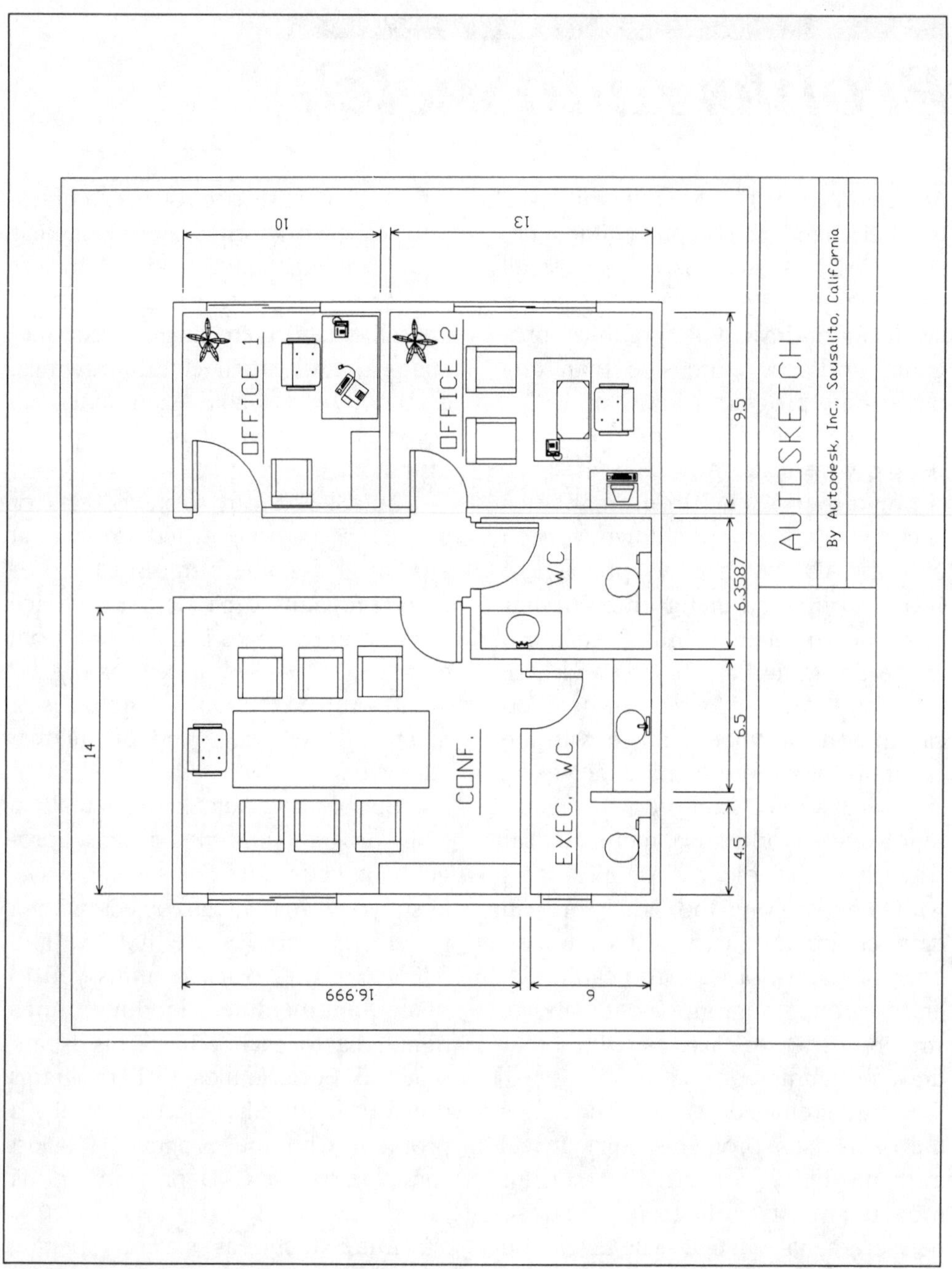

Figure 1: A sample page created with AutoSketch. (Reduced 31 percent.)

mice can emulate the MS-Mouse), Autodesk device interface pointer (whatever that is), or a Joystick/Koala Pad. The program supports the Hercules Monochrome, Hercules InColor, CGA, and EGA graphics standards. AutoSketch does support a wide variety of output devices, including most dot matrix printers, Houston Instrument plotters, and of course the LaserJet.

One drawback of the program is that text is limited to one style: a sketchy, unfilled type of character more suited to a plotter than a laser printer. You don't have the choice of typestyles offered in GEM Draw Plus or Windows Draw.

AutoSketch is extremely sluggish on a PC or XT, and just adequate for moderate drawings on an AT. GEM Draw Plus is much faster, and even Windows Draw is faster. One exceptionally complex sample included with the program took three and a half minutes to redraw on-screen using an 8 MHz AT. If you were going to use the program heavily, you'd want to have a math co-processor chip in your computer (these chips are optional and can cost several hundred dollars). AutoSketch will work many times faster, provided you buy the $99 version of the program that's designed to work with these special chips.

But hey, the program's only $79 and is the easiest CAD program I've seen. It's an inexpensive alternative to other draw programs generally costing around $300, it works directly with Ventura (as SLD or DXF files) and PageMaker (as HP plotter files), and it's a good introduction to draw and drafting programs in general.

—*Daniel Will-Harris*

Access

AutoSketch
Autodesk
2320 Marinship Way
Sausalito, CA 94965
415/332-2344
Price: $79 ($99 for math co-processor support)

Profile: GEM Draw Plus

GEM (WHICH STANDS for Graphic Environment Manager) Draw Plus is the fastest drawing program for the PC. Lightning speed, even on a standard PC or XT, and ease of use are its biggest assets.

GEM Draw Plus uses drop-down menus like the Mac, and adds a graphic menu along the left side of the screen, similar to the kind Ventura Publisher uses. The bar displays the tools and objects available and controls rulers, viewing sizes, and on-screen and snap-to-grids. The bar makes the program both quicker and more spontaneous than Windows Draw, because you can get at the tools without wasting any time pulling down menus. On the minus side, the bar takes up three quarters of an inch on the screen and can't be removed (it's not much, but it has to be mentioned).

Circles, arcs, rectangles, rounded rectangles, polygons, free-form shapes, lines, and text can all be created with GEM Draw Plus. Any object can be rotated 90 degrees and flipped vertically or horizontally. Many objects can be combined into one

Figure 1: GEM Draw is a fast drawing program that works smoothly with Ventura Publisher. Note the automatic shadow feature, which gives added dimension to drawings.

larger object, which makes manipulating elaborate drawings easier. While the program can shrink or stretch any object, it cannot proportionally resize objects automatically.

GEM Draw Plus can not only create different widths of lines (or invisible lines), but different endings for them as well. There are standard lines, lines with rounded ends, and lines that end in arrows. This feature is especially handy for organization charts and diagrams.

GEM Draw Plus has 39 fill patterns and 8 shades of gray. With an EGA monitor, you have 16 colors to choose from—twice as many as either Micrografx Windows Draw or the HP Drawing Gallery. A unique "shadow" feature automatically makes a shadow of any graphic item. This shadow can add interest to otherwise simple graphics and give them a three-dimensional look that would be tedious to construct by hand.

Six different viewing sizes are available with GEM Draw Plus: full page, half page, actual size, 2x, 4x, and 8x. Keyboard shortcuts are another worthwhile feature, such as using Alt-F to put the current selected object in front of those it overlaps. Alt-R rotates a drawing. These mnemonics are often, but not always, easy to remember. For instance, ^V is how a drawing is saVed.

GEM Draw Plus comes with a copy of the Fontware installation program and two typefaces: Swiss (Helvetica) regular, bold, italic, and bold italic, and Dutch (Times Roman) regular, bold, italic, and bold italic. (These fonts cost $400 if purchased separately from Bitstream). Not only does this mean that printed results are exceptionally sharp, but the type in GEM Draw graphics now imports into Ventura more accurately. If you've made bitmapped fonts, GEM Draw will use them. If you want to conserve disk space, GEM Draw will use its own compressed outline fonts, which are as good as the downloaded fonts except slower. GEM Draw fonts are always sharper and more solid than Windows Draw's plotter-like fonts.

Access

GEM Draw Plus
Digital Research, Inc.
60 Garden Court, Box DRI
Monterey, CA 93942
800/443-4200
Price: $299

GEM Draw Plus works seamlessly with Ventura Publisher because they both run under GEM. When used with Ventura, the page composition program automatically replaces GEM Draw's fonts with downloadable fonts of the closest size possible for higher quality.

Because Draw runs under GEM, it prints swiftly with the LaserJet. A full-page drawing prints at 150 dots per inch in about 30 seconds. The same drawing in Windows Draw could easily take three minutes to print.

Unlike Windows Draw, GEM Draw Plus will not use the LaserJet's resident fonts or cartridge fonts. Another limitation is that it will not create drawings larger than a single page. Neither of these deficiencies are significant when using the program for desktop publishing applications such as newsletters or documentation. On the plus side, GEM Draw Plus is substantially faster than Windows Draw, an especially important consideration if you intend to do anything more complex than the simplest of drawings. Even on an AT-type computer, the speed difference is dramatic.

GEM Draw Plus has a small but thorough manual and comes with a modest selection of clip art. For an additional $39.95, you can get the GEM Draw Business Library, which offers a good assortment of clip art containing 21 organization charts (which can be customized and expanded), 55 distinctive borders, 130 engineering and flow chart symbols, and various maps, buildings, trucks, cars, phones, and cameras.

The program has one serious omission—no undo feature. Many graphics programs now allow you to undo the last change, such as moving or resizing an object. While speed and versatility are strong points, the program would be improved by the inclusion of the convenient undo feature. Overall, GEM Draw Plus is the draw program that works best with Ventura Publisher.

—Daniel Will-Harris

Profile: Halo DPE

WORKING WITH HALO DPE (Desktop Publishing Editor) is different than working with most graphics programs, because there's not a single word on-screen—just a collection of occasionally cryptic icons, so you almost have to learn a new graphic language. But learning Halo can be worth it.

For instance, PC Paintbrush is somewhat Mac-like. It has pull-down menus along the top of the screen listing various features, as well as icons along the left and bottom of the screen. You use a combination of the menus and icons to produce your results.

Halo uses only icons. Pressing the left mouse button activates the particular icon the pointer is on. Pressing the right mouse button brings up more icons representing variations of a particular icon. This can be either perplexing or stimulating, depending on how easily you learn the program.

Halo DPE lets you edit a graphic larger than your screen, and like Publisher's Paintbrush, requires expanded memory to use the largest graphic area. With 640K however, Halo gives you a larger workspace than Publisher's Paintbrush.

While Halo almost matches PC Paintbrush feature for feature, type is

Figure 1: Halo is completely icon driven, with no words on-screen at all. This can make working either fast or confusing. Halo supports scanners and uses high-quality fonts.

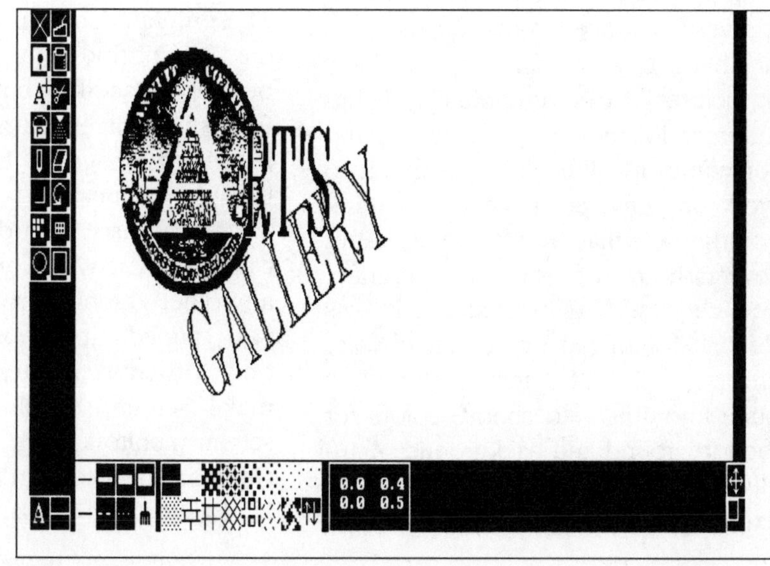

the area in which Halo DPE excels. Halo DPE comes with excellent fonts—so good you could use them as headlines with your page composition program. Like Publisher's Paintbrush, you can place text at any angle.

While it is possible to create an entire PC-published page with Halo DPE alone, it's not realistic. To create a page, you would first write the text in your word processing program and save it as an ASCII file. Then Halo would read the file and set the type. Unlike text-based page layout programs, however, you can't edit the text once it's on-screen.

Like PC Paintbrush, Halo DPE can control scanners and save directly in either IMG (for Ventura) or TIFF (for PageMaker) file formats. Halo also reads these formats, which means you can edit any of the most widely used graphic file formats with it.

Halo DPE is a paint program for the very advanced computer user. It's not hard, but because it speaks only in pictures, it can be confusing. It has a tremendous number of features, and sometimes it's difficult to get things to work properly, even when you think you know what you're doing. After several hours of using the program, and checking in the manual, it was difficult for me to figure out how to create shadows for text. I still don't quite know how to choose colors for the foreground and background. Actually, I do know how, but I still have to experiment until I get it right.

Access

Halo DPE
Media Cybernetics
8484 Georgia Ave. #200
Silver Spring, MD 20910
800/446-4250
Price: $199

As long as you can figure out how to use it, Halo DPE is a remarkable graphics tool. The one area where Halo DPE is lacking compared with PC or Publisher's Paintbrush is in choice of patterns. PC Paintbrush has 32 standard patterns on-screen, with several other sets of patterns you can read off the disk. Halo DPE has a scant 10 patterns, none of which is a fine, even shade of gray (a pattern I find essential).

Don't take any of this as negative. The program isn't hard, it's just different. I don't find using the program to be very Mac-like, but rather almost futuristic, where you are relating to a graphics program by using only graphics commands.

Halo also includes a program called GRAB, which will read almost any other graphics program screen, so you can edit it. Halo's GRAB is the only program I know of that will make screen snapshots from large-screen monitors, such as the full-page Genius. The program is simpler than PC Paintbrush's Frieze screen capture utility in that you press Alt-PrintScrn, and a file is automatically named and saved. Another program called SHOW lets you create on-screen slide shows, with images created or grabbed with Halo.

Halo DPE works with almost every graphics card and monitor known to man, every mouse, every pointing device, and most dot matrix and laser printers.

I like Halo. I find it captivating, but I'm a little in awe of it. It's robust and useful, and strangely different from most other paint programs. I recommend it to the savvy computer user who enjoys a challenge and will find its progressive features stimulating.

—Daniel Will-Harris

Profile: PC Paintbrush & Family

THE GRANDDADDY OF PC paint programs is still the greatest. With support for almost every conceivable monitor, mouse, and printer, and the industry-standard PCX file format, PC Paintbrush is the most flexible and useful paint program for the PC.

It provides the most control in creating or editing graphics scanned from within the program. The interface is intuitive, the performance is good, and the "spray paint" feature is a godsend for lightening overly dark scanned images.

PC Paintbrush also has the largest assortment of fill patterns on any PC-based paint program, including six tones of gray that are invaluable for shading. You can also create your own fill patterns at any time. With an EGA graphics board and monitor, you can have up to 16 colors at a time. The program even works beautifully with full-page monitors, a necessity for most desktop publishing.

A version of PC Paintbrush should go on your "must-have" list for PC publishing, no matter what page composition software you choose, even if

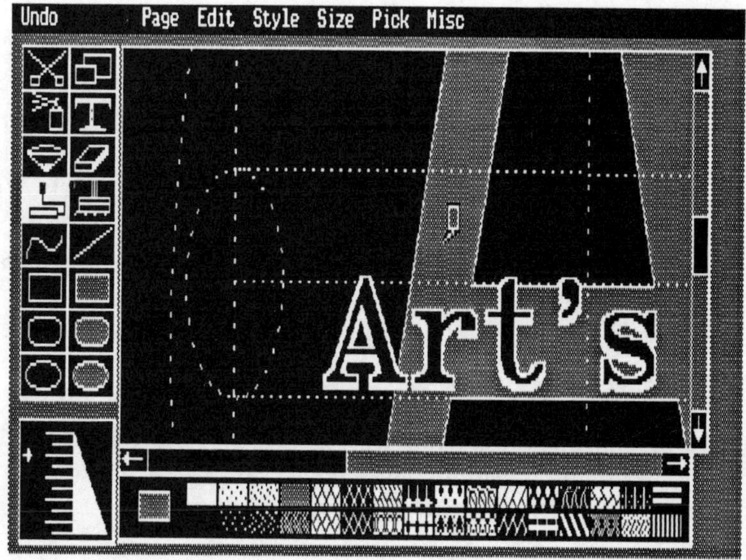

Figure 1: PC Paintbrush is the most popular and most versatile paint program for the PC. It has scanner support and includes fine shades of gray, invaluable for editing.

you aren't good at painting yourself (or painting, yourself). All MS-DOS page composition programs will accept graphics created or edited with PC Paintbrush. Also, most PC clip-art programs provide their art in PC Paintbrush format.

PC Paintbrush is also available in a Windows version. Like any Windows program, you can use the C\lipboard to transfer to and from other Windows programs, and run it concurrently with other programs such as PageMaker. The Windows version does not include scanner or grayscale support and is sluggish compared with the stand-alone version.

As with any paint program, you'll need more than the minimum 512K of memory in your LaserJet if you want to print graphics larger than a third of a page. The rule of thumb is that a full-page image at 300-dpi resolution requires a megabyte of free memory in the printer.

The Great Communicator

Even if you never create a graphic with PC Paintbrush, you'll still need one of the program's most important features: the ability to grab, right off the screen, graphics created by other programs. This makes it an indispensable tool for integrating the graphics from many noncompatible programs, but does not work with all the monitors the program supports. (Keep in mind that the resolution of graphics PC Paintbrush reads from the screen will only be as high as that of the monitor they were taken from. Most often, this is lower than graphics created directly by a graphics program.)

Access

PC Paintbrush family
Z-Soft
450 Franklin Road #100
Marietta, CA 30067
404/980-1950
Prices: PC Paintbrush $95, PC Paintbrush Plus $149, PC Paintbrush for Windows $84, PC Paintbrush Plus Designer Series $185, Publisher's Paintbrush $285

The Rest of the Family

PC Paintbrush Plus comes with Chart Interpreter, which can read the PIC files that 1-2-3 and Symphony create. It will then draw graphs that are higher resolution and more attractive than the originals. You can edit them using PC Paintbrush's extensive set of tools and use these charts in any page composition program. PC Paintbrush Plus Designer Series adds a slide show program, and two additional disks of fonts. PC Paintbrush Plus also supports a gray-scale PCX format.

Publisher's Paintbrush is the top of the line. It looks and acts just like PC Paintbrush, but it includes additional features, including much higher quality type (for creating extra large headlines or text as graphics). It also gives you the ability to have type at any angle and even control the angle of italics. Publisher's Paintbrush can also use outline fonts created with Publisher's Type Foundry, giving you especially high quality type. Publisher's Paintbrush lets you edit at the 300-dpi resolution of the LaserJet, rather than at the resolution of your screen, so you can control, dot by dot, what your printer prints.

With Publisher's Paintbrush, you can zoom out to four different views, so even the largest graphic can be seen and edited at one time. This is a feature you yearn for when you are working with large, scanned images. It also supports the gray-scale PCX format.

One warning: Unlike PC Paintbrush, which will use a hard disk as storage when editing graphics larger than one screen, Publisher's Paintbrush requires expanded memory for this. If you have the extra memory (ZSoft recommends as much as two megabytes), Publisher's Paintbrush will run fast, with lots of work space. If you don't, the size of graphics you can edit will be limited.

—Daniel Will-Harris

Profile: SLed

SLED IS A FASCINATING hybrid of a paint program—a graphics power tool. The name stands for Signature/Logo Editor, but that's a misnomer, because it makes it sound as if that's all SLed will do. Not only can you do the normal paint kind of things, but this multifaceted program lets you insert 300-dpi bitmapped fonts into a graphic, edit fonts as if they were graphics, and read and write images in not only PCX and IMG formats, but as downloadable fonts for use with word processing programs.

Why would anyone want to save a graphic as a downloadable font? Suppose it's your logo, or signature. If you're using a word processing program, all you have to do is select that font, type a few letters (SLed tells you which ones), and your logo or signature, appears on the printed page. No fancy footwork or an additional page composition program is necessary. SLed comes with a program that creates printer drivers using these fonts for Word and WordPerfect. As word processing programs get more savvy in the graphics department, this element of the program will become less important. Currently, however, with often-used graphics, this can be easier to use than the way word pro-

Figure 1: SLed lets you insert 300-dpi bitmapped downloadable fonts into your graphics. You can manipulate and reverse the fonts. LaserJet users can use SLed to create reversed type.

cessing programs require you to insert graphics.

The program is quite fast and responsive and lets you work with graphics larger than your screen, which is good because it doesn't support large high-resolution screens. Whereas PC Paintbrush won't let you mark an area larger than the screen for a block, SLed lets you select large areas to be blocked and manipulated, flipped, skewed, or reversed. You can paste blocks as either transparent or opaque, a feature lacking in PC Paintbrush, but you cannot create a "lasso" block.

SLed includes full scanner support and allows you to resize the work area if a graphic becomes larger than you expected. SLed has four zoom levels, and you can work in all except the most reduced. In addition to circles and rectangles, SLed has curve, ellipse, and parallelogram features. Unfortunately, SLed lacks an undo feature, and there are no fill patterns other than black and white.

SLed's most useful and unique feature is the way it allows you to manipulate bitmapped type. You can enlarge it, reduce it, make it bolder, or make it lighter. You can write the font back to its original file, make a new file, or use the new type as part of a graphic. I don't know of any other program for the PC that lets you use high-resolution fonts directly in a graphic, or manipulate them in such immediate, graphic ways.

Access

SLed
VS Software
P.O. Box 6158
Little Rock, AR 72216
501/376-2083
Price: $149.95

If you have a LaserJet and desperately want reversed type, SLed can take your downloadable fonts and either create an entirely new reversed font (which will print correctly on a LaserJet) or just reverse a headline or a single character. SLed also lets you incorporate any LaserJet bitmapped fonts into a PostScript-printed page by saving them as paint files.

SLed does have its limitations. It supports only the keyboard, Microsoft mouse (and compatibles, although the PC Mouse wouldn't work, even in MS-Mouse mode), and SummaSketch tablet. Unless you have CGA, EGA, or Hercules graphics, you're out of luck. The majority of PC publishers have these pieces of equipment, but more hardware support would be an improvement. Overall, SLed is a very handy program, especially when you want to play with bitmapped type.

—Daniel Will-Harris

Profile: Windows Designer

DESIGNER JEANS. DESIGNER colors. Designer telephones—everything's got the word "designer" tacked onto it lately, but Windows Designer actually deserves the name. It's a serious tool for serious artists, but one easy enough to be used by beginners. Adobe Illustrator started a computer graphics revolution by allowing complex curves to be created and edited on a personal computer. But Illustrator runs only on the Mac. Designer gives equal control over curves, runs on an AT or 386, and is easier to understand and use. Designer is the most versatile, most (I don't use this word often) powerful graphics program for the PC.

Even though Designer runs under Windows, it's not the slug that many Windows programs are. On an AT, it responds quickly and has a light touch. You can interrupt the screen redraw at any time to change your view or issue a command. This means you don't have to sit around waiting for a complex graphic to redraw, and makes the program much more efficient.

Because of its ability to generate complex graphics, Designer is one program that can really benefit if you upgrade your LaserJet with the JetScript or PS Jet PostScript controller. But it does work with the LaserJet Plus or LaserJet II. Like Illustrator, Designer allows you to trace over scanned bitmapped images, creating high-resolution object graphics. As with Illustrator, you can rotate PostScript fonts to any angle. While some of PostScript's more specialized commands are not supported (such as fountains), Designer is a real graphics dynamo.

Designer uses many of the same commands as its less talented sibling, Windows Draw. But it adds sophisticated curves, the ability to mix object-oriented and bitmapped graphics (though you can't edit the bitmapped graphics), rotate anything to any angle, and mix your own colors from a palette of up to 3.6 million (although you can display only as many as your screen will support). It also has scanned-image support (through the Windows Clipboard), an extra large working area (up to 48 letter-size pages), and myriad other thoughtfully conceived details.

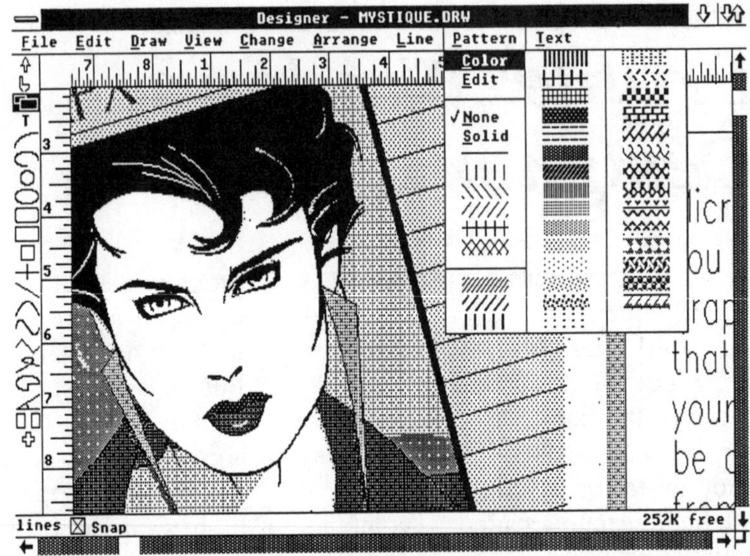

Figure 1: Designer has a range of fill patterns, as shown here.

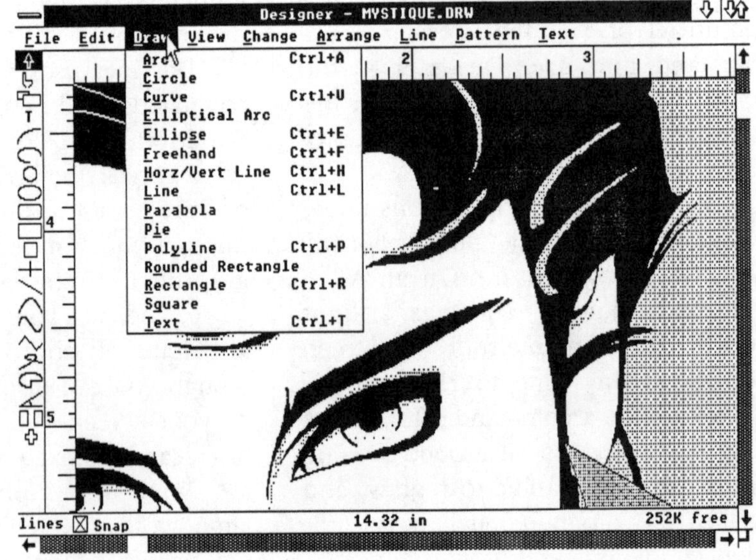

Figure 2: The program also has a wide variety of drawing tools, each of which can be selected either from the menu or with key combinations.

Designer uses any mouse and any monitor supported by Windows, and its files can be imported directly into PageMaker or any other Windows application. You can also create Encapsulated PostScript (EPS) files for use with Ventura Publisher or PageMaker, or save graphics in Windows Draw format.

Designer is the first object graphics program I've used (including Illustrator) that is really comfortable for creating complex graphics. It works in a logical and intuitive manner and offers countless little ways to make things easier.

As well providing the traditional snap-to ruler, Designer lets you snap objects to each other for a perfect fit. You can connect irregularly shaped objects and fill them with any of the standard 39 patterns or a pattern of your own design. You can give each object a name, creating an inventory of stock parts you can call up at will. You can do a form of search and replace, whereby Designer replaces one symbol with another, matching the size and attributes of the original.

Curve Master

But it's the manipulation of curves that makes Designer a great tool. Illustrator uses an effective but rather peculiar and complex technique for working with curves. They don't draw the way you expect, and they don't edit the way you expect. But in Designer, curves draw the way you think they will, and it's easy to edit them. You can select a single curve or all the curves in an object. You can add new edit points or delete them. You can make curves smooth or "unsmooth."

While you cannot edit bitmaps, you can stretch, crop, or change their color. The bitmaps become part of the Designer file and print on any device. Tracing a scanned image yields good results, because once you've traced the lines, you can easily edit them with precision. If you then delete the bitmap, you have an object graphic that will print at the highest resolution of the printer.

The rotation feature is especially keen. You can rotate any object, text or graphic, in tenths of a degree. You can set the exact rotation numerically in a menu or rotate with the mouse.

The number of features is remarkable. You can draw spline and parabolic curves, freehand lines, squares, circles, rectangles, and rounded rectangles. There are 16 different line

Access

Windows Designer
Micrografx Inc.
1820 N. Greenville Ave.
Richardson, TX 75081
214/234-1769
Price: $695

endings to choose from. You can set line widths from 1/1000 inch to 1 inch. You can measure any line in anything from millimeters to miles, seconds to years—perfect for doing time charts.

You can't enter text directly into the page. If you choose to add text to a graphic, a small text-editing window will appear, allowing multiple-line text editing. You can import ASCII files (or Windows Clipboard Text), and Designer has word wrap. You can select sizes up to 100 points, and when you use the JetScript PostScript upgrade, you have access to the 35 built-in fonts.

You can define up to 64 layers, and each can be named. Each layer can be restricted to a certain color. You are not limited in your choice of zoom levels.

Clip Art

Designer includes a clip art library, consisting of over 400 useful symbols such as maps, landmarks, furniture, computer components, animals, planes, borders, flags, familiar objects, signs of the zodiac, and space vehicles. These drawings are remarkably intricate and well rendered, and they offer a wide variety. Over 3,000 professional looking images are available separately from Micrografx, for $49.95 per set of about 400. Also included is a conversion program that translates to and from AutoCad DXF format (a format Ventura uses directly).

Micrografx promises to introduce a utility to convert Designer files into GEM line art format (which Ventura uses directly), CGM, Freelance, Mac PICT file, Micrografx PIC, and AutoCAD file formats. The program will be

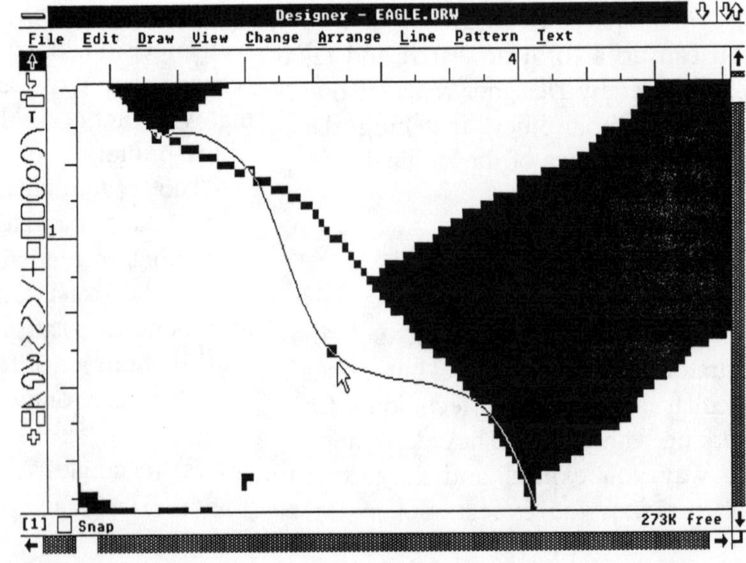

Figure 3: Windows Designer lets you trace scanned images, as seen here. You can manipulate a single point on a curve so that a traced graphic can be edited to perfection.

bi-directional and include batch processing to convert groups of files automatically. A new PostScript driver proposes to print four-color separations from Designer files, and support all Adobe fonts.

If you want to do something simple, the basic tools are available in an on-screen palette. More complex features are located within the menus, but are never buried several layers down. The scope of this program would be overwhelming if it weren't so well-designed.

—Daniel Will-Harris

Profile: Windows Draw

WINDOWS DRAW WAS the precursor of Windows Designer, and while it is a good general-purpose draw program, it pales in comparison. Still, it's more complex, powerful, and multifaceted than GEM Draw, and it has a lower price tag.

Windows Draw requires an AT or 386, and all the standard draw-features are in this program, plus a few other tricks. A single drawing can be as large as 12 pages—great for banners and signs; 1-2-3 and Symphony PIC files can be read to create graphs; and it has a pie-chart feature to create precise slices.

It also has the facility to choose between graphics fonts, which can be sized and stretched, or built-in printer fonts, for the sharpest possible text. When used with a LaserJet, all font cartridges can be used. If you upgrade your LaserJet to PostScript with JetScript or PS Jet, you'll be able to use Times Roman and Helvetica. PostScript fonts up to 72 points can be selected but can't be rotated to print vertically. The plotter-like fonts are sketchy, and when built-in printer fonts are not an option, the Windows Draw fonts will not be as sharp as the fonts included with GEM Draw.

Windows Draw has an important feature that GEM Draw lacks: the ability to enlarge or reduce graphic elements proportionally. If you choose the handles on the corners, the graphic you are resizing will shrink or grow symmetrically, which keeps the scale intact. This makes rescaling graphics easier.

Windows Draw also has a important undo feature, which effectively undoes the last change made, no matter how big or small. Like Designer, Draw allows you to zoom in on any portion of your drawing, rather than having set zoom levels. Draw comes with the same excellent clip art that Designer includes.

Patience Required

Windows Draw is not without a few flaws. It runs much slower than GEM Draw. If you create very complicated drawings with many individual objects, it can become bothersome to watch them re-draw on the screen. A piece of clip art depicting a tiger comes with the program and took 20

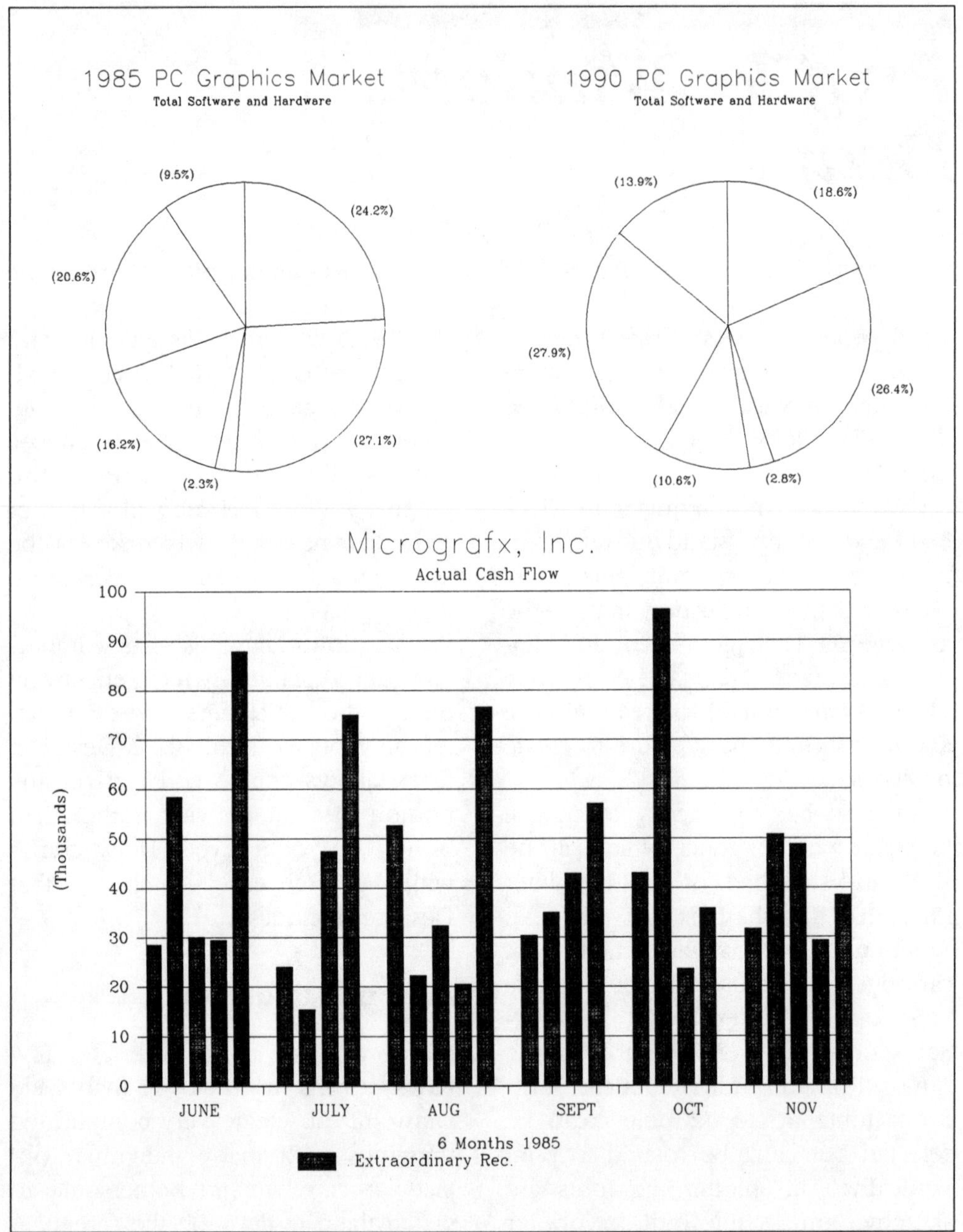

Figure 1: These charts were generated in Lotus, then imported into Windows Draw for printing at 300 dpi. (Reduced 27 percent.)

seconds each time the screen was redrawn on an AT-compatible. Since Windows Draw redraws the screen often, this can add up. When printing a page at 300 dots per inch on a LaserJet, it can easily take seven minutes.

Because Draw runs under Windows, it supports a vast number of monitors, including full-page displays, such as the MDS Genius. Windows Draw also works directly with PageMaker.

There are two ways to use Windows Draw files with Ventura. The first is to install a HP plotter driver and print to disk. Ventura will convert this file into a GEM Draw file. The second uses an additional program called Windows Convert ($99), which transforms Windows Draw files to AutoCAD DXF format. Ventura provides a conversion program from DXF to the GEM Draw format it reads directly. This works for most basic graphics, but complex graphics become too large to convert properly into GEM format.

—Daniel Will-Harris

Access

Windows Draw
Micrografx, Inc.
1820 N. Greenville Ave.
Richardson, TX 75081
214/234-1769
Price: $299

CHAPTER EIGHT

Clip Art

CLIP ART IS A term used in the graphic arts to refer to commercially available collections (usually books) of standard images that can be cut out—*clipped*—and used as illustrations. Since the most common use of such pictures is for advertisements, the collections tend to be commercially oriented, though you can find almost any sort of picture if you look hard enough. There are now thousands of pieces of clip art available on PC-formatted disks. More are coming out all the time as the massive collections that have already been created for the Macintosh get converted.

The vast majority of clip art is in the bitmapped format recognized by paint programs, especially the PC Paintbrush PCX format. Much of this bitmapped clip art was directly converted from the commercial collections already available to graphic artists. Often the images look rather dated (which is fine if you want you publication to have a small-town, 1950s flavor, but somewhat frustrating otherwise). However, the quality is rapidly improving.

The cream of the crop of clip art tends to be that stored in the object graphics format recognized by draw programs. Unfortunately, for best results with this type of clip art youll need to upgrade your LaserJet with a PostScript enhancement. The reason is that the LaserJet's native language, PCL is severely limited in the variety of graphics operations it includes. PCL includes commands for vertical and horizontal lines and shaded or patterned rectangles. But it does not include more sophisticated graphics operations such as arcs and curves.

Generally speaking, you'll be using clip art in conjunction with a desktop publishing program such as PageMaker or Ventura Publisher. Both of these should recognize any format in which your clip art is stored. If not, refer to Chapter 9, "Graphics Conversion Programs."

Figure 1: Examples of clip art provided with GEM Draw Plus. This clip art is in draw art format (each picture stored as a geometrical description).

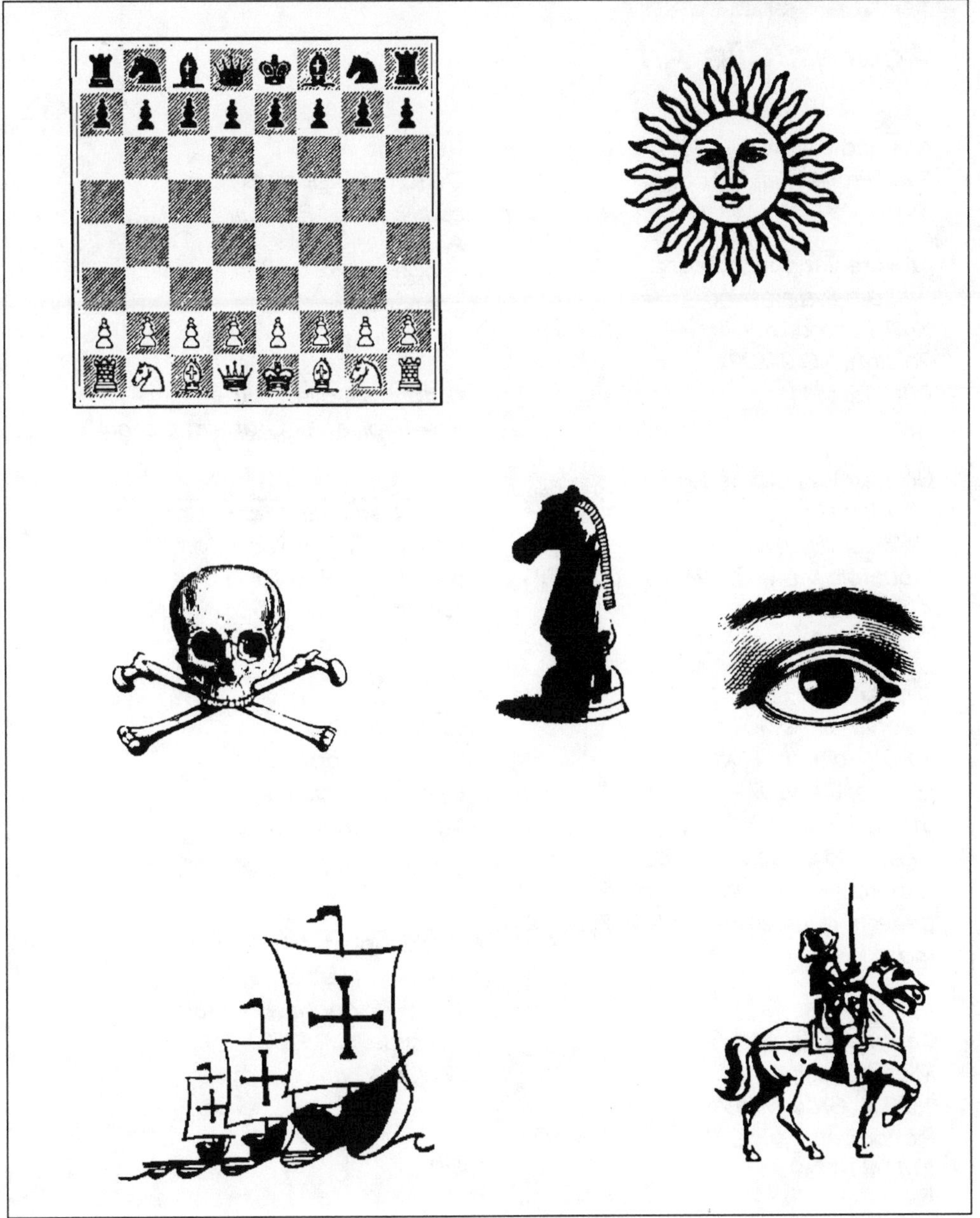

Figure 2: These samples of clip art are from the PC Quik-Art collection. They are stored in paint, or bitmap format (each picture is stored as a pattern of dots). In all, the collection includes over 50,000 symbols and pictures.

Access: Clip Art

Arts and Letters
See "Profile: Arts & Letters"

Artware Graphics Library
Artware Systems, Inc.
3741 Benson Dr.
Raleigh, NC 27609
919/872-6511

ClickArt Portfolio Series
T/Maker Co.
1973 Landings Dr.
Mountain View, CA 94043
415/962-0195

Clip Art
Stephen & Associates
10106 Halberns Blvd.
Santee, CA 92071
619/562-5161
Description: semiconductor, architectural, hydraluic/pneumatic, and general purpose symbols in PCX format

Designer Clip Art
Micrografx, Inc.
1820 N. Greenville Ave.
Richardson, TX 75081
214/234-1769
Description: 20 clip art packages are available

Desk Top Art
Dynamic Graphics, Inc.
600 N. Forest Park Dr.
Peoria, IL 61614
309/688-3075
309/688-8800

Graphics Gallery 2.0
See "Profile: HP Graphics Gallery"

High Resolution Image Libraries
Network Technology Corp.
6825 Lamp Post Lane
Alexandria, VA 22306
703/765-4506

Logos On-Line
Software Complement
8 Pennsylvania Ave.
Matamoras, PA 18336
717/491-2492

MacGraphics 2.0 (for the PC)
GoldMind Publishing
12155 Magnolia Ave. #3B
Riverside, CA 92503
714/785-8685

MacMemories Series
ImageWorld, Inc.
P.O. Box 10415
Eugene, OR 97440
503/485-0395

PC Quik-Art
PC Quik-Art, Inc.
394 S. Milledge Ave. #200
Athens, GA 30606
800/523-1796
404/543-1779
Description: Clip art in PC Paintbrush (PCC) format.

PS Portfolio
Spellbinder Art Library
Lexisoft, Inc.
P.O. Box 1950
Davis, CA 95617
916/758-3630

Publisher's PicturePaks
Marketing Graphics Incorporated
401 E. Main St.
Richmond, VA 23219
804/788-8844
Description: Clip art in PCX and CGM format. Three editions are available: Executive and Management, Finance and Administration, and Sales and Marketing. Each contains approximately 200 pictures.

Profile: Arts & Letters

ARTS & LETTERS, FROM Computer Support Corporation (makers of Diagraph), is an elaborate clip art manipulation program that runs under Windows. The program comes with over 2,200 professionally drawn pieces of clip art, with thousands more available. A&L runs quickly despite Windows, and you can interrupt the screen redraw at any time to execute a command. This speeds the program substantially.

To use Arts & Letters, you start by consulting the list of clip art. Type in the number of the artwork and it appears on-screen. From here you can size it, slant it, flip it horizontally or vertically, rotate it to any angle, put it in the front or back, change the line or fill, or group it with other objects. Freehand drawing is limited to lines, connected lines, and polygons. You cannot draw curves freehand. A&L uses eight standard colors, but also allows you mix colors.

Text manipulation is excellent, with 15 high-resolution typefaces (unfortunately, only 2 of these are serif fonts, similar to Times Roman medium and bold). Another 17 typefaces are optional, and these display faces range from a version of Broadway to "Quadrata." These fonts can be filled with a variety of patterns and gray tones, rotated to any angle, and outlined or reversed. Arts & Letters is a good way to add typographic tricks to LaserJet or even PostScript pages.

While Arts & Letters runs easily and smoothly, there are some annoying failings. There is no freehand drawing. An optional "symbol editor" will be introduced for this purpose, but that will be an additional expense. Unlike Drawing Gallery, where even the predesigned clip art can be broken down into component parts for customization, an Arts & Letters symbol cannot be broken down. It can be manipulated, and filled with different patterns or colors, but it can't be broken apart, if you wanted to remove a piece of it. It would however, be possible to cover it up with something else, but that's not the best way to work with one of these programs. Also, A&L doesn't use the Windows 2.0 keyboard interface, so the only keyboard shortcuts are to the main menus, not the items on them.

A&L converts its files into EPS, Aldus EPS (which includes a screen representation), and CGM, a format Ventura should read. Unfortunately, Ventura 1.1 reverses everything: white becomes black, and vice versa. Computer Support says it is creating a correct CGM file, and that the fault is in

Ventura, but this is of little help if you want to use it with Ventura. You must create everything the opposite of how you really want it, and this is silly.

But A&L is still a practical program, especially for Windows and PageMaker users. The clip art and type effects are excellent, and the program is simple to use. LaserJet users will especially appreciate A&L's type effects, and its easy integration into other Windows applications makes it a useful program for anyone who can't draw but needs good illustrations.

—Daniel Will-Harris

Access

Arts & Letters
Computer Support Corporation
15926 Midway Road
Dallas, TX 75244
214/661-8960
Price: $395

Profile: Graphics Gallery

HEWLETT-PACKARD HAS come out with a useful package of graphics programs called the Gallery Collection. It comprises two parts, Drawing Gallery and Charting Gallery. The strength of drawing Gallery is that it comes with 300 professional-looking images, ranging from simple shapes to an elegant, classical set of "initial caps" (fancy capital letters). These images are especially designed for creating presentation graphics and organization charts. Thousands of additional clip art images are available for $95 per set.

Fifteen different fonts are included with Drawing Gallery—in both serif and sans serif typefaces, with italic, outline, and extra bold. A particularly useful feature allows any font to be rotated to any angle.

While the program won't use internal printer fonts, the graphics fonts included are so well-defined and sharp, especially when printed at 300 dots per inch, that they look like downloadable fonts. You cannot, however, do reverse type, so be forewarned.

Figure 1: HP Drawing Gallery is an elaborate clip-art manipulator. It comes with high-resolution fonts that can be printed at any angle.

Drawing Gallery lets you take the basic shapes and items included and fill them with patterns and gray shades, stretch them, enlarge or reduce them proportionally, or flip them. Unlike GEM and Windows Draw, Drawing Gallery is based on the clip-art graphic items included with the program rather than freehand drawing—in fact, it is not possible to make free-form artwork unless you assemble it from the geometric pieces provided.

Still, the quality of the clip art is so high that this would be a good program for someone without artistic ambitions or talent, but with the need for attractive graphics. Drawing Gallery is also particularly good at creating organization charts because a special feature moves connecting lines when other items are moved.

While Drawing Gallery is helpful for the user who will depend on clip art, it has drawbacks, such as limited hardware support and the ability to work only on CGA, EGA, Hercules, AT&T and Vectra displays. It supports both the LaserJet family and PostScript printers.

Drawing Gallery can create files that are compatible with both PageMaker and Ventura. You can make either PCX or TIFF files, but these are paint-type files, so while the program works like a draw program, its files, when sized for use in desktop publishing, lose the high quality found in other draw programs. If you are using Ventura and want the advantages of a draw-type file, you can print to disk in HP Plotter format and Ventura will convert the file to GEM draw format, but you cannot get proper gray tones with this method.

—Daniel Will-Harris

Access

Graphics Gallery 2.0
Hewlett-Packard Personal Software Division
3410 Central Expressway
Santa Clara, CA 95051
408/749-9500
Price: $495 (for Drawing Gallery and Charting Gallery)

CHAPTER NINE

Graphics Conversion Programs

LIKE WORD PROCESSING programs, every graphics program seems to have its own file format. But unlike word processor files, which all use the same basic ASCII characters, graphics file formats are completely dissimilar.

Some programs can read and write several formats. SLed can read PC Paintbrush (PCX) files and convert them into GEM Paint (IMG) files and vice versa, and HotShot Graphics can take its own files and convert them to PCX and Tagged Image File Format (TIFF) files. Ventura converts PCX files into GEM IMG files.

The Graphics Link

But what do you do if you need to convert a file? The Graphics Link, from PC Quik Art, converts to and from PCX, Windows Paint, EGA Paint, TIFF, IMG, PC Paint Plus, Halo DPE, MacPaint, and Bload or Bsave (BASIC graphics formats). You can convert many files at a time using the batch feature. Conversion takes from one to three minutes, depending on the size and format of the graphic. You can also reverse or resize graphics. The Graphics Link is reliable and useful.

HiJaak

HiJaak, from Inset Systems, not only converts file formats, but will also intercept the output of any program on its way to a LaserJet. This lets you capture and convert large images at full 300-dpi resolution. HiJaak includes a screen-capture utility in CGA, EGA, Hercules, AT&T 6300 and Toshiba 3100 modes, and supports graphics created on the Amiga. HiJaak converts to and from Amiga, CompuServe GIF, LaserJet, Inset, MacPaint, PC Paintbrush, TIFF, NewsMaster, PrintMaster, and ASCII text. In addition, it will convert from Lotus PIC files and to encapsulated PostScript. HiJaak works directly with Inset, to merge graphics with applications that normally don't support them.

—Daniel Will-Harris

Access

The Graphics Link
PC Quik Art
394 Milledge Ave.
Athens, GA 30606
800/523-1796
Price: $99

HiJaak
Inset Systems, Inc.
12 Mill Plain Rd.
Danbury, CT 06811
203/794-0396
Price: $79

4

DESKTOP PUBLISHING

Section Focus

Desktop publishing has been the subject of a great deal of hype, but it really boils down to two capabilities: being able to mix graphics and text on a page, and having access to commercial quality fonts. In this group of chapters, we start with an overview of the various approaches to desktop publishing and the wide variety of software products that are available to choose from.

If you're like most people, your long list of page layout programs will soon boil down to two products: PageMaker and Ventura Publisher. Since the vast majority of desktop publishers end up using one of these two excellent programs, we devote a separate chapter to each.

CHAPTER TEN

Desktop Publishing

IN 1985, A REMARKABLE new program called PageMaker appeared for the Apple Macintosh and the Apple LaserWriter. Surprisingly inexpensive, PageMaker was also easy to use—a combination that until then had not been achieved in any personal computer publishing software. Within minutes of sitting down with PageMaker, people with no special training were creating sophisticated page layouts that incorporated multicolumn text and graphics. As with many software introductions, PageMaker was accompanied by a great deal of hype. The president of the company, Paul Brainerd, claimed that an entirely new category of software, which he termed "desktop publishing," had come into being.

In this instance, the hype was on target. Although PageMaker wasn't actually the first attempt to bring powerful publishing tools to the personal computer, it was the first to catch on. Just as Brainerd had predicted, PageMaker did create an entirely new category of software, one closely honed to the capabilities of laser printers. The instant success of PageMaker led to a chorus of requests from owners of IBM PCs and LaserJets for a similarly powerful program that could operate with their equipment. With the Macintosh world leading the way and the PC world in hot pursuit, a flood of desktop publishing products soon appeared.

In fact, so many products are now available that claim to offer "desktop publishing" capabilities that it's become quite confusing for buyers to sort out the differences among them. In this chapter we'll look at several categories of software.

First, what is meant by "desktop publishing" anyway? In a nutshell, it refers to software and hardware tools that make it possible to create com-

Resources for Desktop Publishers

Magazines

Over the past three years, desktop publishing has grown into a virtual subindustry. The best way to catch up on the latest happenings is to check out the periodicals that have sprung up to cover the subject, especially Publish! and Personal Publishing. Both magazines also sell back issues (while they last). Back issues are a real gold mine—taken as a whole, they're a better buy than any book.

- **Personal Publishing**
  Hitchcock Publishing Company
  25W550 Geneva Rd.
  Wheaton, IL 60188-2292
  Subscriptions: $24 for 12 issues; back issues available
  The best source of the latest news. In general, Personal Publishing is more detailed than Publish!
- **Publish!**
  PCW Communications
  501 Second St.
  San Francisco, CA 94107
  Subscriptions: $39.90 for 12 issues; back issues available
  Stronger on design than Personal Publishing.

Books

For more general background, some good survey books are available, though they tend to become quickly outdated if not frequently revised.

- **The Art of Desktop Publishing**
  Tony Bove, Cheryl Rhodes, and Wes Thomas
  Bantam Books, New York
  Price: $18.95
  A good general survey, though heavily weighted toward the Macintosh.

- **Desktop Publishing With Style**
  by Daniel Will-Harris
  And Books, South Bend, IN
  Price: $19.95
  Specifically focused on desktop publishing with the IBM PC and heavily emphasizing the HP LaserJet.
- **Looking Good in Print**
  by Roger Parker
  Ventana Press, Chapel Hill, NC
  Price: $23.95
  This is the best book available on basic design techniques for desktop publishing.
- **Publishing From the Desktop**
  by John Seybold and Fritz Dressler
  Bantam Books, New York
  Price: $19.95
  This is the book to read if you want to understand the foundations of desktop publishing, including typography and the workings of laser printers and scanners.

Newsletters

If you're interested in keeping up on the latest developments, there are lots of newsletters to choose from, but *The Seybold Report on Desktop Publishing* is far and away the most comprehensive.

- **The Seybold Report on Desktop Publishing**
  Seybold Publications, Inc.
  Box 644
  Media, PA 19063
  215/565-2480
  Subscriptions: $192 for 12 monthly issues U.S.; $198 Canada; $210 foreign

Organizations

- **The National Association of Desktop Publishers (NADTP)**
  P.O. Box 508
  Kenmore Station
  Boston, MA 02215-9998
  NADTP is an independent, nonprofit trade association of desktop publishing professionals. Membership is $75, and benefits include a periodical called the NADTP Journal, access to the NADTP Round-Table on the GEnie network, and substantial discounts on a large selection of desktop publishing books and trade shows.

Bulletin Boards

- BBS Buena Park 714/821-5014
- Cooperworks/Jamestown Software 608/271-3685
- DataCom Super Systems 813/796-5627
- Desktop Publishing Electric 512/250-1316
- The Desktop Publisher 415/856-2771
- East Coast PubNet 301/277-5990
- The Eastern Publisher Exchange 813/989-1087
- Form Feed BBS 201/869-1327
- The Other Woman 707/938-3508
- Publisher Information Service 312/342-6919
- Ruppel Set][606/781-4478
- Tardis BBD 609/448-1361
- The Well 415/332-6106
- Western Publisher's Exchange 714/739-5150

plex illustrated documents without manual pasteup.

Before PageMaker, there were a number of programs for creating illustrated documents with a personal computer and a LaserJet, but they required you to insert complex formatting codes into passages of text—a tedious and painstaking process, since it required you to visualize in your mind the effect of those codes on the appearance of the page.

WYSIWYG

PageMaker introduced a much more effective way of laying out pages, an approach dubbed WYSIWYG, for "what you see (on-screen) is what you get (on paper)." WYSIWYG is important because it gives you instant feedback on the appearance of your page as you work. Since much of the work of formatting a page is trial and error, it's nice to be able to correct your errors on the screen rather than wait till a page is printed out.

The most successful desktop publishing programs, including PageMaker and Ventura Publisher at the professional level and PFS: First Publisher at the introductory level, use the WYSIWYG approach.

Preview Mode

Despite the attraction of the WYSIWYG approach, many programs are still based on older technology. For example, all the leading word processing programs currently on the market were first developed at a time when most monitors were capable of displaying only text; hence, they use a character-based approach.

Lately, some word processing programs like WordPerfect and Microsoft Word have been adding a "preview mode." After you work on formatting your page for a while, you press a particular key combination and the program shows you an on-screen representation of the final appearance of your page. In some instances, such as with the Microsoft Word's PageView utility, it's possible to make adjustments to the appearance of the document, such as changing margins or moving pictures on the page.

Style Sheets

Just as word processors have adopted techniques developed for desktop publishing, such as a WYSIWYG preview mode, desktop publishing has similarly been learning from word processing. Typically, most desktop publishing programs allow you to enter and edit text directly on your pages. And it won't be long before desktop publishing programs begin offering such word processing features as search/replace and spell checking.

Perhaps the best example of an innovation that has migrated from word processing to desktop publish-

Ventura or PageMaker?

According to market observers, Ventura Publisher has outsold PageMaker by a considerable margin. Still, in deciding which program fits your needs, you should consider both. Here are some criteria to guide your decision.

Type of documents: Conventional wisdom has it that PageMaker is for short documents and Ventura is for long documents. Actually, that's not necessarily the case. In the hands of someone experienced with the program, Ventura is faster than PageMaker for whipping out a newsletter or a business form. However, for a beginner or a casual user, PageMaker might be quicker because it has an easier learning curve. For long documents such as books, technical manuals, and catalogs, Ventura is better.

Operating environment: PageMaker runs under Microsoft Windows, while Ventura works with DOS (it incorporates a version of Digital Research's GEM, which is hidden from the user of the program).

Speed: Ventura is faster than PageMaker, which means that you can use it comfortably on an AT-class computer or even an XT-class computer. In contrast, you need at least an AT-class computer to run PageMaker, and preferably a 80386 computer.

Ease of learning: PageMaker is easier to learn than Ventura. The organization of the program is less complex and there are fewer menus and functions. For that reason, if you intend to use a desktop publishing program only occasionally, you'll be better off with PageMaker.

LaserJet support: In general, both PageMaker and Ventura work well with the LaserJet. Ventura is more convenient, however, because the program provides sets of Swiss (similar to Helvetica) and Dutch (similar to Times Roman) fonts, so you can use the program without purchasing and installing any additional soft fonts. Ventura works with only the F cartridge, while PageMaker works with any font cartridge.

Integration with graphics and word processing programs: Neither PageMaker nor Ventura is intended to serve as a stand-alone program. Rather, you create your text using your favorite word processor, your pictures using a graphics program, and then use the desktop publishing program to knit together text and graphics on formatted pages. Both Ventura and PageMaker work with a wide selection of word processor and graphics formats.

ing are style sheets, which first appeared in Microsoft Word and then moved into Ventura Publisher and PageMaker. A style sheet is a collection of instructions for formatting different kinds of material. For example, one style might apply to titles, another to captions, another to subheads, and another to footers. To format a passage of text, you simply label it with the appropriate style. In the case of Ventura Publisher, this is as simple as pointing at the text, clicking, and then pointing at the name of the style in a handy sidebar and clicking again.

Word Publishing

The upshot of the cross-fertilization that has been going on between word processing and desktop publishing is a blurring of the two categories. Those eager to invent new terms have coined one for this border region: word publishing. A good example is WordPerfect 5.0, which still works great for regular word processing but also allows you to import graphics, shrink and even rotate them, use multiple fonts on a single line, and preview your formatted pages before printing them.

Code-based Programs

Even though most users have voted with their pocketbooks for WYSIWYG programs—in particular PageMaker and Ventura—a number of programs still use the older, code-based approach.

These programs fall into two camps. Some are high-end programs such as LaserScript, PC Tex, and MicroTex that offer special capabilities not found in mainstream products, such as the ability to format mathematical equations. Because programs like Ventura are so much easier to use, you should consider these code-based programs only if you need to print something that the mainstream software can't handle.

At the other end of the code-based program spectrum is the sort of software that you often see advertised in small ads for $49.95. Beware! Typically, such programs are only usable by the person who created them. While these programs are cheap, they're definitely not a bargain. Because they require you to embed commands in your text files but provide no way to preview the effect of those commands, getting a page to look the way you want it to becomes a slow, laborious process of repeated trial printouts.

Where they diverge is in the type of documents for which they are best suited, with some better for long documents with uniform formats and others better for short documents with unique pages.

Valley Dining Guide

What's Inside

2	*Seafood*
3	*Gourmet*
4	*Family Fare*
5	*Mexican Food*
6	*Italian Cuisine*
7	*Chinese Food*
8	*Indian Food*
9	*Cajun Food*
11	*Pizza Parlors*

With over 300 restaurants in the Lakeshore Valley, the area has a variety of cuisine that rivals many of the larger metropolitan areas of the world. But, of course, variety isn't everything. Not only do we have a wide variety of restaurants to choose from, but the quality of food in the valley is superb. Would you believe we have three 5-star restaurants within a square mile area? For a community this size, that's incredible!

Since we do have so many fine restaurants to tempt your palate, it can get a bit confusing when deciding where to dine. Where do you take your sweetheart for a romantic evening, or what restaurant serves seafood *and* burritos? To help you decide, we've compiled this exhaustive list of the finest Lakeshore Valley eating establishments. The restaurant listings help give you a flavor of each eatery and all include sample menu items and a description of the house specialty. The price range, location (with map), hours of business, phone number and many other tidbits of information are also included to help you plan your next evening on the town. Enjoy!

Figure 1: A page created with PageMaker (reduced by 31 percent).

Selecting a Program

Although there are several dozen desktop publishing programs on the market, Ventura Publisher and PageMaker probably account for about 80 percent of the packages sold. So if you're like most people, choosing a program boils down to deciding which of those two to buy. For some advice, see the sidebard "Ventura or PageMaker?"

If your requirements are fairly typical, either Ventura or PageMaker will be a good choice. Here are some instances in which you might want to look beyond the leaders:

- **Casual use:** If you just want a cheap program to play around with at home and print up an occasional club newsletter or party invitation, get PFS: First Publisher.
- **Databases:** ByLine is a good choice if you want to easily import information from dBASE and Lotus into your documents. Ventura can also be used to format databases, but more steps are involved than with ByLine.
- **Mathematical equations:** So far, neither Ventura nor PageMaker can automatically manage the complexities of equation formatting. Get PC Tex or MicroTex.
- **Simple graphics:** If all you're interested in is adding an occasional chart or table to an otherwise unsophisticated document, you'll do just as well with WordPerfect 5.0 as with any of the current crop of desktop publishing programs.

Access: Desktop Publishing

ByLine
Ashton-Tate Corp.
20101 Hamilton Ave.
Torrance, CA 90502
213/329-8000
Price: $295
Description: A WYSIWYG program with less powerful graphic and typographic features than Ventura or PageMaker. Its most interesting feature is that it allows you to import dBASE or Lotus files without going through an intermediate conversion process.

EPAW
Network Technology Corp.
6825 Lamp Post Lane
Alexandria, VA 22306
703/765-4506
Price: $1,295

EROFF
Elan Computer Group, Inc.
410 Cambridge Ave., Suite A
Palo Alto, CA 94306
415/322-2450
Price: $795 - $4,995

Exact
Technical Support Software
72 Kent St. #110
Brookline, MA 02146
617/734-4130
Price: $475
Description: A code-base program designed for technical documents.

First Impression
Megahaus Corp.
6215 Ferris Square
San Diego, CA 92121
619/450-1230
Price: $895
Description: A WYSIWYG program designed for long documents.

Front Page Personal Publisher
Haba/Arrays, Inc.
6711 Valjean Ave.
Van Nuys, CA 91406
818/994-1899
Price: $199

GEM Desktop Publisher
Digital Research, Inc.
60 Garden Court, Box DRI
Monterey, CA 93942
408/649-3896
Price: $395
Description: Similar to Ventura Publisher but with fewer capabilities.

Laser Press
Award Software, Inc.
130 Knowles Dr.
Los Gatos, CA 95030
408/370-7979
Price: $198
Description: A low-end code-based program.

□ EROFF™ Desktop Typesetter □

Eroff is a professional quality publishing system based on an enhanced version of AT&T's Documenter's Workbench™ release 2.0. *Eroff*™ is the ideal solution for users developing medium or long doumentation. *Eroff*™ supports the entire HP LaserJet family including the **HP LaserJet, HP LaserJet Plus, HP LaserJet Series II,** and **HP LaserJet 2000.** As you can see below, *Eroff*™ has the most *complete* tool set available for medium and large scale documentation requirements, and Elan also makes this package available on a very wide variety of computer systems from personal computers to mainframes under *both* the **UNIX®** and **MS-DOS®** operating systems. For document proofing, screen *previewers* and impact printer support is also available.

Charts and Tables

Eroff contains a sophisticated, yet easy to use mechanism, *tbl,* for table creation. Simply describe the layout of the table and input the table contents. *Eroff* takes care of adjusting, aligning, boxing, centering, etc. Here's an example...

Composition of Foods			
Food	*Percent by Weight*		
	Protein	Fat	Carbo-hydrate
Apples	.4	.5	13.0
Lima beans	7.5	.8	22.0
Milk	3.3	4.0	5.0
Mushrooms	3.5	.4	6.0
Rye bread	9.0	.6	52.7

Mathematics

Sophisticated mathematics a requirement? *Eroff* includes a powerful yet easy to use tool, *eqn,* for entering complex math equations. Even a novice can produce complicated equations like these ...

$$G(z) = e^{\ln G(z)} = \exp\left(\sum_{k\geq 1} \frac{S_k z^k}{k}\right) = \prod_{k\geq 1} e^{S_k z^k/k}$$

$$= \left(1 + S_1 z + \frac{S_1^2 z^2}{2!} + \frac{S_2 z^2}{2} + \frac{S_2^2 z^4}{2^2 \cdot 2!} + \cdots\right)$$

$$= \sum_{m\geq 0} \left(\sum_{\substack{k_1,k_2,\cdots,k_m \geq 0 \\ k_1+2k_2+\cdots+mk_m}} \frac{S_1^{k_1}}{1^{k_1} k_1!} \cdots \frac{S_m^{k_m}}{m^{k_m} k_m!} \right) z^m$$

Diagrams

Tired of *cutting-and-pasting* or waiting for the art department? With *Eroff,* diagrams can be created and positioned along with your text. The diagram facility, *pic,* uses simple English-like commands such as *box, arrow from box to circle, move down,* etc.

Plots & Graphs

Simple numeric data may be converted to typeset plots and graphs using the plot and graph tool *grap* in *Eroff.* Here's an example...

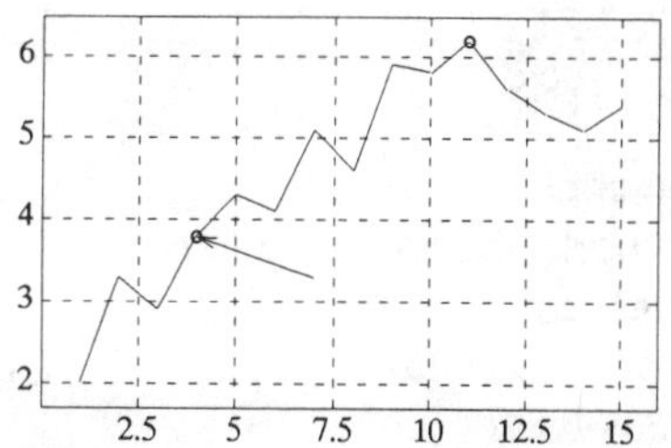

Images

And here's cause for celebration - now any *bitmap* graphic image such as a chart, symbols, logos, art, scanned picture, etc. from a wide variety of sources, such as a scanner, paint program, CAD/ CAM or other graphic system, may be included *directly* into your document without the need to *cut-and-paste* pictures to your printed documents.

Availability

Eroff is available *now* on a variety of machines:

- IBM-PC under MS-DOS, Xenix® and Microport
- AT&T 3B1, 3B2, 3B5, 3B15, 3B20
- HP-9000 Series 200, 300, 500, and 800
- A wide variety of UNIX® systems.

for the complete HP LaserJet family:

- HP LaserJet and LaserJet Plus
- HP LaserJet 500 Plus
- HP LaserJet Series II
- HP LaserJet 2000

Figure 2: A page created with EROFF (reduced by 23 percent)

Laser Print Plus
Janus Associates
94 Chestnut St.
Boston, MA 02108
617/720-5085
Price: $395

Laser-Set
Laser Technologies Int'l, Inc.
15403 E. Alondra Blvd.
La Mirada, CA 90638
714/739-2478
Price: $199.95

LaserScript
Command Technology Corp.
1900 Mountain Blvd.
Oakland, CA 94611
415/339-3530
Price: $695
Description: A code-based program designed for very long, highly-structured publications.

LaserType
Reon Technology
Box 191
Cochiti Lake, NM 87041
505/465-2990
Price: $400

MagicSeries
Computer Editype Systems
509 Cathedral Pkwy #10-A
New York, NY 10025
800/251-2223
212/222-8148
Price: $99 - $149
Description: A low-end, code-based program.

Manuscript
Lotus Development Corp.
55 Cambridge Pkwy.
Cambridge, MA 02142
800/343-5414
617/577-8500
Price: $495
Description: A technical word processor with special features for equations.

MicroTex
Addison-Wesley Publishing Co.
EMS Division
6 Jacob Way
Reading, MA 01867
617/944-6795
Price: $495
Description: An implementation of Donald Knuth's Tex formatting language; excellent for typesetting mathematical equations. Code-based with preview mode.

MP-XL
Micro Print-X, Inc.
P.O. Box 581
119 North 8th St.
Ballinger, TX 76821
915/365-2343
Price: $395

News Master
Unison World
2150 Shattuck Ave. #902
Berkeley, CA 94704
415/848-6670

LaserScript™— The Solution To LARGE Document Production!

GRAPHICS	
Placement	Float figures and tables with associated text: • Top or bottom of page • Top or bottom of column • Inline
Illus-trations	Include graphics generated by: • AutoCAD (like the nozzle below) • In•a•Vision • Windows Draw and LOTUS 123
Tables	This table demonstrates **some** of the capabilities: • Individual table cells may contain any desired text, lists, or graphics. • Individual table cells may be shaded. • Variable-width ruled lines may be drawn between cells and around the table. • Adjacent cells may be grouped in any arrangement.
Screens	Capture text screens with Dan Bricklin's DEMO program to automatically include them in your documentation.
DESIGN	
Page Composition	Contains all of the features for creating an individual user style for books, technical manuals or even letters • User designed headers, footers • Unlimited multiple columns and gutters • Variable margins, spacing, type sizes and leading • Macros allow page styles to vary endlessly
Emphasized Text	Underscore, *Italic*, **Bold**, Super^{script}, CAPS, Sub$_{script}$, **BOLD CAPS**, and `font changes`
Camera Ready Copy	• Crop-marks • Physical page numbers reduce the likelihood of lost pages • Duplex layout and page imposition
SPECIAL FEATURES	
Rules and Rev. Bars	Rules may vary in length, thickness, shading and style. Revision bars are vertical rules and can indicate level.
Icons & Key Caps	LaserScript provides a font which includes these special symbols: ● ○ ■ □ ▲ △ ♦ ◊ © ® ™ ↘ ✓ [A]-[Z] [0]-[9] [↑] [↓] [←] [→] [⇥] [⇤] [↵] [PG UP] [PG DN] [HOME] [END] [INS] [DEL] [ESC] [ALT] [CTRL] [SHIFT] [SYS REQ] [BKSP] [F1]-[F24]

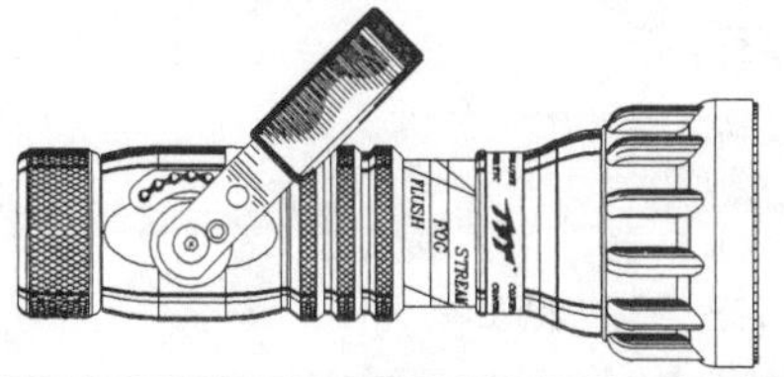

DOCUMENT FORMATTING	
Cross-References	Cross references are generated automatically, and reference both forward and backward within a manuscript.
Lists	**Numbered** The style may be: 1. Arabic 2. Alphabetic—upper or lower case 3. Roman—upper or lower case **Definition** The item being defined may be placed: • To the left of the definition (as in this list) • Above the definition body text **Bulleted** With several styles of bullets **Simple** Used to itemize or organize data **Note:** Automatically formats notes within lists **Warning:** Automatically formats warnings within lists
Headings	• Chapter, Section, and Subsection • Automatically placed into Table of Contents • Automatically entered into the Index • May be numbered in the style of user's choice
Table of Contents	• Automatic and multi-level • Creates additional separate Figure and Table Lists • User specified style
Index	• Multi level, automatically built and formatted • Index entries may also be manually inserted by a user • User specified output style
Footnotes	Automatically numbered and placed at the bottom of the page or at the end of a chapter.
Page Numbering	LaserScript completely automates page numbering in the following formats: • Sequential (from front to back) • Page numbering by chapter (1-1, 1-2, 2-1,...,) Pages can be numbered in Arabic, alphabetic, or Roman format, the same as *Headings*
Hyphenation & Justification	Automatic hyphenation, justification, kerning, tracking, and word-space optimization—all under user control. Also, a user hyphenation-exception dictionary is available.

LARGE DOCUMENTS

Now you can produce professional looking large documents on your PC.

With LaserScript's powerful formatting and sophisticated publishing features, a 600 page manual is as easy to produce as this one-page summary. (We composed this with LaserScript and printed it on an HP LaserJet+ with HP's AC soft fonts).

LaserScript is the solution to large document production.

CTC Command Technology Corporation

1900 Mountain Boulevard
Oakland, CA 94611
(415)339-3530 Telex:509330

Figure 3: A page created with LaserScript (reduced by 33 percent).

Price: $99.95
Description: A WYSIWYG program intended only for casual use. Not as good as PFS: First Publisher.

The Newsroom Pro
Springboard
7808 Creekridge Circle
Minneapolis, MN 55435
612/944-3912
Price: $129
Description: A WYSIWYG program intended only for casual use. Not as good as PFS: First Publisher.

Office Publisher
Laser Friendly, Inc.
930 Benecia Ave.
Sunnyvale, CA 94086
408/730-1921
Price: $995
Description: A high-end WYSIWYG program. Better than Ventura at creating tables, but generally slower and more awkward than Ventura.

PageMaker
Aldus Corp.
411 First Ave. S. #200
Seattle, WA 98104
206/622-5500
Price: $795
Description: A powerful, easy-to-use WYSIWYG program. Not as fast as Ventura.

Page Perfect
IMSI
1299 Fourth St.
San Rafael, CA 94901
415/454-7101
Price: $495

PageWriter
The Computer Group
1717 W. Beltline Hwy.
Madison, WI 53713
608/273-1803
Price: $495

PC Tex
Personal Tex, Inc.
12 Madrona
Mill Valley, CA 94941
415/388-8853
Price: $249
Description: An implementation of Donald Knuth's Tex formatting language; excellent for typesetting mathematical equations. Code-based with preview mode.

PFS: First Publisher
Software Publishing
1901 Landings Dr.
P.O. Box 7210
Mountain View, CA 94039
415/962-8910
Price: $99
Description: The best of the low-end WYSIWYG programs. Not intended for professional use.

PowerText Formatter
Beaman Porter, Inc.
417 Halstead Ave.
Harrison, NY 10528
800/431-0007
914/835-3156
Price: $149.95

LOTUS MANUSCRIPT

A Word and Document Processor for Technical Professionals

Lotus Manuscript is a word and document processor designed to write technical proposals and reports as easily as it writes a memo. Using charts, tables, graphics, equations and sophisticated page layouts as communication tools, Manuscript helps you to actively convey your message to the reader.

Full Range of Word Processing
All word processing features required to produce documents ranging from a one page memo to an 800 page technical specification including: Cut, copy, paste, search and replace and spelling checker are provided.

Technical Document Support
Manuscript has an integrated outliner which can be decimal, Roman numeral or alphabetic. The table of contents is automatically generated as are table of tables and table of figures and the index. Sections can be cross-referenced and three types of footnotes are available. Document compare allows you to print a document with change bars in the margins and/or text notations to show the revisions since the last edit session. The table editor creates simple to complex tables using columns. Columns may be inserted, deleted, moved and sized.

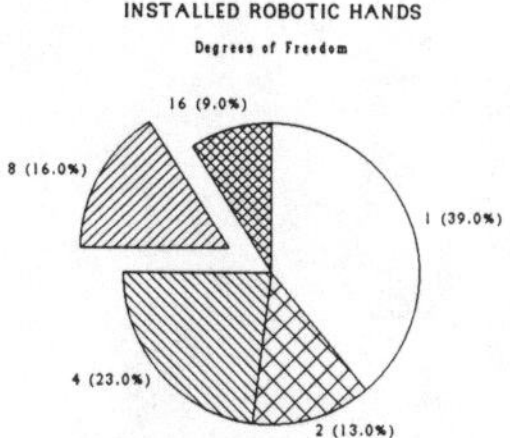

Lotus 1-2-3, Symphony Interface
Incorporate worksheet or graphics files with your text. Once included in a file, you can further enhance worksheet and graphics files with boxes, rules or by changing the column layout.

Mixing Text with Graphics
Import graphics files from Lotus 1-2-3 and Symphony as well Freelance Plus and bit-mapped images from desktop scanners to support your text.

Equations and Greek symbols
To incorporate equations, you type the word equivalent of the mathematical symbols. Manuscript will construct the equation for you.

$$E = E^{o} + 2.3\frac{RT}{n_i F}\log\left(A_i + \sum_{j=1}^{i} K_{ij}A_j\right)$$

Document/Page Layout Preview
Before printing your document, review the layout to check the positioning of graphics and equations. Document Preview shows you a representation of an 8 1/2 x 11 inch page of your document. Magnify areas of text to check hyphenation, line endings and page breaks.

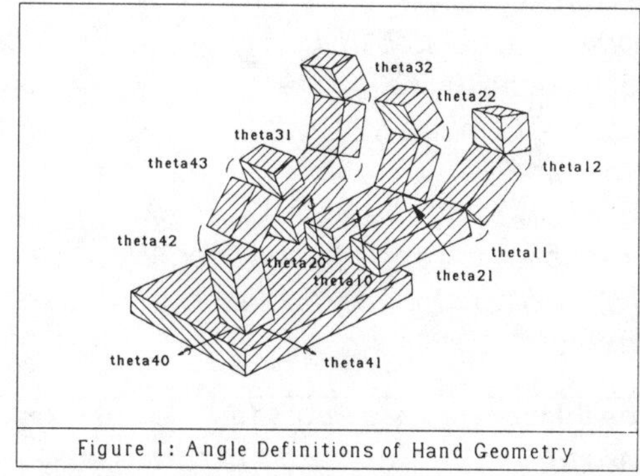

Figure 1: Angle Definitions of Hand Geometry

Print Formatter
The print formatter lays out the pages, justifies the copy using micro-justification, and has sophisticated widow and orphan control. It places and sizes any graphics and makes all the font and linespace changes requested. You easily design the layout for title pages, table of contents, first, even and odd pages and the index.

Printer Support
Manuscript is designed to take full advantage of your printer's capabilities. It supports a full range of printers from dot matrix and letter quality to laser.[1]

Figure 4: A page created with Lotus Manuscript (reduced by 29 percent).

Printrix
Data Transforms
616 Washington
Denver, CO 80203
303/832-1501
Price: $165
Description: A code-based program that uses its own fonts rather than LaserJet soft fonts.

ScenicWriter
Scenicsoft, Inc.
100 Second Ave. S.
Edmonds, WA 98020
800/422-2994
Price: $695
Description: A code-based program. Quite difficult to use.

scLaserPlus
Pursang Corp.
Software Channels Division
1320 Yonge St. #301
Toronto, Canada M4T 1X2
416/967-4290
Price: $495
Description: A code-based, non-WYSIWYG program. Easy to use but inflexible.

Spellbinder Desktop Publisher
Lexisoft, Inc.
P.O. Box 1950
Davis, CA 95617
916/758-3630
Price: $695
Description: A code-based program. Quite difficult to use.

SuperPage II
Bestinfo
1400 N. Providence Rd. #117
Media, PA 19063
215/891-6500
Price: $8,250

SuperPrint
Janus Associates
94 Chestnut St.
Boston, MA 02108
617/720-5085
Price: $695

Ventura Publisher
Xerox Corp.
P.O. Box 24
Rochester, NY 14692
800/832-6979
Price: $895
Description: The most popular desktop publishing program. Uses a WYSIWYG interface and style sheets. Fast and packed with features.

Profile: Xerox Ventura Publisher

RIGHT AWAY, WE'LL confess our bias. We like Ventura Publisher. So much, in fact, that one of the authors wrote a separate book about the program (Ventura Tips and Tricks). Our interest in the program goes back to the experience of laying out the first edition of *LaserJet Unlimited* in 1986. At that time, the tools available to us were Microsoft Word, a light table, a waxer, and an X-acto knife. Needless to say, we were eager to find a software tool that would make it possible to do a book-size project like *LaserJet Unlimited* without all the fussy manual pasteup work. Ventura proved to be that tool.

Ventura has several big advantages over other desktop publishing software, especially for LaserJet owners:

- It's clearly the fastest program on the market. In desktop publishing, speed means smoothness, and smoothness means ease of use. Notice I didn't say "ease of learning." Ventura takes longer to learn than PageMaker, but once you've become familiar with how it works, you'll find it a very comfortable tool.
- For LaserJet Plus and LaserJet II owners, Ventura comes with a built-in set of fonts that are automatically downloaded to the printer when needed. Provided your needs are met by this selection of fonts, you can forget about the chores of buying fonts and learning to download them. It's all taken care of.
- Ventura's typographic and page layout capabilities are unmatched by any program on the PC or the Macintosh.

Ventura does have some significant drawbacks. First, it's not cheap (but so far that's been somewhat mitigated by heavy discounting). Of greater importance is the difficulty of learning the program. Most people find Ventura far from intuitive, and it's sensible to set aside a few weeks for getting accustomed to the way the program operates. Still, it's worth the effort.

Not only is Ventura a program with publishing muscle to burn—better, in fact, than anything available on the Macintosh—it's one of the rare programs that demolishes a good deal of the conventional wisdom about what is and isn't possible on the IBM PC.

Until Ventura came along, most people assumed that the new breed of high-powered WYSIWYG publishing programs would need more horsepower than the standard IBM PC or XT. Such programs would mandate owning an AT-class computer or better, they warned, because the PC just couldn't handle the complexity of multiple-font WYSIWYG text and graphics. Surprise! Although its performance is definitely superior on an AT, its speed on an XT is quite acceptable. Many people tend to compare programs according to how many features they offer (and Ventura can go toe-to-toe with any program in that regard), it's really the speed that makes Ventura such a great tool.

Ventura allows a seemingly endless range of hardware and software choices. It supports all the graphics monitor standards, several scanners, most major word processors, and numerous graphics formats.

What's It Good For?

It's true that Ventura is ideally suited for a particular sort of work, namely, producing those long, highly structured manuals known as "technical documentation." Ventura gives the tech-doc folks exactly what they need in a publishing program: automatic chapter, page, subhead, caption, and footnote numbering; automatic table of contents and index generation; easy merging of computer-generated graphics and scanned images with text; and compatibility with multiple word processor files.

But Ventura fits the bill quite nicely for other sorts of documents as well. Forms, for instance. Ventura actually works better than any of the specialized forms generation programs I've seen on the PC. For whipping up a quick invoice or order form, it's quicker, more accurate, and allows more options for boxes and shading. Ventura also functions nicely as a page makeup program for newsletter-style layouts, in which two or three articles begin on the first page and then flow independently onto subsequent pages. A survey done by the Ventura Users of North America in the Spring of 1988 showed that newsletters were the largest application category among Ventura users (29 percent used Ventura for that purpose) followed by manuals (19 percent) and advertising material (15 percent).

Behind the Magic

The key to Ventura's performance is that the program includes a run-time version of Digital Research's GEM environment. Those unacquainted with GEM needn't worry—Ventura boots from the DOS command line in normal fashion. Behind the scenes, GEM takes care of the details of writing to

NUTS

Deluxe Assortment **Spring 1987**

1. Peanut

A tasty, unique assortment from plantations in Africa and Southeast Asia. And, yes, from Georgia too!

2. Brazil Nut

Exclusively from South America, these Brazils are fat, hard-shelled and delicious. They'll be much in demand.

3. Hazelnut

Cakes, cookies, ice cream, chocolate, salads. They'll never taste better than with this delicious French variety.

4. Almond

They're popular and they're versatile. Available whole, sliced or chopped, they're equally at home in Mom's favorite recipes.

5. Pecan

Another great favorite in the bakery. And our own superb pecans will satisfy even the most discriminating tastes.

6. Pistachio

With an unusually subtle and delicate flavor, these perennial favorites will be perfect for either sweet or savory dishes.

7. Walnut

Blond English Walnuts are just one of the many varieties available, in the best nut-cracking tradition.

8. Chestnut

Superior varieties from our own plantations in Italy and France. All the best for more than seasonal consumption.

Figure 1: This page is free-form, unlike the typical Ventura document, which is more structured. It shows, however, that Ventura can handle free-form layouts. (Reduced by 35 percent.)

the screen and providing drivers for various printers.

If you've ever used a Macintosh, you may experience déjà vu the first time you see the main Ventura screen. Like the Macintosh, Ventura uses a pull-down command line along the top of the screen. Each command on the top line represents a menu, whose commands are selected by pointing and clicking with the mouse. In addition, Ventura places some commands along the left side of the screen: the four mode icons at the upper left, and below that a panel used for showing character-formatting or text-tagging options. For many functions, Ventura does allow keyboard commands, but these are intended to augment the use of the mouse, not replace it. If your mouse gets broken, it's possible to move around the screen using cursor keys, but for all practical purposes you need a mouse.

While new to many PC users, the point-and-click way of working should be easy to grasp, though it may take awhile for the neophyte to feel comfortable. Navigating the screen, for example, isn't like the easy scrolling of a word processor. Instead of PgUp and PgDn, you have to go to the side of the screen with the mouse and click on a scroll bar.

More daunting than the Macintosh-like interface are the four modes used by the program—Frames, Tagging, Text, and Graphics. Before attempting any operation in Ventura, you must first make sure that the program is set to one of these four modes.

Frame Job

The first and most basic mode is framing. Frames are essentially boxes, with borders that may be visible or invisible. Every page itself is a frame, and to this first underlying frame, more frames can be added to hold elements of text or graphics. To insert a graphic on a page, you first activate frame mode, then use the mouse to draw a rectangular frame. After you select the Load Text/Graphics command from the Frame menu and type the name of the file containing the graphic, the picture appears on the screen within the frame.

Ventura's use of frames provides you with unending freedom to make changes and adjustments in a document. For example, at any time, you can reposition a frame by pointing anywhere within it with the mouse, clicking a mouse button, and then dragging the mouse (with frame in tow) to its new home. Text automatically hyphenates and reformats text around the new frame.

When you first begin using the program, you may find that frames are a source of some consternation. After some practice, selecting the appropriate frame before altering the page becomes as automatic as pressing the backslash key in Lotus or the Ctrl key in WordStar.

Not all frame operations are performed with the mouse. For instance, once you have used the mouse to drag a frame to a new location, you can position it more precisely by typing specific coordinates into the frame menu. Likewise, the menu lets you select whether you want a border around the frame, background shades, the widths of margins, and more. This interplay between mouse-work for rough positioning and command selection, and menus for fine adjustments is a recurrent theme in the design of Ventura, and accounts for the seamless feel of the program.

Word Processor Friendly

Once you have specified the parameters of the underlying frame (the page itself), you can begin adding text and pictures. When you highlight the text icon, Ventura becomes a word processor: the cursor takes the shape of a marker and you can directly enter text onto the screen.

Rather than typing text directly into Ventura, most people will probably prefer to generate text using their familiar word processing program, and then load the text into Ventura for formatting. Ventura can convert files in any of the major word processing formats—Microsoft Word, WordPerfect, WordStar, MultiMate, Xerox Writer—as well as plain ASCII files. Files from different word processors can be used in a single document. For the most part, any character formatting such as bold, italics, underlining, or superscript specified in the original document is preserved by Ventura. Other sorts of formatting, such as line spacing, are ignored. Tabs in original files may cause problems. Ventura will attempt to recognize them but may not interpret them in exactly the same way as the word processor does.

Perhaps the most welcome aspect of Ventura's method of handling both text and graphics files is that it preserves them in their original formats, rather than translating them into a new Ventura format. To store formatting information, Ventura creates a separate file containing pointers to other files. This method of file handling makes it possible to cope with one of the traditional bugaboos of the technical documentation department—the infamous last-minute change. It allows companies to move back and forth from word-processed to formatted versions of a document as a document travels through successive revisions, thus eliminating the need to rekey changes made during formatting back into the original files. Finally, the method saves disk space, since a single version of a file is used both for word processing and for Ventura formatting.

Dressing Up the Type

When first poured onto the page, all text flows into the predetermined columns, and with character attributes such as boldface preserved from the word processor. Otherwise, it is unformatted. To add the appropriate typographic information, such as typeface, type size, leading (line spacing), and centering, as well as additional niceties such as bullets and drop caps, you need to switch to Ventura's Tagging mode (by selecting the Tag icon). Those who have mastered Microsoft Word's method of style-sheet formatting will have no trouble getting used to Ventura's use of tags, but others may find this to be an additional source of confusion. You first place text on a page either by typing it in directly or by importing it from a text file created by a word processor. You then select a style sheet, which comprises a list of formats, such as "Chapter Title" or "Subhead." Tagging merely involves highlighting a block of text with the mouse, and then clicking the mouse on the name of the appropriate tag. Alternatively, tagging can be done using function keys, a much faster approach.

Each tag contains all the information necessary to format a block of text: font information (typeface, type style, type size), line spacing, justification (left, right, centered, or fully justified), etc. You can change the formatting instructions associated with a tag at any time: all text labeled with that tag automatically assumes the new format.

Worth a Thousand

Pictures created by graphics programs or digitized by a scanner are loaded into frames using the same command used to load pictures. Ventura recognizes two types of pictures, those stored in bitmapped form (as patterns of dots)—Ventura calls these Images—and those stored in object form (as geometric commands)—called Line Art by the program.

Your choice for graphics includes the following formats: PC Paintbrush, MacPaint, MacDraw, CGM, VideoShow, Lotus 1-2-3, AutoCAD SLD files, Mentor Graphics, GEM Draw, and GEM Paint. Once loaded into a frame,

Figure 2: Contributor Daniel Will-Harris's used Ventura to create the ad on the facing page (reduced by 41 percent) for his Ventura style sheet collection. The sample pages were scanned and then loaded into Ventura as graphic images. (By the way, at a couple bucks a pop, these style sheets are one of the LaserJet steal/deals of the Millenium! Send in your order to Box 480265, Los Angeles, CA 90048 today. —An unsolicited testimonial.)

a graphic can be easily cropped, merely by using the mouse to move the edge of its frame. You can also stretch or shrink images by selecting new scaling factors. While you cannot drive a scanner directly from Ventura, PC Paintbrush does include a command to drive a scanner. Thus, to include such an image in a Ventura document, you first scan it using PC Paintbrush (or your own scanner software), then load the Paintbrush file into Ventura.

Drawing Your Own

Although it tends to be overshadowed by the more impressive graphics exported from other programs, Ventura's own internal graphics mode provides some extremely useful features. When you highlight the Graphics icon, Ventura assumes the role of a simple drawing program, allowing you to draw lines, boxes, circles, and special text-holding boxes. The left panel shows the graphics tools: the arrow (for moving items), rectangles, rounded-corner rectangles, circles, and box text. Once you have selected any of the graphics options, you can draw the shape on the screen using the mouse. From the Graphics menu, you can then select such graphics attributes as line thickness and shading pattern. Graphics can be clumped together by holding down the Shift key while you click on them successively with the mouse—allowing a group to be moved together.

Two graphics operations of particular note are Ventura's invisible grid lines and its Box Text command. Within the Graphics menu, specifying horizontal and vertical grid and turning the Snap-To option on allows you to align graphics precisely on an unseen grid. For more free-form positioning, you can turn the Snap-To option off.

While the Box Text command may be initially overlooked by many users of the program, but it is one of the most useful features of the program. When you draw a box on screen after selecting the Box Text icon, the box contains the words "Box Text." You can replace these words with text of your own, and center, right justify, or left justify it. By joining Box Text boxes together, you can quickly create tables and forms. Ventura's own graphics operations also provide a useful means for enhancing imported graphics with labels and arrows.

Advanced Pagination and Typography

With each upgrade, Ventura has added an increasing number of powerful typographic features, allowing you full control over kerning, spaces between letters, and spaces between words. Hyphenation is also powerful, and if desired (such as when working on French and English in adjacent columns) you can use two hyphenation routines at once. The hyphenation routine is based on an algorithm, with an expandable exceptions dictionary. In addition, you can insert optional hyphens in a document. For measuring, you can select among inches, centimeters, and picas. Leading can be altered only at the paragraph level, and the program does not provide any tracking or spaceband control.

Ventura's pagination capabilities are truly exceptional. Once you have established margins, number of columns, and other parameters of the first page of a document, Ventura will automatically create as many pages as are necessary to contain the manuscript. A frame can contain up to eight columns, which may be of equal or unequal widths and may be separated by vertical rules. You can lay pages out in either portrait (upright) or landscape (sideways) orientation, and can set up distinct parameters for left and right pages. Whereas many desktop publishing programs balk at documents longer than 12 or 16 pages, Ventura can handle veritable tomes. Scores of chapters can be chained together—that is, printed in a single batch, with all numbering preserved in sequence. Automatic numbering applies to almost anything you might think of: pages, captions, footnotes, and up to eight levels of subheads.

One excellent feature is the ability to "anchor" graphics vis-a-vis text. Anchoring, a capability of some high-end batch pagination programs, allows graphics to be tied to specific locations in text. Thus, when a document is revised and pagination changes, the graphics automatically reposition themselves to stay with the text to which they have been attached.

Included among Ventura's pagination controls are some inconspicuous but highly useful touches. One provides you the capability to attach captions to figures, so that when you move a figure the caption automatically moves as well. Another lets you specify three types of text within a header or footer: left justified, right justified, and centered—all on the same line. Yet another lets you select whether you want a document collated, and whether you want it printed in forward or backward order. Finally, the program allows for column balancing, which evens out the length of columns on the final page of a multicolumn document.

As icing on the pagination cake, the program can automatically prepare a table of contents and an index for your document (the latter, of course, depends on you marking the appropriate entries in the text).

Hardware

All publishing systems are agglomerations of hardware: monitors, printers, scanners, computers, and other devices. In essence, the job of a program like Ventura is to act as a skilled master of ceremonies, introducing different acts, helping them look their best, and combining them all into a seamless show.

The program requires a hard disk and a graphics adapter. While any adapter from a CGA on up to expensive full-page monitors is acceptable, you'll find that the better the monitor, the easier the program is to use. On the CGA, text can generally be read only in enlarged view, which makes it necessary at times to switch back and forth from full-page to enlarged views. With a Hercules board or an EGA, operations are somewhat more convenient, since smaller text can be read in Normal mode. But if you spend much time with the program, you'll find yourself craving one of the new high-resolution, full-page monitors. Using anything less feels somewhat cramped, like word processing on an 8-line laptop after cutting your computing teeth on a regular display.

With Ventura you can get by without a mouse by using keyboard alternatives, but the no-mouse option is mainly theoretical. If your mouse is out of order, you can still move around on the screen using the cursor keys and can substitute the Home key for the mouse button. But keyboard operations are excruciatingly slow. For those who are still dragging their feet, it's time to make friends with a mouse.

Using Ventura with the Classic LaserJet

Ventura can be used with any member of the LaserJet family. Its capabilities on the original LaserJet, however, mainly serve to highlight the shortcomings of the printer. You can use Ventura with the basic LaserJet, but only if you have the F font cartridge. That cartridge provides one display font (14.4-point HELV), three text fonts (10-point TMS RMN in regular, bold, and italic), and one footnote font (8-point TMS RMN). Though limited, this range of sizes is suitable for letters, memoranda, simple reports, and some technical documentation.

With the basic LaserJet, you cannot print text in landscape mode, and graphics are severely limited by the 59K of available printer memory. If you select other fonts and try to print them on the original LaserJet, Ventura will render them at a crude 75-dpi resolution.

To get better results with a basic LaserJet, your best bet is to upgrade it with a LaserMaster CAPCard (see discussion below and in "Profile: LaserMaster CAPCard").

Installing Ventura for the LaserJet Plus and LaserJet II

In contrast to its font limitations on the basic LaserJet, Ventura is almost perfectly suited for either the LaserJet Plus or the LaserJet II. The reason is that the program comes bundled with its own set of LaserJet soft fonts, including Dutch (similar to TMS RMN or Times Roman) and Swiss (similar to HELV or Helvetica) in sizes ranging from 8 to 24 points. These add about 2MB to the 1MB of storage space that Ventura normally requires on a hard disk.

These models differ from the original LaserJet in that they have more memory and can be used with soft fonts. The basic 512K configuration of these printers is adequate, although you will encounter some limitations in printing very large graphics, in combining more than a few fonts on a page and in combining graphics and several fonts on a page.

To avoid such potential limitations, install an extra 1MB of memory in your LaserJet II or retrofit your LaserJet Plus with a LaserMaster CAPCard.

Installing Ventura for the LaserJet Plus or LaserJet II is the same. You'll have the option of installing for 300-dpi or 150-dpi output. Install for 300-dpi first to make it your default. When Ventura asks, "Add Another Printer?" respond "Yes" and select the 150-dpi option. When you're using the program, everything will work fine with the 300-dpi option, but if memory is insufficient for a page, you can use the Printer Preferences selection from the Options menu to switch to the 150-dpi option. This will reduce the amount of memory needed for pictures by causing them to be printed at the coarser 150-dpi resolution and thereby allowing your page to print. Fonts will not be printed at the lower resolution, just graphics.

Using Ventura with Upgraded LaserJets

Ventura works with any of the popular upgrades for the LaserJet, including HP's JetScript PostScript controller, the LaserMaster CAPCard, and the JLaserPlus board. With JetScript, you get a great deal of convenience in working with fonts, since the JetScript itself comes with 35 built-in typefaces and all these are already installed in Ventura. Just select the PostScript printer option when you install the program. Printing speed with JetScript is slower than with the LaserJet Plus or LaserJet II.

If you're interested in fast printing, the CAPCard definitely beats out every other option for printing with Ventura. What makes it an even better companion to Ventura is that you can select any size font from within Ventura and the CAPCard will generate it on the fly using a built-in version of Bitstream's Fontware. That makes the

Typeface	Sizes Provided with Ventura	Sizes in VS Ventura Supplemental FontPak
Dutch Medium	6, 8, 10, 12	14, 18, 20, 24, 30
Dutch Italic	10, 12	6, 8, 14, 18, 20, 24, 30
Dutch Bold	10, 12, 14, 18, 24	6, 8, 20, 30
Dutch Bold Italic	none	6, 8, 10, 12, 14, 18, 20, 24, 30
Swiss Medium	6, 8, 10, 12	14, 18, 20, 24, 30
Swiss Italic	10, 12	6, 8, 14, 18, 20, 24, 30
Swiss Bold	10, 12, 14, 18, 24	6, 8, 20, 30
Swiss Bold Italic	none	6, 8, 10, 12, 14, 18, 20, 24, 30

Figure 3: The VS Ventura Supplemental FontPak fills out the selection of fonts provided with Ventura. With the supplemental set, you have a uniform selection from 6 to 30 points for the Dutch (Times Roman) and Swiss (Helvetica) families.

CAPCard as convenient in handling fonts as any PostScript printer.

Adding New Fonts

Since Ventura comes with a set of Swiss and Dutch Fonts, you don't necessarily need to install new fonts for the program. You might want to do so, however, if you want to use other typefaces or if you want a greater selection of sizes for Swiss and Dutch.

The procedure for adding new fonts for Ventura is as follows:

- Purchase fonts from Hewlett-Packard or from a third-party supplier (for sources, see Appendix E, "Font Directory.") Usually, the package of fonts you buy will come with printer fonts, screen fonts, and Ventura width tables (WID files). Screen fonts are nice to have but not essential (except for symbol fonts and fonts for non-European languages). Width tables are also nice to get along with your fonts. If they're not provided, you'll need to create them using SoftCraft's WYSIFonts or the utilities provided with Ventura's.
- Copy the WID files, the screen font files (if any), and the printer font files into the \VENTURA subdirectory on your hard disk.
- Load Ventura.
- From the Options menu select Set Printer Info. If using screen fonts other than those with the EGA extension, backspace across

the letters EGA in the dialog box and type the new extension. Select the desired printer and the width table that you wish to expand.

- From the Options menu select Add/Remove Fonts. Select Merge Width Tables.
- In the Item Selector dialog box, select the name of the new width table you wish to merge with the current width table.

VS Supplemental FontPak

Although Ventura does provide Swiss and Dutch fonts ranging from 6 to 24 points, the collection has quite a few gaps. As shown in Figure 3, medium weights are only provided in 6, 8, 10, and 12; italics are only provided in 10, 12, 14, and 18; bolds are only available for 10, 12, 14, 18, and 24; and bold italics are not available at all. With the VS Supplemental FontPak, you can have all the missing weights, including a full set of 30-point fonts. These are provided in CG Triumvirate (which closely matches Swiss) and CG Times (which closely matches Dutch).

VP/Fonts

Currently, Ventura width tables are not provided with the soft fonts sold by Hewlett-Packard. To make the installation of such fonts somewhat easier, a program called VP/Fonts is available. The utility prompts you for the names and sizes of the fonts you wish to install, and produces the Ventura WID files automatically. Note that the program works only with fonts sold by Hewlett-Packard itself, not with those sold by third-party vendors like VS Software, SoftCraft, and Conographic.

Access

VS Ventura Supplemental FontPak
VS Software
P.O. Box 6158
Little Rock, AR 72216
501/376-2083

VP/Fonts
The Laser Edge
360 - 17th Street
Oakland, CA 94612
415/835-1581

Changing Printers in Ventura

You can have multiple laser printers installed for Ventura: for example, a PostScript printer and a LaserJet Series II. Changing from one printer to another involves two steps:

- Selecting Set Printer Info from the Options menu and selecting the name of the printer from the list of available devices.
- Selecting the box that reads Change Printer Width Table.

Note that in the list of available width tables, one of the options is OUTPUT. This is the default printer, which is the same as the first printer you selected during the installation process. Thus, if you installed Ventura for the HP LaserJet Plus and then for a PostScript printer, OUTPUT.WID stands for the LaserJet Plus.

Profile: PageMaker

ALDUS PRESIDENT PAUL Brainerd coined the term "desktop publishing," and the program he conceived has set the standard for other programs since its introduction on the Macintosh in 1985. The PC version of PageMaker appeared in early 1987 and resembles the Macintosh version very closely.

The PC version of PageMaker hasn't been as popular as had been expected, probably because of the runaway popularity of Ventura. Still PageMaker is an excellent program, and with release 3.0 it now offers style sheets, one of the main features that caused many people to select Ventura. In addition, the new release provides a new Soft Font Installer, which dramatically eases the work of adding new fonts to PageMaker (see discussion of Font Installer below).

Windows: Pro and Con

The first thing you should know about PageMaker is that it runs under Microsoft Windows. That might be a plus if you're already using other Windows applications, such as Excel, Windows Designer, and Publisher's Type Foundry. Windows is also nice because it takes care of the font handling for all your applications, so you don't have to worry about how to install the LaserJet for each one independently. Finally, if you get used to Windows now, you'll be getting prepared for OS/2's Presentation Manager.

On the down side, Windows requires a fast computer and a lot of memory and storage. Your computer should have at least an 80286 microprocessor (AT clone or PS/2 Systems 30, 50, and 60) or, preferably, an 80386 microprocessor. Several megabytes of RAM are also recommended. No matter how good your hardware, you'll inevitably find that PageMaker runs slower than Ventura, simply because GEM (the basis of Ventura) provides leaner, more efficient graphics kernel than Windows.

The Pasteup Metaphor

Your compensation for going through the trouble of installing Windows on your computer and for putting up with PageMaker's slower speed is that the program uses a wonderfully intuitive approach to creating pages. Note that we said *pages*, not *documents.* The program is set up to resemble a graphic artist's pasteup table, so the emphasis is much more on working with one page at a time rather than, as is the case with Ventura, setting up

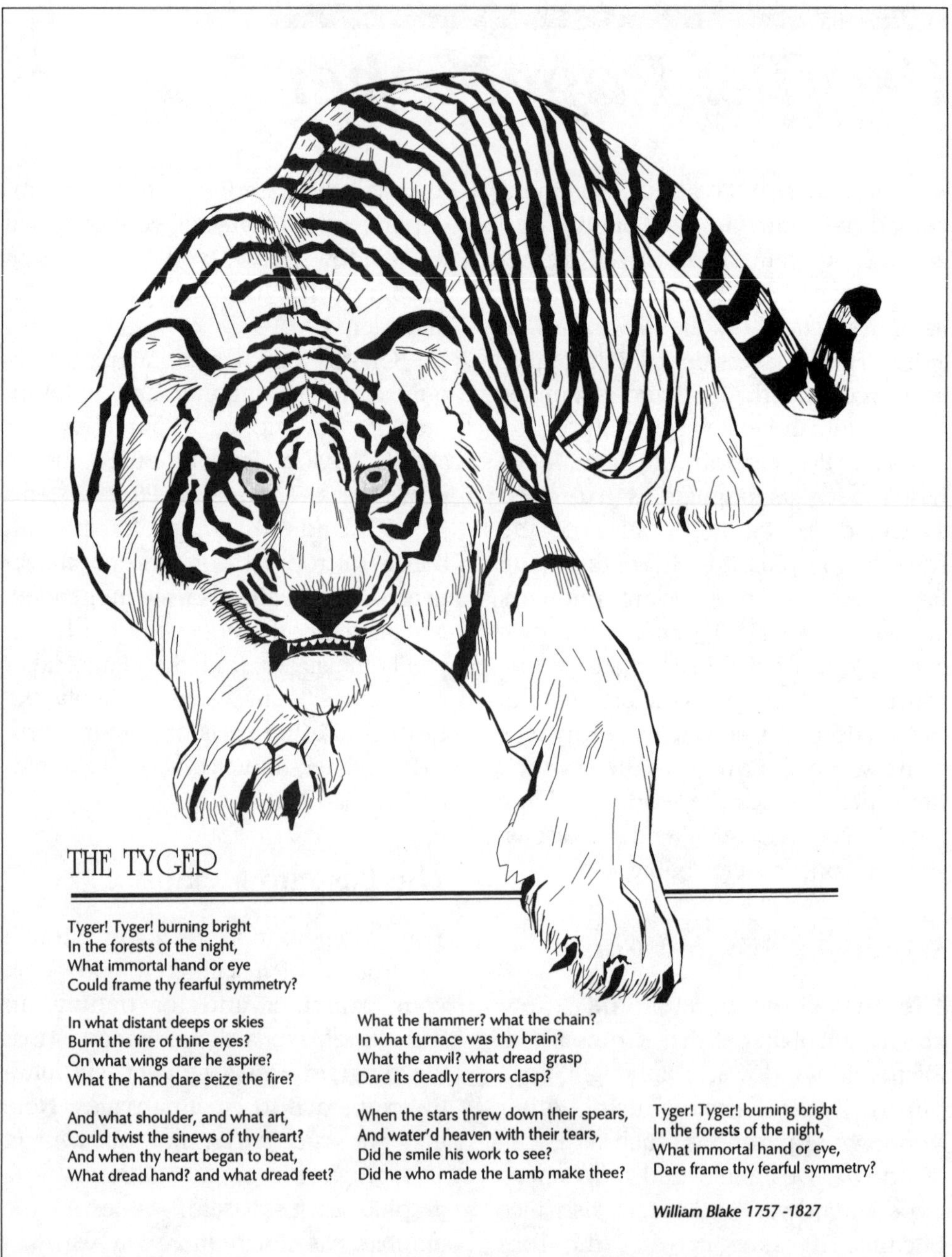

THE TYGER

Tyger! Tyger! burning bright
In the forests of the night,
What immortal hand or eye
Could frame thy fearful symmetry?

In what distant deeps or skies
Burnt the fire of thine eyes?
On what wings dare he aspire?
What the hand dare seize the fire?

And what shoulder, and what art,
Could twist the sinews of thy heart?
And when thy heart began to beat,
What dread hand? and what dread feet?

What the hammer? what the chain?
In what furnace was thy brain?
What the anvil? what dread grasp
Dare its deadly terrors clasp?

When the stars threw down their spears,
And water'd heaven with their tears,
Did he smile his work to see?
Did he who made the Lamb make thee?

Tyger! Tyger! burning bright
In the forests of the night,
What immortal hand or eye,
Dare frame thy fearful symmetry?

William Blake 1757 -1827

Figure 1: A sample page printed with PageMaker. (Reduced 35 percent.)

the entire document in one fell swoop. However, with release 3.0, you do have the option of having text flow automatically forward onto new pages, thus wiping out one of PageMaker's previous disadvantages vis-a-vis Ventura.

The opening screen embodies the pasteup metaphor. In the upper-right corner is the toolbox containing, from left to right, tools for selecting elements to move, drawing lines, typing letters, creating boxes, and cropping pictures. Using these tools in conjunction with the menu selections along the top of the page, you proceed to produce one page at a time.

Importing Text

To incorporate text into a PageMaker document, you start outside PageMaker in your familiar word processing program. PageMaker recognizes all the popular programs for the PC: WordStar, MultiMate, WordPerfect, Microsoft Word, XyWrite, as well as any program (including Samna and IBM DisplayWrite) that uses the DCA file format. Of course, plain ASCII text can also be loaded.

Within PageMaker, you mark the upper-left corner of your intended text block and "paste" text onto a page with the Place command. PageMaker lays down a column, displaying a small plus sign at the bottom of the column if there is more text in the file than could fit in that column.

To move the column, you simply grab it with the selection tool and use the mouse to drag it to a new location. To stretch or shrink the column, you use the mouse to select one of the corners and move it as desired. To lay down another column, you first click on the plus sign, then move the cursor to the new location and double click.

Formatting Text

Once you have positioned your text as desired, you can proceed to apply typographic formatting to it. PageMaker makes it easy to change the font and leading (line spacing), as well as allowing control over typographic niceties such as hanging and nested indents, kerning, letter spacing, and word spacing. The program also automatically hyphenates your text, though you can override the hyphenation if desired.

Adding Graphics

The procedure for adding graphics is similar to that used to put text on a page. PageMaker allows graphics to be imported from a broad selection of programs. The list includes AutoCAD, PIC files from Lotus 1-2-3, Windows Draw, Windows Paint, In*A*Vision, HPGL, and Aldus's TIFF format.

In addition to importing graphics, you can also draw your own simple graphics within the program.

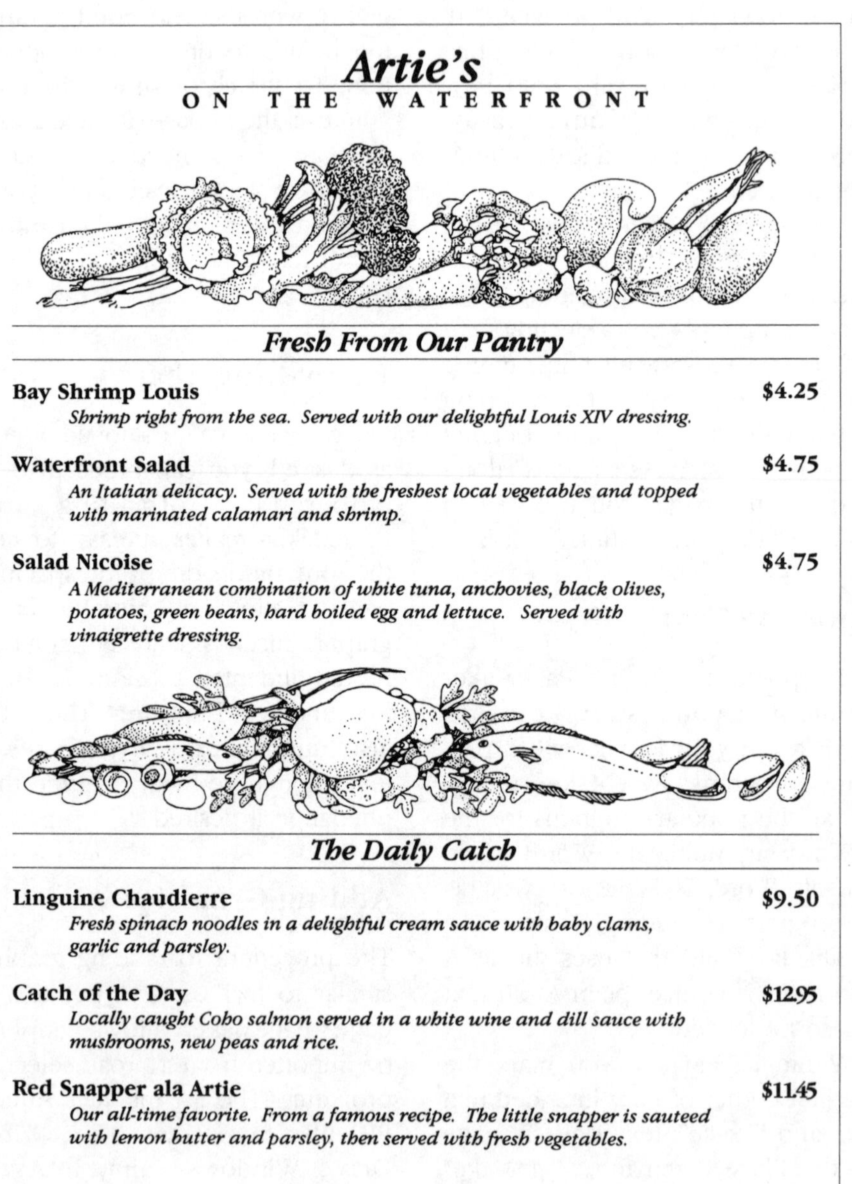

Artie's
ON THE WATERFRONT
Fresh From Our Pantry
Bay Shrimp Louis $4.25
Shrimp right from the sea. Served with our delightful Louis XIV dressing.
Waterfront Salad $4.75
An Italian delicacy. Served with the freshest local vegetables and topped with marinated calamari and shrimp.
Salad Nicoise $4.75
A Mediterranean combination of white tuna, anchovies, black olives, potatoes, green beans, hard boiled egg and lettuce. Served with vinaigrette dressing.
The Daily Catch
Linguine Chaudierre $9.50
Fresh spinach noodles in a delightful cream sauce with baby clams, garlic and parsley.
Catch of the Day $12.95
Locally caught Coho salmon served in a white wine and dill sauce with mushrooms, new peas and rice.
Red Snapper ala Artie $11.45
Our all-time favorite. From a famous recipe. The little snapper is sauteed with lemon butter and parsley, then served with fresh vegetables.

Figure 2: A sample page printed with PageMaker. (Reduced 35 percent.)

PageMaker has separate drawing tools for lines, rectangles, rounded-corner rectangles, and circles. It also has numerous options for varying the width of border lines and adding shades or patterns to internally generated graphics.

Special Features

Some of the best aspects of PageMaker are easy to miss. Here's a sampling:

- **Tiling.** The actual document you're printing does not need to have any relation to the size of your paper. If you specify that the document is smaller than the paper, PageMaker will print crop marks to indicate the corners. If the document is larger than the paper, PageMaker will print it using a technique called tiling. Tiling simply means that each page is printed in sections, with the sections overlapping like tiles on a roof. Paste the tiles together and you can create large documents—even tabloid size.
- **The Pasteboard.** This refers to an area outside your pages where you can temporarily store pictures or text passages.
- **The Undo command.** Conspicuously absent in Ventura.
- **On-screen help.** Also absent in Ventura.
- **Diagonal lines.** One of the line drawing tools creates only horizontal, vertical, and 45-degree lines.
- **Word processor compatibility.** Not only can PageMaker be used with a variety of word processors, it also preserves much of the formatting done within the word processor, such as italic type.
- **Automatic scrolling.** If you move the cursor near the edge of the page, PageMaker automatically scrolls the page.
- **Spreads.** PageMaker lets you place a graphic so that it straddles facing pages.

LaserJet Notes

Unlike Ventura, which only works with the F cartridge, PageMaker can be used with all the HP font cartridges supported by Windows. Most people, however, will want to use the program with soft fonts. Unlike Ventura, which comes bundled with a good range of Dutch (Times Roman) and Swiss (Helvetica) soft fonts, no soft fonts are provided with PageMaker. However, Aldus does bundle PageMaker with a free copy of Bitstream's Fontware font-generating software, which you can use to create printer fonts and matching screen fonts of any size. (See "Profile: Fontware.")

Soft Font Installer

In previous releases of PageMaker, installing new soft fonts was a difficult, almost forbidding process. Release 3.0, however, includes a new feature called the Soft Font Installer that lets you install new soft fonts without even leaving PageMaker.

To use the Soft Font Installer, select Printer Setup from the File menu, select Setup from the printer-specific dialog box, and select Fonts. Now place the floppy disk containing your new fonts in drive A. When you select Add fonts, PageMaker will display the names of all the fonts on the floppy disk. To select one of them, you merely click on its name, select Add, and confirm the name of the hard disk subdirectory into which the fonts are to be transferred.

One of the beauties of this built-in font management utility is that you don't have to provide it with the PFM (Printer Font Metric) files usually demanded by Windows. The reason is that the Soft Font Installer is smart enough to generate the PFM files for you, although in some cases (where the utility does not recognize the name of the font) you may have to assist it by entering information in a dialog box about the font's name and typeface family.

The Soft Font Installer gives you the option of installing fonts in permanent or temporary status. Permanent status means that once loaded into the printer, they will remain there until the power is turned off. Temporary means that PageMaker will download them anew each time it prints the document. Obviously, you save time with permanent fonts, since they only have to be downloaded once, but you need to make sure that you don't exceed the amount of memory available in your printer for storing fonts.

One of the bells (or is it a whistle?) of PageMaker 3.0's Soft Font Installer is that it lets you copy fonts *from one LaserJet to another.* It seems unlikely that many people will ever need this feature (and we don't know of any other application or font management utility that provides it), but don't you get a warm, fuzzy feeling just knowing that it's there?

5

SPREADSHEETS, DATABASES, AND FORMS

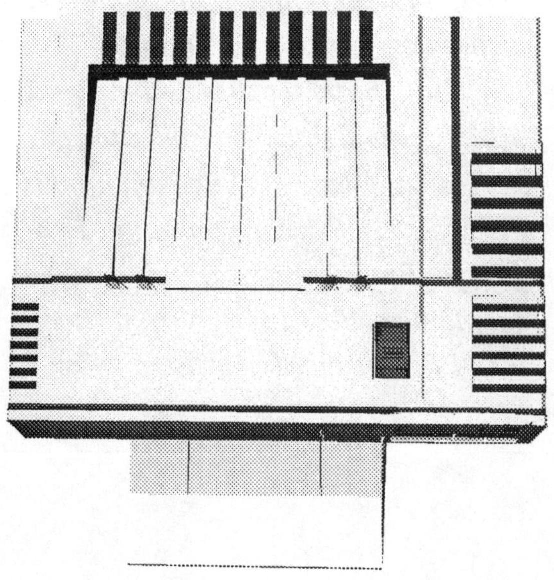

Section Focus

Hundreds of thousands of offices use the LaserJet as their workhorse for printing spreadsheets, database reports, and forms—including standard government tax forms and schedules. For these applications, the LaserJet gives you more flexibility than you've ever had before. You can change the size of fonts to fit more data on a page, print sideways, and enhance your printouts with rules, boxes, and shading.

With both Lotus 1-2-3 and dBASE, you'll have to roll up your sleeves and learn a little bit about the LaserJet's Printer Command Language. But if you start with some simple objectives and go from there, you'll find it's well worth the effort.

Profile: Lotus 1-2-3

WITH ITS KNACK for speedy printing, its ability to print wide spreadsheets sideways on a single sheet of paper, and its selection of type styles and sizes, the LaserJet theoretically makes an excellent companion to Lotus 1-2-3. We say theoretically because translating that potential into reality can be difficult, due to that fact that 1-2-3 releases 1A and 2.0 were not designed with commands for properly controlling the LaserJet. To get Lotus working properly with the printer, you have to take matters into your own hands, picking up where the designers of 1-2-3 left off.

In this chapter we'll explain a quick and simple way to get Lotus 1-2-3 working with the LaserJet. Then we'll look at some ways for getting the Lotus/LaserJet combination to perform some fancier tricks. Finally, we'll describe how to get the best results with 1-2-3 graphics.

A Quick Solution

The following steps will set up the LaserJet so that it prints in landscape mode (i.e., sideways across the length of the paper) using the internal Courier font.

Here are the steps to follow:

- From DOS, use the cd command to change to your Lotus subdirectory.
- Type **`Install`**. If this does not get you into the Lotus Install menu, the reason is that the necessary installation files are not present in your hard disk. In that case, place the Lotus Utility disk in drive A: and type A:INSTALL.
- Select Change Selected Equipment and press Enter.
- Select Text Printer and press Enter.
- Scroll to Unlisted and press Enter. (That's right, choose Unlisted rather than HP LaserJet. The reason is that the LaserJet driver supplied by Lotus actually gets in the way more than it helps.)
- Select No Backspace and press Enter.
- Select Exit.
- Save your changes.
- Name the setup file "123."
- Exit Install.
- Load 1-2-3.
- Load your worksheet.

- Type **/ W G D P** (for Worksheet Global Default Printer).
- Type **P 45** Enter (to set the page length).
- Type **R 1Ø6** Enter (to set the right margin).
- Type **S \Ø27E\Ø27&l1O** Enter.
- Type **Q U** (this makes the changes in the default parameters permanent).
- Type **Q** to return to your worksheet.
- Type **/ P P** (for Print Printer).
- Select the desired range.
- Type **G** (for Go).

If your worksheet is less than a page, the Form Feed light on the Control Panel will light up but no page will emerge. To eject the page, press the ON LINE key and then FORM FEED.

> ### *Tip: Confusing Codes*
>
> *In all printer codes that you enter, make sure you do the following:*
>
> - *Don't confuse the lowercase letter l with the numeral 1.*
> - *Don't confuse the capital letter O with the numeral Ø.*
> - *Always type a letter in capitals if that is called for.*

If your worksheet has multiple pages, you'll get all but the final page. To eject that page, press ON LINE and then press FORM FEED.

Another Quick Solution

If you're having trouble making Lotus print on the LaserJet and aren't interested in fooling around with the LaserJet's PCL codes, a good solution is to purchase a utility that makes the LaserJet emulate a Diablo or Epson printer. You can then install Lotus for use with that printer and let the utility program worry about the rest.

The best such utility on the market is LaserControl, which is described in Part 1 of this book under "Profile: LaserControl." One bonus of the program is that it lets you print out your Lotus graphs at twice the resolution you'd get otherwise.

Some Options

The steps described above set the printer so that it prints using the landscape Courier font that is internal to all models of the LaserJet. You can program other options into 1-2-3, referring to the sidebar, "How to Build a Setup String."

Strange Gaps

If your worksheet has strange gaps when you print it, there are two possible solutions.

- Printing a new worksheet while the FORM FEED light is on can cause a gap in the middle of the page. Make sure that the FORM FEED light is not on when you start printing a new page. If the light is on, it means that the last page of the previous spreadsheet is still in the printer. Press the ON LINE button, then the FORM FEED button, then the ON LINE button again before printing.
- Another cause of a gap is that Lotus is trying to format the worksheet in a way that the LaserJet cannot understand. To solve the problem, type **/ P P O O U**.

More Control with Embedded Codes

The tip for including a blank line containing the | |\027 code is an example of embedding codes in a worksheet. Using embedding codes is only possible in Release 2.0 or later, not Lotus 1A. Embedded codes are handy for changing fonts within a spreadsheet.

Here's how to create an embedded code:

- Type two vertical bars (| |) in a cell. It must be the first cell in the row and the rest of the row must be blank. The first vertical bar will be hidden, so you'll only see one on the screen.

Tip: Printing the Last Page

Here are three ways to get the last page of your spreadsheet to come out of the printer.

- *Issue the Print Printer Page command.*
- *Press the ON LINE button, press the FORM FEED button, then press the ON LINE button.*
- *This method ejects the last page without pressing the ON LINE and FORM FEED buttons. It works with 1-2-3 Release 2.0 or later only, not with Release 1A. On a blank line at the bottom of your worksheet, type | |\Ø12. All other cells in the line should be blank. Note: The vertical bar character is on the same key that has the \ character. When you type the two vertical bars into the worksheet, the first will be hidden, so what you see on the screen will be |\012. When you print the worksheet, include the line containing | |\012 in your range. Note: The line containing the | |\Ø12 must be the very last line in your range.*

How to Build a Setup String

You can build your own setup string, using a "boxcar" approach. The "train" (the final setup string) is created by plugging in the desired value for each boxcar.

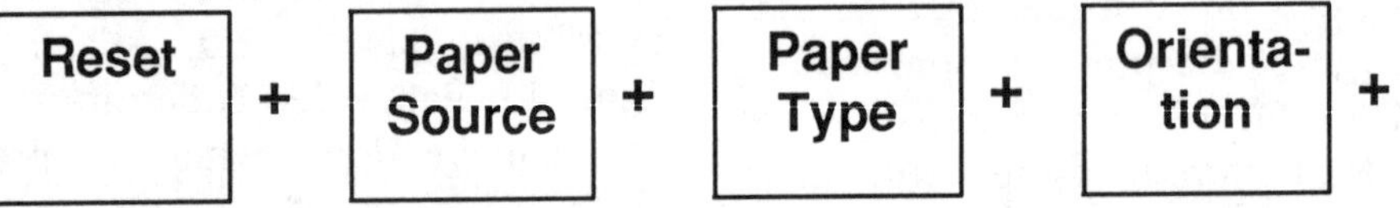

Line Spacing + Font = Setup String

What to Plug in

Reset	\Ø27E
Paper Source	
Tray	\Ø27&*l*1h
Manual	\Ø27&*l*2h
Paper Type	
Letter	66p
Legal	84p
Orientation	
Portrait	Øo
Landscape	1o
Line Spacing	
6 Lines per Inch	6D
8 Lines per Inch	8D
Font	
Courier	\Ø27(8u\Ø27&kØS
Line Printer	\Ø27(8u\Ø27&k2S

Example

Suppose you wanted to print a spreadsheet on legal-size paper, manually fed into the printer, in landscape mode using the Line Printer font at 8 lines per inch. The set up string would be:
\Ø27E\Ø27&l2h84p1o8D\Ø27(8U\Ø27&k2S

Notes

- For this technique to work properly, the LaserJet must start out with its factory default settings intact. If you have changed those settings, you can restore them by holding down the ENTER / RESET MENU key for about 5 seconds.
- To keep things simple, we have left out the VMI parameter, which you might also want to include in a setup string in place of the line-per-inch commands. In place of 6D or 8D, you substitute #C, where # stands for the number of 1/48-inch increments in each line. For example, the value 8C is the same as 6 lines per inch.
- All four fonts that can be selected using these codes (landscape and portrait Courier and landscape and portrait Line Printer) are resident in the LaserJet II. In the classic LaserJet, only landscape and portrait Courier are resident. In the LaserJet Plus, only landcape and portrait Courier and portrait Line Printer are resident.
- To select other cartridge or soft fonts in place of Courier and Line Printer, refer to Chapter 18, "Selecting Fonts with PCL."
- Note that the maximum length of a setup string is 39 characters. This can pose a problem if you're trying to specify all possible parameters to select a font. You'll have to be judicious and specify only the minimum number of parameters necessary to select a font, or else embed the font selection codes within the spreadsheet.

- Type the escape character. In HP's PCL charts this will appear as ^{E}c. In the tables provided in the back of this book it is represented by a caret (^). In Lotus, the escape character is represented as \027.
- Type the remainder of the code, paying particular attention to distinguishing the letter *l* from the numeral 1, and the letter O from the numeral Ø. Also, if letters are capitalized in the PCL tables, make sure you keep the capitalization.
- The embedded code should occupy a line of its own, with all other cells on that line remaining blank.

A Case of the Wobblies

If you are using proportional typefaces such as TMS RMN or HELV, you'll find that your columns are not staying in alignment. The reason is that with these fonts, each character takes up different amounts of space. When Lotus tries to align the columns by counting spaces, it ends up with slight differences in positioning for different rows.

Wobblies Solution 1: Edit the Font

One solution to the problem of wobbly alignment is to use a font editor to change your font so that all the widths are the same. While this may sound like a daunting task, it may not be much work if you'll only be printing number, since in most proportional fonts all numerical characters have the same width. If that is the case, all you'll have to do is change the width of the space character to match the width of the numerals and you're in business. For more information on font editors, refer to Chapter 17, "Font Editing."

Wobblies Solution 2: Transfer to a Word Processor

Another solution is to transfer your spreadsheet into your word processor and then use the formatting capabilities of the word program to designate fonts and align columns. With Microsoft Word 4.0, you can directly transfer a Lotus worksheet file into Word using Word's Library Link command. This command automatically places tab characters in the spreadsheet file to separate cells. You can then easily align the columns by setting tabs within Word and then printing.

Wobblies Solution 3: Transfer to Ventura Publisher

You can't load Lotus WKS files directly into Ventura. To load a worksheet, first print it to a disk file, set-

Access: Lotus 1-2-3 Tools

JetFont 1-2-3 cartridge
Computer Peripherals, Inc.
667 Rancho Conejo Blvd.
Newbury Park, CA 91320
800/854-7600
Price: $325

JetSet 1.2
Intex Solutions, Inc.
161 Highland Ave.
Needham, MA 02194
617/449-6222
Price: $79.95

Tabin
Corel Systems Corporation
Corel Bldg.
1600 Carling Ave.
Ottawa, Ontario
Canada K1Z 7M4
613/728-8200
Price: $99

Unlocking the LaserJet Using Symphony andLotus 1-2-3
by Howard & Janelle Gluckman
WizzyWays Publishing
1943 Chilton Dr.
Glendale, CA 91201
Price: $24.95

XVP Tabs, Version 2
The Laser Edge
360 17th St. #203
Oakland, CA 94612
415/835-1581
Price: $89

Super Cartridge 1
IQ Engineering
P.O. Box 60955
Sunnyvale, CA 94086
408/733-1161
Price: $699

ting the margins to 0, then load that file into Ventura, selecting XyWrite as the type of file. The drawback of this method is that you have to manually replace all the spaces that separate the columns of the worksheet with tab characters, a laborious process. However, there are two utilities that automatically perform the substitution of tabs for spaces. One is XVP/Tabs, Release 2. The other is Tabin.

JetSet

Another utility specifically designed for enhancing 1-2-3's LaserJet capabilities is JetSet, from Intex Solutions, Inc.—not to be confused with Jet-Set from Probe Software (a general-purpose printer setup utility) or JetSet II from DataMate Company (a setup and text-formatting program). Intex's JetSet lets you set margins and fonts for your spreadsheet without leaving 1-2-3. The program is memory-resident, popping into view when you press a hot-key combination. Both soft fonts and cartridge fonts can be selected from a menu without typing any codes. As of version 1.2, the program can handle multiple, non-contiguous print ranges, works with Symphony spreadsheets, recognizes spreadsheet borders, and can be used with all HP cartridges as well as with the Lotica font on the JetFont 1-2-3 cartridge (see below).

Lotica

Lotica is a new font designed by Xiphias, a digital font foundry, specifically for maximum legibility at small sizes. When we say small, we do mean *small.* The JetFont 1-2-3 cartridge includes 12-, 16-, 21-, and 30-character-per-inch (cpi) versions of Lotica. With the smallest HP cartridge font, 8.5-point compressed Line Printer, you're limited to printing 173 characters on a sheet of letter-sized paper in landscape mode. But with 21-cpi Lotica, you can print 220 characters, and with 30-cpi Lotica you can go all the way to 1-2-3's maximum of 240 characters across the paper. Of course, 30 characters per inch is pushing the limits of legibility, but Lotica manages to carry it off.

IQ's Super Cartridge 1

Another source of micro-fonts is IQ Engineering's Super Cartridge 1. This cartridge contains a total of 55 fonts, among which are 4.5-point Letter Gothic and 5-point Line Printer. With these tiny, but legible, fonts, you can print up to the full 220-character Lotus limit on standard paper. To assist in formatting, IQ includes a utility called FONTSEL. To use it, you first print your spreadsheet to a disk file, then run FONTSEL and choose the number of rows and columns for the spreadsheet.

Other Resources

Believe it or not, there's a book on the market that is devoted exclusively to the topic of printing on a LaserJet with Lotus 1-2-3 and Symphony. It's called Unlocking the LaserJet Using Symphony and Lotus 1-2-3. The premise of the authors (certified Lotus hackers) is that you can do virtually anything with this program, including fancy graphic effects. The book begins with clear, simple explanations of PCL codes that are definitely aimed at beginners; however, from there it pushes relentlessly forward into such advanced technical areas as macros for generating graphics and managing soft fonts. There's even a chapter that explains how to create your own fonts in Symphony!

New Drivers from Phoenix

You can obtain improved drivers for Lotus 1-2-3 releases 1A, 2.0, and 2.01 and Symphony releases 1.0, 1.1, and 1.2 from Phoenix Technology (800/843-4784). The cost of the drivers is $25.

Printing 1-2-3 Graphics

To use Lotus 1-2-3's PrintGraph module with the LaserJet, you have to install the LaserJet as your graphics printer.

- From the DOS prompt, use the cd command to change to your Lotus subdirectory.
- Type **`Install`**. If this does not get you into the Lotus Install menu, the reason is that the necessary installation files are not present in your hard disk. In that case, place the Lotus Utility disk in drive A and type **`A:INSTALL`**.
- Select Change Selected Equipment and press Enter.
- Select Graphics Printer and press Enter.
- Select HP.
- Select 2686A LaserJet if you only want 75-dpi graphics. If you want 100- or 300-dpi graphics, select 2686 LaserJet Plus.
- Select Save Changes and press Enter.
- Select Exit.
- Run 1-2-3 and type **`/ W G D P`**.
- Set the parameters to the #1 Interface. Select No for Auto Linefeed. Set the default left margin to 0. Set the default right margin to 80. Set the default top margin to 0. Set the default bottom margin to 0. Set the default page length to 60. Set wait to No. Leave the default Setup String blank. For Name, select the number that corresponds to Unlisted, no backspace.
- Type **`Q U`** to quit and update.

Now when you use PrintGraph, you'll have the option of either 100- or 300-dpi resolution for your charts. Note that if you have 512K of memory in your LaserJet, you're limited to charts of one-third the size of the page when printing at 300-dpi resolution. When you print at 100-dpi, there are no size limitations.

If you have 1-2-3 versions prior to release 2, you'll be limited to 75-dpi graphics. To get better resolution, get LaserControl and follow the directions for using high-resolution Epson emulation. For details, see "Profile: LaserControl" in Part 1 of this book. Alternatively, you can import Lotus graphs and charts into Windows Draw, as illustrated in "Profile: Windows Draw."

Profile: dBASE

BESIDES ITS SPEED and quiet operation, the LaserJet's ability to format output and print in landscape mode makes it useful for dBASE operations such as printing reports or labels. dBASE IV, the most recent version of dBASE, incorporates a printer driver that makes it easy to talk to a LaserJet, although this driver supports only basic formatting commands and may not be entirely sufficient for your needs. (If it isn't, you can use PCL, the LaserJet's internal command set, in conjunction with the dBASE programming language to make your LaserJet do nearly anything. For details, see the second half of this chapter, and Chapter 19, "Programming the LaserJet with PCL.") Installing dBASE IV to use this driver is the first step to success; the second is to learn what this driver will and won't do for you. Both topics are covered in the first sections of this chapter. Using dBASE IV commands to actually send information to the printer is discussed in the second half of this chapter.

Because of the cost and memory requirements of dBASE IV, many people still choose to use one of the older versions of dBASE that they may own: dBASE II, dBASE III, or dBASE III Plus. All these releases lack drivers for the LaserJet. The latter sections of this chapter cover tips that let you use these earlier versions of dBASE reasonably well with a LaserJet.

Installing dBASE IV for the LaserJet

The first step in getting dBASE IV properly installed to use its LaserJet printer drivers is to make sure that those drivers are accessible. If you're installing dBASE IV for the first time, follow the normal installation instructions provided with it. When prompted, specify that you have a Hewlett-Packard LaserJet and the model, and dBASE will automatically copy the appropriate printer drivers to your hard disk and note that it should use them when requested to.

If you have already installed dBASE, or if dBASE can't seem to remember that you want it to talk to a LaserJet, the first thing to do is ensure that it can find the driver file. Whatever directory you have installed dBASE on should also contain the drivers, which have file names beginning with "HP." From DOS you can verify this by changing to that directory using the CD command, then entering:

```
DIR HP*.*
```

If the files are not there, you can use the COPY command of DOS to copy them from the dBASE system disks to your dBASE directory.

There are several ways to instruct dBASE to use a driver, once that driver is accessible. The easiest way is through dBASE IV's internal system variables, of which several are reserved for controlling the printer.

From the dBASE IV prompt (which you can access from the "Assistant" or Control Center by pressing F10 to get to the top menu, then choosing Exit and Exit to dBASE Prompt), enter the command

```
STORE "<driver>" TO _PDRIVER
```

where <driver> is the full file name of the driver, such as HPLASL.CR. If you've entered this command correctly and dBASE can find the driver, it will respond with the message: "Printer driver installed," followed by the name of the driver.

You can easily ensure that the driver has indeed been activated by entering these commands:

```
SET TALK OFF
SET PRINT ON
? 'This should be in bold'
STYLE "B"
SET PRINT OFF
EJECT
```

The sentence, when the sheet of paper is ejected from the LaserJet, should appear in bold if a bold font is available in the LaserJet.

Covering the Basics

The dBASE IV printer drivers let you accomplish the basics with your LaserJet, and we do mean basics. The driver will automatically deal with the LaserJet's image area (solving potential problems of your reports printing with unexpected breaks between pages) and will let you format your printed output as italic, bold, or regular. It is not, however, very suitable for mixed formats with many type sizes and styles. (For this, you will have to resort to PCL codes.)

The basic way to use dBASE IV's LaserJet drivers is with the STYLE keyword which has been added to the ? and ?? output commands. These commands let you output the contents of a memory variable, database field, or expression to your screen or to your printer if you have used the SET PRINT ON command. There are two possible attributes for the ?...STYLE command, "B" for Bold, and "I" for Italic. For example, if you have a database with a field titled NAME, and you want to print the name in bold, after issuing SET PRINT ON you could do so using:

```
? NAME STYLE "B"
```

A minor variation is to use two question marks rather than one. This has the effect of suppressing carriage return and line feed.

dBASE and LaserJet Escape Sequences

If you're using dBASE II, III, or III Plus rather than dBASE IV, or if you need to go beyond the capabilities of the dBASE IV printer drivers, you need to send PCL codes to your printer. Fortunately, this is easy to do using any version of dBASE. These codes are also referred to as "escape sequences" because they always begin with the escape character, ASCII 27. Since it is possible to use the CHR( ) function of dBASE to send any character, you can send the escape character with the function CHR(27).

To send an entire escape sequence, use an output command to send output to the printer, followed by CHR(27) and whatever other characters you need to send. These characters must be contained in double or single quotes, since they form a character string. For example, if you want to send Escape-E, the sequence that resets the LaserJet to its default parameters, you would first SET PRINT ON to make sure the sequence reached the printer, and then issue the following command:

```
? CHR(27) + 'E'
```

Once you have determined the escape sequences you need for various tasks, it's best to store them in memory variables. When you need to send a control string, you can use the ? command and the substitution function (&) to retrieve the contents of the memory variable. The & function causes dBASE to substitute into a command line the evaluated contents of the variable following the &, rather than the variable itself.

For example, the LaserJet escape sequence to select landscape mode is ^&l1O (where ^ stands for the escape character). The corresponding dBASE string is

```
CHR(27) + '&l1O'
```

You can store this sequence to a memory variable named LJETLAND by using the command

```
STORE "CHR(27) + '&l1O'" TO
LJETLAND
```

After that, you can send the string whenever you need to merely by entering

```
? &LJETLAND
```

after issuing the SET PRINT ON command. If you left out the &, what would be sent to the printer would be the character string CHR(27) + '&*l*1O' (which would have no effect and would just be printed) rather than the desired escape character followed by &*l*1O.

A Memory Variable Sample

Once you've taken the time to figure out the memory variables you need and have created them, you'll want to be able to access them easily and re-use them, rather than having to create then anew each time you need them. This is especially true if you want to use many escape sequences, such as would be required to select landscape mode, select a font, specify line spacing, and set margins. Using the SAVE and RESTORE commands of dBASE, you can save memory variables to a .MEM file on disk and recall them whenever you need them. This can save much time and effort.

Because of the syntax of the SAVE and RESTORE commands, you'll find it useful to give your LaserJet memory variables similar names, so that you can easily distinguish them from your other memory variables. For example, you might want to name your variables LJET1, LJET2, LJET3, and so on. This will let you utilize the ALL LIKE clause of the SAVE command, so you can save all the memory variables whose names begin with LJET. This naming convention will also make it easier to locate your memory variables in the list displayed by a LIST MEMORY command, if you're ever trying to determine the exact contents of your LaserJet memory variables. Note that it's also a useful habit to make sure that your names connote something, such as LJETLAND for the variable that will hold the instructions that switch the LaserJet into landscape mode.

The following example of dBASE commands takes the simple string used to switch the LaserJet into landscape mode, and stores it to a memory variable named LJETLAND. It then saves it (and any other memory variables with names beginning with LJET) to a .MEM file called LJETCODE.MEM, then restores them and sends LJETLAND to the printer. The ADDITIVE clause of the RESTORE FROM command ensures that any other already active memory variables aren't overwritten or erased by the RESTORE command.

```
Store "CHR(27) + '&l1O'" to
LJETLAND
Save To LJETCODE All Like
LJET* Restore From LJETCODE
Additive
Set Print On
? &LJETLAND
Set Print Off
```

Of course, normally you wouldn't save a memory variable and then immediately restore it. This example is merely to give you some ideas about how you can manage your memory variables effectively. Also, while you can type in this entire sequence of commands interactively, if you have to do this every time you wish to switch the LaserJet into landscape mode, it will become tedious. You'll find it easier to use a text editor in ASCII mode to type the sequence of commands into a file, thereby creating a small program. (You can use the MODIFY COMMAND instruction of dBASE to invoke dBASE's built-in editor, if you like. It's not very full-featured, but it's handy.) By default, a dBASE program should have a .PRG extension, and its name should always connote what the program does. For example, you may wish to type the command sequence shown on the previous page into a file called LANDMODE.PRG, indicating that it is a program to switch the LaserJet into landscape mode. Once you have created a dBASE program, you can run it whenever you want by simply entering

DO *program name*

from the dBASE prompt.

The dBASE Output Commands

Users of dBASE II, III, or III Plus have three basic ways to output information. Normally output is sent just to your PC's screen, but if you use the SET PRINT ON command, output will go to the printer as well. The three commands for accomplishing this are the ? command, the ?? command, and the @...SAY... command. Using the @...SAY... command, you can specify screen or page coordinates where you want the output to appear. All these commands will let you use the CHR(27) and & macro-substitution techniques described earlier. dBASE IV users have additional flexibility, because that program includes a few more ways to get escape sequences to the LaserJet.

Since dBASE IV supports printer drivers that filter and adjust all output to a printer, it's possible that the printer driver may get in your way if you're trying to accomplish some fancy PCL formatting. A way around this is the dBASE IV ??? command, which sends output directly to the printer (obviating the need for SET PRINT ON) and ensures that the information it outputs will not be modified by the printer driver. This eliminates the possibility of the LaserJet being given conflicting PCL instructions by both your commands and the driver.

Another dBASE IV nicety for sending PCL instructions is the ON PAGE command. This lets you specify an element that should occur on every new page that is printed, at a particular line. Normally you may only have one command executed per line, but if you embed a series of commands in a procedure or program, you may execute that series of commands by calling the program or procedure from the ON PAGE line.

For example, you may wish your printed output to have a shaded rectangle appearing on certain lines of the page. Chapter 19, "Programming the LaserJet with PCL," contains a sample dBASE III Plus program that prints a special pattern called a rule. The program that is given defines a rule that is only one dot high and 300 dots wide, so that when this rectangle prints it looks like a straight line. You could just as easily change the rule specification to print a rule 30 dots high. When this 30-by-300-dot rule printed, it would appear as a solid rectangle. You could embed the dBASE commands accomplishing this in a dBASE program called RULE.PRG. Then, if you wanted the rule to print on line 30 of every page, you could use the dBASE command

```
ON PAGE AT LINE 30 DO RULE
```

dBASE Reports

There are two ways that people use dBASE to obtain reports from a database. Most commonly, people use the CREATE REPORT command to create a report form describing what data should be reported and how it should appear on the printed page. Once a report form exists, the REPORT FORM ... TO PRINT command runs the report and sends it to the printer. While this procedure works, there is a limit to the sophistication of the reports that can be produced. A second means of obtaining a report is to write a dBASE program to output the data; this way, you can obtain just about any report you could possibly imagine. The program can also incorporate LaserJet formatting commands, including commands to switch between landscape and portrait mode, select fonts, and set margins.

The dBASE III Plus report form command lets you incorporate short "expressions," or character strings, into your reports. In this way you can embed the CHR(27) function, which sends the escape character, followed by whatever other characters you need. After entering CREATE REPORT at the dBASE prompt, you will see a pull-down menu allowing you to choose between Options, Groups, Columns, and a few other choices. The Columns menu lets you edit Contents, Heading, and Width. After using the cursor keys to select Contents and pressing Enter, you will be able to enter the contents you want for a given report column, starting with column 1. Here you could put in an escape sequence expressed as a dBASE expression. For example, the escape sequence to select a font by its font ID number (after the ID number has been assigned) is Ec(#X, where # is the font ID. If we have defined a font ID as 15, in dBASE we can express the escape sequence to select that font as CHR(27) + '(15X'. If you wanted column 1 to be printed in this font, and wanted it to include a field named FIELD1, you could specify the column contents as: CHR(27) + '(15X' + FIELD1.

The problem with using the dBASE report form in this way is that the expressions you embed cannot be very long and cannot contain memory variables. Also, the only places where an expression may be entered is within a column, or as a column heading, or as a page title. One way around these limitations is to combine the report form approach with the programming approach. Use the CREATE REPORT command to define how you want your data to appear, and any necessary LaserJet formatting codes, but don't use it to put in LaserJet setup instructions. Next, write a simple program that sends the necessary setup escape sequences to the LaserJet, then runs the report using the REPORT FORM ... TO PRINT command.

In the next example, we're pretending a museum is printing a report listing financial supporters, their addresses, and the amounts and dates of their contributions. The report itself is contained in a report form file called ENDOW.FRM. However, the report must be printed in landscape mode. We'll use the LJETLAND memory variable mentioned earlier to hold the escape sequence that puts the LaserJet into landscape mode. LJETLAND's contents have previously been stored in the memory file LJETCODE. The program activates LJETLAND by restoring it from this memory file, then sends it to the printer using the & substitution function. The program prints the report using the REPORT command.

```
* put printer into landscape
mode
Restore From LJETCODE
Additive
Set Print On
? &LJETLAND
Set Print Off
* note LaserJet will eject a
blank page at this point
* there is nothing you can
do about that
Report To Print Form ENDOW
* reset printer to portrait
mode
Set Print On
? CHR(27) + 'E'
Set Print Off
Return
```

This is a simple example, but it does illustrate the concept. For example, if you wanted to switch to boldface type, prior to issuing the REPORT command you would use the CHR( ) command to send the necessary escape sequence.

dBASE IV users have more flexibility because dBASE IV actually generates a program from CREATE REPORT. You can modify this resulting program and insert any formatting instructions you desire. Put them in right before the ? and ?? commands that output the fields and memory variable expressions you want to modify. Use MODIFY COMMAND, dBASE's built-in text editor, to edit the program that results from CREATE REPORT. Find the first output line you want to format, move the cursor to the beginning of that line, and enter a Ctrl-N. This will give you a blank line upon which to work. Type ??? followed by CHR(27) and the rest of the escape sequence you want to send. Repeat this for every ? or ?? output line you want to modify.

dBASE and Labels

Another function that database programs like dBASE are frequently used for is printing labels, such as mailing labels. The LaserJet is particularly well suited for labels in some respects, because it is fast and quiet, and because its formatting capabilities can make your labels much more attractive. Using it for labels may require new work procedures from you, though, because the LaserJet does not accept the continuous-form labels you are probably accustomed to using. Instead, you must use special laser printer sheet labels, as described in Chapter 22, "Label Sheets."

After you have found labels that won't jam your printer, the next step is to get dBASE to print the labels two or three across. As with reports (and nearly everything else in dBASE), there are two ways to do this: using a built-in dBASE command, CREATE LABEL; and writing your own program.

Using CREATE LABEL to embed escape sequences in dBASE's label-printing capability is very similar to the techniques described above for CREATE REPORT. CREATE LABEL invokes a pull-down menu system offering you the choice of Options and Contents. The Options choices will allow you to specify the layout of the labels you will be printing on. The Contents submenu allows you to specify the label contents you want to print. Use the arrow keys to select Contents, and press Enter. Then use the arrow keys to select the label line you would like to specify. After pressing Enter, you will be able to specify the actual contents for that line. Here you may enter a legal dBASE expression as was described under CREATE REPORT.

There are some major problems with this approach. Again, the length of your expressions are limited to 254 characters, and you may not include memory variables. One drastic way to work around this in dBASE III Plus is to use the TO FILE option of LABEL FORM to print the labels to a file you specify. You may then use a text editor to insert formatting codes. A more pressing problem is that the label sheets designed specifically for laser printers do not match the dBASE III Plus predefined label size, and they have a row of half-labels at the top of the sheet that dBASE doesn't know about. If you try to use the LABEL FORM command to print on these, you will lose your first row of data and the next will print between two rows of labels.

dBASE IV users have more flexibility, because under dBASE IV, CREATE LABEL generates a modifiable program rather than just a label form. You may use MODIFY COMMAND to edit this program, inserting formatting commands around the output commands you are interested in and, if necessary, accommodating the label size. If you use dBASE III, III Plus, or II, don't despair, though. You can always write your own label program to accomplish fancy formatting of your labels.

Creating a Label Printing Program

The program shown in the following pages, BOLDNAME.PRG, is written in dBASE III and will also run under dBASE IV. It prints three labels horizontally and ten vertically, using 10-point Tms Rmn bold for names and 10-point Tms Rmn medium for addresses. It is designed for the label sheets sold specifically for laser printers.

The program first establishes Tms Rmn bold as the primary font and Tms Rmn medium as the secondary font. When it comes time to switch between fonts, the program uses the Shift-In and Shift-Out commands. (If more than two fonts are being used, it is easier to a font by ID number when that font is needed, rather than Shift-In and Shift-Out.) BOLDNAME.PRG builds up print lines by iterating and adding data from the next database record. A potential problem is that the fonts being used are proportionally spaced; hence the characters are not of uniform width. To keep the columns aligned, the program uses an escape sequence that prints each column at an absolute position. The necessary commands are stored to the memory variables COLPOS1, COLPOS2, and COLPOS3. If you will not be using proportionally spaced fonts, you can modify the program to ignore the cursor positioning commands.

P. Picasso
344 Eden Gates Road
Cloud 211
Heaven, CA 94563

Attila Big
Conquerers All
24 Conquer Lane
Grave 11
Hunville, IO 63427

Blimpo Boy
Big Stuff, Inc.
23 Cake Road
Suite 5
Hippoville, CA 99999

Becky Ballerina
47 Tutu Way
Tschaikovsky, AK 23445

Paul Bunyan
Gyppo Axe, Inc.
345 Big Axe Road
Tent 4
Lumberland, OR 93494

Venus de Milo
Granite Designs
37 Rue d'Artagnan
Paris, TX 56778

Casy McBat
Mudville 9
#1 Home Plate
Stadium Villa Apartments
Mudville, WI 34502

Jesse James
Infamy Row
#304
Badlands, NM 84563

Jermaine Germane
Scotia Florists
890 Relevant Road
Pertinent, NC 29880

Wyatt Earp
U.S. Marshall's Office
U.S. Marshall's Office
245 Main Street
Tombstone, AZ 93220

Jasmine Jockey
JJ Riders
Paddock 1
Horse 3
Derbyville, KY 32440

John Paul Jones
Captain's Quarters
Bon Homme Richard
At Sea, AS 00000

Lisa Mona
Intrigue Agency
43 Convinci Ln.
Canals, FL 33456

Blackbeard
Privateer's Association
The Barber's Shop
7 Terror Wave
Carribean Sea, CS 00000

Little Miss Muffet
PTA
Tuffet #4
Bo Peep Way
MotherGoose, NJ 08540

Joe Football
55 Sunday Circle
Apt. 28
Couch Spud, ID 89734

A. E. VanVillinger
Dutch Treat, Inc.
345 Yehuda Lane
New Amsterdam, NJ 08345

Thor Thunder
33 Cataclysm Street
Blue Moon, NH 02543

Shiva Destroyer
9087 Dancer Lane
Endit, IL 43362

Barney Blarney
Green Ale Importers
34 Stowe Ln.
Boston, MA 03456

Franny Filibuster
U.S. Senate
Capitol Hill
Washington, DC 02345

J. Ive Knott
Truth, Inc.
345 Serious Way
Suite 01
Sternness, CT 23490

Cruella DeVille
Spotted Furs, Inc.
345 Ominous Road
D'urbanville, IL 45678

Glinda Wester
Witches of Oz
Star Route
Westerville, Oz 01010

Harry Hacker
Late Nite Bytes
EBBS 404
Hachituate, DE 30342

Priscilla Prissy
Picky Models Co.
34 Madison Avenue
Suite 4367
New York, NY 10023

Lurch Demon
Butlers for Hire
657 Adams Way
Haunted, CT 02345

Nicky Knight
Templar Associates
878 Heraldic Way
Charger, ND 78693

Rayleen Charanne Davoe
98 Cowgirl Place
Sticks, KY 43256

Joe "Pink" Fun
Plastic Flowers = Profits
22 Arbor Lane
Suite 3
Fakeville, MN 65789

Figure 1: Sample output of the label program shown in the following pages.

```
* LASRLABL.PRG
*
* A program to print labels on Avery 5260 label sheets,
* holding 3 columns and 10 rows of labels per sheet
*
* variables colpos1, colpos2, colpos3 hold escape
* sequences positioning print cursor at label columns
* 1, 2, and 3 respectively
*
* variables line1, line2, line3, line4, line5 hold a
* built-up line of data
*
* variables regular, boldface hold escape sequences to
* select regular and boldface fonts (tms rmn)
*
* variable col holds numeric version of current label
* column while ccol holds character version of current
* label column
*
* variable linecount holds numeric version of current
* line in label row while lineccount holds character
* version of current line in label row
*
* database NAMES.DBF has structure:
* Name      - 32
* Company   - 25
* Address1 - 32
* Address2 - 32
* City      - 18
* State     - 2
* ZIP       - 10
```

Figure 2: LASRLABL.PRG, a dBASE III program that prints labels on Avery 5260 label sheets.

```
SET TALK OFF
SET PRINT ON
boldface = "chr(27) + '&l0O' + chr(27) + '(0U' +
chr(27) + ;
'(s1p10v0s1b5T'"
regular  = "chr(27) + '(s0B'"
col       = 1
ccol      = STR(col,1)
* first, initialize print lines as blank
line1     = '  '
line2     = '  '
line3     = '  '
line4     = '  '
line5     = '  '
* first column of labels is at position120 decipoints
colpos1 = chr(27) + '&a120H'
* second column of labels is at position 2160 decipoints
colpos2 = chr(27) + '&a2160'
* third column of labels is at position 4200 decipoints
colpos3 = chr(27) + '&a4200H'
USE Names
DO WHILE (.NOT. EOF())
ccol = STR(col,1)
linecount = 1
lineccount = STR(linecount,1)
* if name isn't blank, add it to the info already
* stored on the current line and increment the line
* counter (move to next line)
IF (Name  '  ')
line&lineccount = line&lineccount + colpos&ccol + Name
linecount = linecount + 1
lineccount = STR(linecount,1)
ENDIF (Name  '  ')
```

```
* if company isn't blank, add it to the info already
* stored on tht line and increment the line counter
IF (Company  '  ')
line&lineccount = line&lineccount + colpos&ccol +
Company
linecount = linecount + 1
lineccount = STR(linecount,1)
ENDIF (Company  '  ')
* if address1 isn't blank, add it to the information
* already stored on the current line and increment the
* line counter
IF (Address1  '  ')
line&lineccount = line&lineccount + colpos&ccol +
Address1
linecount = linecount + 1
lineccount = STR(linecount,1)
ENDIF (Address1  '  ')
* if address2 isn't blank, add it to the information
* already  stored on the current line and increment the
* line counter
IF (Address2  '  ')
line&lineccount = line&lineccount + colpos&ccol +
Address2
linecount = linecount + 1
lineccount = STR(linecount,1)
ENDIF (Address2  '  ')
* add city, a comma, the state, and zip to current line
* and increment counter
line&lineccount = line&lineccount + colpos&ccol +
TRIM(City) +      ;
', ' + State + '  ' + Zip
linecount = linecount + 1
lineccount = STR(linecount,1)
* now, make up for any blank lines (assuming 6 lines
```

```
* desired per label)
DO WHILE (linecount  6)
line&lineccount = colpos&ccol + line&lineccount
linecount = linecount + 1
lineccount = STR(linecount,1)
ENDDO (linecount  6)
SKIP
* do housekeeping on column number: increment column
* number and check to see if it goes over 3; if it does,
* print all the lines, reset them to blanks, and reset
* the column counter to 1
col = col + 1
IF (COL  3 .OR. EOF())
* switch line 1 into boldface
line1 = &boldface + line1
* switch line2 and following lines into regular
line2 = &regular + line2
? line1
? line2
? line3
? line4
? line5
? ' '
col   = 1
line1 = '  '
line2 = '  '
line3 = '  '
line4 = '  '
line5 = '  '
ENDIF (COL  3 .OR. EOF())
ENDDO (.NOT. EOF())
SET PRINT OFF
SET TALK ON
EJECT
```

CHAPTER ELEVEN

Form and Tax Preparation Software

FORMS GENERATION REPRESENTS a specialized application within desktop publishing, one that calls for a particular set of capabilities. These include the ability to create horizontal and vertical ruling lines, boxes, and shaded rectangles; position text either on its own or within boxes; use multiple fonts on a page; and merge information from a database program such as dBASE and to print a form simultaneously with embedded data. A good forms program will let you specify the position in which you want data to appear and then will provide a procedure for easily merging this data from popular database formats.

Of course, it is not enough for a program merely to have these capabilities; they must also be relatively easy to implement. For example, one of the most common needs in generating a form is to create a large number of identical boxes. It should be possible to accomplish that with just a few keystrokes or movements of the mouse.

The Generic Approach

Although there are a large number of forms programs that work with the LaserJet, users of desktop publishing programs (Ventura Publisher, ByLine, Office Publisher, and PageMaker), word processors that include line drawing (Microsoft Word 4.0, WordPerfect 5.0), drawing programs (Windows Draw, GEM Draw), and graphics based spreadsheets (Excel) may find it easier to use those programs for forms than to use one of the specialized packages. Office Pub-

Access: Form Programs

Form Easy
FormScan
Graphics Development Int'l
20 C Pimentel Court #4
Novato, CA 94947
415/382-6600
Price: $495 Form Easy, $495 Formscan
Notes: More or less WYSIWYG (doesn't require a graphics monitor). Supports data merging.

FormMaker II
QMS
P.O. Box 81250
Mobile, AL 36689
205/633-4300
Price: $495
Notes: Menu driven WYSIWYG. Supports data merging. Rich in features but not as easy to use as some other programs.

Form Set
Orbit Enterprises, Inc.
799 Roosevelt Rd., Bldg. 6, Suite 1
Glen Ellyn, IL 60137
312/469-3405
Price: $189.95

FormsManager DB
Software Concepts, Inc.
45 Church St.
Stanford, CT 06906
203/357-0522
Price: $399
FormSet
Orbit Enterprises, Inc.
799 Roosevelt Rd., Bldg. 6, Suite 1
Glen Ellyn, IL 60137
312/469-3405
Price: $189.95
Notes: While this program does have a preview feature, it requires you to create your form using codes rather than by drawing directly onscreen.

Form Tool
Bloc Development Corp.
1301 Dade Blvd.
Miami Beach, FL 33139
305/531-5486
Price: $95
Notes: Menu-driven layout; supports merging with dBASE data

Formworxl, Fill & File
Formworx Corp.
1365 Massachusetts Ave.
Arlington, MA 02174
800/992-0085
617/641-0400
Price: $95 Formworx, $149 with Fill & File

IPrint: The Laser Office
IPrompt
Indigo Software Ltd.
1568 Carling Ave.
Ottawa, Ontario
Canada K1Z 7M5
800/267-9976
613/594-3026
Price: $349.95 IPrint, $249.95 IPrompt
Notes: See "Profile: IPrint."
Also available from HP Direct Marketing Division, 800/538-8787
HP Part Number 35188D

Lasersoft/PC
Lasersoft/Complete
Business Systems Int'l, Inc.
2094 Osborne St.
Canoga Park, CA 91304
818/998-7227
Price: Lasersoft/PC $375, Lasersoft/Complete $495

Lasertex Electronic Forms Tools
Network Technology Corp.
6825 Lamp Post Lane
Alexandria, VA 22306
703/765-4506
Price: $295

Polaris Forms
Polaris Software
613 West Valley Parkway #323
Escondido, CA 92025
800/338-5943,
800/231-3531 California
619/743-7800
Price: $149
Notes: Not WYSIWYG; hard to use because of the need to enter formatting codes.

Visual Forms
Forms Library Disks
Deeresoft, Inc.
P.O. Box 1360
Melbourne, FL 32902
305/768-2477
Price: $89.95 Visual Forms, $24.95 Forms Library Disks
Notes: In its review of nine forms programs, Publish! *magazine rated this the easiest to use. The library disks provide you with precooked forms.*

lisher is especially well suited for creating forms because it includes commands for automatically creating stacked boxes to fill a designated area. ByLine is especially handy for forms because it allows you to import data directly from dBASE. With Ventura Publisher, you can use the Box Text feature of Graphics mode, setting up an underlying grid so that the boxes are of a uniform size. With Excel, you can easily create boxes in a grid, controlling line thickness and box shading.

For example, at Peachpit Press, we use a "twice through the printer" method to create invoice forms and fill in the data. First, we create the form in Ventura Publisher and print enough blank forms for a few weeks. Each week, we enter our data in dBXL (a dBASE III clone) and merge the data into Microsoft Word, where we add formatting information such as fonts and location on the page. Using Word, we position each data field so that it will be printed at the appropriatie location on the blank form. Finally, we load the blank forms in the LaserJet's paper tray and print the data for the current week's batch.

On-Screen Entry

Of course, using page makeup or graphics programs to create your forms only gives you the form itself. Where specialized forms programs come in handy is in automating the process of adding data to a form. Many programs let you see your form onscreen as you enter the data.

If you do use one of the programs that allows you to fill in the blanks onscreen (Visual Forms and FormSet are two examples), you'll find it extremely useful to incorporate a full-screen monitor into your setup. Otherwise, you (or whoever has the job of filling in the data) will constantly being scrolling around the page. Surprisingly, most forms programs don't provide drivers for full screen monitors; the big exception is FormMaker II, which works well with the Genius monitor.

Merging from a Database

While being able to filling out forms onscreen is useful, many organizations routinely enter information in a database and then wish to selectively merge this information into a form. Most forms programs (including FormEasy, FormMaker II, FormScan, FormTool, Formworx with Fill & File, IPrint, and Polaris Forms) let you do this, although setting up the form with all the data fields correctly positioned may take some doing.

Scanning Support

Creating your own forms is fine, but what do you do with preprinted forms that you want to fill out using the LaserJet? A clever solution devised

Customer (Bill To) :
Manhattan Exports
1800 Express Circle
Miami, FL 12345

SHIP TO:
Norris Manufacturing Co.
455 Tiki Boulevard
Honolulu, Hawaii 11234

South Seas Shipping Company
6 Embarcadero Center
San Francisco, CA
812/644-0991
Telex: 922900

Sales Order #	Purchase Order #	Ship Via *	Date	Terms	Customer #
M44566	813369	Best Way	05-05-86	Net 30 Days	H5112

QTY. ORDERED	ITEM NO.	DESCRIPTION	UNIT PRICE	DISCOUNT %	EXTENDED PRICE
300 cases	4612	Herbal Tea 100/10 per case	$34.62		$10,387.50
640 cases	1457	Paper Products	$34.62	4.62	$19,200.00
				Tax	2,461.20
				TOTAL	$32,048.70

Special Handling Instructions:

THIS FORM WAS CREATED USING
FormMaker® II Software

FormMaker Software, Inc.
57 S. Schillinger Road
Mobile, Alabama 36608
205/633-3676

(Accounting Use Only)

Customer No.
Way Bill No.
Ship Date:
Invoice No.

Serial #(s)

Figure 1: A sample page printed with FormMaker II.

by Graphics Development International is its Formscan program. With this software, you enter the form into your computer by scanning it. You can use a number of scanners, including HP's ScanJet, the Canon IX-12, Datacopy 700, and Dest. Then, viewing your form onscreen, you can denote fields for entering data.

While the advantages of this approach are obvious, there are a few disadvantages. Because the computer must manage a very large bitmap, you'll need plenty of memory in your computer, and the need to handle all that data will slow such functions as scrolling around the form. It's recommended that you use this program with the JLaser board; otherwise, printing a form is excessively slow.

WYSIWYG or Coding

Specialized forms packages can be divided into two categories: WYSIWYG (what you see is what you get) programs and non-WYSIWYG, code-based programs. For creating forms, we strongly recommend the the WYSIWYG approach. It's simply much faster, since you can see the results of your work onscreen as you create the form. With the non-WYSIWYG approach, you use a word processor to type the text portion of your form and then insert codes into the text file indicating the parameters of the ruling lines, boxes, and other graphic elements of the form.

Creating a form always requires a good deal of adjusting and fine-tuning before all the elements of the page are satisfactory. Because of the nature of form generation, non-WYSIWYG programs are generally impractical because you have to print so many copies of the form before you get it right.

One of the best of the WYSIWYG programs, IPrint, is described in "Profile: IPrint."

Tax Preparation Software

Because of its ability to print data merged with actual tax forms, the LaserJet has emerged as an important tool for accountants and tax preparers. With such packages as Lacerte Tax Preparation Software 1040, the user enters raw tax data and the program not only makes the appropriate tax calculations from that data but also prints the completed forms.

Such software almost always uses the T font cartridge. This includes the Helv bold typeface in a range of sizes: 14 point, 12 point, 10 point, and 8 point; and Helv regular weight in 8 point and 6 point. It also includes the Tax Linedraw font, which contains all the line-drawing and shading characters needed to construct a standard tax form.

While tax preparation programs work well, few seem to be well optimized for speed. For a busy accountant, there's nothing more frustrating

FORM 1040 Department of the Treasury – Internal Revenue Service
U.S. Individual Income Tax Return 1986

For the year January 1 – December 31, 1986, or other tax year beginning , 1986, ending , 19 . OMB No. 1545-0074

Use IRS label. Other-wise, please print or type.	
Your first name and initial (if joint return, also give spouse's name and initial) Last name	Your social security number
JOHN A. AND MARY B. TAXPAYER	111-11-1111
Present home address (number and street or rural route). (If you have a P.O. Box, see page 4 of Instructions.)	Spouse's social security number
1234 MAIN STREET	222-22-2222
City, town or post office, state, and ZIP code	If this address is different from the one shown on your 1985 return, check here ▶
LONG BEACH, CA 90807	

Presidential Election Campaign

	Yes		No	
Do you want $1 to go to this fund?	Yes	X	No	Note: Checking "Yes" will not change your tax or reduce your refund.
If joint return, does your spouse want $1 to go to this fund?	Yes	X	No	

Filing Status (Check only one box.) — For Privacy Act and Paperwork Reduction Act Notice, see Instructions.

1		Single
2	X	Married filing joint return (even if only one had income)
3		Married filing separate return. Enter spouse's soc. sec. no. above & name here:
4		Head of household (with qualifying person). (See page 5 of Instructions.) If the qualifying person is your unmarried child but not your dependent, enter child's name here:
5		Qualifying widow(er) with dependent child (year spouse died ▶ 19). (See page 6 of instructions.)

Exemptions (Always check the box labeled Yourself. Check other boxes if they apply.)

6a	X	Yourself		65 or over		Blind	Enter number of boxes checked on 6a and b ▶ 2
b	X	Spouse		65 or over		Blind	

c First names of your dependent children who lived with you:
MARK, KAREN, CHRIS — Enter number of children listed on 6c ▶ 3

d First names of your dependent children who did not live with you (see page 6):
(If pre-1985 agreement, check here ▶ ☐.) — Enter number of children listed on 6d ▶

e Other dependents:

(1) Name	(2) Relationship	(3) Number of months lived in your home	(4) Did depend. have income of $1,080 or more?	(5) Did you provide more than 1/2 of dependent's support?

Enter number of other dependents ▶

f Total number of exemptions claimed (also complete line 36). — Add numbers entered in boxes above ▶ 5

Income (Please attach Copy B of your Forms W-2, W-2G, and W-2P here. If you do not have a W-2, see page 4 of Instructions. Please attach check or money order here.)

Line	Description		Line	Amount
7	Wages, salaries, tips, etc. (attach Form(s) W-2.)		7	50000
8	Interest income (also attach Schedule B if over $400)		8	1473
9a	Dividends (attach Sch. B if over $400) 352, 9b Exclusion 200			
c	Subtract line 9b from line 9a and enter the result		9c	152
10	Taxable refunds of state and local income taxes, if any, from the worksheet on page 9		10	
11	Alimony received		11	
12	Business income or (loss)(attach Schedule C)		12	
13	Capital gain or (loss)(attach Schedule D)		13	160
14	40% of capital gain distributions not reported on line 13 (see page 9 of instructions)		14	
15	Other gains or (losses)(attach Form 4797)		15	
16	Fully taxable pensions, IRA distributions, and annuities not reported on line 17 (see page 9)		16	
17a	Other pensions and annuities, incl. rollovers. Total received	17a		
b	Taxable amount, if any, from the worksheet on page 10 of instructions		17b	
18	Rents, royalties, partnerships, estates, trusts, etc. (attach Schedule E)		18	-17000
19	Farm income or (loss)(attach Schedule F)		19	
20a	Unemployment compensation (insurance). Total received	20a		
b	Taxable amount, if any, from the worksheet on page 10 of instructions		20b	
21a	Social security benefits (see page 10)	21a		
b	Taxable amount, from worksheet on page 11 { Tax-exempt interest }		21b	
22	Other income (list type and amount)		22	
23	Add the amounts shown in the far right column for lines 7 - 22. This is your **total income** ▶		23	34785

Adjustments to Income (See Instructions on page 11.)

Line	Description	Line	Amount		
24	Moving expenses (attach Form 3903 or 3903F)	24	2500		
25	Employee business expenses (attach Form 2106)	25			
26	IRA deduction, from the worksheet on page 12	26	4000		
27	Keogh retirement plan and self-employed SEP deduction	27			
28	Penalty on early withdrawal of savings	28			
29	Alimony paid (recipient's last name and social security no.)	29			
30	Deduction for a married couple when both work (Sch. W)	30	1800		
31	Add lines 24 through 30. **Total adjustments** ▶			31	8300

Adjusted Gross Income

Line	Description	Line	Amount
32	Subtract line 31 from line 23. This is your **adjusted gross income**. If this line is less than $11,000 and a child lived with you, see "Earned Income Credit" (line 58) on page 16 of Instructions. If you want IRS to figure your tax, see page 13 of instructions ▶	32	26485

Figure 2: An IRS 1040 form printed with Lacerte Tax Software.

than to wait while the computer downloads the tax form to the printer and the printer processes and prints the form. Two techniques can speed up the process: the use of LaserJet macros and the use of an accelerator board. When you shop for tax preparation software, you should try to find a package that has added support for both.

LaserJet Macros: One of the lesser-used capabilities of the LaserJet Plus and LaserJet II is the ability to store a series of commands (such as a tax form) within the printer under a brief name. The stored group of commands, known as a "macro," can then be executed by sending a brief command to the printer. If a tax form is stored as a macro, then all the application has to send to the printer is the specific data needed to fill in the blanks. The LaserJet then merges the two and prints the form much more quickly, since it saves the time needed to repeatedly transmit the entire form.

Accelerator Boards: Using the LaserJet in conjunction with an accelerator board such as the LaserMaster CAPCard dramatically speed the printing process. The catch is that a special driver must be written to enable the application to work with the accelererator. It's expected that many tax packages will add such drivers in the near future, so this is something that should definitely be on your list of questions when you shop for soft-

Access: Tax Preparation Software

1040 Solution
1120 Solution
Creative Solutions, Inc.
230 Collingwood, Suite 250
Ann Arbor, MI 48103
313/995-8811
Price: 1040 Solution $1495 , 1120 Solution $695

A-PlusTax 1040
Arthur Anderson & Co.
630 South Orange Ave.
Sarasota, FL 33577
800/872-1040
Price: $1495 to $1995

Corporate 1120
Corporate 1120S
CPAID
1061 Fraternity Circle
Kent, OH 44240
216/678-9015
Price: $500 each

Glowstx Tax Processing System
Orion Microsystems, Inc.
Lafayette Bldg. #910

5th & Chestnut St.
Philadelphia, PA 19106
215/928-1119
Price: $1295 to $1995

Lacerte Tax Preparation Software 1040
Lacerte Software Corporation
3447 Atlantic Ave.
Long Beach, CA 90807
800/331-8614
213/595-0901
Price: $2000

Laser Tax Form Software
Nelco Tax Forms
P.O. Box 10208
3130 South Ridge Rd.
Green Bay, WI 54307-0208
414/337-1000
Price: $100 to $400

Master Tax
CPAID
1061 Fraternity Circle
Kent, OH 44240
216/678-9015
Price: $1795

Partnership 1065
CPAID
1061 Fraternity Circle
Kent, OH 44240
216/678-9015
Price: $500

PC/Professional Tax Partner
Best Programs, Inc.
2700 S. Quincy Rd.
Arlington, VA 22206
800/368-2405
Price: $995

State Programs
CPAID
1061 Fraternity Circle
Kent, OH 44240
216/678-9015
Price: $400 to $600

Tax Refund System
UFS Good-Year, Inc.
534 Burmont Rd.
Drexel Hill, PA 19026
215/623-6140
Price: $399.95

Tax Resources 1120
Tax Resources Ten40
Tax Resources, Inc.
1111 North Loop West #920
Houston, TX 77008
713/868-2937
Price: $495

Volts Tax Preparation & Planning
Hanson Software Systems
1344 E. Katella Ave.
Anaheim, CA 92805
714/385-1556
Price: $975

ware. For more information on accelerator boards, see Chapter 27, "Upgrade Options."

Profile: IPrint

IPRINT IS ONE of the more seasoned LaserJet applications. It offers a unique WYSIWYG interface that is easily learned and quite powerful. The ability of this program to combine text and graphics makes it especially well suited for creating forms.

The product comprises three modules. IFORM lets you design forms interactively. The program provides a menu of icons, including a circle, a vertical line, a horizontal line, a rectangle, a diagonal line, a rectangle with rounded corners, and a shaded area. By selecting these icons with a mouse (or using the cursor keys), you can create on-screen the graphical elements of a form. You can also create text and move it into the form. Text that appears on a form cannot actually be read on-screen, however, unless you zoom in close. Once elements have been created on the form, you can select a rectangular area and move or copy elements to new locations. A zoom command lets you select an area and magnify it to full-screen size.

The second module, IPRINT, lets you send the form you have created to the LaserJet Plus for printing. It also allows you to merge your data files into data fields on forms created by IFORM.

The third module, IDOC, allows you to combine individual forms on a page or print documents that consist of several forms on more than one page.

Especially noteworthy is IFORM's ability to let you create and then store logos. You can define a logo using PC Paint; alternatively, you can draw its shape in an ASCII text file using asterisks or another character to represent dots printed by the LaserJet. The program lets you display names of up to 14 predefined logos. To include a logo in a document, you select it from the list using the mouse or the cursor keys. You can print logos at varying sizes by changing the resolution.

The user interface of IPrint is reminiscent to that of the Macintosh. Like the Mac, IPrint uses a mouse (or the cursor keys) to control cursor movements and, like the Mac, works with icons and pull-down menus. To create a rectangle, for example, you select the rectangle icon, then move the cursor onto the screen and stretch the rectangle to the size you want. Graphics and text elements are not fixed on the page. You can move them around as independent objects or lay one inside or overlapping another.

RESERVATION REQUEST
INDIGO SOFTWARE LTD.

IPRINT CORPORATE TRAVEL

NAME OF TRAVELER OR GUEST	EMPLOYEE NUMBER	DIV/CORP. DEPT.	BUDGET CENTER	DATE SUBMITTED
Barry H. Gillespie	12345	345	456	87/08/01

TELEPHONE NUMBERS	SECRETARY'S NAME	EXTENSION
Office Ext. 1357 Area Code 613 Home 728-0016	Carma	1358

DATES	DATE TICKET NEEDED: 87/08/05	LOCATION UB-40	BUILDING 23	ROOM 2345

TRAVEL	FROM	TO	FLIGHT No.	TIME DEPART	TIME ARRIVE	F/B	
87/08/06	New York	San Francisco	234	09:00	11:00	a1	
87/08/09	San Francisco	New York	235	17:00	02:00	a2	

CAR SERV.	FROM	TO	NAME OF PASSENGER	TIME	

HOTEL		HOTEL/MOTEL	CITY - ADDRESS	TELEPHONE	
IN 87/08/06	OUT 87/08/08	Embarcadero Hilton	Embarcadero Center San Francisco	415-555-1234	
IN	OUT				
IN	OUT				

GUEST	☐ INDIGO TO PAY FOR GUEST HOTEL BILL	☐ GUEST WILL PAY OWN HOTEL BILL	

CAR RENTAL		LOCATION (City/Airport)	CAR RENTAL PREFERENCE	CAR TYPE	PURPOSE OF TRIP:
PICK UP 87/08/06	RETURN 87/08/09	San Francisco Bay AirPort	Hertz	Mid-Size	Visit major clients in bay area for 2 days.
PICK UP	RETURN				
PICK UP	RETURN				

SPECIAL INSTRUCTIONS:	REQUESTED BY:
None	Barry H. Gillespie
	APPROVED BY (Print or Type): John Gleed
	SIGNATURE FOR APPROVAL:

FOR TRAVEL DEPARTMENT USE ONLY: SABRE LOCATOR NUMBER ______ TICKET NUMBER ______ COST OF TICKET ______

AIRLINE/OTHER REMARKS:

Figure 1: A sample form created using IPrint. (Reduced by 33 percent.)

For graphics, IPrint has several features that allow precise positioning. One enables you to define the increments of vertical and horizontal position down to one-thousandth of an inch. Another feature lets you zoom in on a portion of the screen for detail work. To facilitate drawing and placement, the program lets you draw on-screen lines that do not print.

To enter a passage of text on a form, you select the text icon, causing a box to appear at the top of the screen. You enter text in the box and then position it at the appropriate location using the mouse or cursor keys.

Access

IPrint: The Laser Office
Indigo Software Ltd.
1568 Carling AVe.
Ottawa, Ontario
Canada K1Z 7M5
613/728-0016
HP Direct: 800/537-8787
Price: $349.95
HP Part No. 35188D

Profile: Lasersoft/PC

LASERSOFT/PC IS A menu-driven forms-generation package originally developed for Xerox laser printers. By means of a menu interface, it lets you create simple forms and forms that can be merged with data. Graphical elements are created by specifying location and dimension; the package does not let you draw on-screen with a mouse.

From the main menu of Lasersoft/PC, you can move to any of the four principle components of the program: LaserJet setup, font management, forms composition, and data merging.

Using the Setup menu, you can specify margins, page length, the increments of horizontal and vertical motion that you want to work with, number of copies to print, whether to wrap lines, and type of paper.

With the Font menu, you can create a "catalog" of the fonts on each cartridge that you use with the LaserJet. To create a new catalog, you need to enter the escape sequence, orientation, spacing, point size, and pitch of the font.

You can choose either to create a new form or to redesign one that you previously created and stored. For each form, Lasersoft/PC keeps track of parameters such as margins, paper size, orientation, and fonts used on the page. To build a form you work from the Form Design menu, which lets you choose options such as boxes, horizontal lines, vertical lines, and text by pressing the appropriate function key.

To create an element on the screen, you need to know its intended size and location on the page. The manual suggests first drawing your form on paper and then using a transparent overlay grid sheet (provided in the Lasersoft/PC package) to determine the coordinates of graphic elements. To create a box, for example, you enter the coordinates of its top left and the bottom left corners, and specify the width of the vertical and horizontal lines. Once you have created the box, you can repeat it elsewhere on the page using the Repeat command.

Text is entered on the form by first determining the font and the starting location. You can then enter a line (80 characters) of text at a time. You can adjust the location of each line of text in increments of 1/720 inch.

The data merging feature lets you combine the output of any other program with a form and print the two on the same page. While this is a useful feature, it leaves to you the task of figuring out a way to position the data you are merging so that it appears in the right location on the form. In this respect it is much less sophisticated that the mail-merge module of most word processing packages, which automatically insert the merged data at the proper location in the document. However, a new version of the program, Lasersoft/Complete, makes it possible to enter data, performs mathematical calculations on the data, and automatically places it in the correct location on the form.

Access

Lasersoft/PC
Lasersoft/Complete
Business Systems Int'l
2094 Osborne St.
Canoga Park, CA 91304
818/998-7227
Price: Lasersoft/PC $375, Lasersoft/Complete $495

6

FONTS

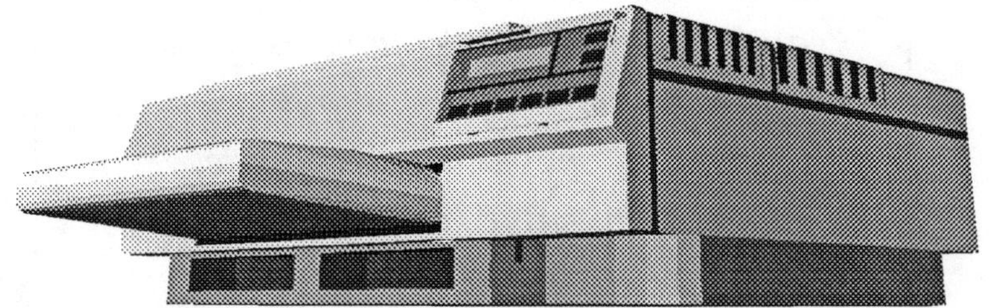

Section Focus

The LaserJet uses three kinds of fonts: resident fonts (built into the printer), cartridge fonts, and soft fonts (distributed on floppy disks and downloaded into the printer's memory).

This section provides background information on fonts and introduces you to tools for managing your font collection. These tools include font generators, font editors, and utilities for downloading fonts and modifying applications to work with new fonts. There's also a guide to selecting fonts using the LaserJet's Printer Command Language. For a list of font cartridge escape codes and a directory of font vendors, see the appendices.

CHAPTER TWELVE

Typographic Background

THE FIRST STEP in using laser printer fonts is to become acquainted with some of the concepts that have evolved over the past few centuries to describe type.

Font Versus Typeface

First, let's clear up some confusion that occasionally arises between the terms *font* and *typeface.* Typeface refers to a particular design, such as Letter Gothic. A font, on the other hand, is the actual implementation of that design in a specific collection of characters—something you buy at a computer store, take home, and install on your computer.

For the ordinary user of type, the distinction between these two terms is only of interest for the purpose of knowing which word to use in a particular context. For the type designer, however, there are legal implications also, and since tools such as font editors are becoming widely available, it's worth touching on these briefly.

In the United States, there is no way for a designer of type to protect his or her original designs except by trademarking the name of the design. Thus, while many companies have come out with their versions of Times Roman, only the Allied Corporation, which owns the trademark on the name, can refer to its fonts as "Times Roman." Other companies will refer to their versions as "similar to Times Roman" or something of that nature.

Fonts, on the other hand, are protected by copyright just like any other software. In other words, you can create a font that looks like someone else's, but you can't simply steal their font and call it your own.

Classifying Type

There are many ways to classify type: according to the function it is intended to serve, according to the families of closely related designs, according to whether the characters contain certain decorative elements, etc. We'll now look at these various methods in turn.

Basic Typeface Groups

As the name implies, text faces are those used primarily for ordinary text. Since the principle design aim is maximum readability, these faces avoid design elements that would detract from their basic purpose.

Display faces are specially designed for use in titles and headlines. Generally, such faces are bold and dramatic. Their aim is to draw attention, so they tend to be darker and more striking than plain text faces. Frequently, the bold version of a text face is used as a display face.

Decorative faces are highly distinctive, used for special purposes such as advertisements and diplomas. Often, they are derived from fancy calligraphic styles and are used for such items as greeting cards.

Increasingly, fonts are becoming available that do not comprise alphabetic characters but instead contain special symbols. Traditionally, font vendors have referred to fonts made up of special-purpose symbols as pi fonts. The application of such fonts is only limited by the imagination: advertisements, mathematics, music scores, chemical structures, crossword puzzles, chess boards, architectural diagrams, and so forth. Another category is known as dingbats. Like pi fonts, dingbats contain nonalphabetic characters, but of a more playful and decorative nature.

Serif Versus Sans Serif

Another way of classifying typefaces is in terms of the way they are drawn, and here there are two basic categories. Serif fonts are those whose characters include serifs, which are small strokes that accentuate the corners or tips of characters. Characters that lack serifs are called sans serif; in addition, their strokes tend to be more even.

Generally, it's a good idea to use serif type for text and reserve sans serif type for titles or for short passages or tables, where a contrasting appearance to plain text is desired.

While it has been proposed that serifs actually assist readers by providing the eye with visual clues, studies have shown that serif type is more readable for those who grew up reading text in serif type, while sans serif type is more readable for those who grew up with sans serif. In this country, of course, virtually everyone is accustomed to reading text set in serif type. In Europe, however, the use of sans serif typefaces for ordinary text is more common and acceptable.

Families

A "type family" refers to variations on a typeface, typically the following four: roman, italic, bold, and bold italic. Other variations on the central theme are possible, including condensed, obliqued, extended, rounded, and a spectrum of weights from very light to very dark. In a popular family such as Helvetica, there may be as many as three dozen distinct typefaces within a single type family.

Note that the term "roman" means upright characters. Thus, the typeface Times Roman is the upright variation of the Times family. Note also the difference between an obliqued typeface, which is merely a slanted version of a roman typeface, and italic, which is a separate design derived from calligraphic letterforms.

Measurement Units

Rather than using either the English or the metric system, typographers use points and picas for measuring type. Since there are 72 points or 6 picas per inch, the typographic measuring system is appropriately scaled for its purpose and allows you to almost always avoid using fractions.

Type is measured from the top of the tallest ascender to the bottom of the lowest descender. Typically, 10-point, 11-point, or 12-point type is used for text, while 6-point to 8-point type is used for footnotes. The display type used in most publications is at least 24 points, and may range above 100 points.

Because of differences in design among different fonts, point sizes can be deceptive. For example, 10-point Helvetica looks larger than 10-point Times Roman because the lowercase letters in Helvetica are large relative to the descenders and ascenders. Thus, before deciding on which point size to use for a document, make sure you check actual samples of the font.

Spacing

So far we've talked about the anatomy of type itself: how type is classified and measured. However, the quality of typeset text does not depend only on the design of the typeface or the rendering of the characters at particular sizes, it also depends on how well the letters are spaced. Even a beautiful typeface will be rendered ugly if the spacing is not correct. Type should be set so that it is neither too tight nor too loose—a challenge given the often conflicting need to justify a line. We'll now take a look at some of the methods for controlling spacing.

Monospacing Versus Proportional Spacing

Typefaces originally designed for typewriters are monospaced, which means simply that all characters require the same amount of space. The fonts used by low-cost computer monitors are monospaced, as are the two most popular typewriter typefaces: Courier and Prestige Elite.

In a monospaced font, spaces are standardized at the same width as a character. The spacing for a font is called its "pitch," measured in characters per inch.

Of course, pitch has meaning only for fonts whose characters are fixed in width, typewriter-style, such as the Courier font built into the LaserJet. Most typographic fonts are proportionally spaced, which means that the width of characters varies, as does the spacing between characters.

In general, the goal of typesetting with a proportional font is to end up with an even rhythm of white and black.

For a block of text to look right, certain letter pairs must have their spacing adjusted. Usually this means pushing them together, as is necessary if a W is next to an A. This sort of pairwise adjustment is called kerning. Some font vendors build this information into each font as a table of values for the amount of horizontal adjustment necessary for selected character combinations. Applications programs with automatic kerning capabilities can then read this information and make the appropriate adjustments.

Justification

As if things weren't complex enough already, typographers have something else to worry about: justification. Justification refers to setting text so that it is flush against either one or both margins. "Left justified" means flush on the left and ragged on the right, "right justified" means flush on the right and ragged on the left, and "justified" means flush on both sides.

There are several techniques for justifying type. The first is to hyphenate words. The second is to adjust the spacing between words. Of course, adding too much space between words may give text an undesirable appearance. Lines in which the amount of space between words exceeds a certain desirable maximum are referred to as "loose lines." To deal with a loose line, a typographic system can resort to the third technique, increasing the amount of space between letters within words. This is known as "letter spacing." This final technique is generally available in desktop publishing software such as Ventura and PageMaker, but not in word processing programs.

Leading

While the bulk of the work of setting type relates to adjusting the horizontal distance between characters on a line, the distance between lines of text must also be adjusted. This factor, called leading, is measured from baseline to baseline. With a typewriter, leading was not a big concern: your options were one line, one and a half lines, or two lines. With type of varying sizes, however, leading must be controlled in finer increments. When specifying how a given block of text is to be set, typographers will write a fraction such as 10/12 (pronounced "10 on 12"). This means that a 10-point font is to be used with 12 points separating the baselines of text.

CHAPTER THIRTEEN

LaserJet Font Basics

IF YOU LOOKED at a character printed by the LaserJet, you would see that it is actually a mosaic made up of hundreds of closely fitted dots, arranged in neat rows and columns packed 300 to an inch. The technical term for that mosaic is a "bitmap," since each dot on the page has a one-to-one correspondence, or mapping, to a digital bit stored in computer memory. Since digital bits are either 0's or 1's, the correspondence is very simple: for each 1 stored in the computer, the printer will print a dot; for each 0 stored in the computer, the printer will leave a white space.

Thus, a laser printer font is merely a computer file that contains all the bitmaps needed to print a full set of characters and symbols. Besides the bit maps themselves, that file also includes a header with various sorts of information identifying the font: typeface name, point size, etc.

Where Fonts Are Stored

Like any other computer files, fonts can be stored in a variety of locations. These include

- The permanent memory of the laser printer itself,
- A font cartridge,
- Floppy disks or the hard disk of the computer.

Resident Fonts

"Resident font" is the term for a font that is permanently stored in the ROM (Read-Only Memory) of the LaserJet. Table 1 lists the resident fonts for the LaserJet, the LaserJet Plus, and the LaserJet II.

Cartridge Fonts

The original LaserJet and the LaserJet Plus had a single slot for inserting a

Resident Fonts

Original LaserJet*

Courier 12-pt medium, portrait orientation
Courier 12-pt medium, landscape orientationm

LaserJet Plus**

Courier 12-pt medium, portrait orientation
Courier 12-pt medium, landscape orientation
Line printer 8.5-pt medium, portrait orientation

LaserJet II***

Courier 12-pt medium, portrait orientation
Courier 12-pt medium, landscape orientation
Courier 12-pt bold, portrait orientation
Courier 12-pt bold, landscape orientation
Line printer 8.5-pt medium, portrait orientation
Line printer 8.5-pt medium, landscape orientation

---

*All fonts in Roman-8 symbol set only

**All fonts in Roman-8, USASCII, and Rom. Ext. symbol sets

***All fonts in the following symbol sets: Roman-8, IBM-US, IBM-DN, ECMA-94, Denmark/Norway, ISO IRV, ISO United Kingdom, ANSI ASCII, ISO Swedish, ISO Swedish: names, JIS ASCII, ISO Italian, ISO Portuguese, ISO Spanish, ISO German, ISO 100 Latin 1, ISO French, ISO Chinese, ISO Norwegian v1, ISO Norwegian v2, ISO French, ISO Portuguese: IBM, ISO Spanish: IBM, HP German, HP Spanish.

Table 1: Resident fonts.

font cartridge; the LaserJet II has two such slots. Originally, purchasing such cartridges was the only way to extend your selection of fonts, since the first LaserJets did not allow fonts to be downloaded into the printer from floppy disks. Hewlett-Packard sells a full line of font cartridges, as listed in Appendix E, "Annotated Font Directory." In addition, other companies have begun marketing their own cartridges. For example, the Super Cartridge from IQ Engineering packs in almost all the fonts offered on the entire line of HP cartridges, though the selection of character sets is more limited than HP's. Another useful third-party font cartridge is JetFont 123 from Computer Peripherals, Inc. This cartridge includes Lotica, a typeface designed for good legibility at very small sizes, in sizes as small as 30 characters per inch—perfect for fitting a big spreadsheet on a single page. A third example is a company called GNU Business Systems, which can create your own custom font cartridge with any font from the Bitstream Fontware library. (For access information on the Super Cartridge, JetFont 123, and GNU cartridges, see Appendix E, "Font Directory.")

The biggest advantage of font cartridges is their simplicity. Once you plug the cartridge into the printer and adjust your software to recognize the fonts contained on it, the cartridge can be considered a permanent part of your system. No need to download fonts from the computer every morning.

Cartridges do have some drawbacks, however. One is that they do not last indefinitely. Another is that they can be damaged by static electricity or by being pulled out of the LaserJet while the printer is online. To maximize the life of font cartridges, make sure you take the printer offline (by pressing the ON LINE button once) before you insert or remove a cartridge. Even better, only insert or remove a cartridge when the printer is turned off.

Another drawback of cartridges is that the selection of fonts on the cartridge is rigid. You can't move fonts from one cartridge to another. However, that problem is somewhat alleviated by the fact that the LaserJet II has two slots and by the fact that some software applications allow you to mix soft fonts and cartridge fonts on the same page.

Soft Fonts

"Soft fonts" is the term for fonts that are sold on floppy disks. Such fonts can be purchased either from Hewlett-Packard or from one of the many third-party font manufacturers listed in the next chapter. They can be used with the LaserJet Plus or LaserJet II, but not with the original LaserJet.

One advantage of soft fonts is that they are relatively inexpensive;

another is that they are more flexible than cartridge fonts, since you can mix fonts from one floppy disk with fonts from another. Generally, the best way to work is to copy fonts from the floppy onto a special directory of the hard disk reserved for that purpose.

The disadvantage of soft fonts is that they must be transferred, or "downloaded," from the floppy disk or hard disk into the LaserJet's RAM (random access memory) before they can be used. Since anything in RAM disappears once the printer's power is turned off, you have to download the soft fonts you need each time you turn the power back on. Some programs, such as Microsoft Word and Ventura Publisher, take care of the downloading process automatically. Others require you to perform the task manually. For instructions on downloading, see Chapter 15, "Downloading Fonts and Building Drivers."

Fonts downloaded into memory reduce the amount of RAM available for other purposes, such as storing overlay forms. Therefore, you need to be careful that you download only the fonts you need for each job and remove those not needed.

Character Sets

A character set or symbol set is the collection of symbols used in a font. Keyboard characters like letters, numbers, and punctuation marks and other special symbols like math symbols all belong to character sets.

Most character sets include all the characters found on a standard computer keyboard, but they differ greatly in what else they contain. For example, you have the option of using a variety of foreign language character sets for the resident fonts contained in the LaserJet II. All of these sets include the basic keyboard characters, but each provides a particular collection of accented characters.

In addition, some character sets provide important typographic symbols that others lack. The Roman-8 set, for example, is missing true typographic (i.e., open and closed) quotation marks as well as several other symbols.

Seven-Bit Sets and Eight-Bit Sets

Before we go any farther, let's explain a piece of terminology that you may occasionally encounter in navigating the world of fonts: the terms "7-bit fonts" and "8-bit fonts."

Typically, character sets have either 128 or 256 members. Character sets with 128 members are called seven-bit sets, because it takes only seven binary digits to represent any number from 0 to 127. Character sets with 256 members are called eight-bit sets, because with eight binary digits you can represent any number from 0 to 255. Frequently, you'll hear the characters above 127 referred to as "high-bit" characters. The term "high-bit" refers to the fact that in order to represent numbers in the range 127 to 255 using binary notation, the eighth bit of every byte—the "high bit"—must be turned on. The term "extended ASCII characters" also refers to characters above 127.

ASCII

The most basic character set is the ASCII set (American Standard Code for Information Interchange). Numbers 0 to 31 of the ASCII set are reserved for unprintable control characters. Numbers 33 through 127 include the standard upper- and lowercase letters of the English alphabet as well as the punctuation marks and symbols found on a standard computer keyboard—92 characters in all. Many other character sets, including the Roman-8, IBM, and Ventura sets described below, are extensions of ASCII. They match the ASCII set in the range below 128, differing in the characters they provide in the 128 to 255 range. Thus, with any of the fonts that use these character sets, when you type a k on the keyboard, you see a k on the screen and a k is printed by the printer.

Many fonts, especially in large point sizes, include only the ASCII character set. The reason is that this reduces the amount of storage necessary to hold them. This applies to many third-party fonts for the HP LaserJet as well as to Hewlett-Packard's own soft fonts numbered 33412AC (TmsRmn/Helv), 33412AE (TmsRmn/Helv), 33412RA (ITC Garamond), 33412SA (Century Schoolbook), 33412TA (Zapf Humanist 601), and 33412UA (Headline Typefaces).

Conspicuously absent from the ASCII set are any typographic characters not found on the keyboard. These include true open and closed quotation marks (" and "), the em dash (—), copyright and trademark symbols (©, ®, and ™), European characters (such as ä, à, and å), commercial symbols (such as ¢, £, and ¥), and typographic symbols (such as ‡ and ¶).

The Roman-8 Character Set

The Roman-8 set is an 8-bit character set used by Hewlett-Packard for many of its cartridge and soft fonts. Cartridges A, B, C, D, E, F, J, L, M, N, P, Q, U, V, W, and X all use this font. It is also the character set used in most of Hewlett-Packard's soft fonts.

The high-bit characters of the Roman-8 set are mainly European and currency symbols. Missing are a number of important typographic and commercial symbols, including ", ", §, ‡, †, ¶, ©, ®, and ™. Finally, the set lacks a satisfactory bullet character.

Note that although the Roman-8 set shares many of the high-bit characters used by the IBM set, the two assign them different numbers. Because of this difference in encoding methods, a command that elicits a particular character on the screen may cause a different character to be printed. This is important to keep in mind when you are using symbols in the 128 to 255 range.

The Roman Extension Character Set

This character set is made up of the upper half of the Roman-8 character set, i.e., the characters numbered 128 to 255. Thus, it lacks the keyboard characters. The advantage of using Roman Ext. is that you can type non-keyboard characters directly from a standard keyboard, provided you have a table showing the correspondence between the members of the Roman Extension set and the keyboard characters.

The IBM Character Set

Another common character set is the one used by most personal computer monitors and by the fonts in Hewlett-Packard's Y cartridge. It is an eight-bit set. Elements 0 through 31, the ASCII control characters, are represented on the screen by smiling faces, hearts, spades, etc. Elements 32 through 127 are the same as the ASCII printable characters. Elements 128 through 255 are roughly divided into three groups of foreign characters, graphic shapes, and mathematical symbols.

The Ventura Character Set

The character set used by the printer and screen fonts provided with the Xerox Ventura Publisher package is referred to as the Ventura or International set. It is an 8-bit character set that includes a full complement of typographic symbols missing from the standard computer keyboard as well as characters needed by some European languages: Spanish, French, Italian, and German. The full set is shown in Appendix E of the Ventura manual.

European Character Sets

With the LaserJet II, you can select a number of European language character sets using the control panel. To do so, press the ON LINE key to take the printer off-line. When you do so, the ON LINE light will go out. Next, press and hold the MENU key for about 5 seconds. The LED panel will display: "SYM SET =" followed by the abbreviated name of the currently selected character set. Now press the plus or minus button until the character set you wish to use is displayed on the display panel. Select the change by pressing the ENTER/RESET MENU button. To activate the new default, press and hold the CON-

TINUE / RESET button for about three seconds.

European characters are also contained in the C font cartridge, including those needed for printing French, German, and Italian.

Miscellaneous Character Sets

Increasingly, fonts are becoming available that contain none of the keyboard characters but instead are made up entirely of special symbols. A good example is the Symbol font provided with Ventura Publisher, an 8-bit font. It includes a number of scientific and mathematic symbols, the Greek alphabet (uppercase and lowercase), and a variety of miscellaneous symbols.

Other miscellaneous fonts, all of which are slight variations of the ASCII character set, include the following: (1) the Line Draw character set, found on the G, H, T, U, V, W, and X font cartridges; (2) the Legal character set on the G and H font cartridges; (3) the Math8, Math8a, Math7, PiFont, and PiFonta character sets on the J cartridge; and (4) the optical character and barcode character sets on the W and X cartridges.

Font Names

People are often surprised when they order fonts at how many files are on the font disks. The reason for all the files is that a separate file is required to store each point size, style (italic, roman, bold, bold italic), and orientation (portrait or landscape).

To keep track of all these files, it helps to be able to decipher their names. Since DOS only allows eight letters for the name of a file and three letters for the extension, these names are somewhat cryptic. The purpose of this chapter is to explain their meaning.

Note: To the LaserJet, it doesn't really matter what you name a particular font file. That's because the LaserJet doesn't look at font file names when it is searching for the right font to print; instead it looks at the contents of the font header, which is stored inside the font file. However, to many software programs—such as font editing programs, programs that convert fonts from one format to another, and font downloading programs—the names of the font files do matter, especially the extension. For that reason, be careful if you decide to rename your font files.

There is no one system for naming font files. In this chapter we'll describe the formats used by Hewlett-Packard, SoftCraft, and Bitstream. Still other formats are used by other companies.

Hewlett-Packard Font Format

Soft fonts purchased from Hewlett-Packard use the following font format:

aabbbcpn.ffg

aa stands for the typeface, such as tr for Dutch (Times Roman) and hv for Swiss (Helvetica).

bbb stands for the point size multiplied by 10. For example, 140 means 14.0 points and 095 means 9.5 points

c stands for the style of the font (r for roman, i for italic, b for bold, and x for bold italic).

The letters **pn** simply indicate that this is a printer font. These two letters always appear in HP font names.

ff stands for the character set, such as r8 for Roman-8 and us for USASCII.

g stands for orientation, either p for portrait or l for landscape.

SoftCraft Font Format

Fonts sold by SoftCraft use the following format:

aabccddd.fon

aa stands for the typeface.

b is only present if the font is a style other than roman: i for italic, b for bold, x for bold italic.

cc stands for the character set.

ddd stands for the point size, such as 10 points or 14 points (note, if a font size is a decimal such as 10.5 points, the .5 is dropped in the file name).

fon is always the extension.

CHAPTER FOURTEEN

Font Generators

ALTHOUGH FONT GENERATORS are the newest type of LaserJet software to arrive on the scene, they are probably the most important. The reason is simple. Before font generators were available, the LaserJet could only print fonts at fixed sizes. If you wanted 12-point type, you had to buy a 12-point font. If you wanted 13-point type, you had to buy a separate 13-point font. With a generator, you simply buy a master outline for the typeface you wish to use, and the font-generating program will generate any size font you want.

The big benefit in this new technology is the unlimited flexibility it gives you to use fonts of any size, not just those sizes available from font vendors.

Not all font generators are created equal. The task of generating a good-looking font from a font outline requires sophisticated algorithms; otherwise, the result is jagged, uneven characters.

Fontware

Currently, the generator that offers the highest-quality output and the largest selection of typefaces is Bitstream's Fontware, described in "Profile: Fontware." Currently, Fontware installation programs are being given away with Microsoft Word 4.0, PageMaker 3.0, WordPerfect 5.0, GEM, PagePerfect, Lotus Manuscript, the LaserMaster CAPCard, the JLaser board, and Moniterm's high-resolution monitors. Typically, the installation kits come with one or two master font outlines to get you started. You can buy additional font packages from Bitstream.

Type Director

At this writing, another major font generating product, called Type Director, was nearing introduction. Developed by Compugraphic Corporation, Type Director uses a proprietary technology called "Intellifont." Compugraphic's technology is impor-

Access: Font Generators

Alphabets
Wilkes Publishing Corp.
25251 Paseo de Alicia, #229
Laguna Hills, CA 92653
714/855-0730
Price: $195

Fontpac
Metro Software
2509 N. Campbell #214
Tucson, AZ 85719
800/621-1137
Price: $150

Fontware
see "Profile: Fontware"

Glyphix Basics, Glyphix WordPerfect Font Manager, Glyphix MS Word Font Manager, Glyphix Pop 'n Print
see "Profile: Glyphix"

GPA Soft Font Generator
Gradco Systems, Inc.
7 Morgan
Irvine, CA 92718
714/770-1223
Price: $495

tant to LaserJet owners for two reasons. One reason is that Hewlett-Packard has licensed the Intellifont technology for use in future HP products. The other reason is that Type Director will make Compugraphic's vast library of commercial fonts accessible for laser printing.

While Fontware and Type Director are certainly destined to dominate the market, those interested in saving money may look into several font generators of lesser renown: Glyphix, GPA Soft Font Generator, Alphabets, and Fontpac. Of these, Glyphix was first on the scene and has had the most time to evolve.

Fonts on the Fly

Even though font generators offer a great deal of flexibility, they still require you to go through awkward procedures and keep track of all sorts of annoying details. Fortunately, two companies have come up with software that takes care of all the gory details and makes the use of fonts of any size almost completely automatic.

One such program is the Glyphix MS Word font manager. You decide on the fonts you wish to include in your document and Glyphix generates and downloads them during printing. A related program is Glyphix Pop 'n Print. This program is loaded into memory, where it takes up about 40K.

At any time you can pop it up from within another application, use it to generate a font, and download the font—all without leaving the application.

Another "fonts on the fly" program, from LaserMaster Corporation, works in conjunction with Ventura Publisher. Once you've gone through a one-time installation procedure, you can select any size font from the Ventura or Word menu. The software automatically generates that font from its master outline and downloads it to the printer.

It sounds perfect, but there are a few drawbacks of the system. One is that to run LaserMaster's "fonts on the fly" software for Ventura, you have to be using the LaserMaster CAPCard accelerator board. It is described in Part 8 of this book in "Profile: LaserMaster CAPCard." The other drawback is that fonts generated via the fonts on the fly option should only be used for fonts greater than 18 points. In smaller sizes the quality is slightly lower than regular fonts.

Profile: Fontware

GIVE 'EM THE RAZORS, then sell 'em the razor blades. That's the tried and true strategy being used to promote Fontware. Currently, Fontware installation kits are being offered free to owners of Microsoft Word 4.0, PageMaker 3.0, WordPerfect 5.0, GEM, PagePerfect, Lotus Manuscript, the LaserMaster CAPCard, the JLaser board, and Moniterm's high-resolution monitors. That's probably just for starters—by the time you read this many more companies may be bundling Fontware with their products. Along with the free installation package, you're usually provided with two or three sample font outlines. Additional outlines cost approximately $195 per package, which usually contain the regular, bold, italic, and bold italic versions of a single typeface.

Background

The development work behind Fontware actually predates the LaserJet itself. Bitstream, the company that created Fontware, was organized in 1981 as the world's first digital type foundry. Initially, the company concentrated on supplying type for expensive typesetting equipment, but with the arrival of laser printers it began supplying type to the manufacturers of those systems. For example, most of the cartridge and downloadable fonts sold by Hewlett-Packard were developed by Bitstream.

By introducing a method of generating fonts from outlines, Bitstream has attempted to do what many experts had said was impossible. In the past, many typographers have claimed that any efforts to create fonts at specific sizes from master outlines would be doomed to failure. The reason is that after a character is converted from an outline into a bitmap (i.e., a dot pattern), its appearance and legibility can be improved by a typographic expert who makes subtle changes in the dot pattern.

Far from being a superfluous nicety, these subtle changes dramatically improve the appearance of a font, especially at normal text sizes (14 points and below), from one that appears rough and amateurish to one that looks as good as allowable, given the constraints of printer resolution.

The technology embodied in Fontware actually amounts to a set of artificial intelligence algorithms that check the results of the outline-to-bitmap conversions and make minor revisions, just like the typographic ex-

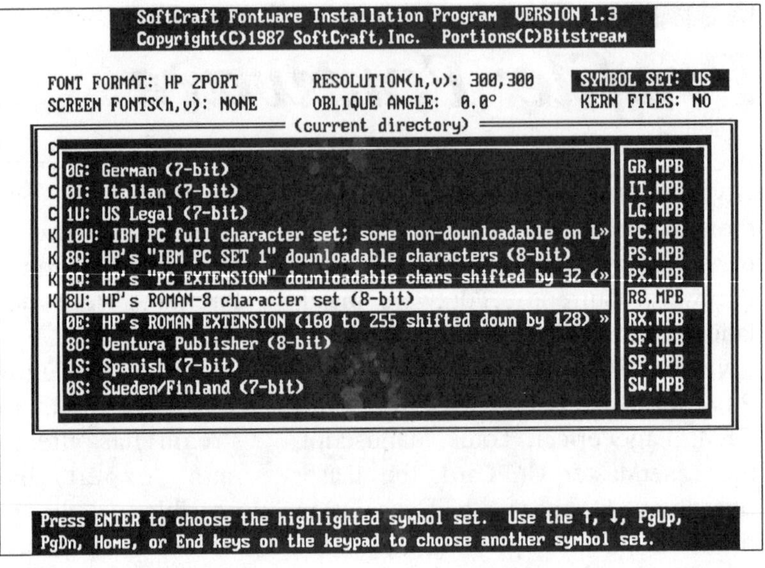

Figure 1: Fontware provides a scrolling list of the available symbol sets for the font you wish to generate.

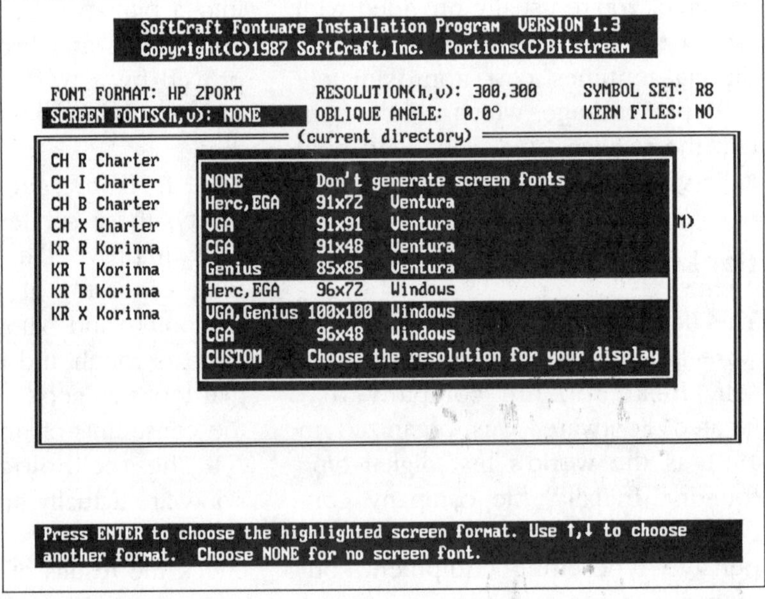

Figure 2: You have the option of installing screen fonts for several display standards. Not generating screen fonts saves space on your hard disk. Use EGA for big-screen monitors like the Viking I.

pert. Other font-generating software is beginning to incorporate such algorithms, but the technology developed by Bitstream is still unsurpassed.

Creating a Font

There are a growing number of Fontware installation kits for various programs. Although there are superficial differences between them, they all work in essentially the same way. As a user, your main concern is to provide Fontware with the specifications it needs to generate the font (or fonts) you want. Among the specifications to be aware of are the following:

- Printer
- Monitor
- Typeface
- Sizes
- Character set

Printer

Some versions of Fontware, such as SoftCraft's, support only the LaserJet Plus and the LaserJet II. Other versions, including the one marketed by Bitstream itself, also support other laser printers and laser printer enhancement boards. If you have one of those versions, you can continue using Fontware if you upgrade your LaserJet to PostScript with the Jet-Script board.

Access

Fontware
Bitstream, Inc.
Athenaeum House
215 First St.
Cambridge, MA 02142
617/497-7514
Price: Installation kits for software applications $95 each, font packages $195 each

Monitor

If you use Fontware to generate fonts for a WYSIWYG desktop publishing package such as Ventura or PageMaker, you may also want to generate screen fonts that match your printer fonts. The advantage of having screen fonts to match your printer fonts is that you'll be able to get a nearly WYSIWYG view of your page while you're working in your page makeup program.

The disadvantage of having screen fonts is that they take up room on your hard disk and, more important, can take up RAM that your page makeup program would otherwise have available for other purposes. Ventura, for example, slows down if too many screen fonts are installed, so you'll need to be judicious.

Fontware can take care of this task for all the graphics display standards (CGA, EGA, Hercules, VGA) as

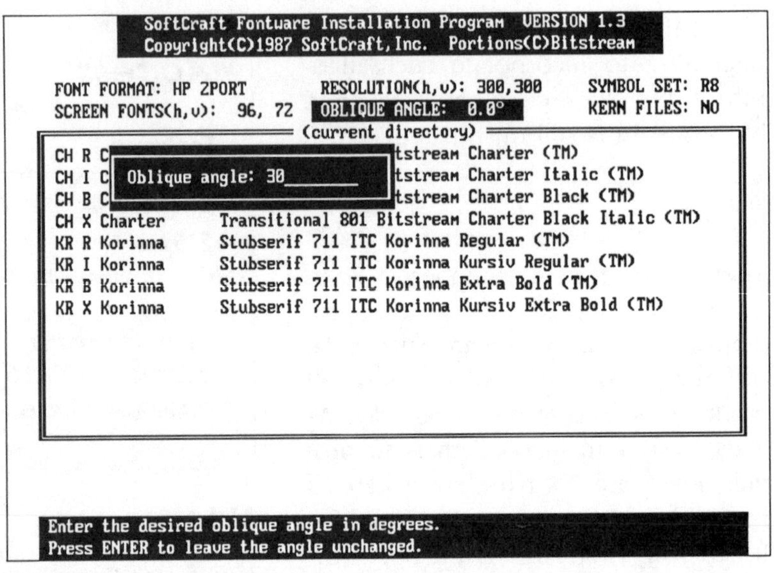

Figure 3: If you wish, you can generate a font in which all the characters are slanted at a uniform angle. This technique is called "obliquing."

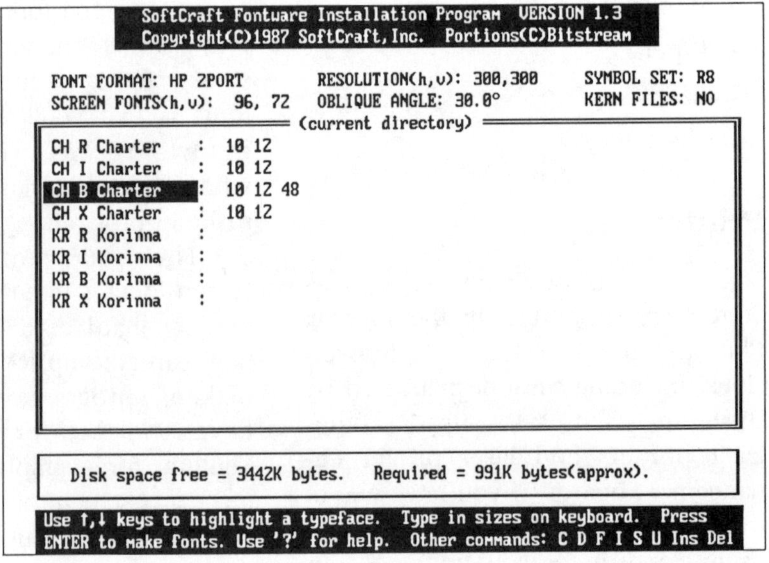

Figure 4: On the final selection screen, you select the fonts and sizes. On the bottom you can see the amount of free space on your hard disk and the amount needed for the selected fonts.

abcdefghijklmnopqrstuvwxyz
ABCDEFGHIJKLMNOPQRSTUVWXYZ
1234567890&$£%.,:;-!?"

abcdefghijklmnopqrstuvwxyz
ABCDEFGHIJKLMNOPQRSTUVWXYZ
1234567890&$£%.,:;-!?"

abcdefghijklmnopqrstuvwxyz
ABCDEFGHIJKLMNOPQRSTUVWXYZ
1234567890&$£%.,:;-!?"

abcdefghijklmnopqrstuvwxyz
ABCDEFGHIJKLMNOPQRSTUVWXYZ
1234567890&$£%.,:;-!?"

Figure 5: The Bitstream Charter family, a new set of typefaces designed by Bitstream's Mattthew Carter for optimal appearance at laser printer resolution.

well as for a number of high-resolution monitors (Viking 1, Sigma LaserView, Wyse 700 or Amdex 1200, Genius, and others).

Typeface

At this writing, outlines were available for more than 30 typeface families, and within most of these families there are four variations: roman, italic, bold, and bold italic. The families include Swiss (similar to Helvetica), Dutch (similar to Times Roman), Century Schoolbook, Zapf Calligraphic, Futura Light, Swiss Light, Futura Book, Futura Medium, Courier, Letter Gothic, Prestige, ITC Avant Garde, Zapf Humanist, ITC Garamond, ITC Souvenir, ITC Korinna, ITC Galliard, Bitstream Cooper Black, Broadway, University Roman, and Cloister Black. Most of these typefaces are already popular in commercial typography. In addition, Bitstream's Matthew Carter has developed the Charter family, which is designed to be especially crisp and legible when rendered by a laser printer.

Of course, to use any of these typefaces you'll have to shell out $195 for the outline package—no trifle if all you want to do is print an occasional caption in that particular font.

Sizes

To generate Fontware fonts, you need to specify the sizes you want. Because of the amount of memory each font requires once you have generated it, you'll need to be judicious and not clog your hard disk with too many sizes. Memory requirements for fonts are described below. Note that the maximum size Fontware font you can use with a LaserJet Plus is about 36 points; with a LaserJet II it is about 72 points. The former limit is due to the hardware; the latter is due to Fontware.

Character Set or Symbol Set

As discussed in Chapter 14, "LaserJet Font Basics," a character set or symbol set is the specific collection of symbols that together constitute a font. The character sets generated by Fontware all include the English alphabet, but they differ in the remaining characters they provide, such as punctuation marks, special symbols, and foreign accented characters.

With the version of Fontware marketed by Bitstream, you can generate the VP US character set (116 characters), the VP International character set (190 characters) or the PostScript Outline character set (186 characters). With the version marketed by SoftCraft, you can generate ten 7-bit character sets (USASCII, ECMA,

Font Storage Requirements

Font Name and Symbol Set	Kb
6-pt Charter regular, USASCII symbol set	6
12-pt Charter regular, USASCII symbol set	25
24-pt Charter regular, USASCII symbol set	103
36-pt Charter regular, USASCII symbol set	232
72-pt Charter bold, USASCII symbol set	930
72-pt Charter bold, Roman-8 symbol set	1,840

Figure 6: Amount of hard disk storage required for typical fonts of varying sizes.

Typeface / Applications	Directions	Forms	Newsletters—Text	Newsletters—Headlines	Instruction Manuals	Proposals	Flyers	Books	Catalogs	Office Correspondence	Presentation Materials
ITC Avant Garde Gothic	●		●	●			●				●
Baskerville			●			●		●			
Century Schoolbook			●	●		●		●	●		●
Bitstream Charter	●			●					●	●	●
Dutch			●			●		●			
Futura Book	●	●					●		●		●
Futura Medium	●		●	●	●		●		●		●
ITC Galliard			●			●		●			
ITC Garamond			●			●		●			
ITC Garamond Condensed			●	●		●					
Goudy Old Style			●					●			
Headlines 1				●			●				●
Headlines 2				●			●				●
Headlines 3				●			●				●
ITC Korinna			●				●				●
Swiss	●	●	●	●	●		●		●		●
Swiss Condensed	●	●		●	●				●		
Zapf Calligraphic			●		●	●		●			●
Zapf Humanist	●		●		●			●	●	●	

Figure 7: This table is distributed by Bitstream to provide some general guidelines for selecting typefaces.

UK, French, German, Italian, Spanish, Swedish/Finnish, Danish/Norwegian, and Legal). You can also generate the following 8-bit sets: SoftCraft, IBM PC, HP Roman-8, HP Roman Extension, Windows/ANSI, Ventura, HP IBM PC, and HP IBM PC Extension.

In selecting which character set to generate, you can refer to complete tables of characters in the back of the FontWare documentation. For example, if you want true typographic quotation marks, you should use the Ventura or the Windows/ANSI set and avoid the Roman-8 or IBM PC sets.

A major consideration in selecting a character set is the amount of memory that will be required. Generally, large fonts are used only in headlines and do not require special characters. So to save the amount of memory needed, you should choose USASCII, the character set with the smallest number of elements (just the keyboard characters, numbers, and punctuation marks).

Storage Requirements

The amount of storage required for various fonts is shown in the table below. Note that the amount of memory increases proportionally to the square of the point size—in other words, it takes about four times as much memory to store a 24-point font as to store a 12-point font, other factors being equal.

Using a Font with Software

Once you've generated a font, you'll still need to download it to the printer and create a driver for your software application. Depending on the version of Fontware you are using, one or both of these tasks may be handled more or less automatically. For example, Bitstream's version of Fontware for Ventura creates the necessary Ventura WID file when it generates a font. If your Fontware package does not take care of downloading and drivers for a particular application, you'll have to take of these tasks yourself. Refer to Chapter 15, "Downloading Fonts and Building Drivers."

Profile: Glyphix

WHEN IT COMES to font generators, there's no doubt that products based on Bitstream's Fontware technology or on Compugraphic's Intellifont technology will rule the roost for the forseeable future. But if any low-end competitor does survive, it will likely be Glyphix. The program stands out for two reasons:

- Glyphix's master font outlines are quite cheap, and the quality, as shown in Figure 1, is respectable. While the master outlines for a single typeface family cost about $195 with Fontware, you can get four typeface families for Glyphix for only $100.
- Versions of Glyphix for Microsoft Word and WordPerfect (and soon for Ventura and PageMaker), generate fonts on the fly from within the application program, so there's no need to precompile the fonts you need or use up space on your hard disk.

Determining Parameters

As is the case with other font generators, Glyphix uses master outlines to produce bitmapped fonts at specific sizes. Glyphix works like a police artist. You give it the details—typeface, point size, fill pattern, and so forth—and it puts these together to build you a font. When you start the program, all the parameters that make up a font are listed in a menu on the right side of the screen. These include typeface, orientation, size, expansion (for creating extra-wide or compressed type), weight, degree of slanting, and fill pattern.

You start by selecting the typeface. A Helvetica-style typeface called Helvette comes with the program. Three additional styles—Roman (similar to Times Roman), Chancelor (similar to Zapf Chancery, a typeface with a calligraphic appearance), and Rockland (a blocky font similar to Lubalin Graph). The next parameter, and obviously one of the most crucial, is size. Glyphix allows you to create fonts as large as 60 points.

Next comes the expansion ratio. With this control you can compress a font so that it takes up as little as one-quarter the normal horizontal space, or expand it so that it takes four times the normal space. The control for weight, i.e. the boldness or lightness of the type, provides a range from -5 (for very light type) to 9 (for very heavy type). The default is 0, which produces normal type.

Roman

ABCDEFGHIJKLMNOPQRSTUVWXYZ
abcdefghijklmnopqrstuvwxyz
0123456789
~'!@#$%^&*()-_=+\|[{]};:'",<.>/?

Roman is the most popular font to use for small type.

Helvette

ABCDEFGHIJKLMNOPQRSTUVWXYZ
abcdefghijklmnopqrstuvwxyz
0123456789
~'!@#$%^&*()-_=+\|[{]};:'",<.>/?

Helvette complements Roman well when used in headlines.

Rockland

ABCDEFGHIJKLMNOPQRSTUVWXYZ
abcdefghijklmnopqrstuvwxyz
0123456789
~`!@#$%^&*()-_=+\|[{]};:'",<.>/?

The blocky look of Rockland makes strong, bold headlines.

Chancelor

ABCDEFGHIJKLMNOPQRSTUVWXYZ
abcdefghijklmnopqrstuvwxyz
0123456789
~'!@#$%^&*()-_=+\|[{]};:'",<.>/?

The handwritten look of Chancelor conveys a personal touch.

With Glyphix's fill pattern option, you can put a decorative spin on workaday typefaces like Helvetica. The fill patterns include black; five shades of gray; horizontal, vertical, or diagonal stripes; cross hatching; and tiny squares. Finally, the slant parameter lets you specify a tilt of up to 25 degrees, an effect known to typographers as "obliquing."

Once you've decided on the parameters you want, you can press Test Print to get immediate feedback on your design. In less than a minute, Glyphix generates the entire character set for the font and prints out a sample. If you like the results, pressing Soft Font File loads the file onto your hard disk for future use; alternatively Download File loads it into immediately into the printer.

Convenient, yes—but what about quality? While slightly lower than Fontware, Glyphix fonts are acceptable for most purposes, and the appearance has definitely improved since the first release of the product.

Integrating with Software

The final question is: Will I be able to use it with my software? As noted above, you can use Glyphix to generate fonts on the fly from within Microsoft Word or WordPerfect, by separately purchasing an $80 Font Manager for each of those programs. With the Font Manager, your fonts are generated and downloaded automatically without the intermediate step of creating a file on your hard disk. And Glyphix also creates the necessary Word or WordPerfect driver, so you'll still be able to print nicely justified columns. Amazingly enough, the RAM-resident version of Glyphix takes up only about 40K of RAM, so it's feasible to run it in this fashion

Access

Glyphix Basics, Glyphix Basics II, Glyphix Book Faces, Glyphix Sans Serif Faces, Glyphix Decorative Faces, Glyphix Fixed Faces, Glyphix WordPerfect Font Manager, Glyphix MS Word Font Manager, Glyphix Pop 'n' Print
SWFTE International
Box 5773
Wilmington, DE 19808
800/237-9383
302/733-0956
Price: $79.95 WordPerfect Font Manager, $79.95 MS Word Font Manager, all others $99.95

Figure 1 (Facing Page): This example—reduced 18 percent—shows fonts generated from the four outlines provided with Glyphix: Roman (Times Roman), Helvette (Helvetica), Rockland (Lubalin Graph), and Chancelor (Zapf Chancery).

without depriving your application of the memory it needs.

With other programs, you'll need to generate your fonts outside the application and then use a font utility to create the necessary drivers. This need not be a difficult process. For example, with Ventura Publisher, I generated a new font, tested it with Glyphix, downloaded it to my hard disk, built a new Ventura width table, reformatted a document to contain the new font in a headline, and printed it—all in less than 10 minutes.

For those willing to make some comprises in type quality for a big savings in money and time, Glyphix should be a valuable supplement to your LaserJet tool chest.

CHAPTER FIFTEEN

Downloading Fonts and Building Drivers

ONCE YOU HAVE purchased a set of fonts or created them with a font generator such as Fontware, you are ready for the final two steps: transferring them to the printer and teaching your software applications to recognize them.

Downloading Fonts

The process of transferring fonts from a storage location such as a floppy disk into a laser printer is called downloading. This is often done transparently and automatically by the software program. If so, you're in luck. If not, you'll have to do the downloading yourself using one of the do-it-yourself methods or one of the software utilities described in this chapter.

In some cases, even if your application does have the ability to automatically download the fonts it needs, you still may want to perform the process manually because downloading a set of fonts once at the beginning of the day is more efficient than having the software load them repeatedly each time it needs them. Once you have downloaded the fonts, you can turn the automatic downloading feature of your software off.

Which Fonts Must Be Downloaded?

Some fonts are permanently stored in the LaserJet and therefore don't have to be downloaded. Other fonts are contained in cartridges and also don't have to be downloaded. Downloading is only necessary for soft fonts, whether stored on floppy disks or on your computer's hard disk.

Creating Drivers

Once you have downloaded fonts into the printer, the next step is to teach your software application to recognize them. With most programs, this task is handled by a *driver,* a separate software module containing information needed by the application to work with a certain printer.

It used to be that when you bought a software application such as a word processing program, it would be provided with a driver for several different printers. For example, one driver would be for the Epson FX-80, another for the Diablo 640, and so forth. Now, it's not unusual for a major software application such as Microsoft Word or WordPerfect to come with 20 or 30 drivers for the LaserJet alone. Each driver works with a particular font cartridge or set of soft fonts.

Even with that many drivers provided, it's still likely that if you purchase a new set of soft fonts, none of the drivers will work and you'll have to generate an entirely new driver. For that purpose, you'll need to buy a special utility program.

Before we take a look at the available utilities, let's consider some cases in which it *won't* be necessary for you to purchase a driver generating utility:

- If you're using HP's own soft fonts with Microsoft Word 4.0 or WordPerfect 5.0. The reason is that both these programs come with drivers for HP's full set of soft fonts.
- If you're using WordStar 2000. That program is bundled with its own font utility (Conofonts Manager), which both downloads fonts from any vendor and creates WordStar 2000 drivers for them.
- If you're using Ventura. Fonts almost always come with the WID files used by Ventura. As long as the WID files are available, you won't need any separate program to generate drivers.
- If you're using fonts purchased from VS Software with Microsoft Word or WordPerfect. VS Software provides the Word Processor Tool Kit with all its soft fonts and with its FontGen font editing program. The Word Processor Tool Kit takes care of downloading and builds drivers for Microsoft Word and WordPerfect.

Survey of Utilities

If you find that you do need to purchase a utility for downloading your fonts and building drivers, you need to get one that makes the process as easy as possible. As described below, there are a number of utility programs available for that purpose. In selecting such a program, here are some features to look for:

- Does the utility automatically list your fonts and allow you to select the ones you want? If not, you'll have to make sure you keep careful notes on your font names—a tedious and error-prone task.
- Does the utility let you create a setup file that will download a group of fonts at once? If not, you'll waste a lot of time downloading each font separately.
- Does the utility create drivers for your software application? If not, you'll only be able to download the fonts but not print with them.

FontLoad

FontLoad, Hewlett-Packard's own font-downloading utility, does meet the first two criteria above but not the third. Therefore, if you choose this utility and want to use the fonts with programs such as Microsoft Word or WordPerfect, you'll need to obtain an additional utility that builds printer drivers. For details on FontLoad, see the profile on the program that follows this chapter.

Laser Fonts

This is probably the best of the font downloading and driver generation utilities. It is described in "Profile: Laser Fonts."

Glyphix Font Managers

The Glyphix Font Managers for WordPerfect and Microsoft Word are unique in that they let you generate and download fonts from within the word processing program. However, they can only be used with Glyphix's own font outlines, not with fonts from other vendors.

Font Control

This program is less convenient to use than HP's FontLoad or SoftCraft's Laser Fonts. Rather than automatically listing the names of the fonts on your disk, it requires you to type them in and thus does not meet the first criterion listed above. Typing font names manually is difficult for two reasons. First, it is easy to make a mistake, and if you incorrectly enter even one character of the font name, the font will not load correctly. Also, to know what names to type you have to keep notes on the contents of the directories that contain your fonts.

In addition to downloading fonts, Font Control creates drivers for Microsoft Word and WordStar 2000, but not for WordPerfect.

Two useful features of Font Control are that it lets you mix soft fonts and cartridge fonts on a single page and it runs on a Novell Network.

Laser Word Processor Tool Kit

This program is provided free with VS Software's FontGen and with any of the fonts sold by VS Software. You can also purchase it separately for $50. Besides downloading fonts to the printer, it builds drivers for Microsoft Word, WordPerfect, and Spellbinder.

In its current release, the program is not as easy to use as Font Control or Conofonts Manager, because it does not meet Criteria 1. On the other hand, at $50 it's the best value of any of the available utilities.

Conofonts Manager

In a world where clumsy, simple utility programs are the norm, the capabililties of the ittle-known Conofonts Manager are a pleasant surprise. The program is entirely menu-driven, using a unique windowing interface. It's straightforward and easy to use.

Conofonts Manager meets all three criteria listed above. You don't have to remember the names of your fonts, because it does that for you. You can create "sets" of fonts, so you don't have to tediously download one font at a time. Finally, Conofonts Manager creates the necessary drivers for MultiMate Advantage II, WordPerfect, WordStar 2000, and Microsoft Word.

If your application does not have a LaserJet driver, you can still use Conofonts Manager to designate a "primary" font and download it to the printer. You can then use your application to print with that font, though you won't be able to switch from that font to any others.

ID Numbers

All font-downloading utilities will give you the option of choosing an ID number for each font. You can safely ignore this ID number under the following circumstances:

- if your software application already provides a driver that lets you access the font you are downloading, or
- if you are using a utility that lets you generate a driver for the font.

You'll need to pay attention to the ID number (i.e., make a note of what number you have assigned) under the following circumstances:

- if you will be selecting the font with the control panel, or
- if you will be selecting the font using PCL commands.

Permanent/Temporary

If you specify that the fonts you are downloading are permanent, they will remain in the printer until the power is turned off. If you specify that the fonts are to be temporary, they will be erased from the printer's memory any time it receives a soft reset (Escape E). Many application programs automatically transmit a soft reset to the printer at the end of printing. You can also send a soft reset manually by pressing the ON LINE key on the Control Panel to take the printer off-line and then pressing and holding the CONTINUE RESET key for about five seconds.

Batch Files

Once you have created a setup file with a downloading utility, it is a convenient practice to make the downloading procedure a batch file that is executed at the beginning of each day or each working session. For example, if the LaserJet is shared by a work group, the group can decide what fonts it wants to have available and give one person the responsibility to download those fonts every day.

Manual Downloading

Despite the many utility programs on the market that take care of downloading fonts, you may still find it necessary to do the downloading yourself. To do this, you'll have to figure out how to create a one-character file containing the escape character (ASCII 27). This is described in Chapter 19, "Programming the LaserJet with PCL." Once you have created the one-character file, save it as ESCAPE. Then do the following steps:

- From the DOS prompt, type
  COPY ESCAPE+CON PRN
  ***c8D**
  Ctrl-Z
  This assigns the number 8 as the font ID for the font you are going to download. You can use any number in place of 8.
- Type
  copy/b *fontname* prn
  This downloads the font into the printer. The /b option is necessary to keep the file clear of any extraneous characters that DOS would otherwise attach to it.
- Type
  COPY ESCAPE+ CON
  ***c5F**
  Ctrl-Z
  This makes the font permanent (so that it will not be deleted by a soft reset, which many applications routinely send to the printer).

Access: Font Management Utilities

ConoFonts Manager
Conographics Corporation
16802 Aston
Irvine, CA 92714
714/474-1188
Price: $70

FontLoad
See "Profile: FontLoad"

Glyphix
See "Profile: Glyphix"

Laser Fonts
See "Profile: Laser Fonts"

Polaris Font Control
Polaris Software
613 West Valley Pkwy #323
Escondido, CA 92025
619/743-7800
Price: $99

VS Laser Word Processor Tool Kit
VS Software
2101 S. Broadway
Little Rock, AR 72216
501/376-2083
Price: $50 or free with font purchase

Memory Limitations

In a LaserJet Plus or LaserJet II without added memory, a maximum of about 395Kb is available for storing fonts and graphics; however, as a practical matter you should avoid downloading more than 290Kb of fonts. That's not much, when you consider that a single 12-point font will typically take up about 15Kb to 25Kb and a 24-point font will require 100Kb or more. Memory limitations are especially important in a work group, where it's virtually mandatory that everyone agree upon a set of fonts that will be downloaded to the printer.

Another limitation of the LaserJet Plus and the LaserJet II is that no more than 32 fonts can be downloaded at once, and no more than 16 fonts can be printed on a single page.

There are two significant differences between the LaserJet Plus and the LaserJet II. One is that while the LaserJet Plus is limited to 30-point or 36-point type (depending on the number of characters in the font), the LaserJet II is limited to 655-point type.

Profile: FontLoad

ALTHOUGH HP'S FONTLOAD is not as capable as some of the utilities on the market that also create drivers for word processing programs, it is a very useful tool if all you need to do is download a set of fonts. Here is the procedure for downloading a font with FontLoad.

- Type
  CD \directory name
  to switch to the subdirectory containing the FontLoad program
- Type
  FLOAD
  to load the program
- Press F1 to tell FontLoad that you are creating a new "setup" (i.e., a collection of fonts to be downloaded).
- Type
  directory name
  to indicate the directory on your hard disk containing your soft fonts. For example, if the fonts are located in the directory FONTS in the C: driver, type
  \FONTS
- In response, FontLoad will display a list of all the soft fonts in that subdirectory.
- Move the cursor to the font you want to download and press F1 to select it. If you want to download another font as well,

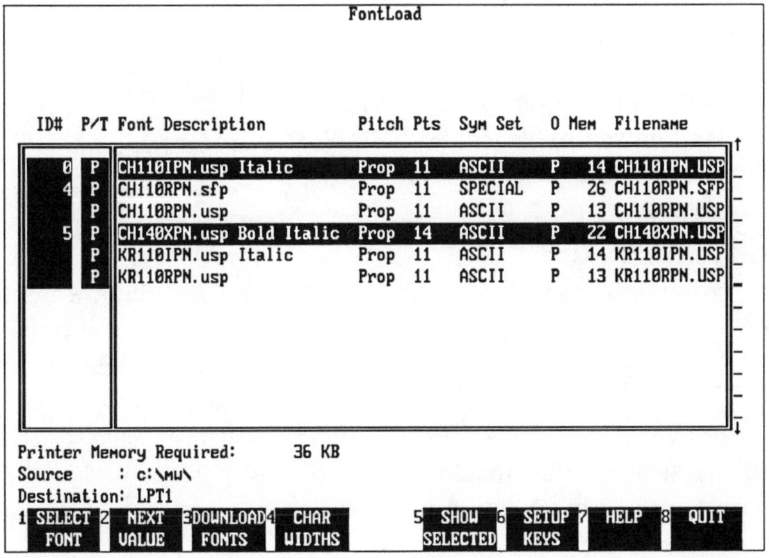

Figure 1: This is the main menu for FontLoad. The commands shown at the bottom of the screen are selected by pressing the function keys.

move the cursor to it and press F1 again. FontLoad will show which fonts you have selected by displaying their names in black rather than light type.

- FontLoad will automatically assign each font an ID number (indicated by the number in the first column) and a Permanent or Temporary Status (indicated by a P or a T in the second column). You can change these values if you wish, using the cursor and the F2 key.
- Press F6 to switch the menu to show the Setup Commands.
- Press F3 to save your setup, and type in the file name you wish to use for the setup.
- Exit FontLoad.
- Hereafter, each time you wish to download the set of fonts you included in the Setup File, you merely type
  *path***FLOAD** *path\setname*
  For example, if both FontLoad and a setup file called SETUP1 are in the directory FONTS in the C: drive, type

```
C:\FONTS\FLOAD
C:\FONTS\SETUP1
```

Automatic Font Listing

As shown in the above scenario, one of the features that makes FontLoad easy to use is that it automatically displays the names of the fonts that are contained in a specified directory. All you have to do is press the right function key to pick the set of fonts you wish to download or save in a permanent setup file.

Make sure you avoid any font-downloading program that makes you remember and type in font names rather than showing them automatically.

Access

FontLoad
Hewlett-Packard Company
Boise Division
11311 Chinden Blvd.
Boise, ID 83707
800/538-8787
408/738 4133 California
Price: $20
HP Part No. 33407

Batch Files

Rather than starting from square one every time you want to download some fonts, it's a good idea to create batch files for automatically downloading a set of fonts to the printer. Let's suppose your setup file, called FONTSET1, and the FontLoad program are both stored in the C: drive in directory LJ. To create the batch file from DOS, type

```
COPY CON DOWNLOAD.BAT
```

```
c:\LJ\FLOAD c:\LJ\FONTSET1
^Z
```

Once you have set up the file with the above commands, all you have to do is type DOWNLOAD (or include the command DOWNLOAD as a separate line in your Autoexec.bat file) to transmit FONTSET1 to the printer.

Profile: Laser Fonts

OF ALL THE FONT utilities on the market, SoftCraft's Laser Fonts is the most capable. Previously, Laser Fonts was somewhat more difficult to use than other such programs because it required you to manually type in the names of any fonts you wanted to work with. As of Version 3, however, everything is done by means of easy-to-use menus—a big improvement.

Here are some of the tasks that Laser Fonts takes care of:

- Downloading fonts one at a time. You can do this straight from the Laser Fonts menus, or else you can create a batch file to make the process automatic.
- Downloading a set of fonts. Same thing: use the menus or set up a batch file for automatic operation.
- Creating drivers for Microsoft Word and WordPerfect. You can either set up separate drivers for your fonts or merge the new drivers with your old drivers.
- Keeping track of how much memory your font set will take up and warning you if you go over the printer or word processor limit.
- Resetting the printer.
- Deleting downloaded fonts.

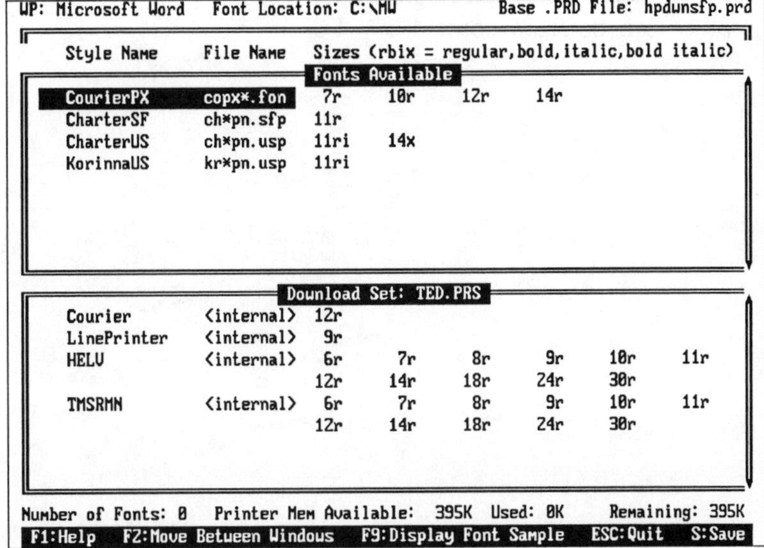

Figure 1: The font-selection menu for Laser Fonts. Available fonts are shown at the top, and the fonts that you want to add to your word processor are at the bottom.

- Activating manual or automatic paper feed.
- Ejecting a page.
- Switching to portrait or landscape orientation.
- Selecting legal- or letter-size paper.
- Selecting number of copies.
- Selecting a font by ID number.
- Printing a test string (any text you choose to print to test your font selection).

As shown in Figure 1, the Laser Fonts display has two windows. The top window shows all the fonts in your directory. The bottom window shows the fonts in your download set.

Laser Fonts Version 3 comes with a utility called Laser Graphics, which prepares graphics images for including in documents created by Microsoft Word 4.0 and WordPerfect 5.0. Such graphics can be from Lotus 1-2-3, PC Paintbrush, or captured screens.

Access

Laser Fonts, Version 3.0
SoftCraft, Inc.
16 N. Carroll St. #500
Madison, WI 53703
608/257-3300
Price: $180

CHAPTER SIXTEEN

Screen Fonts

THE PHILOSOPHY UNDERLYING the new generation of desktop publishing programs such as PageMaker and Ventura Publisher is called WYSIWYG, or What You See Is What You Get.

In order for this to happen, the type shown on the display has to look the same as the type that is printed. Also, the relative widths taken up by each character should be the same for the type shown on the screen as for the printed type. Otherwise, the widths of lines would differ and the two versions of the document would not match.

If the resolution of the display was the same as the resolution of the printer, there would be no problem, because the same font files could be used for both the display and the printer. But the resolutions do not match. While the LaserJet prints 300 dots per inch, the resolution of monitors ranges from around 50 to 150 dpi.

Besides the difference in resolution, the shape of the dots differs. Printer dots are square, but some monitors such as the EGA and the VGA use rectangular dots.

Because of these discrepancies between monitor and printer, WYSIWYG programs such as Ventura and PageMaker require that you install separate screen fonts to match your printer fonts.

Screen Fonts and DTP

Both Ventura and Windows provide a basic set of default screen fonts. Ventura comes with its own Dutch (same as Times Roman) and Swiss (same as Helvetica) screen fonts, so if you're just using those two fonts to print, you don't have to worry about installing screen fonts. If you purchase other printer fonts, for example Garamond or Futura, you can go ahead and use them without worrying about installing matching screen fonts. The reason is that Ventura will default to either Dutch (for serif fonts like Garamond) or Swiss (for sans serif fonts like Futura). In other words, the program uses Dutch and Swiss as generic serif and sans serif screen fonts.

In fact, even if you did have the option of installing screen fonts for your printer, you still might want to go on using the generic fonts. Why? Because screen fonts eat up valuable memory that your computer would otherwise use to hold large documents. Also, by eating up memory, screen fonts often slow the computer down signficantly.

The choice is yours: Stick to the generic fonts when you want to maximize the speed of the program and the size of the document it can handle; use screen fonts when you want to do onscreen manual kerning and when you need to accurately preview letter spacing.

To summarize, having a screen font to match every printer font with Ventura or PageMaker and Windows is nice if you can manage it, but don't forget that there are trade-offs.

Screen Font Software

Several software programs are available for generating screen fonts. One is Bitstream's Fontware, which can be set up to generate matching screen fonts whenever it generates printer fonts. The other is SoftCraft's WYSIfonts!, which is capable of analyzing an existing printer font and then automatically generating a screen font to match it. Basically, Fontware is useful for generating screen fonts that match new printer fonts. For older printer fonts that lack screen fonts, use WYSIfonts!. For more details, see "Profile: WYSIfonts!," and "Profile: Fontware."

Profile: WYSIfonts!

THIS PROGRAM HELPS Ventura and PageMaker users beef up the What You See side of the WYSIWYG equation. If you're using fonts with those programs that don't come with matching screen fonts, WYSIfonts! can create them and also assist with the installation process.

Another benefit of the program is that it makes it easier to install new fonts into either Ventura or PageMaker.

Here are some simple guidelines to help you decide whether you need WYSIfonts!:

- If you're using Ventura with only the Dutch (Times Roman), Swiss (Helvetica), Symbol, and Courier typefaces supplied with the program, you don't need WYSIfonts! because the program includes matching screen fonts for those typefaces.
- If you're using Bitstream's Fontware to add fonts to Ventura and PageMaker, you don't need WYSIfonts! to generate screen fonts because Fontware takes care of generating matching screen fonts if you ask it to. However, WYSIfonts! can make installing the screen and printer fonts much easier.
- If you're adding fonts to Ventura from sources other than Bitstream's Fontware, you don't have to have matching screen fonts in order to print, but using WYSIfonts! will make installation easier and will give you a better representation of your page on the screen.
- If you're adding fonts to PageMaker or other Windows applications from vendors other than Bitstream, WYSIfonts! will make installation easier.

As the above guidelines show, WYSIfonts! really has a twofold purpose. First, it generates screen fonts. Second, it makes installation of *any* fonts (screen or printer) a good deal easier with Ventura or Windows.

Access

WYSIfonts!
SoftCraft, Inc.
16 N. Carroll Street
Suite 500
Madison, WI 53703
800/351-0500
608/257-3300
Price: $95

One caution that you should be aware of is that the quality of the screen fonts created by WYSIfonts! is not as good as the screen fonts provided with Ventura and PageMaker or generated by Fontware. This is due to the automatic process used by WYSIfonts! to compress 300-dpi printer fonts to 75-dpi screen fonts. Generally, the results are legible, but not perfect. Since you're only using the screen fonts to proof your pages, the lower quality doesn't matter much. However, if you do want to tune up the screen fonts, you can do so with the SoftCraft Font Editor or Publisher's Type Foundry.

CHAPTER SEVENTEEN

Font Editors and Enhancers

TYPE IS THE ACHILLES' heel of any laser printer. You might spend hundreds of dollars assembling a collection of fonts, and then find that it is useless because it lacks a character you need, such as the trademark symbol or the ballot box symbol, or true typographic quotation marks (ones that open and close).

Basically, a font is nothing more than a collection of one or two hundred pictures, each assigned a numerical code. A font editor is a software tool that lets you blow up individual characters on your computer display and change or replace them. In the past, font-editing software tended to be so difficult to use that few people took advantage of it. Now, well-designed, powerful products such as Publisher's Type Foundry and the SoftCraft Font Editor have made font editing accessible to everyone.

Most people use font editors such as Publisher's Type Foundry for the simple purpose of adding a few missing symbols to an existing commercial font. However, as with the computer itself, surprising new uses for a font editor may occur to you once you become familiar with the tool. With practice, you might go beyond merely altering an existing font and try your hand at developing a new font from scratch. While it's not likely that your new font will woo the *London Times* away from Times Roman, newly designed fonts are popping up every day for such diverse uses as publishing text in South Asian languages, printing chemical symbols, and providing numerous unusual symbols used in technical documentation.

Here are some of the things one might do with a font-editing program:

- Add your corporate logo to an existing font. For example, you could replace a little-used keyboard character such as ~ or ^

with the logo. Using the revised font, you could insert the logo into a document simply by typing that character.

- Add typographic characters such as true quotations marks or the registered trademark symbol to a font (such as any of the Hewlett-Packard fonts that use the ASCII character set) that lacks these elements.
- Add dingbats—special symbols such as the pointing hand frequently used in advertisements—to an existing font.
- Create an entirely new font for a non-European language.
- Design a new typeface.

As you can see, the tasks that might be attempted with a font-editing program range from simple tasks like adding a single new character for an existing font to complex projects creating an entirely new font from scratch.

All Font Editors Are Not Created Equal

Over the past few years, the state of the art in font-editing software has advanced greatly. Unfortunately, many obsolete programs are still on the market, waiting to snag the unsuspecting buyer. The crudest programs are those that must be used in conjunction with an ASCII text editor or word processing program. With the editor, you create each character as a pattern of dots or asterisks. You then save this pattern as a text file and

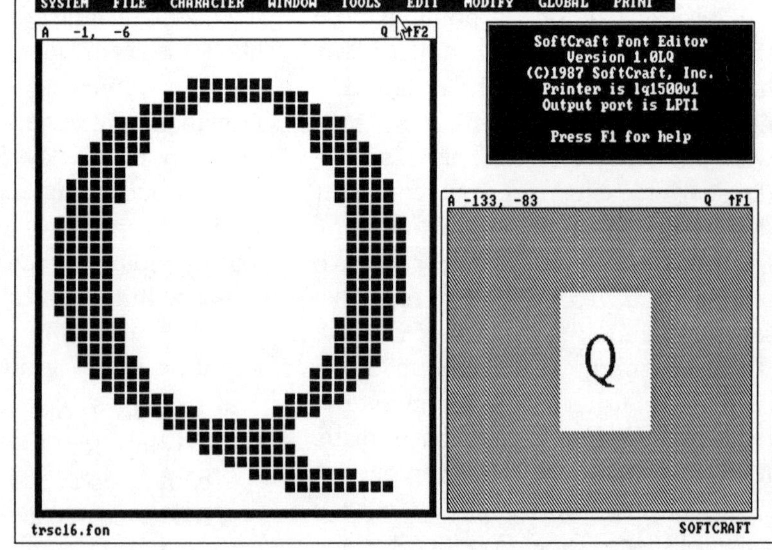

Figure 1: The SoftCraft Font Editor. On the left is the main editing window. On the right is a view of the current character. Tools are selected from the top menu bar.

merge it into an existing font using the font-editing program. Obviously, using this sort of font-editing system is tedious and slow. An example is SoftCraft's Efont program.

In contrast, the newest font-editing programs work much like painting programs. Using a mouse (or, alternatively, the keyboard), you draw your character on the screen using pens or brushes of adjustable thickness, line-drawing tools, and even tools to automatically create circles, ovals, and polygons.

Of all the programs on the market, the two with the most highly developed interface and set of tools are the SoftCraft Font Editor (SCFE) and Publisher's Type Foundry (PTF). Either tool makes it easy to carry out a task such as creating a logo or special symbol and merging it into an existing font. Where they diverge is in price and in advanced features. PTF is actually two programs, an outline editor and a bitmap editor. SCFE is a bitmap editor only. The following is a point-by-point comparison:

- SCFE does not require Microsoft Windows; PTF does.
- SCFE costs $290; PTF costs $495.
- SCFE edits only bitmap fonts, PTF edits bitmap fonts or outline fonts. The PTF outline-editing module is its strongest feature. It makes it possible to use PTF for creating PostScript fonts, which SCFE cannot do. It also can be brought into play in conjunction with the bitmap editor for generating bitmap fonts.
- SCFE includes tools for drawing ellipses, circles, polygons, and lines. PTF only includes tools in its bitmap module for drawing lines and polygons.

Because of the interesting potential of using the bitmap editor and the outline editor in tandem, we discuss Publisher's Type Foundry in greater detail in the next chapter.

Font Enhancers

Font enhancers are programs that are closely related to font editors. Rather than enabling you to freely alter a font, these programs let you apply special effects to existing fonts. With SoftCraft's Font Effects, for example, you can apply a variety of patterns to a font, including shades, stripes, checkerboard squares, basketweave, spots, and bricks. You can also shrink, stretch, reverse, or slant a font. Finally, you can alter the background of the font, apply a shadow, turn a font into an outline, and more.

Access: Font Editors and Enhancers

Font Effects
SoftCraft, Inc.
16 N. Carroll St. #500
Madison, WI 53703
800/351-0500
Price: $95

FontGen IV+
VS Software
P.O. Box 6158
2101 South Broadway
Little Rock, AR 72206
501/376-2083
Price: $250

FontMaster
Cooperative Office Systems
207 Holly Road
Edgewater, MD 21037
301/261-7570
Price: $150

MagicSeries: MagicFont
Computer Editype Systems
509 Cathedral Pkwy #10-A
New York, NY 10025
800/251-2223
212/222-8148
Price: $59

Profont Editing System
FontCenter
509 Marin St. #227
Thousand Oaks, CA 91360
805/373-1919
Price: $400

Publisher's Type Foundry
See "Profile: Publisher's Type Foundry"

SoftCraft Font Editor
SoftCraft, Inc.
16 N. Carroll St. #500
Madison, WI 53703
800/351-0500
Price: $290

Profile: Publisher's Type Foundry

THIS EXTREMELY POWERFUL program has two modules. One lets you work with outline fonts, which can then be used on PostScript printers. The other works with bitmapped fonts, which can then be used on PCL LaserJets. The remarkable thing is that it lets you move things back and forth between the two.

In order to be usable with all types of laser printers, a font editor must be a switch-hitter. Printers that incorporate the PostScript page description language work with characters stored in outline format, i.e., as scalable mathematic descriptions. Other printers, including the LaserJet, work with characters stored as bit maps, i.e., as stored patterns of dots that cannot be scaled.

While previous font editors have been available on the PC, all have worked exclusively with bitmap fonts. Type Foundry is new in that it lets you work with either outlines or bitmaps. Surprisingly, the Bitmap Editor and the Outline Editor actually are best used in tandem, whether your final product happens to be a bitmap font or an outline font.

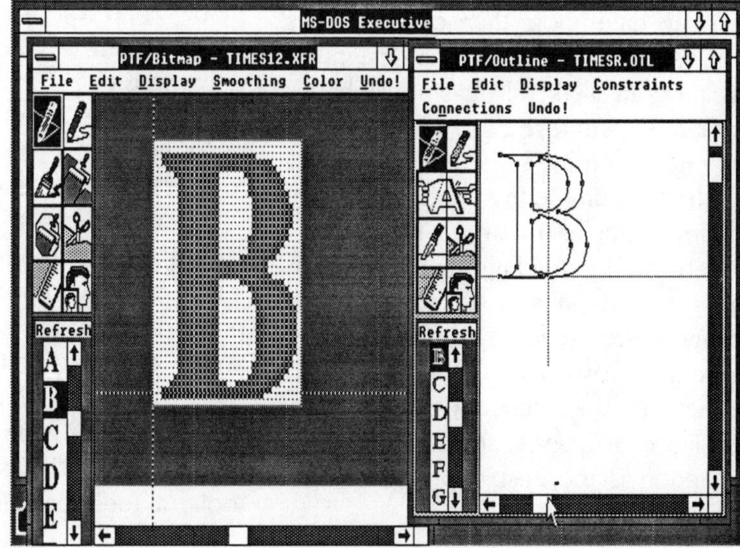

Figure 1: You can operate the Bitmap Editor and the Outline Editor in tandem by having them open in adjacent windows and moving characters back and forth from one to the other.

This pooling of talents is the most interesting feature of Type Foundry. For example, you might start in the Outline Editor drawing outlines of the characters you wish to add to a font, then switch to the Bitmap Editor for final cleanup. Alternatively, you might start by scanning in characters from paper, load them into the Bitmap Editor, automatically generate outlines, resize these outlines, then transfer them back to the Bitmap Editor for cleanup.

Whether you start with the Bitmap or the Outline Editor, the basic interface is similar. On the upper left are your drawing tools, on the lower left a scroll bar from which you select your font. On top are the menus. Most of the screen is devoted to a drawing area. If this area is not enough for your character, you can use scroll bars on the right and on the bottom. Because this is a Windows application, you can have more than one application open at a time, and the design of the program makes it feasible to have both the Outline Editor and the Bitmap Editor on the screen side-by-side.

In the simple case of altering a single character in an existing font, you begin by loading that font into the program. Most laser printer font formats are acceptable, including those sold by Bitstream and by the numerous third-party vendors that specialize in LaserJet fonts. The major exception is the PostScript fonts from

Access

Publisher's Type Foundry
ZSoft Corporation
450 Franklin Rd. #100
Marietta, GA 30067
404/428-0008
Price: $495

Adobe Systems, which use a propriety format.

As with all other procedures in Type Foundry, loading a new font is done Windows-style: by using the mouse to pull down a window-shade menu and then select the desired command name.

Once a font is loaded, the characters it comprises can be seen in a scroll bar on the left side of the screen. Clicking on one of these with the mouse causes the character to appear, enlarged, in the work area, where it can be altered using various drawing tools.

With the Bitmap Editor, those tools include a straight-line drawing tool, a freehand drawing tool, a tool for drawing blocks, a fill tool that "pours" pixels into any enclosed area, a tool for drawing polygons, a cut and paste tool, a tape measure, and a zoom feature. With the Outline Editor, the tools are a line-drawing tool, a tool for drawing Bezier curves, a tool for changing the shape of existing tools, a tool for selecting sections of the font, a tool for dividing one curve into two separate curves, a tool for moving parts of the font, a tape measure, and a zoom view.

Like many crafts, that of creating laser printer fonts combines some art and some attention to technical nuts and bolts. Using the graphics tools is the fun part of Type Foundry. The knuckle-skinning part arrives when it comes time to take care of the myriad technical details involved in converting fonts from one format to another and in specifying the technical parameters that make a font internally consistent and that allow it to be identified and used in the laser printer.

For dealing with the technical side of things, Type Foundry provides several dialog boxes. In the Font Description dialog box, you classify your font according to family, weight, character set, point size, and the resolution of your laser printer. In the Font Parameters dialog box, you specify the standard character pixel height, the numerical encoding of the font, the vertical space to be stored with the font, the maximum pixel width of the font, etc. Finally, a Global Changes dialog box allows you to apply scaling, slanting, and rotating uniformly to all characters in a font.

Collectively, the various obscure font manipulations possible with these dialog boxes amount to a large degree of power. It's a mixed blessing, because with this many options, you'll probably find mastering Type Foundry to be a greater challenge than mastering a complex page layout program like PageMaker or Ventura.

Fortunately, Type Foundry provides not only sheer font manipulation power but also some clever touches. One such innovation is the tape measure, with which you can quickly measure not only horizontal and vertical distances in your work area but also any diagonal distance. Another is the "Gadget Box," a set of tools for flipping, rotating, stretching, and scaling a character. A third is the the "Gravity" feature of the Constraints Menu, which allows you to precisely connect line and curve segments.

Of course, no software program in its first release is without a few stray bugs, and Type Foundry is no exception. For instance, during a simple walk-through of one of the tutorials described in the manual, the computer inexplicably froze up. Another problem is the lack of a few useful features, such as a tool for drawing circles and the ability to display the entire character set of a font. Another helpful addition would be the ability to place two characters next to each other in the working area to create a kerning pair. Finally, a trial-print feature, allowing an immediate printout of a font-in-progress, would make the process of refinement much quicker.

All things considered, however, Publisher's Type Foundry is a milestone in the push to bring PC desktop publishing tools up to the level of their Macintosh counterparts. And as a well-conceived Windows application, it should slide smoothly into your personal toolbox.

Profile: Font Effects

HOW WOULD YOU like to double or triple the size of your LaserJet font library for $90. That's actually what Font Effects can accomplish, and that also happens to be the actual price. As the example on the following page shows, Font Effects is a program that takes a normal, everyday font and applies special effects to it. In the example, shadows, outlining, and patterns were applied to the 30-point Garamond at the top, but this is just a taste of what Font Effects can do. Perhaps most importantly, it can also scale existing fonts, which means you can beef up your library with hard-to-find sizes, and not have to go out and buy additional soft font packages.

The various capabilities of Font Effects are all accessed from a straightforward menu. To get started, you enter the name of the font you wish to modify. If you can't remember the file name, Font Effects lets you search various directories using wildcards, without exiting the program. Next, you type the name of your new font. Right away, you can get to work experimenting with special effects.

The main capabilities of Font Effects are divided between two menu options. The "Effects" option lets you specify the parameters that control the outline of a font, the interior pattern, the background, the shadow, and countless variations on the above. The "Modify" option lets you scale a font by stretching it in the vertical and/or horizontal direction, and also lets you embolden the font or "fillet" it. Fillet refers to adding dots to smooth out jagged edges that result from generating a large font from a smaller one.

All the options would be overwhelming, except for the fact that the program includes a "Description" option that provides a number of precooked settings. In addition, the manual contains a number of easily followed recipes for various sorts of special effects. And if you come up with a new combination of effects that works particularly well, it's an easy matter to add your discovery to the existing selection of recipes. That's just one of the nice touches that keep popping up when you use Font Effects. Another is a context-sensitive help line that is always on display at the bottom of the screen, explaining the meaning of the sometimes cryptic menu options.

When you've decided on a set of parameters, you can proceed to preview your font onscreen and then generate the actual font file on your hard disk. Unfortunately, the generation process takes some time. A

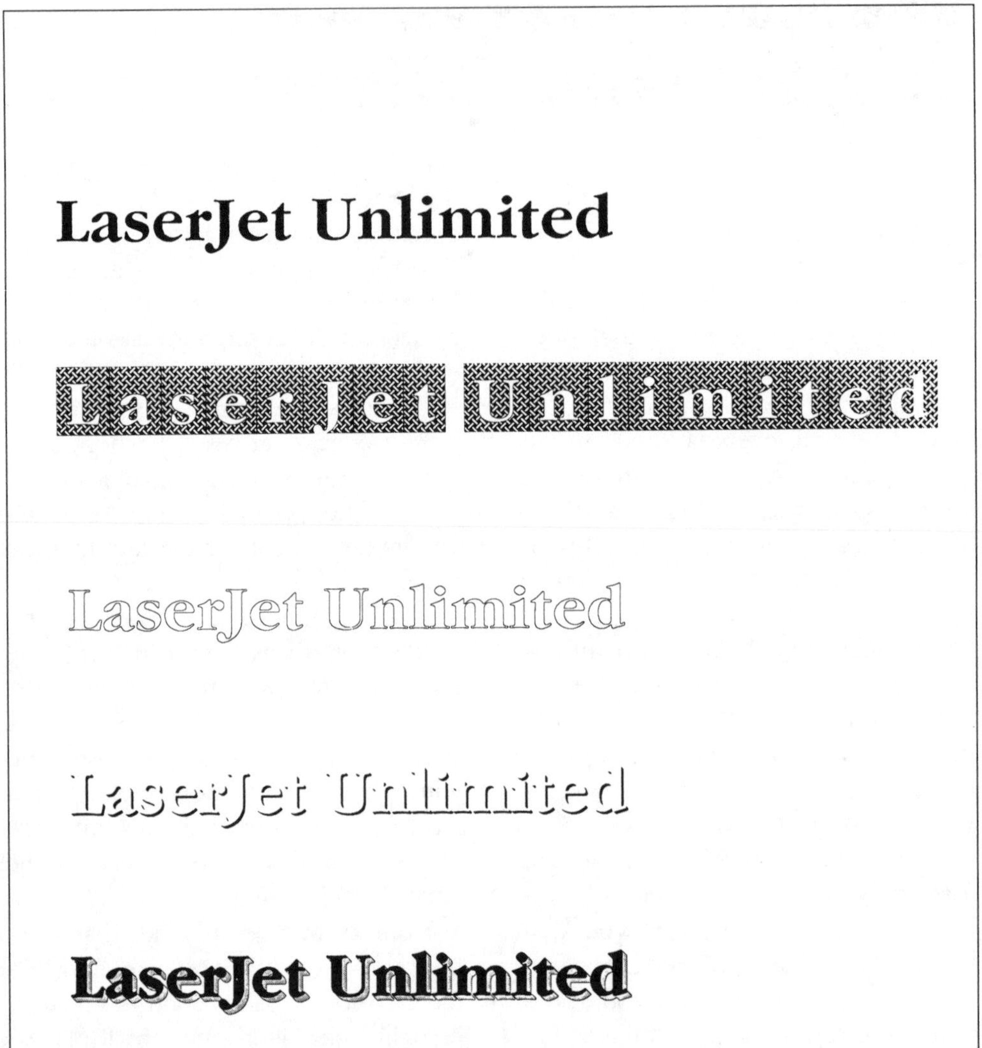

LaserJet Unlimited

LaserJet Unlimited

LaserJet Unlimited

LaserJet Unlimited

LaserJet Unlimited

Figure 1: The top font (30-point Garamond bold) was the original template for the other fonts shown here. The fonts were then downloaded into the LaserJet using SoftCraft's Laser Fonts, and Laser Fonts was also used to create a driver for Microsoft Word.

simple special effect takes about a minute on a 16MHz PC's Limited 386 computer; a complex set of effects that included scaling takes 10 minutes or more. None of the fonts in Figure 1 required any scaling, but on average each took 3 minutes to be generated, even on the fast computer.

Two improvements in the program would make the slow speed more tolerable. One would allow you to print an actual sample of a few of the characters in a font, before you tie up your computer generating the whole font. Another would allow you to run the program in batch mode and generate several fonts at once.

Of course, having generated your fonts, you'll have to figure out how to get your software to work with them. This is easily handled by one of the font management utilities described in Chapter 15 (in the case of word processing programs) or with WYSIfonts! (for Ventura and PageMaker).

Judged on the criterion of "new possibilities per dollar," Font Effects is one of the best values available in LaserJet software. Moreover, the design of the menus makes it easy to learn and use. The only drawback is the speed, but that's not so hard to tolerate when you consider the generally stellar qualities of the program.

Access

Font Effects
SoftCraft, Inc.
16 N. Carroll St. #500
Madison, WI 53703
608/257-3300
Price: $90

CHAPTER EIGHTEEN

Selecting Fonts with PCL

HOW DO YOU get the LaserJet to print in the font of your choice? With the major word processing programs, like WordPerfect and Microsoft Word, it's quite easy, because they provide drivers for all the HP font cartridges and soft fonts. Moreover, as described in Chapter 15, "Downloading Fonts and Building Drivers," there are several utility programs that can build new drivers, allowing WordPerfect and Microsoft Word to work equally smoothly with soft fonts from third-party vendors like SoftCraft and VS Software.

With most applications, however, things aren't so easy. If a LaserJet driver is not available, or if you're using fonts not recognized by the driver, you'll need to use the LaserJet's internal language, PCL (Printer Command Language), to select fonts. The purpose of this chapter is to explain how to construct the necessary codes.

Primary Versus Secondary

Because the strings of characters needed to select a particular font are often rather long, LaserJet font selection codes have gained a degree of notoriety. In fact, however, there's nothing inherently difficult about the process—mastering it just takes some patience and persistence.

Before we begin outlining the steps for setting up the selection codes, we need to explain the difference between primary and secondary fonts. In this chapter as well as in the Appendix C, "Font Cartridge Escape Sequences," the sequences shown in the examples and tables are to select a font as primary. To select a font as secondary, you merely substitute a close parenthesis mark [ )] for the open parenthesis mark [( ]. Once you have selected one font as primary and another as secondary, you can switch from one to another using the single-character Shift In (ASCII 015) or Shift Out (ASCII 014) commands. Shift In switches you to the primary font; Shift Out switches you to the secondaray font.

The Escape Code

As described in Chapter 19, "Programming the LaserJet with PCL," all PCL codes begin with the escape character, ASCII 27. This is designated in the HP manuals as Ec. For more details on the escape character, refer to that chapter.

Two Ways of Selecting

The LaserJet actually can use either of two methods for selecting a font. The first is according to an ID number; the second is according to a description of the font. The advantage of the ID number method is that it only requires very short, simple codes. For example, to select as primary font the font that has been assigned ID number 6, the escape sequence is as follows:

Ec(6X

The drawback of selecting fonts by ID is that ID numbers are not permanent, but instead are assigned to fonts when they are downloaded. So if you do use the ID method of selecting fonts, you have to take notes when you download the fonts so that the number you use to select a given font matches the number you assigned to that font.

The descriptive method of selecting a font takes advantage of the fact that a description of each font is built into the font itself, as part of the header of the font file. When you send a description of the font to the printer (in the form of an escape code), the printer looks into the head-

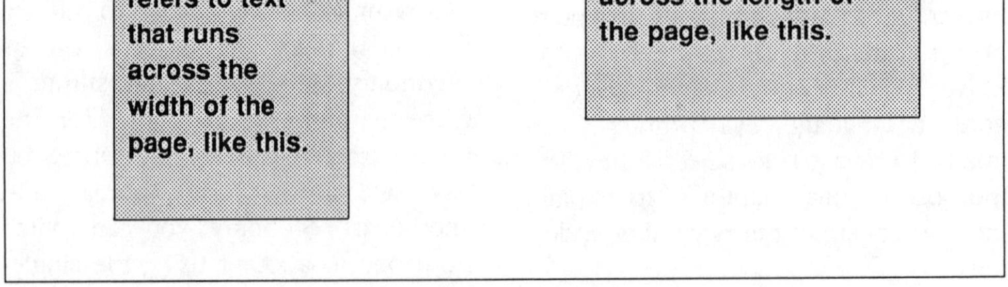

Portrait orientation refers to text that runs across the width of the page, like this.

Landscape orientation refers to text that runs across the length of the page, like this.

ers of each of the fonts that are either resident in the printer, located in one of the cartridges, or downloaded into memory. When it finds the font that most closely matches the description, it uses that font.

The Selection Process

The process of building an escape code for a particular font is rather like the compilation of a police artist drawing used to track down a criminal. At the station, the police artist questions witnesses about each component of the criminal's face: mustache, beard, nose, mouth, chin, haircut, eyes, eyebrows. Likewise, you build an escape sequence by listing all the parameters that describe a font. These are as follows:

Orientation: There are two possibilities here. Portrait refers to pages printed in normal, upright style. Landscape refers to pages printed sideways.

Character or Symbol Set: This is the name of the collection of symbols that make up the font, such as Roman-8 or IBM PC.

Spacing: Depending on the design of the font, this will either be fixed or proportional.

Pitch: This applies only to monospaced fonts and is defined as the number of characters per horizontal inch.

Height: The size of the font, measured approximately from the bottom of the lowest descender to the top of the highest ascender. It is expressed in points (1 point = 1/72 inch).

Style: Upright or italic.

Weight: Bold, medium, or light.

Typeface: The design on which the font is based, such as Letter Gothic or Swiss.

The Priority System

So that the LaserJet can make up its mind when it gets conflicting instructions, the various parameters are ranked according to priority.

The ranking is as follows: (1) orientation, (2) symbol set, (3) proportional versus fixed spacing, (4) pitch, (5) height, (6) style, (7) weight, and (8) typeface.

Under this system, when the LaserJet is handed a description of a font and instructed to print with it, it goes through the following steps:

- It tries to find a font with the same orientation, symbol set, spacing, pitch, height, style, weight, and typeface as the description.
- If no such font can be found, it looks for a font with the same orientation, symbol set, spacing, pitch, height, style, and weight as the description (typeface is dropped as a criterion).
- If no such font can be found, it looks for a font with the same

orientation, symbol set, proportional or fixed spacing, pitch, height, and style as the description (weight and typeface are dropped as criteria).

- If no such font can be found, it looks for a font with the same orientation, symbol set, spacing, and pitch as the description.
- If no such font can be found, it looks for a font with the same orientation, symbol set, and spacing as the description.
- If no such font can be found, it looks for a font with the same orientation and symbol set as the description.
- If no such font can be found, it looks for a font with the same orientation as the description.
- If no such font can be found, it prints the default font.

Building an Escape Code

To build an escape code, you simply look up the code for each parameter and then string them all together. The codes shown below are for selecting the primary font only. To select the secondary font, substitute a close parenthesis sign [ )] for the open parenthesis sign [( ].

(1) Orientation

Ec&lØO Portrait

Ec&l1O Landscape

(2) Character Set

Ec(#

where # is replaced by one of the codes shown in Table 1.

(3) Spacing

Ec(s1P Proportional

Ec(sØP Fixed

(4) Pitch

Ec(s#H

where # is replaced by the pitch, which is a measure of the number of characters per horizontal inch.

(5) Height in Points

Ec(s#V

where # is replaced by the point size of the font.

(6) Style

Ec(sØS Upright

Ec(s1S Italic

(7) Weight

Ec(s#B

where # is replaced by a number ranging from -3 (lightest weight) to 3 (boldest weight).

Codes for Character Set Selection

HP Math7	øA	OCR B	1O
HP Line Draw	øB	ISO 100: ECMA-94 (Latin 1)	øN
ISO 60: Norwegian 1	øD	ISO11: Swedish	øS
ISO 61: Norwegian 2	1D	HP Spanish	1S
HP Roman Extension	øE	ISO 17: Spanish	2S
ISO 4: United Kingdom	1E	ISO 10: Swedish	3S
ISO 25: French	øF	ISO 16: Portuguese	4S
ISO 69: French	1F	ISO 84: Portuguese	5S
HP German	øG	ISO 85: Spanish	6S
ISO 21: German	1G	ISO 6: ASCII	øU
HP Greek8	8G	HP Legal	1U
ISO 15: Italian	øI	ISO 2: IRV	2U
ISO 14: JIS ASCII	øK	OEM-1	7U
HP Katakana	1K	HP Roman-8	8U
ISO 57: Chinese	2K	PC-8	1øU
HP Math7	øM	PC-8 (D/N)	11U
Technical	1M	HP Pi Font	15U
HP Math8	8M		
OCR A	øO		

Table 1: To select a symbol set, you insert these codes in place of # in the escape sequence ^{E}c*(# .*

(8) Typeface

^{E}c(s#T

where # is replaced by one of the codes shown in Table 2.

Compressing an Escape Sequence

Combining all these components can result in a rather long code, but fortunately there are some allowable shortcuts, ways to compress the codes and ways to abbreviate them. You can combine a long string of escape codes into a shorter string according to the following rule:

If the two characters after the ^{E}c are the same in the two sequences you want to combine, then drop the ^{E}c and the two characters from the second seqence. When you do this,

Codes for Typeface Selection

Typeface	Code	Typeface	Code
Line Printer	ø	ITC Garamond	18
Courier	3	Cooper Black	19
Helv	4	Coronet Bold	20
Tms Rmn	5	Broadway	21
Letter Gothic	6	Bauer Bodoni Black Condensed	22
Prestige	8	Century Schoolbook	23
Presentations	11	University Roman	24
Optima	17		

Table 2: To select a typeface for a primary font, you insert these codes in place of # in the escape sequence Ec(s#T .

you need to change the final character of the first code from uppercase to lowercase.

Example:

Ec&a12K and Ec&a8J can be combined into

Ec&a12k8J

More Compression

Another way you can get your codes to take up less space is to include only the parameters that you want to change. For example, if you are using 10-point upright Letter Gothic medium and you want to switch to 10-point Helv, you can use the escape sequence

Ec(s4T

which is the code for Helv. No need for any other parameters.

Caution #1

When you do use an abbreviated selection string, you may be surprised at the results. For example, if you are using Helv italic in medium weight and want to switch to Helv bold, you might try the following sequence:

Ec(s3B

which is the sequence for bold. If you try this, however, you'll find that the LaserJet keeps printing Helv italic medium. The reason is that you didn't send the code to change from italic to upright. Since the style is higher priority than the weight, the LaserJet won't change to bold unless you specify

Ec(s3BEc(s0S

which is the sequence for bold, upright.

Caution #2

When typing escape sequences, be careful to distinguish between the lowercase letter *l* and the numeral 1, and between capital letter O and numeral ø.

7

SPECIAL TOPICS

Section Focus

This group of chapters provides a potpourri of information. It begins with a chapter introducing the set of control codes used by the LaserJet, known as Printer Command Language. Next, three hands-on chapters: how to make screen snapshots, print envelopes, and print label sheets. A chapter on Microsoft Windows explains how to install fonts for use by any application that runs under Windows. Two chapters cover the special software and hardware available for running the LaserJet with the Macintosh and with a medley of other computers. Finally, a chapter on LaserJet shareware discloses some little-known gems.

CHAPTER NINETEEN

Programming the LaserJet with PCL

THE LOW-LEVEL INSTRUCTIONS that control the LaserJet—telling it to change the margin or the number of lines per page, or to switch to a new font—make up the Printer Command Language (PCL). Most people who use the LaserJet never have to learn how to use PCL commands, because most applications come with a LaserJet driver. These drivers translate the output of a program into PCL. If you're not necessarily technically inclined—you don't know the difference between a bit and a byte, and don't care to learn—you may want to stick to software that has good LaserJet drivers, rather than wading through this chapter.

Unfortunately, not every software package has a LaserJet driver, and even those that do may not support all the features you need. For example, the LaserJet can print either horizontally (portrait mode) or vertically (landscape mode) on a sheet of paper, but a particular spreadsheet driver may not offer the ability to access this feature. Sometimes a particular LaserJet utility can be used to compensate for weakness in, or lack of, a driver; many such utilities are profiled throughout this book. But if a utility isn't available, or if you just want to have maximum control over your output, you may want to understand PCL well enough to supply the missing commands. Understanding the theory behind PCL will also help you better understand and predict your LaserJet's behavior in various situations.

Setup Commands and Embedded Commands

Whether you're controlling the LaserJet via a driver, a utility, with the console, directly with PCL commands, or with some combination of these methods, you must first know the difference between setup commands and embedded commands. Both are equally useful, and have their appropriate uses.

Setup commands are sent to the LaserJet as soon as you issue them, and evoke an immediate response from the printer. They are typically sent to the printer just before a document is printed, and are normally issued only once per printing session. Setup commands often specify parameters that control the format of the entire document, such as margins, page length, orientation, and font. (LaserJet II owners often may use the console selection panel as an alternative to sending setup commands.) If you're interested in setup commands, you might explore Chapter 5, "Using Setup Utilities," which describes several software packages that can be used to send them.

Embedded commands, in contrast, are placed within a document or file, and have no effect until that file is printed. For example, if you want to make font changes while printing a document, such as switching to 14-point Helv bold to print a headline and then switching back to your standard typeface for body text, you have to embed, or insert, two control codes within the document. One code, placed directly in front of the headline, instructs the printer to switch to 14-point Helv, and the other code, placed directly after the headline, instructs the LaserJet to switch back to the previous font.

PCL: The Great Escape Sequence

How does the LaserJet distinguish between instructions and material to be printed? The special commands that constitute PCL must somehow be discernible from normal data that is simply meant to be printed. To set them apart, every PCL command starts with a character known as the escape character, ends with a capital letter, and contains one or more characters in between. Each time the LaserJet receives an escape character, it examines the following sequence of characters up to the next capital letter, checking to see if that sequence is one of the commands in the vocabulary of PCL. If so, it executes that command; if not, it ignores it.

Because PCL commands all begin with the escape character, represented by the notation ^{E}c, the commands are also known as escape sequences. The escape character is the 27th character in the ASCII symbol set, so it is also commonly referred to as ASCII 27. In hexadecimal (base 16) and octal (base 8) notation, it is Hex 1B and Oct 033 respectively.

Every LaserJet function has its own escape sequence. For instance, one escape sequence tells the printer to switch to a bold font, another sequence tells the printer to print eight lines per inch rather than six, and yet another tells it that you want to eject a page held in the printer's memory.

Suppose you are using a word processing program and need to print some words in italic type. If your word processor doesn't have a LaserJet driver, one way to do this is to embed two escape sequences in your text, one to shift to italics, the second to shift back to normal upright type:

"...any mans Ec(s1SdeathEc(s0S diminishes Ec(s1Sme,Ec(s0S because I am involved in Ec(s1SMankinde;Ec(s0S And therefore never send to know for whom the Ec(s1SbellEc(s0S tolls; It tolls for Ec(s1Sthee.Ec(s0S
(John Donne)

The printed version looks a lot prettier:

"...any mans *death* diminishes *me*, because I am involved in *Mankinde*; And therefore never send to know for whom the *bell* tolls; It tolls for *thee*."
(John Donne)

Although escape sequences look bizarre to a human, they make perfect sense to the LaserJet and fall into particular categories. Let's now take a look at these groupings, the taxonomy of PCL.

Analyzing PCL: Major Categories

The commands that make up PCL fall into eight major categories: job control, page control, cursor positioning, font selection, font management, font creation, graphics, macros. The escape sequences for all the commands are shown in Appendix D, "Table of PCL Commands." A brief description of each category follows.

Job Control

There are only two commands in this category:

- Soft Reset, EcE. Issuing this command restores the printer to its default settings. It also removes any fonts that have been downloaded in "temporary" status but does not affect fonts that have been downloaded in "permanent" status. If you just want to get rid of temporary fonts, don't issue a soft reset. Instead, use the sequence Ec*c1F, which deletes all the temporary fonts without affecting any printer parameters.
- Number of Copies.

Page Control

These commands control the type of paper that will be printed on, the amount of the page that is available for printing, and the distance between characters and between lines. The commands are as follows:

- Paper Source. The options are the tray, manual feed, and manual envelope feed.
- Page Size or Length. The options here are used to select paper sizes and also envelope types. For a full listing, see Chapter 21, "Envelopes," and the PCL Command Table.
- Orientation. The options are landscape or portrait. Note that you can't mix portrait and landscape printing on a page. Also, when you switch orientations, the LaserJet will start a new page. If orientation is the first command you send to the printer, you'll get a blank page.
- Left Margin. This is measured in columns.
- Right Margin. Ditto.
- Horizontal Margin Reset.
- Top Margin. Measured in number of lines. Note that you can change the thickness of a line using the Vertical Motion Index command.
- Text Length. Number of lines per page.
- Perforation Skip. Adds a line feed or half-line feed at the bottom of a page to avoid losing text within the perforation region expected by many software applications.
- Horizontal Motion Index or HMI. This sets the width of a colum, measured in 1/120-inch increments.
- Vertical Motion Index or VMI. This sets the thickness of a line, measured in 1/48-inch increments.
- Line Spacing. An alternative to VMI for setting the thickness of a line. It is measured in lines per inch.

Cursor Positioning

While it is accepting print information from an application, the LaserJet always keeps track of the currently active position on its logical page, automatically incrementing the position to make room for a character, a tab, a backspace, a carriage return, a half-line feed, a line feed, a form feed, a blank space, or a graphic element. The cursor positioning commands give the application direct control over the active position.

- Horizontal Cursor Positioning. Can be specified in columns, decipoints, or dots. Note that a decipoint is 1/720 inch, a dot is 1/300 inch, and the width of a column is set by the Vertical Motion Index.

- Vertical Cursor Positioning. Can be specified in rows, decipoints, dots.
- Line Termination. There are four options, which determine exactly how the LaserJet is to interpret carriage return, line-feed, and form-feed commands. When you replace # with 0 in the sequence Ec&k#G, issuing the carriage return (ASCII 013) results in a plain carriage return (i.e., moves the cursor to the left margin but does not go to a new line), issuing a line feed (ASCII 10) results in a plain line feed (i.e., moves the cursor to the next print line but does not change the column position), and issuing a form feed (ASCII012) results in a plain form feed (i.e. moves the cursor to the first line at the top of the next page without changing the column position). When you replace # with 1 in the sequence, issuing a carriage return results in a carriage return and a line feed, but issuing a line feed and or a form feed is unaffected. When you replace # with 2 in the sequence, issuing a line feed results in a carriage return and a line feed, issuing a form feed results in a carriage return and a form feed, and carriage return is unaffected. When you replace # with 3, issuing a carriage return results in a carriage return and a line feed, issuing a line feed results in a carriage return and a line feed (i.e., same thing), and issuing a form feed results in a carriage retun and a form feed.
- Push/Pop Cursor. This lets the current position be stored and later retrieved.

Font Selection

This set of commands is explained in detail in Chapter 18, "Selecting Fonts with PCL." It includes the following:

- Orientation
- Symbol Set
- Spacing
- Pitch
- Height
- Style
- Stroke Weight
- Typeface
- Selection by ID Number
- Selection of Default Font
- Transparent Print (allows symbols that represent otherwise unprintable characters to be printed, such as an arrow for ASCII 27)

Font Management

Font management commands make it possible to download fonts, assign ID numbers to fonts, etc.

Embedding the Escape Character

BASIC	You can send the escape character to the printer using BASIC with the two-line program 10 LPRINT CHR$(27) 20 END Of course, you normally would want to include a character string after the ASCII 27, in which case line 10 would include the character string in quotation marks like this: 10 LPRINT CHR$(27);"character string";
dBASE	The CHR() function of dBASE II, dBASE III and III Plus, and dBASE IV allows you to use the ASCII character specified (in decimal form) as the argument of the function. Thus, to send the escape character to the printer, you use the CHR(27) function, after setting communications with the printer using SET PRINT ON or Ctrl-P.
DOS Batch Files	You can use a text processor or word processor to create batch files for all the escape codes you normally use, e.g., TMSRMN10.BAT, COURIER12.BAT, TOPMARG.BAT, ORIENTA.BAT. For those batch files that you use every time you started the printer, you could create a LJSETUP.BAT file and then include its name in your AUTOEXEC.BAT file.
DOS COPY command	From DOS, you cannot send the escape character directly to the printer. If you press the Esc key at the DOS prompt, it merely puts you on a new line. But by using a text editor or a word processor (Word, XyWrite, Volkswriter, WordStar 2000, PC Write—not WordStar) in unformatted mode, you can create a one-character file containing the escape character. If you are using a word processor to create the

Table 1: There is no universal way of embedding the escape character. Each program uses a different method, and in some programs it may simply be impossible.

	file, use the methods indicated above and save the file on your DOS disk as an ASCII file (or unformatted file) and give it the name ESCAPE. To send an escape sequence to the printer type COPY ESCAPE+CON PRN *remainder of escape code* Ctrl-Z This will let you type in the rest of the escape sequence from your keyboard. Note that if you are using the LaserJet with a serial interface you must have already configured the PC to direct its output to the serial port with the two mode commands.
Lotus 1-2-3	1-2-3 allows you to include the escape character in a setup string in the form \027 [the backslash character (\) tells 1-2-3 that the next three characters represent the decimal value of an ASCII character], but versions prior to Release 2 do not provide any means for embedding escape characters within a worksheet. With Release 2, typing a pair of vertical lines (||) in a cell tells the program that the following characters represent ASCII codes. So to include the escape character you enter ||\027 in a cell. You cannot use this method to embed an escape character in a worksheet cell.
Microsoft Word, PC Write, WordStar 2000	You can insert any ASCII character into text by holding down the Alt key while you type the character's three-digit code on the numeric pad. So to include the escape character, hold down the Alt key and type 027 on the number pad. With Word, a leftward pointing arrow will appear on the screen, representing the escape character.
MultiMate	To include any ASCII character in a MultiMate text file, press Alt-A (that is, hold down the Alt key while typing A) and then type the three-digit number of the character. To enter the escape character, press Alt-A and then type 027.

	Note that a printer control sequence must be entered on a line by itself.
Multiplan	To enter an escape character into a file, type ^[. Note that the ^ symbol is entered by typing Shift-6.
PFS:Write	The escape character can be embedded in PFS:Write files in the following form: *P 27*
SideKick	To embed the escape character in a SideKick Notepad, type Ctrl-P Ctrl-[.
Volkswriter	This program lets you enter the escape character directly into text using the Esc key and represents it on-screen with a left-pointing arrow. It also has a special command that lets you "hide" long command codes within text. To embed such codes in a document, type the command ..CMD, making sure that the two periods are in columns 1 and 2. You can enter the escape character and the remainder of the control code, and Volkswriter will send the entire line, verbatim, to the printer.
WordPerfect 3.0	To enter the escape character, press the Format key (Shift-F8), type O for Other, P for Printer Functions, P for Printer Command, and C for Command. Then type <27>. The screen will not show that the escape character has been embedded in text, but it can be seen if you press the Reveal Codes key. WordPerfect also provides another way to insert long control codes into your documents. First create a file for each code. One file might be called TR10It (for Tmns Rmn 10-point italic) and contain the control code <27>&10O<27>(0U<27>(s1p10v1s0b5T Make sure that this file is in unformatted ASCII form. To insert this code into a document you would press the Print Format key, type A for Insert Printer Command, press the Retrieve key, and type the name of the document (e.g., TR10It).

WordStar	If you're using an older version of WordStar, the only way to embed an escape character in a document is by "hiding" it in one of the user-defined function keys (^PQ, ^PW, ^PE, or ^PR). This is done via the Winstall utility on the WordStar disk. To use Winstall, start at the DOS prompt and type WINSTALL WS. Winstall will ask what drive your WordStar files are located on. If you're using WordStar on a floppy disk, type A:. When Winstall asks the name of the file to install, type WS.COM. When you're asked for the name of the file for the installed version, type lws.com. From the main Installation menu, select D, Custom Installation of Printers. From the Printer Installation menu select O, User-Defined Functions. Now enter the hexadecimal code 1B in one of the user-defined function keys (let's assume its ^PR). 1B happens to be the hexadecimal equivalent of ASCII 027, the escape character. Now type X to leave the Function Key menu, X to leave the Installation menu, and X again to leave Winstall. Finally, at the Exit Options menu, press A to save your changes. Now whenever you want to type the escape character, you type Ctrl-PR. ^R will appear on your screen, which stands for the escape character. With Winstall, it's possible to enter longer codes into the WordStar User Defined Functions and into the function keys. The chapter "Profile: WordStar" shows how to build a simple driver for LaserJet cartridge B or F using Winstall.
XyWrite	True to its reputation as the "word processing program for programmers," XyWrite makes it easy to insert the escape character in a text document. You simply press the Esc key and a right-pointing arrow appears on the screen, XyWrite's way of representing ASCII 027.

- Font ID. Used for assigning an ID number to a font upon downloading. You always issuing this command first to identify the font to which you are going to apply other font management operations.
- Font Control. Depending on the parameter, this command is used for deleting soft fonts or assigning them permanent or temporary status.
- Font Selection by ID number

Font Creation

These commands are definitely not needed by the masses—they're only for those who are creating their own soft fonts. If you're using a font-generating or font-editing program, the application will take care of all this automatically. Since the details on using these commands are beyond the scope of this book, we'll simply list them here. For more information, refer to "LaserJet series II Printer Technical Reference Manual."

- Font Descriptor
- Character Descriptor
- Character Code
- Character Descriptor and Data

Graphics

As described in Chapter 4, "How the LaserJet Thinks," there are two categories of LaserJet graphics: bitmapped (also called "raster" graphics) and object. Since in the case of the LaserJet family, object graphics are restricted to defining rectangles and filling them either with patterns or shades of gray, one might also call this type of graphic "rectangle graphics."

- Raster Graphics Resolution (75, 100, 150, or 300 dots per inch). When you select 75, each pixel in a graphic is actually composed of a 4-by-4 box of printer dots. When you select 100, each pixel is composed of a 3-by-3 box. When you select 150, each pixel is composed of a 2-by-2 box of printer dots. And when you select 300, each pixel is represented by a single dot.
- Start Raster Graphics
- Transfer Raster Data
- End Raster Graphics
- Horizontal Rectangle Size (decipoints or dots).
- Vertical Rectangle Size (decipoints or dots).
- Area Fill ID. Lets you specify the ID number of the HP pattern or shade of gray you want to use to print your rectangle. It must be followed by a Fill Rectangle Area command to actually print the rectangle.
- Fill Rectangular Area. Once the rectangle and the fill ID are selected, this lets you specify

whether you want to use a pattern or a shade, and prints the fill.

Macros

Macros are described in greater length at the end of this chapter. Briefly, the commands are as follows:

- Macro ID
- Macro Control. Depending on the parameter used, this command defines, invokes, or deletes a macro.

Putting Escape Sequences to Work

The first step in embedding escape sequences in your files is to figure out how to send the escape character itself to the printer from within your software application. This is not necessarily easy, because unlike other characters used in control codes, ^{E}c is not a normal letter or punctuation mark. You won't find ^{E}c on any computer keyboard (though on most you will find the Esc key).

Unfortunately, most programs reserve this key for some special function, so chances are that pressing it will not insert the escape character into your text. In Microsoft Word, for instance, pressing Esc takes you to the command menu. In Lotus 1-2-3, pressing Esc takes you from a lower-level command menu to a higher-level menu. When you're using such programs you have to find a different way to embed the escape character. Once you determine how to do so, the rest is easy, since all other characters in PCL escape sequences can be typed directly from any keyboard. For tips on embedding the escape character in common applications programs, see Table 1.

Debugging

When a PCL command isn't working, you should first make sure you entered the characters of the command correctly. Some characters look confusingly alike. A lower-case letter *l* looks like a numeral 1 or an uppercase letter I, and a numeral ø might be mistaken for a capital letter O. These characters are not interchangeable,able nor will a lowercase letter suffice when the capital version is required, and vice versa.

After checking that the characters were entered correctly, the next step is to verify that you gave the LaserJet an executable command. If the LaserJet receives a command that it can't execute, it doesn't necessarily ignore the command or issue an error message. Instead, it goes through a series of steps. First, it looks for a close match to the requested feature. The most notable time this may occur is during font selection. If the LaserJet is unable to select exactly the font you specify (whether because you specified it incorrectly or because the printer just cannot access the font requested), it will go with what it deems to be the nearest alternative, based on the hierarchy of attributes.

Only if no alternative can be found will the printer ignore the command. The fact that the LaserJet handles unrecognizable commands in this way—ignoring them rather than issuing an error message—makes it possible to print files that were formatted for the LaserJet on lower-level HP printers with less powerful versions of PCL. For example, if you try to print a LaserJet file on an HP ThinkJet printer, the file will print but any fancy formatting will be ignored.

When in Rome...

The best way to become conversant in PCL is to try your hand at "speaking" it, playing with some simple escape sequences. Here are some examples of how you may use PCL to configure your LaserJet to various settings. We've expressed the sequences for the most part in their "pure" form, independent of the language or mechanism you might use to send them.

We'll start with something fairly simple, controlling the number of copies printed. By default, the LaserJet will print one copy of every page sent to it. You can increase this by sending a simple escape sequence, EC&*l*#X, where # is the number of copies to printed. For example, the sequence EC&l3X instructs the LaserJet to print three copies of every page it receives. Thereafter, anything sent to the printer will be printed in triplicate. To set it back to printing one copy, use EC&*l*1X.

Let's move on to something a bit more difficult. By default, the LaserJet prints six lines of text per page. If you print using different-size fonts but aren't using LaserJet drivers or software that compensates for the different font heights, your printed output may look a little funny. For example, if you print some text in 8.5-point Line Printer at six lines per inch, the letters of the text will have just a bit too much white space above and below them. But printing the same text in the same font at eight lines per inch looks more natural.

It's easy to change the lines of text that are printed per inch. The escape sequence to do so is EC&*l*#D, where # is the number of lines per inch you want (only values of 1, 2, 3, 4, 6, 8, 12, 16, 24, and 48 are allowed, however). You can get more flexible control using the Vertical Motion Index command, for which the escape sequence is EC&*l*#C, where # is the number of 1/48-inch increments per line. Thus, a value of 48 would give you one line per vertical inch, 16 would give you three lines per vertical inch, and 8 would give you six lines per vertical inch.

Telling Your LaserJet Where to Go

Beginning to get the hang of it? Let's try something more ambitious now. But first, let's introduce the concept of the cursor. The LaserJet has a print cursor that is completely analogous to the display cursor on your computer screen. By controlling the position of the print cursor, you can control where a dot or character will be printed on the page.

There are three units in which you can specify the cursor position: in terms of the row or column, in terms of the dots composing an image, and in terms of decipoints (1/720"). For simplicity, we'll stick to rows and columns here, although the techniques are directly transferable. The basic escape sequence to specify the cursor position by rows is Ec&a#R, where # is the row number in which you want the cursor to be positioned. The basic sequence to specify the cursor position by columns is Ec&a#C, where # is the column number in which you want to place the cursor. Note that in both cases these are *absolute* numbers. That means the number is being measured from the upper left corner of the LaserJet's image area. Row 5 is five rows down from the start of the LaserJet's image area, and column 6 is six columns over from the start of the image area. The image area itself is not the upper-left corner of the sheet, but instead begins about 1/2-inch down from the top, and about 1/4-inch in from the left of the sheet.

You can print a silly line approximately in the middle of an 8 1/2" by 11" sheet of paper by sending your LaserJet Ec&a28R, which positions the print cursor at row 28, then Ec&a22C, which positions the cursor at column 22, then the characters: I'm in the milk and the milk's in me!

If you need very fine-grained cursor positioning, you'll probably want to use the cursor positioning escape sequence specifying decipoints or dots. Using them is basically identical to using the column commands.

Graphics: At Play in the Fields of Dots

The cursor positioning commands are particularly useful with graphics commands, of which there are two types on the LaserJet. The first type, object graphics commands, let you print rectangles and fill them with your choice of six patterns and eight shades of gray. This is handy because you can easily use HP's predefined patterns as building blocks rather than having to create those building blocks yourself. Object graphics are supported on the LaserJet Plus and LaserJet II, but not on the original LaserJet.

Of course, you can choose black as the shade for a rectangle. In that case your rectangles become "rules." By sending the proper escape

```
set talk off
set print on
*
* chr(27) sends escape character
*
* send a line as a special kind of "rule"
*
* first, specify rule height, in number of dots
* Here we specify a height of only one dot
* If you wanted it 30 dots high, put in *c30B instead
*
? chr(27) + "*c1B"
*
* now, specify rule width, in number of dots;
* 300 dots is 1 inch at 300 dpi resolution
*
? chr(27) + "*c300A"
*
* now print the rule we've defined
*
? chr(27) + "*c0P"
*
* Now, send the same line using graphics mode commands
* first, set raster resolution
*
? chr(27) + "*t300R"
*
* switch to graphics mode, and specify which column to
* start printing (1 = start at cursor, 0 = start at
* graphics left margin)
*
```

Figure 1: A dBASE program that prints a two thin lines, one using raster graphics and the other using object graphics.

```
? chr(27) + '*r0A'
*
* now, tell LaserJet we will transfer 37 bytes of raster
* graphics
*
? chr(27) + '*b37W'
*
* now print 37 bytes of ASCII 255 on current row;
* note ASCII 255 has all 8 bits on, which makes for an
* uninterrupted line
*
kount = 0
do while kount < 37
?? chr(255)
kount = kount + 1
enddo kount
*
* switch graphics mode off
*
? chr(27) + '*rB'
set print off
eject
```

sequence, you can cause the LaserJet to print a particular predefined pattern or rule you've specified.

If HP's patterns don't suit your needs, or if you're the type of rugged individual who enjoys "doing it yourself," all the way to the level of the individual dot, you can use the second type of LaserJet graphics commands, known as raster graphics.

In text mode, every byte the LaserJet receives causes it to print a corresponding character. For example, when in text mode the LaserJet receives an ASCII 65, it prints an A. In raster graphics mode, the LaserJet acts according to the setting of every bit in the byte, printing a dot for each bit that is on, and leaving a blank space for each bit that is off. Using this capability, you can program the LaserJet to print virtually any pattern.

Raster Graphics: Bitmania

The escape sequence to switch the LaserJet into raster graphics mode is Ec*r1A. This tells the LaserJet that it will begin receiving graphics data, and that it should begin printing that data starting at the current cursor position. A very similar escape sequence, Ec*r0A, can be used if you want the LaserJet to start printing at the left margin of the current line, rather than with the current cursor column. Before you use either of these escape sequences, though, you should tell the LaserJet the resolution at which you want to print the graphics—75, 100, 150, or 300 dots per inch. The escape sequence to do so is Ec*t#R, where # is the desired number. Basically, the larger the number, the smaller the dot the LaserJet will print.

Following these setup procedures, you send the LaserJet the desired data to be printed as graphics, which the LaserJet prints on a single line from left to right. First you tell it how many bytes will print on the current line; the escape sequence for this is Ecb#W, where # is the number of bytes it will get. Then you send it the data for that line. To do this, you need to know your base 2 arithmetic. That is, you need to know the binary or base 2 bit patterns for all the numbers between 0 and 255. For example, in the binary representation of 0, 00000000_2, no bits are on, consequently the corresponding graphic the LaserJet would print for this datum would be eight blanks. In the binary representation of 1, 00000001_2, the far right bit is on and all the rest are off. For this datum the LaserJet would print seven blanks followed by a dot.

After you've sent a line of graphics data, you can use a cursor positioning command to next print at a different position on the page. This might be the next line, or it might be 35 dots back up the page and 27 dots back to the left; it all depends on the image you want to print. When you want to switch out of graphics mode to resume sending text data, issue the escape sequence Ec*rB.

Two Means to an End

The sample dBASE program in Figure 1 prints two simple thin lines. For the first line, the program calls on the built-in LaserJet ability to print a rule. Once the rule has been defined as a 1-by-300-dot image, printing it only requires one command. To print the second line, the program uses raster graphics mode. Doing so takes more work, but reveals the contrast between the two approaches to LaserJet graphics. The second approach also gives you a flavor of how complicated graphics programming can quickly become.

We've tried to keep this discussion of graphics programming simple, so that you could concentrate on the concepts and learn the basics. If you're interested in graphics, you'll want to experiment with the graphics commands in conjunction with the cursor positioning commands. For example, all we've told you about here is how to print graphics on a single row, rather than up and down on the page. But if you master the techniques we've described, and refer to the cursor positioning commands described earlier in this chapter, you'll be able to easily learn the remaining commands required to create your own images.

Overlay Macros

Owners of the LaserJet Plus and LaserJet II have a special incentive to become conversant in PCL, because these printers both support the use of macros. Macros are PCL instructions that have been downloaded to the memory of the LaserJet and assigned an abbreviated name. You can then execute them whenever necessary merely by calling them by name, rather than having to send the PCL commands themselves. The LaserJet will forget them when the power is switched off, but if necessary you can always reload them at the beginning of the next work period, using batch files.

The LaserJet Plus and LaserJet II have three options for executing macros. The first option returns the cursor to its position prior to execution of the macro, but it does not restore other parameters that may have been changed due to the execution of the macro. The second option does the opposite: after executing, it restores any parameters that have changed, but does not return the cursor to its prior position.

The third way of using a macro turns it into something called an overlay, because the downloaded macro resides in memory, overlaying whatever else is there and printing automatically on every page. For convenience, after the macro is executed, the cursor position and any parameters that might have been altered by its execution are restored to their original values. This way of using the macro is safe because it never affects the rest of a document.

You need to issue three commands to create a macro:

- The first command is Ec&f#Y, where # is the ID number for the macro.
- The second command is Ec&f0X, which initiates macro definition and tells the LaserJet that everything to follow (until it receives the command that stops macro definition) will constitute the macro.
- The third command is Ec&f1X,. which marks the end of the macro definition.

To create a macro with an ID number of 9, you would place the combined command Ec&f9YEc&f0X in front of the PCL commands in your file of graphic elements. Then you would go to the end of the file and insert the third command, Ec&f1X. Now save the macro definition as an unformatted file. To place the macro in the LaserJet's memory, issue the DOS command

```
COPY filename LPT1:
```

Once the macro has been downloaded to the LaserJet's memory, you can call it whenever necessary by sending the LaserJet the sequencece Ec&f9YEc&f#X, where # (which may be 2, 3, or 4) indicates the mode in which you wish to execute the macro. Using 2 allows the execution of the macro to change the cursor position and the printer parameters. Using 3 lets the cursor position change, but restores printer parameters to those that were in effect before the macro was executed. Using 4 causes the macro to execute on every page (in overlay mode), and restores both the cursor position and the printer parameters to their values before the macro was executed. When you no longer want an overlay to print, send the Ecf9X sequence to disable the auto macro overlay.

Becoming Fluent

If the discussion in this chapter has merely whetted your appetite for information on PCL, more technical nourishment is available from HP. The LaserJet Printer Technical Reference Manual (HP Part No. 02686-90915) and *LaserJet series II Printer Technical Reference Manual* (HP Part No. 33440-90905) include a full summary of escape sequences for the LaserJet Plus and Series II, respectively, along with some other examples of programming in PCL. A summary of PCL commands is also included in Appendix D of this book. Perusing such a function-oriented list of PCL commands will help give you other ideas for things you can accomplish using PCL.

Anyone developing software for the LaserJet can apply for acceptance in HP's program of support for Independent Software Vendors (ISVs). Additional technical information is available through this program. Another occasional source of information on PCL is the Hewlett-Packard Journal, available at most university engineering libraries or directly from HP at 3000 Hanover St., Palo Alto, California 94304.

CHAPTER TWENTY

Screen Snapshots

FOR MILLIONS OF PC users, pressing Shift-PrtScrn is the quickest route from screen to printer. Using this humble function doesn't require sitting through a training seminar or interacting with an oppressively user-friendly disk tutorial. If you can press those two keys at the same time, you can take a snapshot of your screen and print the result.

A print screen (or screen shot, as it's often called) can serve many purposes. You might use a screen shot to print out a paragraph or a graphic for quick reference, capture a page of electronic mail, or plunk an on-screen image onto paper for a report, manual, or presentation.

Using the techniques described in this chapter, you can produce snake's-tooth-sharp printed screens on the LaserJet from virtually any kind of monitor. Depending on the software, you can also change the aspect ratio, size, resolution, and orientation of a captured image; crop it; and add special effects such as inverse video. You can capture a screen to a disk file and print it out on another system that's connected to a LaserJet. Or you can make your screen shot an illustration by merging it into another document.

Text Screens with the LaserJet II

The simplest way to print a screen is by pressing Shift-PrtScrn. Unfortunately, the results weren't always perfect with versions of the LaserJet prior to the LaserJet II. Because of differences between the IBM character set used by the IBM Monochrome Display (as well as monitors that emulate that display) and the Roman-8 character set used by the printer's default Courier font, some aspects of the screen do not print correctly. In particular, graphics characters such as the border lines around the screen used by most word processors do not print correctly.

With the LaserJet II you can get around the problem by switching the printer to a font that uses a character set exactly matching the IBM character set used by displays in text mode. To switch the printer to the new character set, do the following steps:

- Take the printer off-line by pressing the ON LINE key.
- Press and hold the MENU key for about five seconds, until it reads SYM SET=.
- Press the plus key repeatedly until it reads SYM SET=IBM-US.
- Press the ENTER / RESET MENU key so that an asterisk appears next to IBM-US. Press the ON LINE key. If you attempt to use Shift-PrtScrn at this point, you'll still get the old character set. The reason is that although the character set has been changed, the printer has to be reset to make it permanent. So there's one more step:
- To make the change permanent, press the ON LINE key again, then press and hold the CONTINUE / RESET key for about 5 seconds until the panel reads 07 RESET. When you release the key, the panel will change to READY.

Now the printer is reconfigured so that the IBM-US set is the default character set. Since this character set matches the one used by your display, it's a cinch to capture a text screen. Do the following:

- Verify that the printer is on-line (the ON LINE light is gleaming).
- Press Shift-PrtScrn. The FORM FEED light should go on, indicating that the printer has received the screen, but the paper will not eject yet.
- To eject the page, take the printer off-line by pressing the ON LINE key, then press the FORM FEED key and press the ON LINE key again.

Text Screens: LaserJet and LaserJet Plus

With models earlier than the LaserJet II, there is no way to change the default font used by the printer to one with the IBM-US character set. You can use PrntScrn to make screen shots of text screens on those printers, but borders and other graphics characters won't print correctly.

There are three solutions:

- HP's Y font cartridge. The Y cartridge is a bit pricey at $250. If all you need to do with it is print screen shots, you'd be better off with one of the other options.
- A shareware font distributed by Orbit Enterprises called Font 10. Like the fonts on the Y cartridge, this font uses nearly the same

HP 92286Y Cartridge

Courier 12-point medium (portrait)
```
10 LPRINT CHR$(27);"E";CHR$(27);"(s0S";CHR$(27);"&l6D";
```

Courier 12-point bold (portrait)
```
10 LPRINT CHR$(27);"E";CHR$(27);"(s3B";CHR$(27);"&l6D";
```

Courier 12-point italic (portrait)
```
10 LPRINT CHR$(27);"E";CHR$(27);"(s1S";CHR$(27);"&l6D";
```

Line Printer 8.5-point medium (portrait)
```
10 LPRINT CHR$(27);"E";CHR$(27);"(s16.66H";CHR$(27);"&l8D";
```

Line Printer 8.5-point medium (landscape)
```
10 LPRINT CHR$(27);"E";CHR$(27);"&l1O";CHR$(27);"(s16.66H";CHR$(27);"&l8D";
```

Table 1: The fonts on the HP 92286Y cartridge and the one-line BASIC programs for selecting each.

character set as the IBM Monochrome Monitor standard.

- A screen capture utility.

The Y Cartridge

The fonts contained on the Y cartridge are PC Courier 12-point medium, bold, and italic, and PC Line Printer 8.5-point medium. The PC Courier fonts can only be printed in standard portrait orientation; the PC Line Printer fonts can be printed in either portrait or landscape orientation.

Since PC Courier 12-point medium is the default font on the Y cartridge, you don't need to send any codes to the LaserJet in order to use this font to capture a screen. Simply using DOS's Shift-PrntScrn command from within any program will produce a correct screen shot. Note that screen shots created using this method do not show inverse video areas of the screen, since the PC symbol set used by the Y cartridge does not have characters to represent inverse video.

To capture screens using Y-cartridge fonts other than PC Courier medium, you must first send the appropriate font-selection code to the printer as well as a code to make the line spacing of the printer match that used by the font. For PC Courier fonts, line spacing should be six lines per inch; for the PC Line Printer font, spacing should be eight lines per inch. Table 1 lists the fonts on the Y cartridge as well as a one-line BASIC program for each. The program selects the indicated font and changes line spacing to six lines per inch for PC Courier fonts and eight lines per inch for PC Line Printer fonts.

The Orbit Font 10

Those with older LaserJets (LaserJet, LaserJet Plus) can produce quick, clear character screen prints with the Font 10 disk from Orbit Enterprises. A quick way to load the font into memory is to print the demo program provided with the font.

Access

Font 10
Orbit Enterprises, Inc.
P.O. Box 2875-B
Glen Ellyn, IL 60138
312/469-3405
Price: Free if you send a formatted disk

Screen-Capture Software

If you are using a graphics monitor that follows the IBM Color Graphics Adapter (CGA), IBM Enhanced Graphics Adapter (EGA), Hercules Graphics Card (HGC), or IBM Video Graphics Adapter (VGA) standards, the way to print a screen is to use a utility program that provides that capability.

Currently, there are a number of utilities available for that purpose, including GrafPlus ($49.95), Hotshot Graphics, ($249), Hotshot Grab ($99), Inset ($99), HiJaak ($89), and Pizazz Plus ($149). In addition, screen capture utilities are provided with PC Paintbrush, Publisher's Paintbrush, WordPerfect 5.0, and WordStar 2000, and the Microsoft Windows Clipboard also can be used for capturing screens.

The main criteria for comparing these tools follow.

What Displays Do They Support?

For the most part, all the utilities support the common formats: CGA, EGA, HGC, and VGA. Most support many more formats, but to be sure yours is covered, contact the vendor.

Do They Allow Editing of the Image?

The main difference among the utilities listed above is in how much they allow you to edit the image. At one end of the spectrum is Hotshot Grab, which merely performs screen captures with no alteration. At the other end are Hotshot Graphics and PC Paintbrush, which allow you to treat the screen shot as a graphic image. With these high-end programs you can add text to a screen shot, crop it, convert colors to various gray shades, change some portions to reverse video, draw arrows, type text, erase portions of the picture, change the size of the screen shot, and even draw your own graphics on top of the screen shot.

Note that if the utility supports PCX format, as discussed below, you can also export it into PC Paintbrush or Publisher's Paintbrush for extensive editing.

What Formats Do They Create?

PCX format is the graphics file format used by ZSoft's Paintbrush family of graphics programs. It is also a format recognized by both Ventura Publisher and PageMaker, as well as by most other page layout programs. If you wish to import a graphic into one of those programs, make sure it can save captured screens on disk in PCX format. At this point all of the screen-capture utilities listed above can generate files in PCX format directly, or else provide a conversion utility that changes their proprietary file format to PCX format.

Can They Capture Windows Screens?

In the past, many screen capture utilities did not allow you to take snapshots from within Microsoft Windows. If that capability is important to you, make sure that the utility you select allows it. Pizazz, Hotshot Grab, and Hotshot Graphics allow you to capture Microsoft Windows screens.

Can the Screen Shots Be Merged with Word-Processed Text?

If you want to merge screen shots directly into word processing programs, the best utility to buy is called Inset. However, several word processors now incorporate this function, making it unnecessary to have Inset. For example, WordPerfect provides an excellent utility for capturing graphics screens, described in the sidebar. So does WordStar 2000.

With Microsoft Word, you can buy a utility called PageView that allows you to merge screen shots from either Windows applications or non-Windows applications. (See "Profile: PageView.") If you'd rather not use PageView with Word, Inset would be your next best option.

Adjusting Parameters

All the screen-capture utilities listed here provide some control over

Making Screen Shots with WordPerfect 5.0

WordPerfect 5.0 comes with a utility called GRAB. To get directions on using the utility, type

```
GRAB /h
```

To load the utility into memory, type GRAB. The program will be loaded into memory, where it will occupy 13K. Now you can capture any graphics screen. To do so, load the graphics program, then type

```
ALT-SHIFT-F9
```

A box will appear on the screen. If you press Enter at this point, you'll save the entire screen; however, you can change the size of the box if you want to change a portion of the screen. To move the right and left side of the box, hold down the Shift key while you press the arrow keys. To move the box itself, use the arrow keys. To toggle between moving slow and moving fast, Press Ins.

When you're ready to capture the screen, press Enter. WordPerfect will save the file into the current directory as GRAB.WPG. If there's already a file with that name, it will save it as GRAB1.WPG. If there's already a GRAB1.WPG, it will save it as GRAB2.WPG, etc.

Once you're back in WordPerfect, you can load GRAB.WPG just like any other graphic using ALT-F9. As with any other graphic, you can rotate, stretch, or crop the screen shot.

parameters such as aspect ratio, reverse video, and cropping. Aspect ratio is important because screen pixels are typically rectangular while printer dots are square. This means that screen shots are often too wide and short, requiring adjustment to look right. Most of the utilities do provide settings for aspect ratio.

Some screens look better when white and black are switched, so reverse video is a desirable capability.

Cropping is a good feature to have if you only need to preserve a portion of the screen.

Speed

Speed is critical when you are making a large number of screen shots and

Access: Screen Capture Tools

GrafPlus, Version 3.0
see "Profile: GrafPlus"

HiJaak
Inset Systems, Inc.
12 Mill Plain Road
Danbury, CT 06811
203/794-0396
Price: $89

Hotshot Graphics
see "Profile: Hotshot Graphics"

Inset
Inset Systems, Inc.
12 Mill Plain Road
Danbury, CT 06811
203/794-0333
Price: $99

Pizazz Plus
Application Techniques, Inc.
10 Lomar Park Dr.
Pepperell, MA 01463
617/433-5201
Price: $149

Y font cartridge
Hewlett-Packard
11311 Chinden Blvd.
Boise, ID 83714
800/854-4031
Price: $250

printing them directly. Hotshot Graphics provides several options for speeding up printing. A "no-frills" option allows you to print a screen dump in about 20 seconds with a Centronix interface or 2 minutes with a standard serial interface, rather than the 30 seconds (3 minutes with a serial interface) required by other options.

Memory Requirements

The less memory required by a screen capture utility, the better. GrafPlus is the winner here, requiring only 8K. WordPerfect's GRAB utility requires 12K. GrafPlus uses 21K, Hotshot's Grab program uses 25K and its Wingrab program uses 28K. HiJaak uses 40K. Pizazz Plus uses 40K to 50K, depending on the configuration.

Awkward or Smooth

It's important to be able to adjust parameters such as cropping and aspect ratio without leaving a program and then starting it up again. This is the big drawback of GrafPlus compared with Hotshot, Pizazz, and HiJaak.

Another program that allows screen dumps to be merged with text is Inset. Like GrafPlus, Inset is memory-resident and is activated with the Shift-PrntScrn combination. It saves images to files and then allows the names of the files to be inserted into text files to allow merging of text and graphics. Although the method does work, it is slow and tedious. Typically you have to print a page to adjust the size of gap in the text and the location of the screen dump image.

With Inset, screen dumps can be printed at four levels of magnification, clipping can be performed along all four sides of the image, and images can be printed at four orientations. It allows continuous sizing, allows adjustment of aspect ratio, allows screen shots captured from one type of screen to be viewed on another, and allows editing of screen dumps (including copy, move, fill, line, rectangle, and zoom views). After you merge screen dumps into text pages, you can view them on screen.

Profile: Hotshot Graphics

HOTSHOT GRAPHICS IS actually four programs in one: a screen capture utility, a screen annotating utility, a paint program, and a graphics conversion program.

Screen Capture

The center of Hotshot Graphics is a screen-capture utility that can capture either text screens or graphics screens on a variety of monitors: CGA, EGA, VGA, Wyse 700, MCGA, Hercules, AT&T 6300, and Vega Deluxe. If you're just interested in this aspect of the program, you can purchase Hotshot Grab separately. Unlike many other screen-capture programs, this one can handle regular text screens (such as the Lotus spreadsheet shown in Figure 1) and Microsoft Windows screens (as shown in Figure 2).

Legalized Graffiti

Once you've captured a screen, Hotshot lets you modify it in numerous ways. You can draw arrows, type notes, and otherwise mark up a captured screen. You can also erase por-

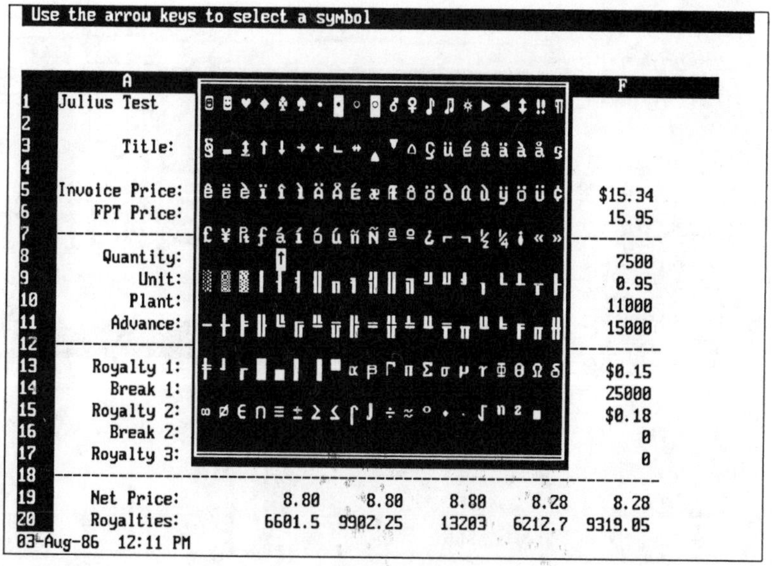

Figure 1: When you're editing a text screen such as this spreadsheet, you can pop up a table of special symbols. These can then be inserted into the captured screen.

tions of the screen. Not only does the utility faithfully reproduce any inverse video portions of the screen, but it also allows you to "paint" inverse video onto the screen to highlight particular passages. In addition, Hotshot will automatically print a border around the screen dump if you want one. You can also add a title to the screen dump. As shown in Figure 1, Hotshot can provide you with a table of special symbols that you can insert into a captured screen. For examples, you might want to insert the British pound sterling sign (£) into a spreadsheet.

More Legalized Graffitti

While annotating a screen is well and good, Hotshot Graphics goes even further, providing a full-fledged paint program, whose drawing tools include lines, boxes, curves, arcs, and circles, and functions such as inverting, flipping, mirroring, ellipses, pixel editing, cropping, panning, and zooming. Not quite all the features are there that you might find in PC Paintbrush, but the capabilities are impressive when you consider that

> ### Access
>
> **Hotshot Graphics**
> **Hotshot Grab**
> *Symsoft*
> *444 First St.*
> *Los Altos, CA 94022*
> *415/941-1552*
> *Price: Hotshot Graphics $249, Hotshot Grab $99*

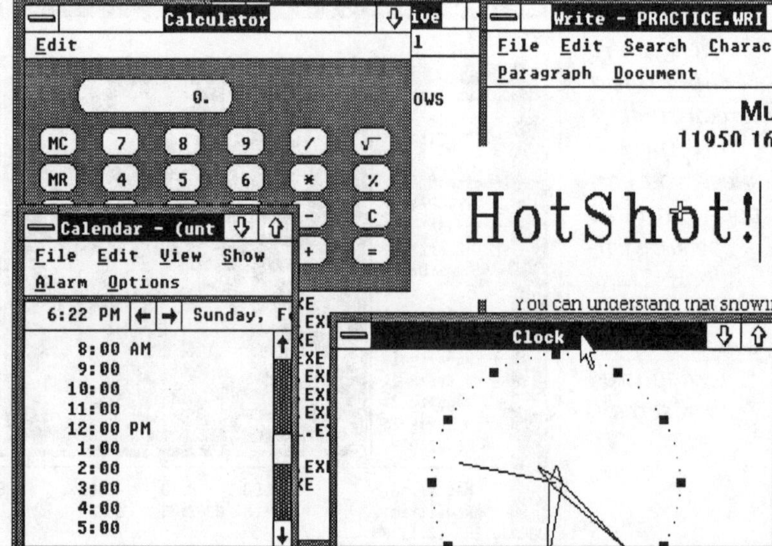

Figure 2: You can edit with 16 colors and add text in four sizes. Here's a screen dump from Windows (including the lovely Windows Clock).

Hotshot is primarily a screen-capture program.

File Conversions

Less flashy than Hotshot's abilities to sling a paintbrush are its workaday file-conversion features. You can convert captured screens to ASCII, PCX, GEM IMG, TIFF, and EPS formats. With the PCX and IMG formats, you can then load captured screens into Ventura (as we've done throughout this book); with PCX and TIFF, you can do the same in PageMaker.

Printing Options

Once you have captured and edited a screen snapshot, you can either merge it into a page layout program or else print directly on the LaserJet. Figure 3 below shows the printing options, which include controls over the position of the image on the page, reversal of black and white, size, thickness of border, etc.

Hotshot Grab

If you don't need all the graphics editing capabilities of Hotshot Graphics, but simply want to make screen snapshots, you can get the much cheaper Hotshot Grab. This package includes WINGRAB, a screen capture utility specifically for Microsoft Windows. It can take snapshots of text or graphics screens, can convert captured screens to different formats, and can reverse black and white in a snapshot. One drawback of

```
Print Options                                        F10-Print
 Size            (S/M/L) L      Inches   width 6.933
                                          height 4.333
 Position            Row  1
                     Col  1
 Print Border?     (Y/N) N
 Print Cursor?     (Y/N) N
 Compressed?       (Y/N) N
 Supress Shades? (Y/N) N
 Inverse?          (Y/N) N
 Auto Form Feed? (Y/N) N
 Number of copies?        1
 Print a title?  (Y/N) N
```

Figure 3: This shows the options available from Hotshot Graphics' print menu.

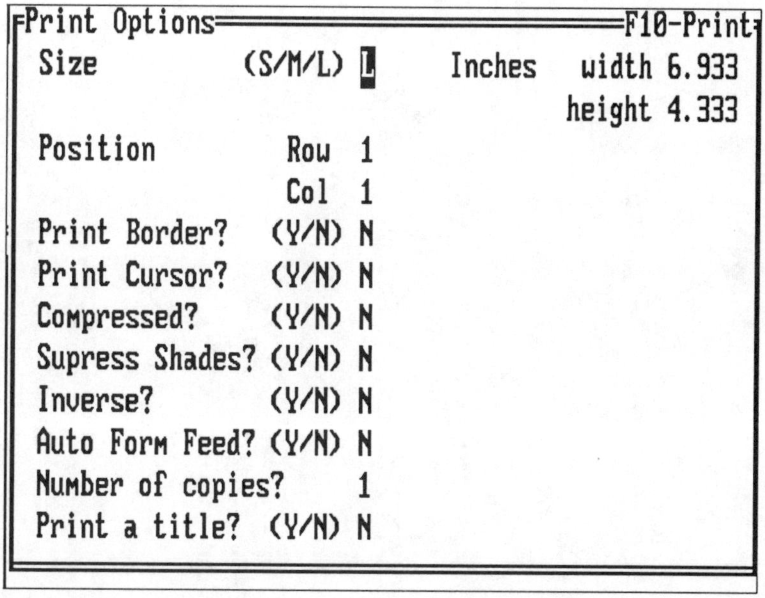

Grab in comparison to Hotshot Graphics is that the type in text screen snapshot printouts is somewhat lower than similar snapshots printed from Hotshot Graphics. The reason is that Hotshot Graphics includes its own 300-dpi font specifically for the purpose of improving the quality of such printouts.

Profile: GrafPlus

ALTHOUGH GRAFPLUS HAS far fewer capabilities than HotShot Graphics, it only costs $49 compared to $249 for HotShot Graphics or $99 for HotShot Grab. If all you need is to capture and print screens without any fancy editing, GrafPlus may be all you require. In addition to letting you print screen shots directly, it can save them in PCX format for merging into Ventura Publisher or PageMaker.

GrafPlus works with a large selection of display adapters, including the following:

- IBM Monochrome Adapter
- IBM Color Graphics Adapter (all modes)
- Tecmar
- Hercules Graphics Adapter (all modes)
- Everex
- 720x350 PC 3270 (720x350 or 360x350)
- Persyst BoB medium and high resolution
- AT&T 6300 medium and high resolution
- Olivetti M24 medium and high resolution
- Sigma Designs Color 400 (640x400) mode
- IBM Professional Graphics Adapter (all modes)
- VMI 8820
- Zenith Z-100 B&W or color
- Verticom M-16 and M-256
- Persyst Bob/16 (640x400)
- IBM Enhanced Graphics Adapter (all modes)

It also handles the unique method used by Lotus for displaying graphics.

Within the GrafPlus package of utilities, Graflasr is the utility specifically designed for making screen snapshots on inkjet and laser printers.

To install Graflasr in memory you type Graflasr from the DOS prompt and then answer several questions about the type of monitor and printer you are using, and about the way you want the screen snapshot to print. To print a Monochrome Adapter character screen, type Y in response to the question, "Print text screen as graphics?" Because it prints reverse video areas, it does a better job reproducing text screens than either the Y cartridge or Orbit Enterprise's Font 10.

After Graflasr is installed, printing a screen snapshot is as easy as pressing Shift-PrntScrn. However, the beauty of the program is the range of options it provides for the appearance of the screen snapshot. Some of the options are provided by the questions that Graflasr asks every time you install it. These include the option of printing with black and white reversed, and the option of printing in portrait or landscape orientation. If you wish to avoid answering the questions every time you install the utility, the GrafPlus manual describes how to indicate them on the command line. For example, typing Graflasr -1 means that you want to print to the LaserJet (printer 1) with black and white reversed.

More options for printing screen snapshots are provided by the EditGraf utility, which alters the default parameters of Graflasr. With EditGraf, you can choose to print the screen snapshot to a file rather than printing it directly. This makes it possible to capture a screen from a program running on a computer that isn't connected to a LaserJet. Later you can print the file on a LaserJet even if the computer connected to the printer is using a different monitor than the one you originally used to make the capture the screen.

Adjusting Parameters

EditGraf allows you to alter the resolution, size, aspect ratio, orientation, and location of the image on the page. It also allows you to set up automatic cropping and change the default resolution to 75, 100, 150, or 300 dots per inch.

The resolution command also affects the size of the image. At 300 dpi the image is one-third the height and one-third the width as at 100 dpi. It is also possible to alter the size of the image by changing the number of horizontal and vertical pixels printed. The best quality is produced when the number of pixels printed is the same number as displayed. With the monochrome adapter that means 720 pixels horizontally and 350 vertically. With the CGA that means 640 horizontally and 200 vertically. With the Hercules that means 720 horizontally and 348 vertically. And with the high-resolution mode of the EGA that means 640 horizontally and 350 vertically.

Aspect ratio refers to the ratio between the horizontal and vertical dimensions of an image. Because the pixels used by most computer monitors are rectangular (taller than they are wide) while the LaserJet prints square dots, images may tend to appear distorted when transferred from

Access

GrafPlus Version 3.0
Jewell Technologies, Inc.
4740 44th Ave SW #203
Seattle, WA 98116
206/937-1081
Price: $49.95

screen to paper. To remedy this, you can alter the ratio of horizontal to vertical pixels using EditGraf. When doing so, avoid reducing the number of either horizontal or vertical pixels below the resolution of the screen, as this will cause some degradation in the quality of the image. Instead, increase the pixels in the dimension that you wish to fatten up.

With Graflasr you have the choice of either portrait (called horizontal) or landscape orientation. You can also place the image in any position on the page. The default location parameters are /027&a200H and /027&a1000V. These position the image approximately 200 decipoints (one decipoint = 1/720-inch) from the left edge of the paper and 1,000 decipoints from the top of the paper. To change these with EditGraf, substitute different numbers for 200 and 1,000. Cropping may also be specified from within EditGraf in response to the questions, "How many horizontal pixels should be clipped?" and "How many vertical pixels should be clipped?" Horizontal clipping applies to the right side of the image; vertical clipping to the bottom.

Black and white may be reversed temporarily during installation of Graflasr or permanently with EditGraf. Normally, the program reverses the colors seen on the monitor, so that white or green letters on a black background print as black letters on paper.

Also included with GrafPlus are several additional utilities designed to assist programmers. These make it possible to issue the Shift-PrntScrn command from programs written in Fortran, Pascal, interpretive BASIC, and compiled BASIC. Finally, the Prtsc.com program allows automatic screen snapshots to be made from within batch files.

CHAPTER TWENTY-ONE

Envelopes

THERE ARE TWO ways to print envelopes with the LaserJet II. One is to use the manual-feed tray and insert them one at a time into the printer. The other is to use the special automatic envelope-feed tray. With either option, you can choose from a range of sizes.

Basic Tips

Because envelopes are thicker and less uniform than standard paper, they're more difficult for the LaserJet to handle. Here are some tips to help you avoid paper jams:

- Whether you're using the envelope tray or the manual feed, you should always lower the rear paper tray on the LaserJet II.
- Use lighter rather than heavier stock, especially if you're having frequent paper jams.

Type of Envelopes

The best type of envelopes to use are those known as "commercial" or "official." These are characterized by diagonal seams and gummed flaps.

There are several types of envelopes you should avoid:

- damaged envelopes
- envelopes of unusual construction: shiny, highly textured, embossed, bulky, multiple-flap, and those with side-seam construction
- envelopes with transparent windows
- envelopes with attachments such as strings or metal clasps
- envelopes with recycled paper (we're not sure why this is a no-no, but HP maintains that they shouldn't be used)
- envelopes with peel-off or pressure-sensitive adhesives

In addition, due to the heat and pressure in the LaserJet, you should

```
EcEEc&l3HEc&l81AEc&a35LEc&l12E
Ec(8UEc(s1p12vs1v4T
Name
Company
Address
```

Figure 1: Contents of an ASCII file that will print the destination address on a standard 4-by-9-inch business (Commercial 10) envelope. The first line of the escape sequence resets the LaserJet, selects landscape orientation, turns on the manual-feed option, selects the envelope dimensions, and sets the margins. The second line, which is optional, selects Helv bold. To print the file, use the command COPY/B (filename) PRN.

avoid "envelopes using paper, inks, adhesives, or other materials that discolor, melt, offset, or release hazardous emissions when exposed to 200 degrees C for 0.1 seconds." (*LaserJet series II Printer Envelope Tray User's Guide*)

Overview of Techniques

In this chapter we'll look at three techniques for printing an envelope:

- creating an ASCII file with escape codes
- using special drivers with Word, WordPerfect, and MultiMate
- using a special envelope utility

ASCII File

The simplest way to print envelopes is to create a plain ASCII file containing the text of the address and the necessary escape codes, then copy the file to the printer. You can create this file with SideKick or with any word processor. Figure 1 shows the contents of a file that will print on a standard business (Commercial 10) envelope. A convenient way to print envelopes is to save this file and then type over it every time you need to print a new envelope.

Building the Escape Sequence

The escape sequence shown on the first line in Figure 1 is built by combining the codes for printer reset, envelope source, page size, orientation, left margin, top margin, and font. (The second line is an optional font selection code.) You'll have to find out how to insert the escape character, Ec, into your files. For information on how to do so with various applications, see Chapter 19, "Programming the LaserJet with PCL." The components of the escape sequence and the options for each component are as follows:

Reset: This is not absolutely necessary but is prudent. The sequence is

Ec E

Source of envelope: This can either be from the manual-feed tray or from the automatic envelope tray.

- The sequence for the manual tray is

  Ec&l3H

- The sequence for the tray is

  Ec&l1H

Page size: There are a four options for page size. They are as follows

- Monarch (3.875 x 7.5 inches)

  Ec&l80A

- Commercial 10 or standard business (4.125 x 9.5 inches)

  Ec&l81A

- International DL 110 x 220 mm

  Ec&l90A

- International C5 162 x 229 mm

  Ec&l91A

Orientation: Envelopes always use landscape orientation:

Ec&l1O

Left margin: This varies, depending on the type of envelope. For commercial envelopes, a good value is 35 columns from the left margin:

Ec&a35L

Top margin: As with the left margin, you may have to experiment with different values here, depending on the type of envelope and the position you want for the address. For commercial envelopes, try 12 lines from the top:

Ec&l12E

Font: You don't need to supply any value here, because the LaserJet will automatically use an available landscape font such as landscape Courier. In Figure 1, we've selected 12-point Helv bold. For font selection codes, refer to Chapter 18, "Selecting Fonts with PCL," and Appendix C, "Font Cartridge Escape Sequences."

Printing

Once you have created your file by selecting from these parameters, save it as an ASCII (unformatted) file. Then copy to the printer. If you are using the manual-feed option, simply push an envelope, stamp end first, between the paper guides. If you are using the envelope tray, make sure it is properly loaded and in place before copying the file to the printer.

Word, WordPerfect, and MultiMate

With each of these word processors, you can print directly without the extra step of creating an ASCII file and copying it to the printer.

MultiMate Advantage II

With MultiMate Advantage II, you'll need to obtain the LJ2ENVTR.PAT Printer Action Table from MultiMate Technical Support (203/247-3445). After installing this printer action table and setting your page length to 45, you'll be able to select a type of envelope from the Document Print Options screen (Alt-3). Before entering the address information, select the Modify Documents Defaults option with F10 and set the lines per page to 45. After entering the address, use a default pitch of 1 for C5, 2 for DL, 3 for Monarch, and 4 for Commercial 10 envelopes. For Commercial 10 envelopes, set the left margin to 035 and the top margin to 010.

Microsoft Word 4.0

With Microsoft Word, you'll need to enter an escape sequence as shown above for the ASCII method, but you should omit the reset command. Select TTYFF as your printer driver with the command Escape-Print-Options-F1. If TTYFF doesn't show up as one of the options, you'll need to copy it from one of the two Microsoft Word Printer disks (it's disk #2 for Word 4.0) into your Microsoft Word subdirectory.

WordPerfect 5.0

With older versions of WordPerfect, printing envelopes required extensive work to create a custom driver, but with WordPerfect 5.0, you can use the regular LaserJet or LaserJet II driver. The following procedure works if you have an envelope tray. If you don't have an envelope tray, you'll have to insert an envelope into the manual-feed tray and press the CONTINUE button on the Control Panel after the FORM FEED light goes on. You may also have to adjust your top margin.

- Type the address into a separate file.
- Move the cursor back to the beginning of the file.
- Press Shift-F8 (Format), select P (Page), select S (Page Size), select E (Envelope), select E again (Envelope), select C (Center top to bottom, or else type in a value for top margin), press Esc, select L (Line), select M (Margins), type in 4" for left margin (or another figure if desired), press Esc.
- Press Ctrl-F8 (Font), select F (Base Font), select a font, press Enter.

- Press Shift-F7 (Print), select S (Select Printer), select the LaserJet or LaserJet II, select F (Full Document).
- The LaserJet will now beep. Press Shift-F7 (Print), select C (Control), select G (Go).

Access

ERMASoft Laser Envelopes
ERM Associates
P.O. Box 1032
Agoura Hills, CA 91301
818/707-3818
Price: $39.95

EnvLJ and GrabPlus

There are several utilities that can assist with envelope printing. Two of these are shareware programs called EnvLJ and GrabPlus. Both are described in Chapter 25, "LaserJet Shareware."

ERMASoft Laser Envelopes

Ideally, an envelope-printing program should show you a picture of an envelope on the screen, allow you to type in the address, and take care of everything else automatically. In fact, that's how ERMASoft Laser Envelopes works.

To start the program you type ENV. Laser Envelopes then asks you if you want to type a return address. If you're using envelopes with a preprinted return address, you can skip this step and type the mailing address. If you want to enhance the address with multiple fonts, you can press F1

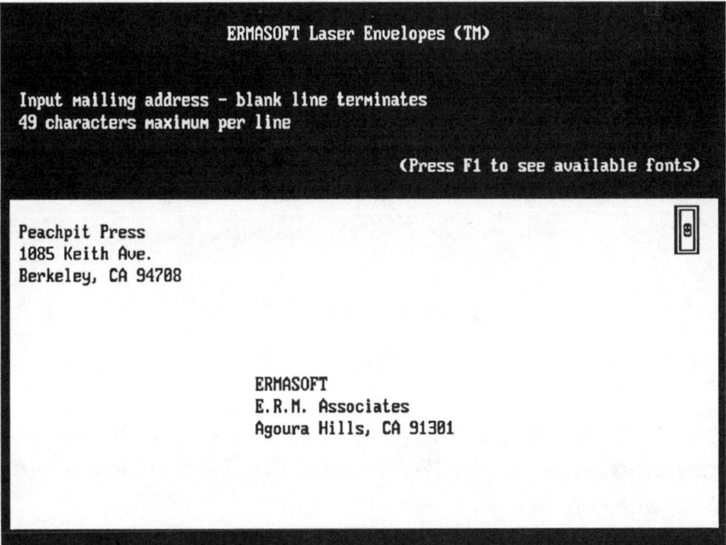

Figure 2: With ERMASoft Laser Envelopes, you type the return address and the destination directly onscreen. Alternatively, the program can "grab" the address from your word processor file.

$^{E}_{c}$E$^{E}_{c}$&l1O$^{E}_{c}$&l3H$^{E}_{c}$&l38E$^{E}_{c}$&a52L
Name
Street/PO
Town, State, Zip

Figure 3: Contents of an ASCII file that prints the destination address on a LaserJet Plus.To print the file, use the command COPY/B (filename) PRN.

$^{E}_{c}$E$^{E}_{c}$&l1O$^{E}_{c}$&l3H$^{E}_{c}$&l27E$^{E}_{c}$&l6L
Name
Street/PO
Town, State, Zip
$^{E}_{c}$c&a52L

(6 line spaces)

Name
Street/PO
Town, State, Zip

Figure 4: Contents of an ASCII file that prints both the return address and the destination on a LaserJet Plus.To print the file, use the command COPY/B (filename) PRN.

to see your options. To print the envelope, you press F3, F4, or F5, depending on the size you want to print.

In addition to using Laser Envelopes in this simple fashion—typing the address directly onto the envelope—the program provides the option of letting you capture an address from within your word processing program. To do this, you install a separate memory-resident module called AddGrab. While you're working in your word processor, you can activate AddGrab by pressing Ctrl-Alt-G. You then use the cursor keys to mark the address you want to print, and AddGrab stores that address for later envelope printing. Using AddGrab, you can capture multiple addresses and then print all the envelopes at the end of your work session using Laser Envelopes.

Printworks for Lasers

As described in the profile in Part 1 of this book, Printworks for PC is a general-purpose utility that provides a variety of functions. One of these, called Memo Writer, lets you type, edit, and print a document containing up to 63 lines.

To print an envelope, use the main Printworks menu to set the following parameters:

- Select landscape font (command A)
- Select envelope feed (command L)
- Set the left margin to column 51 (command [ )
- Set the top margin to 40 (command T)
- Set the page length to 22 (command Q)

Now type 4 to select the Memo Writer. Type the address you want to print on the envelope and type Ctrl-PR. Now you can feed the envelope into the printer.

LaserJet Plus

Figure 3 shows the ASCII file that will print envelopes on the LaserJet Plus (destination address only). Figure 4 shows a different file for envelopes that include the return address. If you want to use a font other than Courier, you'll need to insert that escape sequence as a separate line above the name.

Having created your ASCII file, name it ENVELOPE (or whatever else you want to call it) and save it on your hard disk. Each time you need to print an envelope, type the new address over the previous address, save, and use the DOS COPY/B command to copy it to the printer. The printer will then display a blinking PE on the Control Panel. Position the envelope with the flap side underneath and the stamp end entering the printer first, against the left side of the manual-feed tray (the same side as the indicator panel and the power switch). Gently push the envelope into the feed until you hear a click. The rollers will turn for 5 or 6 seconds, then the printer will pull the envelope into the feed. If you are printing more than one envelope, you can feed another one in as soon as the last is pulled out of the printer. After the LaserJet prints the letter, the PE indicator will turn itself off.

The components of the control code in Figure 3 are as follows:

- the reset command, ^{E}cE
- the command to put the printer in landscape orientation, ^{E}c&l1O
- the command to activate the envelope-feed mechanism, ^{E}c&l3H
- the command to set the top margin, ^{E}c&l#E (where # is the number of rows from the top of the printable area, at six rows per inch)
- the command to set the left margin, ^{E}c&a#L (where # is the number of columns from the left side of the printable area, at ten columns per inch).

CHAPTER TWENTY-TWO

Label Sheets

IF YOU USE your computer to print mailing labels, you'll love and hate the LaserJet. While you can make your labels look much nicer with the LaserJet by selecting attractive fonts or by printing a name in boldface, the LaserJet does have some potential weaknesses when it comes to labels. It's not that you can't print them, but rather that you can't do it in the way you're probably accustomed to. For example, because the LaserJet's printable area is smaller than a full sheet of paper, you won't be able to use the top row of labels on many brands of label sheets you may have used in the past. For this and other reasons, you'll need to get the right kind of label, and learn how to position addresses on a sheet.

Selecting Labels

You can't use the labels that you are probably used to, because the LaserJet doesn't accept continuous (also known as tractor-feed) paper. Instead, you'll have to use sheets of labels. When choosing labels, there are several points to remember. First, Hewlett-Packard has several specific suggestions on the type of labels that you should use. According to HP's "LaserJet Printer Specifications Guide," you should use labels that have an acrylic-based adhesive, which is least likely to break down at the high temperatures the LaserJet uses to fuse toner onto paper. You should also use labels that do not let adhesive come into direct contact with any part of the printer, such as the print drum or rollers. Also, the labels should cover the entire page, with no spaces between them. This reduces the probability that the printer will catch a label and peel it off the sheet.

The type of labels that best fulfill all these conditions are the labels that are sold specifically for use with laser printers. HP makes such labels on an 8.5-by-11-inch sheets, in three label sizes: 92157K, 92157N, and92157P. Your local office supply store should

Access: Labels

Avery 5260/5160, 5261/5161, 5262/5162, 5163, 5164, 5165
Avery Consumer Products Division
777 E. Foothill Blvd.
Azusa, CA 91702
818/969-3311
Description: 5260/5160 are 1 x 2-5/8'' each, come in packs of 25 or 100, and provide 30 labels per page; 5261/5161 are 1 x 4'' each, come in packs of 25 or 100, and provide 20 labels per page; 5262/5162 are 1-1/2 x 4'' each, come in packs of 25 or 100, and provide 14 labels per page; 5163 are 2 x 4'' each, come in packs of 100, and provide 10 labels per page; 5164 are 3-1/3 x 4'' each, come in packs of 100, and provide 6 labels per page; 5165 are 8-1/2 x 11'', come in packs of 100, and provide 1 label per page.

HP 92157K, 92157N, and 92157P
Hewlett-Packard Direct Marketing Division
1324 Kifer Rd.
Sunnyvale, CA 94086
800/538-8787
Description: (See text)

Pro-Tech laser specialties line
James River Corporation
356B Sewall St.
Ludlow, MA 01056
800/521-5035
413/589-7592
Description: 1 by 2 5/8, white: $10.95 for 25, $42.95 for 100; 1 by 2 5/8, clear: $44.95 for 25, $174.95 for 100

have them or be able to order them. Style 92157K comes with thirty 2 5/6" by 1" labels per sheet; this size is generally large enough to accommodate five or six lines, and is the size you're probably most used to using for mailing lists. Style 92157N labels are 1 1/2" by 2 5/6", of which twenty-one can fit on a sheet. Style 92157P offers ten 4 1/4" by 2" labels per sheet. It's well worth it to obtain these laser printer labels, but if for some reason you can't, the labels designed for plain-paper photocopiers can suffice (remember, the LaserJet is a close sibling of Canon copiers). A typical brand of these is Avery's style 5351, which is what most people used before Avery released a laser printer specific style.

There are some significant and some insignificant differences between photocopier labels and laser printer labels. One obvious difference is that at the top of a sheet of laser printer labels is a row of half-height labels. This row accounts for the LaserJet's "unprintable area," a half-inch wide margin at the top and bottom of any sheet, within which the LaserJet cannot print an image. With either laser printer labels or photocopier labels you must adjust your software to account for this margin, but with photocopier labels you waste the top and bottom row of labels. Using laser printer labels, you just waste two half-rows of labels, or one row in all.

One at a Time

There are other subtle, yet ultimately more important, differences between the two types of labels. These differences add up to a warning that you probably shouldn't try to "batch" feed photocopier labels from the input tray, but instead should feed them using the LaserJet's manual-feed mechanism.

This is somewhat frustrating, because we have many times seen laser printer labels successfully batch-fed through the Canon engine that the LaserJet uses. Nonetheless, the LaserJet is an expensive piece of equipment, and we'd rather err on the side of caution and recommend that you feed label sheets manually rather than from the input tray. It's somewhat slower, but it's also safer.

Lower the Tailgate

Whether you decide to print labels manually or by using the input tray, always make sure that you lower the rear output tray first, so that the labels are ejected flat out of the back of the LaserJet and don't have to negotiate the last hairpin bend as they normally would. This greatly increases the chances of your label sheet making it through cleanly.

Feeding Sheets Manually

The method for feeding label sheets manually differs according to whether you own a LaserJet or LaserJet Plus (Canon CX engine), or a LaserJet II (Canon SX engine). If you own a LaserJet or LaserJet Plus, these are the steps:

- Set the printer off-line by pressing the ON LINE button.
- Press the manual feed button, causing PF to appear on the Control Panel.
- Set the printer back on-line (by pressing the ON LINE button again).
- Send the file to the printer.
- Push paper face up into the manual-feed slot along the paper feed guide, with the top of the paper entering first.

- Feed another sheet when the printer displays PF on the Control Panel.

Because the LaserJet II is more flexible regarding mixed paper input, feeding label sheets into a LaserJet II manually is somewhat easier. Simply slide the label sheet into the manual-feed slot atop the regular paper feed tray, with the label side of the sheet face up. The LaserJet II will automatically detect the presence of this sheet and will take it rather than a sheet from the standard paper tray. Note that if you want to print more than a single sheet, you should probably switch the printer into manual-feed mode; otherwise it may beat you to the second sheet and draw one from the regular input tray.

To switch the LaserJet II into manual-feed mode, press the ON LINE button on the Control Panel so that the on-line light goes out. Then press the MENU button twice, until MANUAL FEED=OFF appears in the display. Press the plus key at the top of the console panel once until MANUAL FEED=ON appears in the display, then press the ENTER / RESET MENU button. An asterisk should appear next to the words MANUAL FEED=ON, indicating that this is now the active selection. Press the ON LINE button again; the on-line light should come on and the display should read 00 READY. The printer is now in manual-feed mode. You can switch manual feed off by reversing the steps, until MANUAL FEED=OFF* appears in the display.

Whichever LaserJet model you are using, you can also switch manual feed on by using a software selection instruction, the escape sequence Ec&l2H. The escape sequence Ec&l1H will then switch it back to using the regular input tray. This may be more convenient in some situations and can usually be automatically sent from within your application. (For more information on escape sequences and how to use them with common software products, see Chapter 19, "Programming the LaserJet with PCL.")

The Unprintable Area and Image Position

For an 8.5-by-11-inch sheet, the LaserJet's printable area is about 8- by 10 inches. At six lines per inch, the top two lines are in the unprintable area; at eight lines per inch, the top three. In addition, if any part of a character falls within the unprintable area, none of that character will be printed. If you're not using laser printer specific label sheets with a row of half-labels at the top of the sheet, the unprintable area means that you'll simply have to skip printing on the top row of labels. You might be tempted to pull off the labels on the first line. Don't give in: the entire paper surface must remain smooth and uniform; otherwise you increase the chances of that sheet jamming inside the LaserJet.

Even if you are using laser printer labels that account for the unprintable area with a row of half-labels, you'll still have to make adjustments for this row when using your software. If you're using word processing software, configure your document's margins to incorporate a full half-inch at the top and bottom of each sheet.

Polaris LabelMaker

Polaris LabelMaker is a simple alternative to printing labels using a database program or the mail-merge feature of a word processing program. The program uses dot commands, similar to those used by WordStar, to print labels according to a "matrix file" you have created. This file contains a format for printing your labels. It also contains the name of a text file from which data will be pulled.

You can use LabelMaker if your database program or word processor is capable of writing data files in ASCII format. You also need to ensure that the data is delimited with commas, since this is what LabelMaker looks for when it decides which information to put where. Most database programs have the capability of generating ASCII files with fields separated by an optional delimiter.

A potential drawback of using commas as delimiters is that it precludes the use of commas within fields. LabelMaker takes care of that problem by allowing you to place double quotes around data that includes an embedded comma.

Besides allowing you to create label sheets, LabelMaker includes some other notable features. These include the ability to create lines, boxes, shades, and patterns; to use symbols from the Polaris Symbol Sheet (sold separately for $49.94); and to print envelopes (defined as a label sheet with one label); and to include bar codes on labels using the W and X font cartridges. A special license is available for using LabelMaker with a local area network.

Access: Label Utilities

VPMail
Desktop Publishing Dialog
P.O. Box 558250
Miami, FL 33255
305/577-8394
Price: $25

Polaris LabelMaker
Polaris Software
613 West Valley Parkway
Suite 323
Escondido, CA 92025
619/743-7800
Price: $124

dBASE

Rather than purchasing Polaris Label-Maker, you might also consider writing your own database program to print labels. A sample dBASE program is provided in "Profile: dBASE," in Part 5 of this book.

VPMail

For those using Ventura Publisher, Heintz Dinter (publisher of the Desktop Publishing Dialog newsletter) sells VPMail, which includes Ventura files and an accompanying dBASE program for creating customized 2-by-4-inch labels.

CHAPTER TWENTY-THREE

Microsoft Windows

AN INCREASING NUMBER of top-notch applications now require Microsoft Windows, including Excel, Micrografx Windows Draw, PageMaker, and Publisher's Type Foundry. One of the strengths of the Windows concept is that it provides a common interface between applications and peripheral devices such as the LaserJet, so once you learn the basic procedures for using Windows with the LaserJet, you'll be able to apply this knowledge to whatever new software you use.

Currently, there are two versions of Windows: Windows 2.0 for computers that use the 80286 processor (AT-compatibles) and Windows/386 for computers that use the 80386 processor. The installation procedures and font handling are identical for the two.

Installation

When you install Windows, you have the choice of a number of printers that use HP's Printer Command Language (PCL). These include the Apricot Laser, HP LaserJet, HP LaserJet Plus, HP LaserJet 500 PLUS, HP LaserJet Series II, HP LaserJet 2000, Kyocera F-1010 Laser, and QuadLaser I. If you are using a PCL printer that is not among those listed, you should generally select the LaserJet II. Note that with Windows you can install more than one printer, for example a LaserJet and a dot matrix printer.

If you have already installed Windows and want to add another printer, select CONTROL.EXE from the Windows Executive, select Installation, and from that point onward follow the instructions that Windows provides.

Cartridge Fonts

When you install Windows for any LaserJet printer, all the font cartridges sold by Hewlett-Packard are automatically installed. The method of selecting the particular cartridge you wish to use depends on the application you are using with Windows. With Windows Write, the method is as follows:

- From the File menu select Change Printer. If multiple printers are listed, select PCL or HP LaserJet (even if that is the printer you have already selected). Select OK.
- A dialog box will appear, with font cartridges listed in the lower right. Select the cartridge you wish to use and click on OK.

Now that you have chosen a cartridge, you can use the mouse to select a passage of text and then use the Character menu to format that passage of text in the desired font. If the font you wish to use does not appear among the three fonts listed in the Character menu, select Fonts to see a complete list.

Soft Fonts

To install soft fonts for use by Windows, you need to create a PFM file for each font and you also need to modify the WIN.INI file, which is the master file that stores font parameters and other information used by Win-

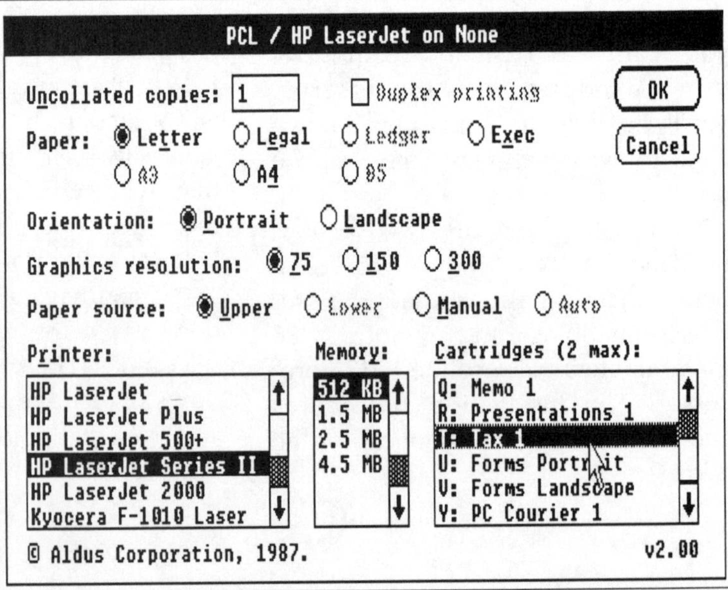

Figure 1: When you select Change Printer from within a Windows application, you have the opportunity to select which PCL printer you want to use as well as which font cartridge.

dows. To create the PFM files and modify WIN.INI, do the following:

- Create a subdirectory named PCLPFM in the Windows directory.
- Copy PCLPFM.EXE from the Windows Fonts disk to the \Windows\PCLPFM subdirectory.
- Copy any soft font files you wish to use to \Windows\PCLPFM. Make a list of the file names of the fonts.
- Run the program PCLPFM.EXE from the Windows DOS Executive (by double-clicking on the name) or from DOS (by typing PCLPFM from the DOS command line).
- When PCLPFM prompts you to enter a file name, you can either type a single file name or process multiple files by using the ? and * wild-card characters. (Note that the ? character takes the place of a single character while the * charcter takes the place of multiple characters.)
- PCLPFM will now generate a file with the PFM extension. In addition, the last character of the file will be changed to P for portrait fonts and L for landscape fonts. (If you are converting multiple fonts, you can stop the conversion process by holding down the Ctrl key and typing C.)
- Next, the program will ask if you would like to create a file called APPNDWIN.INI. Answer Y.
- To complete the procedure, you need to insert APPNDWIN.INI into the correct location within WIN.INI. One way to do this is by using the Windows Notepad.
- From the Windows MS-DOS Executive, bring up APPNDWIN.INI into the Notepad by double-clicking on APPNDWIN.INI.
- Copy the contents into the Clipboard by choosing Select All from the Edit menu and then choosing Copy.
- Load WIN.INI into the Notepad and locate the printer section that refers to the LaserJet. It will look similar to this: [HPPCL,LPT1]. Using Notepad's Paste command (from the Edit menu), insert the text from the Clipboard starting on the line just after the section header.
- Find and delete the end-of-file marker (a small box) from the end of the material you pasted into WIN.INI.
- If you want to have the fonts permanently installed, delete everything from the comma to the end of the line. Then change the font ID number to match the number loaded into the printer.
- Save the new WIN.INI file, close both copies of Notepad, and quit

Windows. Then start Windows again from the DOS command line.

CHAPTER TWENTY-FOUR

Using the LaserJet with the Macintosh

ALTHOUGH THE VAST majority of LaserJet software is designed for IBM PC–compatible computers, it's possible to use the printer with other computers, including the Macintosh. The purpose of this chapter is to survey the tools that are available.

Before we look at the capabilities of the Macintosh-LaserJet connection, it's crucial to stress that everything depends on software. As of this writing, none of the main applications for the Macintosh, including Microsoft Word and PageMaker, had drivers for the LaserJet. That means you simply cannot use these programs directly with the printer. To make the connection, you need a utility program devoted to that purpose.

Graphics

Much like the ImageWriter, the LaserJet can print bitmapped graphics from the screen of the Macintosh at both low and high resolution. The low resolution is 75 pixels per inch, approximately the same as the 72-pixel-per-inch resolution of the Macintosh screen. Note that 75 is a factor of 300, which is the actual number of dots per inch printed by the LaserJet. The LaserJet uses a tiny box, 4 dots wide and 4 dots long, to match one of the Macintosh screen pixels. Because of the difference between the 72-pixel-per-inch resolution of the Mac screen and the 75-dpi resolution of the LaserJet output, an image seen on the screen will be reduced to about 96 percent of its former size when printed on paper.

Text

This is the weak link in the Macintosh-LaserJet connection. Although there are two ways of printing text on the LaserJet from the Mac, neither is completely satisfactory. The first method is to treat text like graphics output—this lets you reproduce the characters as they appear on the Mac screen. The result is a slightly dotty appearance much like ImageWriter output.

The second method is to use the LaserJet's fonts. This gives you much higher quality type; the problem is word spacing. Until a version of Microsoft Word or another word processor appear that better supports text on the LaserJet, this will remain a major stumbling block.

Currently, there are only a handful of utilities that assist in using a Macintosh with the LaserJet. The newest and most powerful is Printworks for the Mac.

Printworks for the Mac

Printworks comes with a serial cable suitable for use with the Macintosh Plus, SE, or II. If you have a Macintosh 512, you can exchange the cable for one that fits that computer. Before installing Printworks, you'll have to change the printer's DIP switches if you have a LaserJet or LaserJet Plus, or use the Control Panel to reconfigure the printer if you have a LaserJet II. The process is described in the Printworks manual. To install Printworks, you need to use the installation program supplied with the product (don't drag the drivers onto your disks, since this will leave resources behind that Printworks needs). Once it is installed, you can activate Printworks by using the Chooser desk accessory, selecting the printer, port, and communication speed.

Once it is installed, you can use Printworks with most Macintosh applications, including MacPaint, MacDraw, MacWrite, Microsoft Word, Microsoft Works, and Excel. Text, bitmapped graphics, and object graphics can all be printed on the same page with no reduction in quality.

Perhaps the most important aspect of Printworks is the Font Adjustment feature, which lets you assign screen fonts to LaserJet fonts. For example, it is recommended that you assign Pica to Courier, Compressed to Line Printer, Times to TMS RMN, and Elite to Prestige Elite.

Another, more limited, program for the Macintosh is HP Laser Program from New Image Technology. Its sole purpose to allow you to print MacPaint documents.

Laserstart

This utility was developed by the same company that created Printworks for the Mac. It is less powerful than Printworks (but also cheaper).

Laserstart makes it possible for the LaserJet to print text and graphics produced by most Macintosh programs. Laserstart is easily installed, modifying the System file and the ImageWriter file in the System Folder. After installation, the ImageWriter file is renamed LaserJet. Note that the LaserJet uses the standard ImageWriter cable with the Macintosh. With Laserstart you cannot use the LaserJet on an AppleTalk network, but you do have the option of connecting the printer to the computer using either the printer or the modem port.

Laserstart lets you select the speed of data transmission between the computer and the printer. If you want to select a data transmission rate other than the standard 9,600 baud, you need to change the settings of the DIP switches inside the printer, as explained in the LaserJet manual. Increasing the rate to 19,200 baud can dramatically reduce the amount of time you have to wait for printed output.

Once you have used Laserstart to modify one of your application programs, such as MacWrite, the modified program will print to the LaserJet. Laserstart supports three printing options: Standard, High, and Draft.

With the Standard option, type and graphics are printed exactly as you see them on the screen, with a four percent reduction. With the High print-quality option, the LaserJet is still replicating what you see on the screen, but at twice the resolution of Standard, i.e., 150 pixels per inch. For graphics, this allows Laserstart to perform a smoothing function. Circles and slanted lines or arcs become less jagged. With this option, you get best results for type if a font twice the size of the one you are printing is defined. To tell if such a font is defined, see if it is highlighted in the pull-down menu.

Draft mode is the Laserstart printing option that lets you use the LaserJet's own fonts rather than the Macintosh fonts. You get best results in this mode if the screen font you use is close to the same size and style of the printer font you are using with the LaserJet. In fact, Laserstart will seek

Access

Printworks for the Mac
Laserstart
Phoenix Technologies
7192 Kalanianaole Hwy. #205
Honolulu, HI 96825
808/396-6368
Also available from Hewlett-Packard Direct: 800/538-8787
HP Part No. Printworks for the Mac 35179P, Laserstart with cable 35179M, Laserstart without cable 35178M
Price: Printworks for the Mac $195, Laserstart with cable $95, Laserstart without cable $65

out a LaserJet font that matches as closely as possible the font you are using on the screen.

Unfortunately, getting good results in Draft mode requires some experimenting with what sizes and styles of type on-screen provide the best results on paper. The basic problem is that type tends to be too spread out, and right justification does not work if your type is proportionally spaced. By carefully selecting the on-screen font, you can achieve fairly tight spacing between words. But there does not seem to be any way to get right justification with proportionally spaced fonts like Tms Rmn, Letter Gothic, or Helv.

Laserstart also adds a new entry to the finder called Print Adjustment. This lets you select the number of copies you wish to print and the type you wish to use for draft printing. The operation of this menu is a bit confusing, however. Even if you select Gothic, you still may get Times Roman.

CHAPTER TWENTY-FIVE

Using the LaserJet with Other Computers

ALTHOUGH THIS BOOK focuses mainly on software for DOS computers, a number of utilities to assist in using the LaserJet with other computers. The following is an inventory of what's available.

Convergent Technologies Workstations

Available from American Computing (505/293-0494), LaserFile Plus is a driver that makes it possible to print on a LaserJet from the word processing software used by the Ngen line of workstations. Similarly, LaserGraphics lets you print charts and pictures from the Art/Chart software that runs on the Ngen. It works with HP font cartridges A, B, D-H, J, L-N, P, U, and V.

Prime Computers

LaserHelper is a program from Cogent Information Systems (201/795-4003) that makes printing on a LaserJet possible from a Prime System running Primos 18.0 or later. It works with HP font cartridges A-H, J-N, P-R, and T-Z.

Another program for Prime Computers (Primos 19 and 20) is Spoolwatch from Watchung Software Group (201/668-0507). It lets you define mnemonics that are translated into LaserJet escape sequences. Soft fonts are not supported, but the program works with cartridges A-F, J-N, P-R, and Y.

Wang

LaserNet-A, from Carr & Associates (312/799-2337) is a program that lets you print on a LaserJet from Wang VS and Wang OIS systems. It supports cartridges A-H, J, L, M, N, and R as well as most of the HP soft fonts. With the program installed, you can use any of the Wang word processing functions as you normally would.

For Wang 2200 Series computers, Laser Optimizer from The Computer Printout (312/799-4510) is an intelligent spooler that sits between the computer and the LaserJet. It supports the A-H and L cartridges.

For Wang PC Word Processing as well as most Wang Core products, the MCS Group Printer Driver from the MCS Group (605/341-6755) makes it possible to control most LaserJet functions from a menu system. The program works with cartridges A-H, J-N, P-R, and U-W.

Another set of programs that supplement the Wang PC are PCS Director Basic Printer Driver and PCS Director Advanced Printer Support, from Amtech Computer Systems (203/659-2635). Features include printer network support, multiple fonts, screen shots, and justified text. The program supports cartridges A-H, K, L, N, P-R, and T-W.

Finally, Printer Driver for Wang PC, from LANworks (617/491-3000) lets you take advantage of every Wang PC word processing feature on the LaserJet. It translates special characters used in the Wang WISCII symbol set to their counterparts in the LaserJet's Roman-8 symbol set.

Burroughs

Available from Gregory Publishing Company (408/727-4660), the Micro Image Printing System (MIPS) outputs word-processed documents created on a Burroughs system and retains attributes such as boldface, italics, overstrike, tabs, headers, and footers when printed on the LaserJet. The program works with cartridges A, B, D-F, L-N, P, and Q but does not support soft fonts.

Power

You can print under UNIX System V from the Power 5/32 line of computers using OfficePower Integrated Office System from Computer Consoles (703/648-3489). Cartridge fonts A-H, J-N, P-R, and T-Z are supported but soft fonts are not.

Z-System, CP/M

PrintStar from Echelon (415/948-3820) lets you print WordStar from a Z-System or CP/M (2.2) computer, such as the Commodore 128, Kaypro CP/M, SB180, and Ampro. You can have up to three fonts per line with the B cartridge, and downloadable soft fonts are also available as an option.

DEC VAX

QROFF, from OCAD Systems (408/727-6671), is a text formatter that can be used in conjunction with most word processors. It allows multiple fonts, justified text, and control over indents and line spacing. Soft fonts are not supported, but you can use the A, B, D, E, F, and L cartridges.

IBM 370, 30XX, 43XX, and 93XX

For these computers that use the VM/SP operating system, Rapid from VM/CMS Unlimited (617/288-4434) lets you print on the LaserJet in serial mode. It supports all the HP cartridge and soft fonts.

NBI

Emulazor, a hardware interface from Brookrock Corporation (800/345-0315), lets you print on the LaserJet from NBI word processing systems. Soft fonts are not supported, but you can use cartridges A-E, G, H, J, L-N, Q, and R. The product supports some LaserJet features such as boldfacing and underlining but does not allow use of proportional fonts.

IBM DisplayWriter

ESI-2646 LaserConnection from Extended Systems (208/322-7163), lets you use the LaserJet with the IBM DisplayWriter word processing workstation as well as with IBM System 34/36/38. It supports all word processor features and also allows landscape printing, envelope printing, and manual feed.

IBM Systems 34/36/38

The GBT series of printer interfaces, from General Business Technology (714/261-1891) comprise special cables and software drivers to connect IBM Systems 34, 36, and 38 to a LaserJet. With the software installed, the LaserJet emulates an IBM 5225 or 5219/3812 printer and can be used with DisplayWrite 36, Textmanagement, or OCL print commands. Soft fonts are not supported, but most cartridge fonts can be used with the product.

The 1181 WP Terminal from I-O Corporation (801/973-6767) is a word processing station that is specifically designed to interface an IBM System 34, 36, or 38 computer to a LaserJet. It provides IBM 5219 emulation and supports DisplayWrite 36 software. It works with most cartridge fonts, but not with soft fonts. I-O Corporation also sells the 8219 SM (Side Mount Module), an interface box that attaches to the side of the LaserJet and causes the printer to emulate an IBM 5219 printer. A third set of products from I-O Corporation are I-O 8225 HP and I-O 8219 HP, which both emulate an IBM 5225 printer.

Available from Micro Trends (205/666-5256), the 3X/Coax Attachment causes the LaserJet to emulate an IBM printer.

Interlynx/5251, from Local Data (213/320-7126), makes it possible to attach up to seven LaserJet printers to an IBM computer via a twinaxial port. The printers will emulate various IBM printers.

IBM 370/43XX/30XX/93XX

The ACX-PM Printer Manager from ACX Software (312/983-5555) works with IBM mainframe computers, emulating 3270 printers.

IRMAPrint, from Digital Communications Association (800/241-IRMA), attaches to the computer using the 3270 controller network via coaxial cable. It supports most of the HP font cartridges and soft fonts.

IBM S1370

The 6287 Protocol Convertor from Agile (415/825-9220) causes a LaserJet to emulate IBM 3287, 3262, 3268, and 5210 printers in BSC and SNA/SDLC applications.

LBI, CPT, Lanier, AM, Jacquard, Philips, Micom, Lexitron, and Raytheon

LaserMate 500, from BDT Products (714/660-1386), is a hardware interface for word processing systems that use a 13-bit parallel interface. It causes a LaserJet to emulate the Qume Sprint 3 protocol.

CHAPTER TWENTY-SIX

LaserJet Shareware Gems

As developer of several commercial LaserJet programs, author of a newsletter on the LaserJet, and electronic bulletin board addict, Joe Beda is the quintessential LaserJet maven. He's tried out scores of LaserJet public domain and Shareware programs; in this chapter, he reveals his favorites.

—TN & MG

THE PERSONAL COMPUTER has spawned many new and innovative ideas. One of these, originally conceived by Andrew Fluegelman, a writer, publisher, programmer, and founding editor of PC World, is that of Freeware or (as it is now more commonly known) Shareware.

Soon after the introduction of the IBM PC, Fluegelman wrote a program called PC-Talk. From his experiences in the book industry, Fluegelman recognized the barriers to commercially marketing his program, and he hit upon an innovative solution. Why not make the program available on bulletin boards, allow users to try it for free, and request those who liked it to send in a registration fee?

As quirky as the idea may sound, it worked. The invitation to freely exchange the program gave it wide exposure, and enough users sent in the requested fee that Fluegelman's work was well rewarded. By now, the Shareware method of distributing software is well established and has been used successfully by a number of software companies, including Buttonware (PC-File and other programs) and QuickSoft (PC-Write).

It should be emphasized that Shareware is not synonymous with public domain software, which refers to programs that were developed to solve a specific problem and, through the generosity of the author, put in the public domain for use by anyone who might require it, free of charge. Shareware authors do expect to receive remuneration for their efforts, though of course the user is on the honor system.

There are many cases of programs that have been released under the Shareware concept that do not warrant a registration fee. This is usually because the software is poorly written but author is just trying to make a few dollars. So, Shareware (registration fee requested) is not necessarily superior to public domain software, and in fact there are duds in both categories. Nonetheless, there are many hundreds of Shareware programs that are excellent utilities. Remember also that beauty is in the eye of the beholder, and one program could be completely useless to one person and an indispensable tool to another.

To find those programs that are truly the gems of the public domain and Shareware universe usually requires a tremendous investment of time to search through and test in increasing multitude of programs that become available each week. The task becomes nearly insurmountable for one person to accomplish. For this reason, the help of a user group or knowledgeable friends and associates is necessary.

Some examples of the good programs available for LaserJets follow. These programs are written to run on IBM or compatible computers using PC/MS-DOS.

Envelope Printing

When your word processor produces a good-looking letter, do you then address the envelope by hand? Do you run over to your trusty old typewriter? Why not also let your LaserJet print your envelopes for you? Here are two great envelope-printing utilities, EnvLJ and GrabPlus.

EnvLJ

EnvLJ shows a screen that looks like the front of an envelope. Simply type in a return address and a mailing address, insert an envelope in your printer, and print your envelope.

EnvLJ works well for a single envelope. EnvLJ also provides a simple database facility for those envelopes that you tend to address over and over: newsletter files, memo addresses, customer lists, bill payments, etc. EnvLJ lets you select one of many data bases that you may have developed. From the selected data base you can choose one, several, or the entire collection of addresses to print at LaserJet speed and quality.

GrabPlus

GrabPlus is a memory resident program that allows you to point at the address in your letter, "grab" it, and then print your envelope. You can choose between two envelopes, large (standard business #10) and small (3 5/8" by 6 1/2").

GrabPlus can be used with any word processor that displays the screen in text mode. (Some WYSIWYG word processors display their screens in graphics mode to better show you what the finished text looks like. Since GrabPlus cannot read from the graphic screen, with these word processors you must enter the address manually.)

GrabPlus also comes with a powerful database function that lets you import names and addresses from your database files, export the data base to your word processor's merge file, and select addresses from the data base using one of five tags that you assign to each address.

In addition, GrabPlus provides for printing the address on your envelope in three different formats. You can position the name field before the company name, after the company name or as an attention line below the city and state line.

Text Printing

Often you may want to print a text file that requires many sheets of paper. If you have many such printouts, storage space can become a significant consideration. You'll find your paper bill can become astronomical, as well, since a LaserJet can print almost as fast as you can fill the paper cassette.

Because the LaserJet can print very clearly and legibly at smaller typefaces, it is not always necessary to print using the default Courier 10 pitch font. If you have a landscape 16.66 font available, you can use one of the next three programs to print, on a single sheet of paper, four pages of 66 lines containing 80 characters. They print two pages side by side for as many pages as necessary to fit the entire document, then instruct you to reinsert the pages into the printer and print two additional pages on the blank side of each sheet.

LJBook

LJBook is written in assembler and is very fast. The program will scan your ASCII text file, tell you how many pages are required, and print the document by feeding the paper through the printer twice. Then simply fold the pages in half and staple. You have a small booklet that contains all the text from your document in a very compact form. LJBook also provides a heading line on each page that can show a file name or title that you supply, the date of printing, and the page number.

Pamphlet

Pamphlet is a program similar to LJBook, but provides additional formatting capability via control codes

Access: LaserJet Shareware

GrabPlus
Paul Mayer
ZPAY Payroll Systems
3516 Ruby Street
Franklin Park, IL 60131
Registration fee: $15 (includes latest version)

LJBook
Vernon D. Buerg
139 White Oak Circle
Petaluma, CA 94952
Registration fee: $15

EnvLJ
Steven Stern
JMB Realty Corporation
900 N. Michigan Avenue
Chicago, IL 60611
Registration fee: $35

Pamphlet
Martin Beattie
9190 Rolling Tree Lane
Fair Oaks, CA 95628
Registration fee: $25 plus $1.50 for latest version

4Print
Korenthal Associates, Inc.
230 West 13th Street
New York, NY 10011
Registration fee: $25 plus $10 for latest version

you embed within the document. These codes allow you to select a different font, or underline words and phrases or print them in bold or italic.

Pamphlet does not provide its own fonts, but it permits you to use any fonts that you have available, including cartridge or soft fonts. The program also will download soft fonts into your printer.

4Print

4Print does not output into a booklet format. It will print four pages on a single sheet of paper, but the format is different. The pages are designed to be punched and inserted into a standard three-ring binder. The program was designed to print program listings that allow you to view four pages at one time. If you're a programmer using a LaserJet to produce reference and documentation, this is the program for you.

Where to Get These Programs

These programs are available on many computer bulletin boards and from user group libraries. If you do not have access to either of these sources, you may wish to contact the author directly.

If you acquire one of these programs and continue to use it after testing the program, please be sure to send the registration fee to the author. These programs reflect untold hours of work on the part of the authors. Show your appreciation by registering your copy of the program. When you register your program, you will be notified of future enhancements to the program. Authors will also certainly be more willing to listen to suggestions for improvements or enhancements if you are a registered user.

—Joe Beda

8

ENHANCEMENTS AND UPGRADES

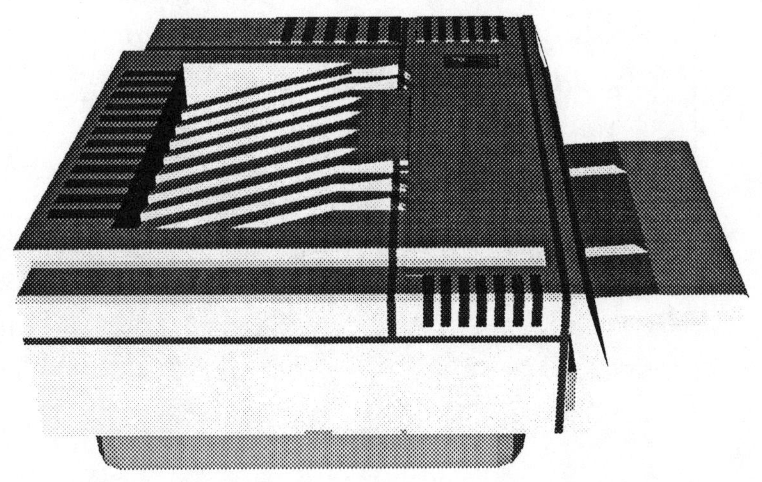

Section Focus

Interested in making your LaserJet faster? Teaching it to speak PostScript? Adding memory? Hooking it up to multiple computers? Running it from a computer at the other end of the hall? Adding a bigger paper tray?

Well, you're in luck. Because of the swelling market for LaserJet add-ons, all these options are available—and more. And unlike previous members of the LaserJet family, the LaserJet II was designed with upgrades in mind, so in most cases you can perform the installation entirely on your own.

CHAPTER TWENTY-SIX

Upgrade Options

FOR OVER A DECADE, one of the main forces that has driven the personal computer phenomenon is the notion of the open system. By now it's taken for granted that when you buy a computer, you're not just getting what you see (the built-in capabilities of the system), but also what you don't see (the future capabilities represented by the empty slots on the bus).

Only two obstacles stand in the way of applying the same principle of expandability to laser printers. The first is the tendency of people to lump lasers into the same category as other printers: mere "peripherals." That perception is changing as it becomes more widely understood that laser printers are actually powerful computers in their own right. All of the printers in the HP LaserJet family use the Motorola 68000 microprocessor, the same chip used in the Macintosh computer. Like personal computers, laser printers also have permanent memory (ROM) and dynamic memory (RAM).

The second obstacle to laser printer upgrades has been the design of the machines themselves. Until recently, the manufacturers didn't take into account the fact that users might want to increase the memory or enhance the speed of their machines.

Fortunately, the design of the LaserJet II explicitly allows for upgrading, for example adding more memory or a faster controller board. Upgrades are available for earlier models as well, but with the LaserJet II, upgrading is simplicity itself.

A number of upgrade options are available: adding memory, adding a PostScript controller (JetScript for LaserJet II printers or PS Jet for older model LaserJets), adding a JLaserPlus board, or adding a LaserMaster CAP-Card controller.

PostScript Upgrades

To understand what PostScript is and does, we have to recall that the architecture of a laser printer is made up of two parts: engine (the machinery that makes the actual marks on paper) and controller (the brains of the printer that control where the engine will make its marks). The controller of the LaserJet family is designed to recognize HP's Printer Command Language, or PCL. While PCL is an effective vehicle for handling most laser printer tasks, it's not intended for some types of complex graphics functions. And although the technology for handling scalable fonts is beginning to arrive for use with PCL, so far it has not been provided as part of PCL itself.

In a nutshell, one might describe PostScript as a more powerful, but slower, alternative to PCL. Whereas PCL comprises a collection of command codes, PostScript is a full-fledged computer language that allows a good deal more complexity, particularly in graphics.

While we could go on at length about the the relative merits of PCL and PostScript, the choice of whether to add a PostScript upgrade to your LaserJet really boils down to a few practical considerations:

- If you're a fan of special-effects graphics and special font effects, go with PostScript.
- If you like to experiment with a variety of type sizes, go with PostScript.

PostScript Clones and Compatibles

Just as there are many implementations of BASIC, C, Pascal, and other computer languages, a number of laser printer controllers with PostScript interpreters are beginning to appear. These interpreters offer two potential advantages over the original PostScript interpreters from Adobe: speed and price. The potential drawbacks of the clones are that they may not be fully compatible with Adobe's PostScript and that they may not deliver as high a quality output, especially in the area of fonts.

Non-PostScript Upgrade Boards

The original non-PostScript upgrade board for the LaserJet was the JLaser from Tall Tree Systems. It became popular with owners of the LaserJet who needed a full megabyte of memory in order to use desktop publishing packages or graphics packages, especially Ventura Publisher, PC Paintbrush, and DR Halo. One big drawback of the JLaser was that it suffered from compatibility problems with various PC compatibles and clones. More recently, the LaserMaster CAPCard has eclipsed the JLaser (as well as the newer JLaserPlus). The reasons are threefold. First, the LaserMaster has none of the compatibility problems that plague the JLaser. Sec-

Access: Upgrades

LaserMaster CAPCard
LaserMaster Corp.
7156 Shady Oak Rd.
Eden Prairie, MN 55344
800/562-7568

JLaserPlus
Tall Tree Systems
2585 E. Bayshore Rd.
P.O. Box 50690
Palo Alto, CA 94303
415/493-1980

PS Jet Plus
The Laser Connection
7852 Schillinger Park W.
Mobile, AL 36608
205/633-7223

PC Publisher Kit
Imagen Corp.
2650 San Tomas Expressway
Santa Clara, CA 95051
408/986-9400

JetScript
Hewlett-Packard Corp.
11311 Chinden Blvd.
Boise, ID 83707
800/752-0900

Conodesk 6000
Conographic Corp.
116802 Aston
Irvine, CA 92714
714/474-9125

ond, the CAPCard is extremely fast, even faster than the JLaser. Third, while the JLaser is limited to 30-point fonts with Ventura Publisher, the CAPCard's driver for Ventura Publisher provides numerous advanced features, including large fonts, scalable fonts on the fly, outline fonts, and even diagonal printing. At this point the CAPCard is clearly the better of the two.

Profile: JetScript

JETSCRIPT IS DESIGNED to provide a PostScript upgrade for LaserJet II printers. The product does not work with older-generation LaserJets such as the original LaserJet, the LaserJet Plus, and the LaserJet 500 PLUS.

JetScript consists of two circuit boards. One is installed in a small slot in the back of the LaserJet II; the other fills a standard slot in the PC. The two are connected with a high-speed cable.

Under the installation procedure, you run an installation program before you install the two boards. The installation program checks the configuration of your computer and tells you how to set the jumpers on the circuit board for the PC. Because of this installation program, configuring the board is much easier than would otherwise be the case.

Two in One

After you've installed JetScript, you really have two printers in one. If desired, you can continue to print just as you normally would, using the printer in LaserJet mode with all your accustomed soft fonts and font cartridges. In this case, printing is directed through the normal printer port. Alternatively, you can use the

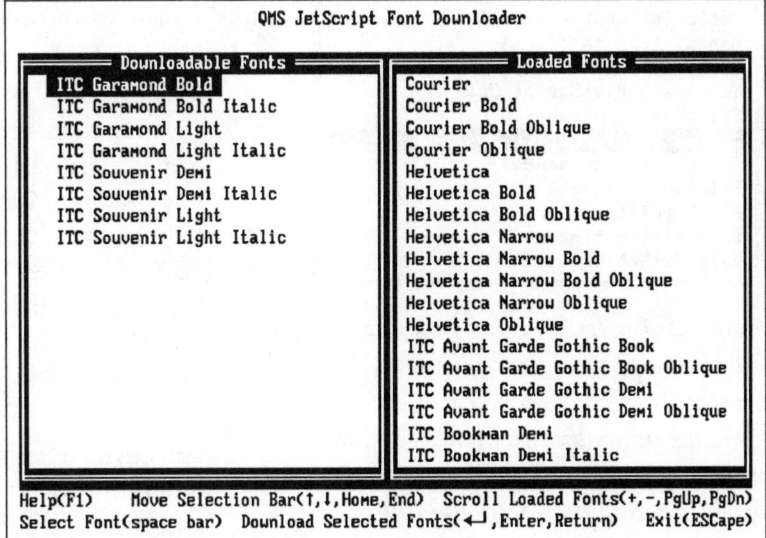

Figure 1: The JetFonts utility displays the resident fonts and the fonts that have already been downloaded on the right. On the left are fonts that you can download by selecting them with the spacebar and then pressing Enter.

printer in PostScript mode, directing printing through the special cable. For example, you could have LPT1: assigned to LaserJet mode and have LPT2: assigned to PostScript mode, and switch back and forth merely by changing the port assignment in your software package.

While other PostScript printers do provide HP emulation, the JetScript approach is superior for three reasons:

- Since you can still use the LaserJet itself rather an emulation, there's no chance of the emulation being slightly faulty.
- Most emulations don't allow you to use font cartridges.
- Most emulations of the LaserJet are slower than the LaserJet itself.

```
QMS JetSet Utility

JetScript status report
Manual feed on/off
Download a PostScript file
Terminate PostScript job
Print samples
JetChat (Interactive PostScript)
Change printer name
Printer alignment
Reset printer alignment
Set printer timeout
Exit JetSet Utility
```

Figure 2: The JetSet utility provides a number of options for controlling the printer. These include JetChat, an interactive utility that lets you program in PostScript directly without separately creating and downloading files.

Performance

When you choose to operate in PostScript mode, you'll find that JetScript outperforms almost any PostScript laser printer on the market. One reason is that it contains 3MB of RAM, in contrast to the 1.5MB provided by some PostScript printers. Another reason is that it uses a high-speed video interface, rather than the much slower serial interface used by most other PostScript printers. Particularly for printing large bitmapped images, but also for downloading fonts, JetScript's high-speed cable makes a tremendous difference.

Nevertheless, the slow speed of PostScript will probably shock you, especially if you've been spoiled by the comparatively fast operation of the LaserJet. Fortunately, there are two simple measures you can take to speed your work up dramatically:

- Always download your fonts at the beginning of your work session rather than let your application download the fonts. For downloading fonts, use the Jetfonts utility that is automatically installed in the \QMSJS directory during the JetScript installation procedure. The JetFonts menu is shown in Figure 1.
- Get hold of LaserTORQ, a high-performance spooling utility that buffers the data you send to JetScript and then takes care of

printing in the background while you return to working with your application. For details, see "Profile: LaserTORQ."

JetSet

One of the best features of the JetScript board is the JetSet utility, whose main menu is shown in Figure 2. This utility has a range of commands for controlling and adjusting the printer, including alignment of the page, downloading PostScript fonts, interactively sending PostScript files to the printer, toggling manual feed, and receiving a status report on the printer. The JetSet utility is accessed by typing JETSET from within the JetScript subdirectory.

Fonts

Like PS Jet Plus, JetScript comes with the same set of standard resident fonts as the Apple LaserWriter Plus, including the Times Roman, Helvetica, Courier, ITC Avant Garde Gothic, Palatino, New Century Schoolbook, Helvetica Narrow, ITC Bookman Light, ITC Zapf Chancery, and Symbol font families. Counting all the variations within each family, a total of 35 fonts are built into the printer.

Profile: PS Jet Plus

PS JET PLUS is an upgrade option that works with LaserJets that use the Canon LBP-CX engine. These include the LaserJet and LaserJet Plus, but not the LaserJet II. The upgrade involves removing the top portion of the laser printer and then connecting up an entirely new top. Once you've completed the work of installing the new top (which takes about an hour), you have a printer that is the functional equivalent of a QMS PS-800 PostScript printer, which itself is slightly superior to the Apple LaserWriter in that it is somewhat faster and 2MB rather than 1.5MB of RAM.

One advantage of the PS Jet approach is that when you're done you can use the printer with either a Macintosh or a PC. In contrast, the JetScript upgrade can only be used with a PC.

PS Jet Plus contains the same typefaces as the Apple LaserWriter Plus: Times Roman, Palatino, ITC Avant Garde Gothic, ITC Bookman, Helvetica Narrow, New Century Schoolbook, ITC Zapf Chancery, and ITC Zapf Dingbats.

Installation

The installation procedure involves unscrewing the top portion of the laser printer, disconnecting its cables, and installing a new top manufactured by the Laser Connection. On an HP LaserJet the removal portion of the task involves unscrewing 12 easily accessible external screws and one slightly difficult internal screw, pulling out a plastic shield that is somewhat tough to budge, and disconnecting three cables. Installing the new top is the same process in reverse.

While a practiced hand could probably make the switch in about 20 minutes, you should budget more time than that to the task and approach it with caution. Our first attempt took an hour and a half; on our second try we did the transplant in just under an hour.

For the most part, the steps of the procedure are clearly described and illustrated. None is difficult, except the removal of a small screw within the printer, for which purpose the Laser Connection thoughtfully provides a magnetized screwdriver with the PS Jet package.

We recommend that you not rely on the magnetic screw driver to hold the small screw. Just to be on the safe side, wrap a loop of tape around the end of the screw driver once you've loosened the screw a few turns. That way the screw will stay attached to the screwdriver until you've drawn it completely out, and you're less likely to get involved with a game of cat and mouse between your needle-nose pliers and a small screw rattling around inside your printer.

Access

PS Jet Plus
Laser Connection
P.O. Box 850296
Mobile, AL 36685
205/633-7223

Operations

Once you've installed the PS Jet, you'll be ready to print. QMS provides a disk with a menu-driven program that configures the PC and provides some demo PostScript files.

Hewlett Packard Graphics Language Emulation

Of course, for all the attractions of having PostScript and HPGL emulation in your printer, there's still one fly in the ointment. What about all the LaserJet software you've got in your library? Will you have to give that up? Fortunately, the answer is no, because PS Jet does provide an emulation of the LaserJet Plus. However, you won't be able to use font cartridges any more, and you may find that font widths don't match quite right.

Profile: LaserMaster CAPCard

THE CAPCARD CAN be used to upgrade either the earlier LaserJet models (Canon LBP-CX engine) or the LaserJet II (Canon LBP-SX engine). In many respects, the CAPCard resembles the JLaser board. Like JLaser, it consists of a board (1.5MB) that is installed in the computer and then connected via a special cable into the back of the LaserJet. The difference is that the CAPCard includes a high-speed raster image processor (RIP), similar to the LaserJet's own controller but much faster. After installing the CAPCard, you can use the LaserJet as usual with your current software, but with software that provides a LaserMaster driver you get the benefit of faster printing.

To see just what the speed difference would be, we created two pages using Xerox Ventura Publisher and then timed how long it took to print them on a LaserJet printer (original model) enhanced with a CAPCard, the same printer enhanced with PS Jet, and on a LaserJet Series II with the basic (512K) memory option. The first test was a single page of a three-column layout with seven different fonts. The page included two vertical lines to separate the columns but did not include any illustrations. For the LaserJet Series II the time was 69 seconds, for the PS Jet it was 150 seconds, and for the CAP/Card it was 30 seconds.

The second test was the same page, adjusted to make room for a 3 by-4-inch bitmapped picture. The LaserJet Series II was unable to print the page due to memory limitations. For the PS Jet the time was 221 seconds, and for the CAPCard it was 45 seconds.

As the results show, the CAPCard was about twice as fast as the LaserJet and five times faster than the PostScript printer. That's a dramatic difference that makes the CAPCard an especially attractive alternative for those users who make heavy use of graphics in their documents.

Access

LaserMaster CAPCard

LaserMaster Corp.
7156 Shady Oak Rd.
Eden Prairie, MN 55344
612/944-6069

Figure 1: Although the CAPCard's font generator uses Bitstream's Fontware technology, it actually goes beyond Fontware in the number of special effects it allows. This sample shows what is possible with the CAPCard's Ventura driver.

Font Generation

In addition to the basic 1.5MB configuration, you can buy an additional 0.5MB module with a built-in font compiler that uses Bitstream's Fontware technology. This module comes with all 35 typefaces used in the Apple LaserWriter Plus and other PostScript printers. Because the font widths are identical to those used by PostScript, you can use the CAPCard as a proofing device prior to typesetting on a Linotronic PostScript typesetter. You can also purchase additional Bitstream font master outlines and generate more fonts of any size.

The CAPCard really shines in conjunction with Ventura Publisher, for which it has a special driver that generates fonts of any size on the fly and also allows you to create a number of special effects, as shown in Figure 1. These include diagonal type, outlined type, type filled with patterns, and rotated type.

CHAPTER TWENTY-NINE

Other Enhancements

BECAUSE OF ITS POPULARITY, the LaserJet has spawned a small subindustry of companies providing a variety of enhancements, large and small. Some of these were designed to address minor deficiencies in the original models of the printer, such as the fact that since paper emerged faceup, documents ended up being printed in reverse order. With the improved design of the LaserJet II, these enhancements are no longer necessary, but others—such as spoolers that speed up printing—are still valuable. This chapter provides a brief survey of what's available.

Paper Feeders

If you tend to do a lot of printing, you may want to avoid having to frequently refill the paper tray. Here's where paper feeders come in. Some of these, such as the JetFeed I, merely provide a larger bin than the LaserJet. Others go much further. For example, MultiFeeder from BDT Products has six bins and costs as much as two LaserJets!

Collators

At the other end of the paper path are collators and other sorts of output trays. These are generally unnecessary for the LaserJet II, due to its capacious output tray, which lets sheets fall face down (and hence in the correct order), but they are a welcome relief for those still using earlier models of the printer.

One simple concept is a bin that hangs below the table and catches sheets as they fall, allowing them to flip over so they end up in the correct order. While this may sound like a simple idea, we've seen at least one example of a tray that simply did not work. The first sheet emerged from the printer and flipped into the V-shaped bin—fine. However, due to the heat of the printer, the paper remained curled momentarily, and when the next sheet came out of the printer it collided with the first and ended up on the floor. After that it was catch as catch can: some pages in the bin, some on the floor. So buy these devices if you must, but (hopefully) get a guarantee that they'll really work as advertised.

Printer-Sharing Devices

As they say in nursery school, sometimes you have to learn to share. The goal of printer-sharing devices is to make this as painless as possible. Generally, they allow three to five computers to share and printer a provide a modest buffer as well, although one product (EZQueue 3000) enables up to 24 PCs to share a single LaserJet.

In selecting a printer-sharing device, select one that performs the switching mechanically and select one that switches electronically. Because of voltage surges from mechanical switches, they have been known to burn out circuit boards. If you use a mechanical switcher, you will void your warranty.

Those with the LaserJet II should look for printer sharing devices that connect directly into that printer's optional I/O slot. Currently, the only products that provide this capability are the Digital Product's LaserBoard, the ShareSpool ESI 2041A from Extended Systems, the Giltronix EZ-Queue laser card, and the Qubit Corporation JetNET/4+1. Of these, the JetNET/4+1 appears to offer the most features, since it is the only sharing device that uses the parallel port, has expandable memory, and fits into the I/O slot.

Buffers and Spoolers

The idea behind a buffer is that your computer can spew out data faster than a printer can absorb and act on it. Without a buffer, you can't go on with your work until the printer is finished. Naturally, this can tie up your work for a long time, especially if you're printing long documents containing lots of pictures. Buffers and spoolers work by quickly receiving the data to be printed and letting you go immediately back to work with your application. Meanwhile, they feed the data to the printer until the job is finished.

The job of buffering can be handled either in software or hardware. If you buy a hardware buffer, it's preferable to get one that allows you to add memory down the road. Another highly desirable feature is the ability to work with the parallel port of the printer rather than the serial port, since parallel printing is so much faster. Finally, if you have a LaserJet II, it's better to buy a hardware buffer that fits into the printer's optional I/O slot. Such units are more convenient and compact, since they don't require a separate box or separate power supply. In addition, they are tailored specifically for the LaserJet II and hence can provide features such as automatically ejecting a page. The best hardware buffer is the JetNET/4+1, which also works as a printer-sharing device.

Software spoolers have the advantage of being able to feed data through the parallel port of the printer, a capability found in few hardware spoolers. One extremely fast software spooler is LaserTORQ, reviewed in "Profile: LaserTORQ" following this chapter.

Cable Extenders

Standard parallel cables are limited to about 10 feet, and standard serial cables to about 50 feet, due to faulty transmissions that result from longer cables. Cable extenders use fiber optics and other technologies (including standard telephone cables) to overcome the distance limitations. In some cases, the computer can be as much as a mile from the printer.

Access: Printer Enhancements

BUFFERS AND SPOOLERS

Buffer Plus
Applied Creative Technology
10529 Olympic Dr. #101
Dallas, TX 75220
800/433-5373
Price: $239 to $269
Description: A 64K buffer box with four programmable function keys. Works with either the parallel or the serial port.

Data Manager I Mega Buffer

Data Manager II Mega Buffer
See Printer-Sharing Devices.

EZQueue
See Printer-Sharing Devices.

Four Channel Buffer
See Printer-Sharing Devices.

JetNET/4+1
See Printer-Sharing Devices.

JetSpool
Computerific, Inc.
316 Fifth Ave.
New York, NY 10001
212/695-2100
Price: $19.95
Description: A software spooler that uses extended memory.

The Juggler
See Printer-Sharing Devices.

LaserBoard
See Printer-Sharing Devices.

LaserTORQ
See "Profile: LaserTORQ"

The Logical Connection
See Printer-Sharing Devices.

MasterLink
See Printer-Sharing Devices.

Mega-Link
See Printer-Sharing Devices.

Printer Optimizer
See Printer-Sharing Devices.

Print Master
See Printer-Sharing Devices.

PrintQ
Software Directions, Inc.

1572 Sussex Turnpike
Randolph, NJ 07869
201/584-8466
Price: $89
Description: A spooler that uses the hard disk. It provides a pop-up status report and takes up 46K of RAM.

Universal Printer Buffer
Universal Printer Buffer Plus
Johnathon Freeman Design, Inc.
P.O. Box 880114
San Francisco, CA 94188
415/822-8451
Price: $249 to $925
Description: The Universal Printer Buffer can have up to 256K memory; the Plus increases that up to 1MB.

VP220 Printer Buffer
See Printer-Sharing Devices.

COLLATORS AND OUTPUT BINS

Collaser
AVN, Inc.
P.O. Box 1036
1036 E. 820 N.
Provo, UT
801/375-8533
Price: $34.50
Description: A paper catcher that flips the paper over as it falls out of the printer, so documents end up in the correct order.

Forms Flipper
BDT Products, Inc.
17152 Armstrong Ave.
Irvine, CA 92417
714/660-1386
Price: $140
Description: An output device for the original LaserJet and LaserJet Plus that holds up to 500 sheets and places them in correct order.

Rightray
Computer Stuff
401 Deerfield Dr.
Mars, PA 16046
412/776-0720
Price: $29.95
Description: This is an output tray for the original LaserJet and the LaserJet Plus that can hold up to 150 sheets in correct order.

CABLE EXTENDERS

Co-Optic Parallel Sub-LAN Link
Co-Optic, Inc.
One First St. #3

Los Altos, CA 94022
415/949-0911
Price: $220
Description: Extends parallel cable up to a mile

Long-Link Parallel Interface Extension 7,000 Feet
Intellicom
9259 Eton
Chatsworth, CA 91311
818/882-8866
Price: $179
Description: Extends parallel cable up to 7000 feet.

Robox Print Extenders
Support Systems International
150 South Second St.
Richmond, CA 94804
415/234-9090
Description: Extends parallel cable more than 100 feet.

PRINTER-SHARING DEVICES

Auto-T Switch Series
Integrated Marketing Corp.
1031-H E. Duane Ave.
Sunnyvale, CA 94086
Price: $149 to $249
Description: Allows up to six computers to share a single printer without manual switching.

BFG4MD
Suncoast/EasyCom, Inc.
P.O. Box 23101
Nashville, TN 37202
815/336-0615
Price: $366
Description: A device that allows more than one computer to share a single LaserJet.

Co-optic Power Share
Co-optic, Inc.
One First St. #3
Los Altos, CA 94022
415/949-0911
Price: $995
Description: Allows multiple computers to share a LaserJet.

Crosspoint 8 Group Data Switch
Server Technology, Inc.
1710 Willow Creek Circle #14
Eugene, OR 97402
800/232-7729
Price: $599.95
Description: Allows up to seven computers to share a LaserJet.

Data Manager I and II Mega Buffer
Integrated Marketing Corp.
1031-H E. Duane Ave.
Sunnyvale, CA 94086

408/730-1112
800/537-5999
Price: $495 to $1,095
Description: Allows up to five computers to share a LaserJet. Includes a 64K buffer.

EZQueue
EZQueue 3000
Giltronix, Inc.
3780 Fabian Way
Palo Alto, CA 94303
800/531-1300
Price: $495 EZQueue, $995 to $3220 EZQueue 3000
Description: The EZQueue handles up to five computers and plugs directly into the back plane of the LaserJet II and features a 256K expandable buffer. The 3000 allows up to 24 computers to share a LaserJet. It can be configured with up to a 2MB buffer.

Four Channel Buffer
Johnathon Freeman Design, Inc.
P.O. Box 880114
San Francisco, CA 94188
415/822-8451
Price: $995 to $1,295
Description: A switcher with four 256K buffers.

JetNET/4+1
Qubit Corporation
544 Weddell Dr. #2
Sunnyvale, CA 94089-2123
408/747-0740
Price: $495
Description: This device fits into the I/O slot of the LaserJet II and allows up to five computers to share the printer. It provides one parallel port and four serial ports. A 256K buffer can be expanded to 512K or 1MB. The device automatically recognizes the last page of a document and ejects it without the need to manually send a Form Feed.

The Juggler
Jewell Technologies, Inc.
4302 S. W. Alaska St. #207
Seattle, WA 98116
206/937-1081
Price: $649 to $999
Description: A switcher with a buffer that can be expanded from 256K to 768K. It can handle up to four computers. An optional module can convert HPGL graphics for printing on the LaserJet.

LaserBoard
Digital Products, Inc.
108 Water St.
Watertown, MA 02172
800/243-2333
617/924-1680
Price: $495
Description: Designed specifically for the LaserJet II, the LaserBoard allows up to three computers to share the printer. It uses the printer's serial port

and includes a non-expandable 250K buffer.

The Logical Connection
Fifth Generation Systems
2691 Richter Ave. #107
Irvine, CA 92714
800/225-2775
714/553-0111
Price: $495
Description: A printer-sharing device that includes a 256K buffer, expandable to 512K.

MasterLink
Advanced Microcomputer Products
15164 Golden West Circle
Westminster, CA 92683
714/893-1335
Price: $395
Description: A printer-sharing device that supports up to three computers and includes a 512K buffer.

Mega-Link
Intellicom
9259 Eton
Chatsworth, CA 91311
818/882-8866
Price: $349
Description: A switch box that includes a 256K buffer, upgradable to 1MB.

Peripheral Sharing Device
Giltronix, Inc.
3780 Fabian Way
Palo Alto, CA 94303
800/531-1300
Price: $340 to $745
Description: There are several models of this printer-sharing device, the 8000 (2 to 14 computers), the 8000P (2 to 7 computers), and the 8000X (2 to 7 computers).

Printdirector MS-1 and MS-10
Digital Products, Inc.
108 Water St.
Watertown, MA 02172
800/243-2333
617/924-1680
Price: $1,195 MS-1, $1,395 MS-10
Description: Printdirector MS-1 includes four serial ports and four parallel ports. MS-10 has ten ports. Both include Printer Management, which assists in control of soft fonts.

Printer Optimizer
Applied Creative Technology
10529 Olympic Dr. #101
Dallas, TX 75220
800/433-5373
Price: $428
Description: A printer-sharing device that includes a programmable buffer. The buffer can range from 64K to 1MB. It includes a front-panel display and a keyboard for programming the device.

Printer Sharing Hardware CA-4 Family

Via West, Inc.
534 North Stone Ave.
Tucson, AZ 85705
602/623-5716
Price: $450 to $550
Description: A device that allows up to 16 computers to share a LaserJet.

Print Master Printer Controllers

Bay Technical Associates, Inc.
P.O. Box 387
200 North 2nd St.
Bay St. Louis, MS 39520
601/467-8231
Price: $795 to $995
Description: A printer-sharing device with a 1MB buffer.

ReadyPort

Zvert Corp.
15234 Transistor Lane
Huntington Beach, CA 92649
714/894-8180
Price: $399 to $995
Description: There are three models, one with three ports, one with six ports, and one with eight ports. All of them allow you to add a memory buffer. They can also be programmed to send a setup string to the printer.

Serial Automatic Scanner

General Interface Systems, Inc.
12919 Alcosta Blvd.
San Ramon, CA 94583
415/866-9600
Price: $169 to $299
Description: A printer-sharing device that allows up to seven computers to use one LaserJet.

Sharespool

Extended Systems, Inc.
P.O. Box 4937
6062 Morris Hill Ln.
Boise, ID 83711
208/322-7163
Price: $495 to $995
Description: Sharespool ESI-2001A is a switcher and spooler that allows up to three computers to share a LaserJet II. The Sharespool ESI 2041A lets four computers share the printer and includes a 256K nonexpandable buffer. Both use the serial port. Sharespool ESI-2076 and 2078 allow up to seven computers to share the printer. Sharespool ESI-2086 and ESI-2088 allow up to three computers to share the printer.

SW2-HP1/SW3-HP1

Gold Key Electronics
11 Cote Ave.
Goffstown, NH 03045
603/625-8518
Price: $549 to $749
Description: Allows up to three computers to share a LaserJet. Also pro-

vides an interface to DECmate applications.

Systematic Printer Sharing System
Systemizer Printer Sharing System
Applied Creative Technology
10529 Olympic Dr. #101
Dallas, TX 75220
800/433-5343
Price: $299 to $349
Description: The Systemizer Network Printer Buffer allows up to 15 computers to share multiple printers. The Systematic Printer-Sharing System is a scaled down version of the Systemizer.

VP220 Printer Buffer
Graftel, Inc.
400 Executive Blvd.
Elmsford, NY 10523
914/592-3700
Price: $995 to $1295
Description: A printer-sharing device that can handle four computers. Includes a buffer of 256K or 512K.

SHEET FEEDERS

JetFeed I and III
Genesis Technology, Inc.
30963 San Benito Court
Hayward, CA 94544
415/489-3700
Price $799 to $999
Description: These products work with both old and new LaserJet models. JetFeed I can feed up to 500 sheets of paper or 100 envelopes into the printer. JetFeed III has two input bins for paper and one input bin for envelopes.

LaserFeeder
BDT Products, Inc.
17152 Armstrong Ave.
Irvine, CA 92417
714/6606-1386
Price: $1,695
Description: This is a combination feeder and output collator that works in both old and new LaserJet models. It has three bins that can hold up to 440 sheets of paper and 60 envelopes, and can collate up to 500 sheets of paper.

MultiFeeder
BDT Products, Inc.
17152 Armstrong Ave.
Irvine, CA 92417
714/6606-1386
Price: $1,695
Description: This sheet feeder works only with the LaserJet and LaserJet Plus. It has six bins for paper plus a bin for envelopes, with a total capacity of 1,400 sheets or 300 en-

velopes. It also can collate 500 sheets of paper.

PaperJet 400
PaperJet 400/DSF
Ziyad, Inc.
100 Ford Rd.
Denville, NJ 07834
201/627-7600
Price: $1,295 to $1,495
Description: The PaperJet 400 adds 350 sheets and 75 envelopes to the capacity of the LaserJet and the LaserJet Plus (not the LaserJet II). The PaperJet 400/DSF is similar to the 400, but can handle varied sizes of paper.

Profile: LaserTORQ

NOTHING EVER SEEMS quite fast enough in our modern world, including our computers and accessories. Although LaserJets are generally far faster than their dot matrix predecessors, we quickly become accustomed to that speed, and soon expect more. It's also a fact that although the LaserJet can theoretically print a page every eight seconds or so, it can much take much longer than that to transfer to the LaserJet the material you wish to print. These delays can seem interminable if you're printing graphics, or if you're downloading fonts in large volumes. An important aspect of these delays is that its usually not because you're dying to see the printed output. Rather, it's because while your computer is tied up sending data to the printer, you can't do anything else with it.

Enter LaserTORQ, from LaserTools. LaserTORQ is a kind of software known as a print spooler, and it can work wonders for your LaserJet printing times. Print spoolers can be thought of as memory reservoirs to which information can be sent, all at once, and held until the printer can process it. Print spoolers evolved in multiuser environments such as a mincomputer or a Local Area Network (LAN), where many users must to

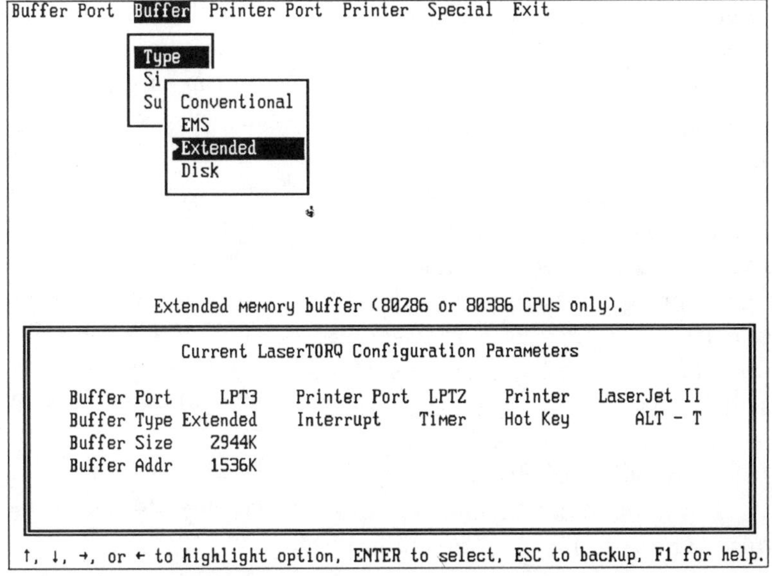

Figure 1: The installation procedure for LaserTORQ allows you to select either conventional memory, expanded memory, extended memory, or the hard disk for the location of the buffer.

share one printer. Picture the scene: late one afternoon Sally wants to print her spreadsheet, Jim his annual report, and Todd his scanned images. A print spooler can accept all their jobs at once, hold them in memory, and feed them one by one to the printer as it finishes a previous job. Because the print spooler looks just like a printer to each user's computer, as soon as the spooler has accepted a particular job that user's computer becomes free to do other work, as if the printing were already finished. The hitch is that each user must wait until his or her turn comes up in the spooler. But without this device, chaos would soon reign as each user tried to beat the other to the printer, and everyone else had to wait.

That Refreshing Twist

LaserTORQ is a kind of spooler, but with a twist. LaserTORQ has been optimized for printing speed rather than harmony in a multiuser office. It lacks some amenities that other multiuser spoolers have, such as job separation. But what LaserTORQ concentrates on, speed, it does very well, and speeds up printing in two ways. First, it offers buffering, as any print spooler does. Second, it many situations it can actually speed up how fast the LaserJet can print pages, using your computer's printer port interrupts.

Buffering improvements work like this. When you send something to your LaserJet, whether it's a font you want to download or a document you want to print, a complex process begins. The LaserJet accepts information, and (in the case of a file to print) begins imaging and printing it, until its memory is full. It then can't accept any more information until has printed a page and purged that page of information from memory, opening up space for a new page. During this process, your computer has to wait. The crying shame is that the faster your computer is, the more it's bound by the LaserJet, or the more you have to wait for the LaserJet to catch up.

LaserTORQ emulates LaserJet memory. When you want to print something, or download fonts, what you really do is send that information to LaserTORQ, which immediately accepts it all, so your computer thinks it's done printing. Acting in the background LaserTORQ will feed the information to the LaserJet as fast as the LaserJet can accept it, and you can meanwhile be using your computer

Access

LaserTORQ
LaserTools Corp.
3025 Buena Vista Way
Berkeley, CA 94708
415/843-2234
Price: $99

for something else. The advantages are obvious.

Help for the Harried

If every morning the first thing you do is download a megabyte of soft fonts into your computer, you might spend several minutes waiting before you can begin to really work. Downloading to LaserTORQ instead takes an average of about ten seconds. That's pretty fast. LaserTORQ also makes a dramatic difference if you're using software that uses many different kinds of fonts, such as PageMaker or Ventura. It also, ironically enough, speeds up the print spooler function of Microsoft Windows, so that your Windows print jobs get done up to twice as fast.

LaserTORQ also offers another major advantage to those of you who print lots of graphics, especially if you have a LaserJet Plus or LaserJet II with only 512K, the minimum amount of memory. When it's processing graphics, LaserTORQ examines every line sent to it and finds an equivalent way to reexpress that line. Usually this alternative expression of the line requires less memory, often as much as 60% less memory. On a large scale this has dramatic effects, and even allows you in most cases to print full pages of 300 dpi graphics on a 512K LaserJet.

9

APPENDICES

APPENDIX A

Answers to Common Questions

The contents of this chapter were prepared by the HP LaserJet Technical Support staff in Boise, Idaho. They answer some of the most frequently asked questions about the LaserJet on the following topics.

- *General questions*
- *Graphics*
- *Fonts*
- *LaserJet II*
- *LaserJet 500 Plus*
- *Error codes*
- *Print quality*
- *EP cartridges*
- *Software*

—TN & MG

GENERAL QUESTIONS

Q: Can my LaserJet printer emulate an Epson or Diablo printer?
A: The LaserJet cannot emulate an Epson or Diablo printer on its own. You'll need to purchase a setup utility such as LaserControl. For details, see Chapter 5, "Setup Utilities," or "Profile: LaserControl."

Q: How do I know when something is in the printer buffer?
A: When the light above the FORM FEED key on the Control Panel is illuminated, there is data in the printer buffer.

Q: When I send data to the printer, why doesn't anything seem to happen? How can I make the LaserJet print my page?

A: Since the LaserJet is a page printer, a page is ejected when one of the following occurs:

- The printer receives a form feed (control character decimal 12), either from the software or from the control panel of the LaserJet.
- The printer reaches the perforation skip region at the bottom of the page. The page is ejected and the printer continues at the top of the next page.
- The printer receives the paper-input escape sequence with a value of zero (Ec&l0H).
- The printer receives a soft reset (EcE). If there is something in memory, a reset ejects the page.
- The printer receives the command to change orientation (Ec&l#O). The printer can only print in one orientation per page. Once data has been received, the printer has started formatting that page. When it receives an orientation change, it ejects the current page and starts formatting a new page in the new orientation.

If none of the above occurs, data remaining in the buffer is not ejected and data received afterward is added to the page currently in the buffer.

Q: Why does the first page of my document print with the correct top margin, but each succeeding page start lower, with a larger top margin?

A: This is often referred to as "creeping text," and results from the number of lines per page in your software application not being set equal to the number of lines per page of the printer. The printer has default margins that equate to 3 lines at the top and bottom of the page, and by default prints 60 lines per page. But most applications default to 66 lines per page. If you set the application program to send only 60 lines to the printer (which translates into 10 inches of image, or text) the problem will be solved. Or, simply adjust the vertical line spacing of the printer to allow 66 lines to print. Do this in your application software, or by sending Ec&17.27C for portrait orientation or Ec&*l*1o5.45C for landscape orientation. Note: 1 is the number one, and *l* is a lowercase L. Note also that the specific value of 66 lines per page assumes a 12-point leading for your type. If you are printing in a smaller type, you will probably want more lines per page.

Q: Why do blank pages eject between pages when I'm printing?

A: Blank pages ejecting between pages while printing usually results when the number of lines per page in your software application is not set equal to the number of lines per page of the printer. Text will either creep down the page as described above or blank pages will eject. See the previous answer to remedy the problem.

Q: I did a print test and it is slightly crooked. How should it be measured to find out if this is within the printer specifications and, if not, what action should be taken?

A: The top and bottom of the print test attempt to print into the non-document portion of the drum, causing misleading results. The test print should be measured from one of the vertical lines to the side of the physical paper both at the top and the bottom. Then subtract to find the difference. Up to 1/16" is within printer specifications, but above this, the printer should be serviced.

Q: How do I use the printer's manual feed feature?

A: When using the original LaserJet or the LaserJet Plus, pressing the MANUAL FEED key on the printer's Control Panel will initiate manual-feed mode. On the LaserJet II, you can initiate manual feed merely by slipping a sheet of paper into the manual feed slot on the top of the paper cartridge. If you want to put the LaserJet II into permanent manual-feed mode, take the printer off-line and press the MENU key twice. The console display will tell you whether manual feed is on or off (the asterisk marks the current selection, so MANUAL FEED=OFF* means that manual feed is off). If you need to change the setting, use the Plus and Minus keys to select your option, then press the ENTER key to save your choice. Then press the ON LINE button twice (to take the LaserJet on- and off-line), and finally press the CONTINUE / RESET key for about three seconds until 07 RESET appears in the display.

Note that many software applications initialize the printer with a soft reset (^{E}cE), which turns manual feed off. The best way to ensure that manual feed mode is initiated is to use the escape sequence ^{E}c&l2H. Upon receipt of this command, the printer's front panel will display the size of paper to be printed. The sheet of paper can then be inserted into the back of the printer (for the LaserJet, LaserJet Plus, or 500 Plus) or in the manual-feed guides on the top of the paper tray (for the LaserJet II). The front panel display will change to double zeros and the printer will pull the paper through.

Q: What paper sizes are supported by the LaserJet printers?

A: Four sizes are supported (without using manual feed): letter size: (8.5 by 11 inches); legal size: (8.5 by 14 inches); European A4: (210 by 297 mm); and European B5: (128 by 257 mm). The LaserJet II also supports the Executive Size (7.25 by 10.5 inches). Smaller sizes can be manually fed.

Q: Why am I missing parts of my documents at the very edge of the printed sheet of paper? Sentences and even words just end abruptly.
A: Your software is attempting to print outside the LaserJet's maximum image area. Adjust your software's page margins to acknowledge the LaserJet's unprintable area of 8 by 10 inches for an 8.5-by-11-inch sheet of paper.

Q: Why doesn't my printer print 8 pages per minute?
A: Your printer's speed depends upon your software application's ability to format the document and transmit it to the printer quickly. Word processing and desktop publishing applications are usually printed slowly because of the special formatting and graphics being used in those documents. If text is provided by your applications to the printer at a rate of 8 pages per minute, your LaserJet will print 8 pages per minute.

Q: Where can I order additional supplies for my printer?
A: You can order additional supplies through Hewlett-Packard Direct Marketing Division (800/538-8787, 408/738-4133 in California). If you want to find the nearest dealer, you can call 800/367-4772 and obtain the name.

Q: Where can I go to have my printer serviced?
A: To obtain the name of the nearest authorized service dealer, call 800/835-4747.

Q: Why can't I get the manual feed to feed envelopes with my LaserJet Plus?
A: Extra-stiff paper requires users to assist the feeding operation. The following are a few suggestions when feeding envelopes:

- Always install one sheet of blank paper in the paper cassette prior to feeding envelopes. The sheet of paper provides a smooth surface at the leading edge of the paper cassette from which to slide the envelopes along.
- Always wait for the PE FEED COMM-10 (or similar envelope-size message) to appear before feeding the envelope. Do not rush the envelopes through the printer.
- Closely inspect the leading edge of the envelopes prior to feeding them into the printer. Ensure the leading edge is flat. Watch for envelope curl and "dog ears." If necessary, flatten the leading edge of the envelope prior to feeding. (It is helpful to place the envelope on a flat, hard surface

and slide your finger along the leading edge of the envelope prior to feeding. This ensures that the edge of the envelope is flat.) It should be noted that envelopes are often packaged and stored in such a manner that envelope damage, e.g., curling, dog ears, paper bow, etc., often occur. Closely inspect the packaging of your envelopes prior to purchase.

- Do not allow too many envelopes to accumulate in the printer's faceup output tray (no more than 10). If too many envelopes are allowed to accumulate, there is a possibility of getting "false paper jams."

Q: What is the benefit of using the Centronics parallel interface on my HP LaserJet Plus, LaserJet 500 Plus, or LaserJet II over the serial interface?
A: Using the parallel interface allows graphics data (raster graphics, downloadable fonts, rules, etc.) to be transferred to the printer up to four times faster than with the serial interface. Using the parallel interface has no effect on the speed at which your text or spreadsheet data will be transferred.

Q: I'm having a problem using my 3.2 version of MS-DOS.
A: We have also recognized a problem with MS-DOS 3.2. It appears that the MODE command does not work correctly. This results in the serial port not being correctly redefined. We suggest that you contact your personal computer dealer regarding the problem, or upgrade your copy of MS-DOS.

Q: The HP LaserJet Plus, LaserJet 500 Plus, and LaserJet II printers offer either serial or parallel interface connections. What is required to switch from one interface to another?
A: First of all, make sure you are using the proper cable to connect your printer to the parallel interface. (For an IBM PC, XT, AT, or compatibles, this cable is HP part number 24542D or 92219K). There are different methods for the different printers:

For the LaserJet Plus and 500 Plus: Change dip switch number 1 (located in the rear of the printer, behind the rear panel) to the ON position. Also make sure that you have removed all MODE commands from your AUTOEXEC.BAT file. For additional information, refer to your *LaserJet Technical Reference Manual,* Appendix C.

For the LaserJet II: Make sure the LaserJet II is off-line, with **00 READY** appearing in the console display. Press the **MENU** key at the lower right of the control panel continuously for about 5 seconds, until **SYM SET** appears in the display. Press it twice more, until **I/O=** appears in the display. If you want an I/O mode other than what is shown in the display, press the Plus or Minus key. Press the **ENTER** key to save your choice, then press the **MENU** key once more, so that **00 READY** again appears in the display. Now press the **CONTINUE / RESET** button (second from the left) and hold it for about three seconds, until **07 RESET** appears in the display.

Q: Is there any way I can create a document on my IBM PC that uses the IBM line-drawing set and have it print correctly on my HP LaserJet printer?
A: For the LaserJet, LaserJet Plus, and 500 Plus, HP offers the HP 92286Y (PC Courier 1) font cartridge. This cartridge contains all the characters associated with the IBM-8 Symbol set. For the LaserJet II printer, the IBM-8 is built-in and can be accessed from the front panel or your software. It may be necessary to reconfigure your software for the Y font cartridge as well. For instructions on how to do this, see Chapter 20, "Screen Snapshots."

GRAPHICS

Q: How can I print 300-by-300 dpi, full-page graphics on the HP laser printers?
A: To print high-resolution, full-page graphics, your printer must have more memory than comes as standard equipment on a LaserJet. For the HP LaserJet, LaserJet Plus, and the 500 Plus printers, you need to order the HP 26054A 2MB upgrade kit. It is field-installable by a technician and consists of a memory board, new front panel display, dual I/O, and new HP LaserJet family manuals. For the LaserJet II printer, you must purchase the HP 33443A 1MB memory board, the HP33444A 2MB memory board, or the HP 33445A 4MB memory board. These LaserJet II boards are customer-installable, or your dealer can do it for you.

Q: How can I tell when a graphics screen dump has completed?
A: There is no direct way to determine that it has completed. On the average, a graphics screen dump takes about 40 seconds. With some packages the message "KEYBOARD LOCKED" will display on the screen while the graphics transfer is taking place and will go off when it is completed, or watch for the ready light to stop blinking on the LaserJet Plus, LaserJet 500 Plus, or LaserJet II.

Q: Does an HP LaserJet printer accept vector graphics commands like a plotter?
A: No, only raster graphics commands. However, vector-to-raster conversion can be accomplished by using a third-party solution such as LaserPlotter by Insight Development Corporation (HP part number 35188A).

Q: I created a graph in portrait mode and it prints fine. When I send the escape sequence to print the same graph in landscape mode, it prints off the page. Why?
A: Sending the escape sequence to change the orientation to landscape will only move the cursor to reflect the starting point of the landscape orientation (the bottom left-hand corner of the page when viewed in portrait orientation). Therefore, after sending the escape sequence for landscape orientation, you must move the cursor to the right at least the length of your graphic image and rotate your data to reflect the landscape orientation. If this process does not take place, your graph will print off the bottom of the page.

Q: Why does my LaserJet print part of my graphics image on one page, and the rest of it on the succeeding page?
A: Your LaserJet does not have enough memory to accommodate the size of your graphics at the resolution you have chosen. Get more memory, or reduce the size of your image or the resolution at which you are printing it.

FONTS

Q: Why is my cartridge font not working?
A: Unlike plugging a new daisy wheel into an impact printer, plugging a new cartridge into the LaserJet does not cause the printer to recognize new fonts. If you change the cartridge, you should:

- Set the printer off-line whenever removing or inserting a cartridge.
- Ensure the cartridge is firmly seated.
- Ensure the font selection procedures in the owner's manual are followed exactly.

Q: What does pressing the CONTINUE / RESET *button do to the fonts I've downloaded?*
A: Pressing RESET erases all temporarily downloaded soft fonts. To erase permanently downloaded fonts, you must turn off the printer or send the command to erase all downloaded fonts (^{E}c*c0F).

Q: I started my print job using the italics character font, then changed to bold; however, I am still getting the italics character font. Why?
A: All font selection is done by priority (See Chapter 18, "Selecting Fonts with PCL.") In this case, the Character Style (upright vs. italic) has a higher priority than Stroke Weight (light, medium, or bold). Therefore, you must turn the Italics *off* before turning Bold *on.*

Q: What are the pros and cons of soft (downloadable) versus hard (cartridge) fonts?
A: Cartridge Advantages:

- Hard fonts are stored entirely in the cartridge, so the fonts are immediately available to the printer.
- No downloading is necessary.
- Printer memory is not utilized. The font cartridge contains all the memory needed to store the font data. Cartridges do not use any of the printer's memory.
- Easy to see what is available. All accessible fonts are shown on the cartridge label.

Soft Font Advantages:

- More versatility in the combinations you can use. You can "mix and match" soft fonts as you wish.
- Costs less. Since there is no hardware involved, you get more fonts for the money.
- The soft font license agreement permits the use of soft fonts on up to three printers.
- There are generally more options in type size when using soft fonts than when using cartridge fonts.

Q: Why can't I access any of the alternate fonts from the 92286B cartridge when I can with the 92286A?
A: The 92286B cartridge uses the USASCII symbol set (this allows more fonts to be contained in the cartridge) and must be specified at the beginning of the print job. The following escape sequence specifies the USASCII symbol set as the primary symbol set: Ec(0U. The LaserJet defaults to the Roman-8 symbol set.

Q: How can I print in compressed type in a landscape orientation?
A: If you have a LaserJet, LaserJet Plus, or 500 Plus, you must use a font cartridge. Several font cartridges contain a compressed line printer font in landscape including the 92286A, 92286B, and 92286L font cartridges. One of these cartridges must first be installed in the printer. The shortest escape sequence needed to access the compressed landscape character font is Ec&l1OEc(s16.6H.

Q: I am using a proportionally spaced font cartridge, but I can't seem to get a justified right margin.
A: Right justification with proportionally spaced fonts is a capability dependent on the software package. To determine which software packages support right justification with proportional fonts, see the *HP LaserJet Printer Family Software and Hardware Solutions Catalog.* If your software is not listed or does not provide right justification, check with the software vendor to see if this feature will be provided on a new release.

HP can supply the software vendor with the metrics of each character font to allow them to incorporate into their software the algorithm to generate a right-justified document.

Q: I don't have a true 12-pitch font cartridge yet, but can I print 12 characters per inch using the default Courier font?
A: The Courier font in the printer is designed to print 10 characters per inch horizontally. The horizontal spacing can be adjusted to compress the Courier font and give the effect of 12 characters per inch. Use the escape sequence Ec&l10H. Remember that this will not be a true 12-pitch font, but a 10-pitch font with the characters printed closer together.

Q: How many different fonts can I print on a page?
A: The original LaserJet allowed up to 8 character fonts of the same orientation on one page, whereas the LaserJet Plus, 500 Plus, and LaserJet II will allow up to 16 character fonts of the same orientation per page. When you change any font characteristic, the printer considers it to be a completely new font (for example, changing the style from upright to italic). The usual result when the 8-font limit is exceeded is incorrect vertical and horizontal spacing for the font printed (often it won't be the one selected).

Q: Even though I have sent the escape sequence to tell the printer I'm manually feeding an envelope, it still doesn't print it properly. Instead, it comes out blank. How do I let my printer know I'm feeding an envelope?
A: The escape sequence Ec&l3H lets the printer know you have adjusted the paper guides on the manual-feed area to fit an envelope. It does not set the printer to the landscape mode, nor does it format the data for you. These steps must also be done to get the envelope to print properly. An 11-line top margin and a 4-inch left margin are the suggested settings to assist you in formatting your envelope.

LASERJET 500 PLUS

Q: How do I access the second paper tray on the HP LaserJet 500 Plus?

A: The paper tray can easily be selected from either the front panel on the printer or via an escape sequence within your document. One of the front control panel options is Auto Select, which will automatically switch paper cassettes if one tray runs out of paper, as long as both trays are the same size. Manual feed is also available.

Q: What is "Job Offset" and how does it work on the HP LaserJet 500 Plus?

A: Job Offset refers to the ability to physically separate different jobs in the output tray. This feature can only be accessed from within your document by sending an escape sequence, and is ideal for separating output when the printer is in a multi-user environment. Job Offset can only be performed when correct-order output is used. This feature should not be confused with Collation, which will separate and arrange multiple copies of the same job (like a photocopier that separates and arranges several copies of a multipage document).

LASERJET II

Q: Why doesn't font selection from the Control Panel work?

A: Most probably, you are doing everything right to make your font choice, but are then forgetting to properly reset the printer to activate your font choice as the default font. For explicit instructions on how to do this see Chapter 3, "The LaserJet II Control Panel."

Q: What fonts do I have available on my LaserJet II printer?

A: Courier 10-pitch and Line Printer 16-pitch in a regular stroke weight with Roman-8, IBM-US, IBM-DN, and ECMA-94 symbol sets in both portrait and landscape orientations. Courier bold is resident in both portrait and landscape.

Q: Even though I have changed the font ID number on the panel of the printer, the printer is not recognizing the change. How do I get the printer to recognize my new font choice?

A: Although you have selected the new font, you still need to reset the printer for it to recognize your new font choice. After selecting the font, press the MENU key until the message 00 READY is displayed. Now hold the CONTINUE/RESET key until 07 RESET is displayed. Release the button and the printer will automatically come back on line.

Q: On the LaserJet II, how do I get to the two levels of menu options?
A: To get to the top level, or "printing level" of the MENU key, first press ON LINE to take the printer off line. Then press MENU and toggle through choices using the Plus and Minus keys. To get to the second level, or "configuration level," press ON LINE to take the printer off-line, then press and hold the MENU key for approximately 4 seconds. When SYM SET= appears, you have reached the second-level menu.

Q: Even though I have a font cartridge installed, my default font is still Courier. How do I get the printer to recognize the default font on the cartridge?
A: When inserting a font cartridge with a new default marker, you must reset the printer before it will recognize your new default font. After taking your printer off-line and inserting your new font cartridge, hold the CONTINUE/RESET button until the message 07 RESET is displayed. Release the button and the printer will automatically come back on-line, recognizing your new default font.

Q: I have performed a font printout and am trying to access the internal font for Courier bold, (listed as #I04 on the Print Fonts Printout). When I use the printer command that is on page A-14 of the LaserJet series II User's Manual for accessing a font by its ID number, Ec(#X, it does not recognize that command. What am I doing wrong?
A: You will not be able to access the internal fonts using the above escape sequence. This sequence is used to access the soft font previously downloaded with that ID number assigned to it.

ERROR CODES

Q: Why am I receiving an Error 40 (line error) when I reboot the operating system in my computer?
A: Many computers will send a string of null characters through the serial interface port when powered up or rebooted. These characters will put the printer in an Error 40 condition. The printer must then be turned off to clear it. It is recommended that the printer always be turned on *after* the computer to eliminate this situation.

Q: I am getting an Error 54. Why?
A: There may be too much paper in the input cassette.

Q: I am receiving an Error 50 when I power on my printer. I have attempted to clear it by turning off the printer for 10 minutes and then turning it back on as it states in the manual, but the error does not clear.

A: An Error 50 will occur most commonly when one or more of the following situations have occurred:

- A power surge caused by a brown out, black out, or a variance exceeding 10 percent.
- A mechanical switchbox is being used with the printer. Mechanical switchboxes can cause voltage and current disturbances. Buffered chips are not a common design feature in RS-232 digital electronic devices, and a significant number of interface boards have failed while using mechanical switchboxes. Therefore, mechanical switchboxes are not recommended. In fact, according to Hewlett-Packard, using a mechanical switchbox device will void the printer warranty.

If you still wish to use a mechanical device, follow the steps to minimize the risk of damage to the printer:

- Check with the switchbox vendor to ensure that the communication lines are protected from voltage and current transients.
- Turn the printer off before rotating the switch or disconnecting system cables.
- Obtain a data line surge protector to provide protection from the disturbances that could be caused by the use of a mechanical switch.

PRINT QUALITY

Q: I'm getting a dark, vertical smear down my page. What's causing this?

A: If the smear appears down the right edge of the paper, you may need to clean or replace your separation belt (if you are using a LaserJet, LaserJet Plus, or LaserJet 500 Plus rather than a LaserJet II.) If the smear appears down the center of the page, you may be using the wrong type of paper (such as 25 percent, 50 percent, or 100 percent cotton) in dry environments. This has been an acute problem in areas where the ambient temperature has been 20 to 40 degrees F (-6.6 to 4.4 degrees C) with a relative humidity of 10 percent to 25 percent. The operating range for the LaserJet is 20 percent to 80 percent relative humidity. Most of the central and eastern U.S. and Canada experience these conditions during winter and may see this problem. The problem occurs when you are using an unsupported paper or a combination of supported and unsupported papers, which may wear the Teflon coating off the Feeder Guide Assembly (part number RG1-0192-000CN), exposing the plastic beneath it. The friction caused by the paper rubbing the Feeder Guide causes a static charge to develop on the part. The static charge attracts the unfused toner and causes the smear.

Q: What kind of paper should I use with my LaserJet printer?
A: The LaserJet is designed to work well with most types of paper, although some variables in their composition may significantly affect print quality and paper handling. Paper manufactured for photocopying (such as Canon NP or Xerox 4024) provides good results for general-purpose applications. For other applications where cotton bond is desirable (i.e., company letterhead), HP has obtained good results using papers such as Gilbert Neu-Tech and Neenah NP. Textured papers with woven or rough finishes may adversely affect print quality. Note: HP does not recommend or advocate the use of any particular paper. The papers mentioned above are only a few that tested well with the LaserJet. Always test paper prior to purchase to ensure desirable performance.

EP CARTRIDGES

Q: When installing the EP (or "toner") cartridge, I flexed the removable tab until it broke off. When I pulled the tab, it broke away from the attached sealing tape. How do I remove the tape?
A: Try grasping the tape with pliers or your hands to remove it. If this doesn't work, you should return the defective cartridge to your local HP dealer. HP will reimburse the dealer for replacing the cartridge.

Q: I replaced my EP cartridge and now nothing is printing. Why not?
A: You probably forgot to remove the sealing tape before inserting the EP cartridge. Refer to Section V of the *LaserJet series II User's Manual.*

Q: How can I extend the toner cartridge's life once the print begins to fade?
A: When your pages begin to show white streaks, remove the EP cartridge and rock it back and forth four or five times to distribute any remaining toner. Replace the cartridge and use it until the print begins to fade again. Once this happens, the cartridge will have to be replaced.

Q: I changed the EP cartridge in my LaserJet (or Plus or 500 Plus) and now my printer fades from left to right. What is wrong?
A: Make sure the doctor pin is in place. The doctor pin holds the doctor blade in place, which allows the toner to distribute evenly across the page. The pin can work itself loose in the shipping process. The doctor pin is located on the end of the cartridge that is inserted into the printer at the upper-left side (11:00 position). If the pin (it resembles a screw) is not in place, you will see a small hole). You can either replace your doctor pin using the pin from your previous EP cartridge or return your cartridge for replacement.

Q: How long can I use my EP cartridge? How can I tell if it needs replacement?

A: The expected life of an EP cartridge for the LaserJet, LaserJet Plus, and 500 Plus is 3,000 pages at 4 percent coverage. Your print will begin to fade when your cartridge needs replacing. Gently rocking the cartridge to distribute any remaining toner will prolong the use of the cartridge. Another indicator of the amount of toner left in this type of EP cartridge is the small window that shows either a green (indicating a new cartridge), yellow, or red background. Keep in mind, however, that the window indicator is based on the number of rotations of the drum of the EP cartridge, not on an exact measurement of toner level.

On the LaserJet II, the estimated life of the EP cartridge is 4000 pages at 4 percent coverage. There is no window on the EP cartridge that is used. The printer will indicate on the display window an error message that states 16 TONER LOW, at which time you should have toner for approximately 100 pages. Follow the instructions on page 5-4 of your *LaserJet series II User's Manual.*

Q: I would like to take advantage of a sale on LaserJet toner cartridges. What is the shelf life of a toner cartridge?
A: The estimated life of a toner cartridge is approximately two years for an unopened cartridge, and six months for an open cartridge. These estimates are based on storage temperatures between 32 to 95 degrees F.

SOFTWARE

Q: Can I run software packages not listed in the "HP LaserJet Software and Hardware Solutions Catalog" on one of the HP LaserJet printers?
A: Print and space applications (databases, spreadsheets, and general business programs) should work well with fixed space fonts. Graphics and word processing packages may re-

quire user modifications or changes on the part of the software vendor. Contact the software vendor for more information.

Q: What languages can I write programmatically to the LaserJet?
A: BASIC has been thoroughly tested and documentation is available in the *LaserJet series II User's Manual.* Fortran, Cobol, C, dBASE, and Pascal have not been tested; howeverc there should not be a problem if the program is written for an HP PCL printer or if the packages were written to only use base-level features (standard control codes). Otherwise they might need to be modified to work with the LaserJet.

Q: How and when should I input an escape sequence or printer command into my application program?
A: In most application programs, printing and formatting features can be accessed directly through menus, setup tables, or commands. Therefore, you don't have to bother with escape sequences—the application sends them for you. In some programs, however, you must input escape sequences or setup strings to access printer features. In these programs, the escape sequence is represented in a variety of different ways (and in most cases, simply pressing the Esc key will not produce the escape character for you). Lotus 1-2-3 uses \027 as the escape character, and others, such as IBM DisplayWrite 4, use the hexadecimal representation, 1B. If your application does require using escape sequences, your software vendor's manual should specify how and will also tell you when and where to input the sequences. Chapter 19, "Programming the LaserJet with PCL," contains a table showing how to embed the escape character with various software products.

Q: Why didn't my escape sequence work when I sent a command for landscape orientation (for example, \027&l1O in Lotus 1-2-3)?
A: Whenever sending escape sequences to your LaserJet, be sure you have not confused the lowercase letter *l* with the number 1 or the uppercase letter I, or the uppercase letter O with the number Ø.

Q: Why can't I print bold with Memomaker?
A: You need to change DEVICE CONFIG, MODEL FIELD from "Special" to "Other." Other is the only field that lets all escape sequences pass through unaltered. Also, you need a font cartridge that supports bold (e.g., 92286A) or a LaserJet II.

Tips, Tricks, and Troubleshooting

This appendix contains a potpourri of notes from our "School of Hard Knocks" file. We'll cover the following topics: (1) solutions to some common problems, (2) ways to save money and make your equipment last longer, (3) simple solutions to not-so-simple problems, (4) cautionary notes, and (5) miscellaneous.

COMMON PROBLEMS

Nothing happening: Sometimes the printer will be on and the control panel will display 00, indicating the printer is ready to receive data, but when you type the print command from your program nothing happens. Here's a checklist of things to do:

- Check the cable connection. If you're using a serial interface, check that the two necessary MODE commands successfully executed (see Chapter 1, "Getting Acquainted."
- If your computer is connected to a switch that lets you send data to more than one printer, make sure that the switch is directing data to the LaserJet.
- Check to see that the printer is on-line, indicated by the orange light above the ON LINE key on the Control Panel. If not, press the button.

Recurring paper jam: If your paper keeps jamming, it may be that the sheets are interfering with each other as they emerge from the printer. It only takes a very slight amount of resistance to make the printer jam.

The best way to see if this is the case is to remove sheets from the tray as soon as they emerge. This should take care of the problem.

The indicator panel displays a paper jam error code (13), but when you open the lid you can't find any stuck piece of paper: If the sheet of paper isn't inside the paper, another place to look is underneath the paper tray. If for some reason the LaserJet can't feed a piece of paper, the rollers tend to force it back underneath the tray. When you remove the paper and reset the printer, the error code should disappear.

Streaks: If vertical streaks appear on the page, it means you're running out of toner. But that doesn't mean you have to throw the toner cartridge away just yet. Take the cartridge out of the printer, hold it by the handle and the opposite side, and rock it back and forth several times using the drum as the axis of rotation. This will redistribute the toner and should let you print as many as several hundred more copies.

Blanks or black stripes: These may have been caused by exposing the EP cartridge to light. For more information see the note under "Caution!" below.

White stripes or faint areas: If the problem is not caused by a lack of toner, it may be caused by a dirty corona wire. A small, green plastic cleaner with a blue tip comes with the printer. On top of an EP cartridge is a long slot covered with black plastic. Insert the blue tip into the slot, holding the cleaner so that the two small holes are facing you. The tip will push the black plastic strip aside while it cleans the hidden corona wire. Move the cleaner from end to end.

Envelopes jamming: The problem is probably that the paper stock you're using is too heavy. Try a lighter (i.e., thinner) stock.

Pages aren't breaking where you want them to: This is a common problem. Typically, pages of text will spill over onto the next page. To fix this you need to make your page length shorter (not longer). With WordStar, change the number of lines per page to 62 by putting the command .PL62 at the top of your document, making sure the period is in the first column. If that doesn't work try .PL60.5. With Microsoft Word, use Escape Format Division to change the upper and lower page margins.

The first line on the page doesn't print: This problem occurs when the tops of letters are extending into the LaserJet's unprintable area. If any portion of a character falls within the unprintable area, none of the character is printed. According to HP's specifications, the margins are .157 inches on the left, .315 inches on the right, and .500 inches top and bottom for letter-size paper. For legal-size paper the margins are the same.

You can find out for yourself by printing a solid page. With the LaserJet Plus you can determine the exact boundaries of the printable area on your printer. Using the PCLPak utility, tell the printer to create a shaded or patterned box that is larger than your page, with initial points set at Y=0 and X=0. The printer will respond by filling up the printable region. By printing out several of these sheets, you can determine the registration of your printer, that is, how much the margins change from one sheet of paper to the next. In our own tests we found that the right and left margins were within a point (1/72 inch) of HP's specified value, and the top margin was within 3 points. To make sure all your characters print, set your margins safely within the printable area.

Difficulty positioning graphics on the page: If you're trying to position lines or graphic elements exactly on the page and aren't succeeding, it may be that you're measuring from the wrong reference point. The LaserJet measures locations on the page from the top left corner of the printable area, not from the corner of the paper. As noted above, the printable area begins .157 inches (11 points) from the left edge of the paper and .500 inches (36 points) from the top edge. These values are identical no matter what size paper you are using. They may vary, however, by a point or two due to the inherent inaccuracy of the paper-feed mechanism.

Mode commands not working: If the two mode commands used to configure your DOS computer for serial communications with the LaserJet aren't working, it may be that you don't have the MODE.COM file on your startup disk or directory. You need to copy the file from the DOS disk onto your startup disk or directory.

Paper is coming out but the pages are blank: If you just replaced the EP cartridge and nothing is printing, you may have neglected to remove the sealing tape.

Microsoft Word style sheets not working: If the printer is not printing in accordance with the style that has been applied from a style sheet, it may be because you previously used the keyboard method of direct formatting on the same document. Styles sent from the keyboard override style sheet formats. To get rid of the old style, you need to highlight the text element and use the "remove style" command, Alt-Spacebar.

Control codes not having desired effect: If an escape sequence sent to the printer doesn't work, first check to make sure you haven't confused the lowercase letter *l* with the numeral 1 or the uppercase I, nor the uppercase O with the numeral 0. Next, check that all the letters of the escape sequence were correctly entered as upper- or lowercase. Third, confirm that the font description you are sending corresponds exactly to the attributes of one of the fonts in a cartridge or one that has been downloaded. Fourth, make sure the font you want exists on your current font cartridge, in the same orientation and size. Fifth, make sure that any escape sequences you've merged share the first three characters (i.e., the escape character plus at least two others). Sixth, make sure that in merged sequences you converted all uppercase letters to lowercase except the final character. Finally, make sure that the escape sequence wasn't broken by a form feed, a line feed, a carriage return, or a space.

Printer won't switch to bold: If you were printing in italics and want to switch to bold, it is not sufficient to send the boldface instruction Ec(s3B. You also need to send the instruction to switch from italic style to upright, Ec(s0S, because style ranks above stroke weight on the hierarchy of font attributes. For more information on this point, see Chapter 18, "Selecting Fonts with PCL."

Printer freezes or shows an error when you reboot: With some computers, including Compaq, Leading Edge, Tandy 1000, and IBM PCjr models, booting or rebooting the computer while the printer is on can cause the printer to display a communications line error and make the computer freeze up. The solution is to take the printer offline whenever you reboot the computer.

Weird symbols: If you're getting weird symbols, you're using the wrong symbol set. Check that the symbol set you have selected corresponds to the symbol set on the cartridge or the soft font. Most likely, you're using Roman Extension when you should be using Roman-8. If the problem occurs when you use the HP Print Screen utility to make a screen shot, the reason is that the graphics characters used by the IBM screen do not match up with the graphics characters on most of the LaserJet font cartridges. Get a font with the IBM character set.

Wrong line spacing: If you're getting double spacing on the printer but only single spacing on the screen, it may be that your text is too wide. When the LaserJet can't fit a screen line onto paper, it wraps characters down to the next line automatically, creating what looks like double-spaced text. Try narrower margins.

Can't print in landscape mode: If you've sent the command to the LaserJet II to print in landscape mode (Ec&l1O) but the printer continues in portrait mode, it didn't get the escape sequence properly. (The LaserJet II contains "built-in" landscape fonts that it will be unable to select only if it is seriously brain-damaged.) On earlier LaserJet models, check to see whether you have a landscape font in that type style on your cartridge or in the soft fonts you've downloaded.

Last page of document missing: If the last page of your document is missing, you can print it by pressing the ON LINE key on the indicator panel (to toggle the printer offline) and then pressing the FORM FEED key. The LaserJet requires a form-feed command in order to eject a page, and many programs do not send a form feed at the termination of a document.

Only a few lines are printed on each page: The problem may be that you accidentally left off a digit when you defined the page length in your word processor, for example setting the page length to 6 rather than 60 lines.

Printer ignores control codes: The problem may be that the application you are using routinely sends a soft reset command (EcE) to the LaserJet before printing. There are two solutions. One is to embed the desired control codes within the text of your document (see Chapter 19, "Programming the LaserJet with PCL"). Another is to use the Prevent Printer Reinitialization command provided by the Printworks for PC utility.

Parts of control codes being printed at the beginning of your documents: The LaserJet will try to execute any escape sequence it encounters, but if the command is not in its lexicon, the printer may treat the sequence like data to be printed. This will always occur if the escape character is missing from the sequence or if you are using an application, such as WordStar, that ignores the escape character.

WAYS TO SAVE MONEY AND PRESERVE THE LIFE OF YOUR EQUIPMENT

EP cartridges: Don't assume you have to change your toner cartridge just because the indicator reads red. In the LaserJet and LaserJet Plus, the indicator automatically turns red after about 3,000 pages, based on revolutions of the drum. (The LaserJet II does not use an indicator color and its cartridge lasts longer—4,000 copies.) HP's estimate of a life of 3,000 pages is based on an assumption of 4 percent print coverage, or 50 characters per line and 40 lines per page. If you are printing a lot of graphics, you may get fewer than 3,000 pages from a cartridge, but most people can expect to get a good deal more than that number. You can wait until streaks begin to appear, and even then it's possible to get several hundred more copies merely by removing the cartridge and rocking it back and forth several times with the drum as the axis of rotation (see "Streaks," above). If you really want to keep track of the amount of toner in the cartridge, you can do so by weighing it from time to time. When new, cartridges contain about 160 grams of toner. If you weigh the cartridge as soon as you buy it, then weigh it again from time to time, you can tell when it's close to running out.

Font cartridges: No matter how well you treat them, font cartridges don't last forever. HP estimates that a cartridge will last about 500 insertions. But there are things you can do to prolong their lives. Since a font cartridge contains ROM chips, which are extremely sensitive to surges in voltage, HP recommends that you set the printer off-line (by pressing the ON LINE key on the Control Panel) when changing a font cartridge. If you want to be extra careful, you can make it a practice to turn the printer entirely off when changing font cartridges.

Paper: Given the natural tendency to run lots of sheets through the printer to get a document looking exactly right, it's not hard to develop a rather expensive paper habit. For rough drafts, it won't harm the printer to print on the blank side of previously printed sheets. Place the printed sheets back into the bin faceup (for LaserJet or LaserJet Plus) or face down (LaserJet II). If there are no bent edges, they will feed back into the printer without any problem and print on the clean side.

SIMPLE SOLUTIONS TO COMPLICATED PROBLEMS

Getting pages to come out in the right order: Jonathan Lazarus of Ziff-Davis Corporation (publishers of *PC Magazine*) has suggested a low-tech solution to the classic problem of reverse-order output on the original LaserJet and LaserJet Plus (LaserJet II owners don't have to worry about this). Lazarus's solution is to remove the output tray and replace it with the cardboard top of an ordinary paper box. You need to find one that jams under the LaserJet's output slot. The result, in the words of the inventor, is that "the top of a sheet of paper coming from the printer falls gently into one end of the box, 'trips,' gently turns over, and falls into the box top with the printed side down." When you remove your document, it is in the correct order.

Speeding up output: The LaserJet can be slow if you print lots of graphics. There are several ways to speed things up:

- Use the Centronics parallel port option of the LaserJet Plus and LaserJet II (two to three times faster than serial port).
- Use the LaserJet Plus and LaserJet II option of switching to 19,200 baud (see manual).
- Get a buffer or spooler (see Chapter 28, "Other Enhancements," and "Profile: LaserTORQ.")
- Invest in the LaserMaster CAPCard (see "Profile: LaserMaster CAPCard").

CAUTION!

Moving the printer: Always remove the EP cartridge before moving the LaserJet. Toner spills are the primary reason for printer malfunctions.

Font cartridges: Font cartridges can be damaged by power fluctuations. Don't pull them out of the printer or insert them when the printer is on-line. Take the printer off-line by pressing the button on the far left of the Control Panel. If you want to be even more careful, turn the printer off entirely when you switch cartridges.

Transparencies: Don't put a new printed sheet into a plastic folder. The toner can be pulled off the paper by the electrostatic attraction of the plastic.

EP cartridges: Don't expose an EP cartridge to normal room light (1,500 lux) for more than five minutes. Although the cartridge has light-blocking shutters, you can damage the drum if you leave the cartridge in strong light for a period of time, causing blank or black stripes to appear on printed sheets. If you do accidentally leave the drum in the light, you may be able to restore it by keeping it in the dark for some time. Direct sunlight is about 10,000 to 30,000 lux, enough to permanently ruin the photosensitive drum. Don't keep an EP cartridge in a car for a period of time; it can be damaged by exhaust fumes.

Mechanical switch boxes: Use electronic rather than mechanical switch boxes, since mechanical switch boxes can cause voltage surges that have been known to burn out circuit boards. Using a mechanical switch box will void the warrenty. For information on electronic switch boxes, see Chapter 29, "Other Enhancements."

MISCELLANEOUS

Since it's not an impact printer, the LaserJet cannot print carbon copies. Because it's a single-sheet feeder, it can't print continuous labels or multisheet forms.

If proportionally spaced TmsRmn is producing different results than you expect in terms of margins and centering, be aware that the TmsRmn in cartridge B is not the same as in cartridge F. In cartridge F the character spacing is much tighter. Drivers for F and A will work with each other, but line spacing will be incorrect. The soft-font version of TmsRmn is very different than either of the cartridge versions, both in letter design and letter spacing.

In landscape mode, for purposes of setting margins, the edge of the sheet that was formerly the left side becomes the top, and the side that was formerly the bottom becomes the side.

APPENDIX C

Font Cartridge Escape Sequences

THIS APPENDIX CONTAINS the escape sequences needed to select the fonts on cartridges A—Z. For background on how to use escape sequences to select fonts, refer to Chapter 18, "Selecting Fonts with PCL," and Chapter 19, "Programming the LaserJet with PCL."

How to Read the Chart

Column 1: Typeface. The options are Courier, Line Printer, Helv, TmsRmn, Prestige, Letter Gothic, and Presentations.
Column 2: Orientation. Fonts may be either portrait (P) or landscape (L).
Column 3: Size. This is measured in points (72 points = 1 inch) from the top of the tallest ascender to the bottom of the lowest descender.
Column 4: Horizontal Spacing. This is either fixed or proportional. If the font uses fixed spacing, the pitch (characters per inch) is also shown.
Column 5: Style and Weight. The first letter indicates style, either upright (U) or italic (I). The second letter indicates the weight, either light (L), medium (M), or bold (B).
Column 6: Character Set. The symbol set or character set is the collection of characters, symbols, and punctuation marks contained in the font. The numbers refer to the table on the following page.
Column 7: Escape Sequence. The sequences shown in this table will select a font as the primary font. To select a font as the *secondary* font, replace all the left parenthesis marks { (} with right parenthesis marks {) }. The caret symbol (^) represents the escape character, ASCII 027, referred to by HP as ^{E}c.

Character Sets

Internal to LaserJet II

(1) HP Math7
(2) HP Line Draw
(3) ISO 60: Norwegian 1
(4) ISO 61: Norwegian 2
(5) HP Roman Extension
(6) ISO 4: United Kingdom
(7) ISO 25: French
(8) ISO 69: French
(9) HP German
(10) ISO 21: German
(11) HP Greek8
(12) ISO 15: Italian
(13) ISO 14: JIS ASCII
(14) HP Katakana
(15) ISO 57: Chinese
(16) HP Math7
(17) Technical
(18) HP Math 8
(19) ISO 100: ECMA-94 (Latin 1)
(20) OCR A
(21) OCR B
(22) ISO 11: Swedish
(23) HP Spanish
(24) ISO 17: Spanish
(25) ISO 10: Swedish
(26) ISO 16: Portuguese
(27) ISO 84: Portuguese
(28) ISO 85: Spanish
(29) ISO 6: ASCII
(30) HP Legal
(31) ISO 2: IRV
(32) OEM-1
(33) HP Roman8
(34) PC-8
(35) PC-8 (D/N)
(36) HP Pi Font
(37) HP Math 8A

Cartridge-Based

(38) HP Math 8B
(39) PC Line
(40) Bar 3 of 9
(41) OCR-B Extension
(42) PC Extension
(43) PC Set 1

Cartridge 92286A

Courier	P	12.00	Fixed 10	I/L	(33)	^&lØO^(8U^(sØp1Øh12vØs-3b3T
Courier	P	12.00	Fixed 10	U/M	(33)	^&lØO^(8U^(sØp1Øh12vØsØb3T
Line Printer	L	8.50	Fixed 16.66	U/L	(33)	^&l1O^(8U^(sØp16.66h8.5vØs-3bØT

Cartridge 92286B

Helv	P	14.40	Prop	U/B	(29)	^&lØO^(ØU^(s1p14.4vØs3b4T
Tms Rmn	P	10.00	Prop	U/B	(29)	^&lØO^(ØU^(s1p1ØvØs3b5T
Tms Rmn	P	8.00	Prop	U/L	(29)	^&lØO^(ØU^(s1p8vØs-3b5T
Tms Rmn	P	10.00	Prop	U/M	(29)	^&lØO^(ØU^(s1p1ØvØsØb5T
Tms Rmn	P	10.00	Prop	I/M	(29)	^&lØO^(ØU^(s1p1Øv1sØb5T
Line Printer	L	8.50	Fixed 16.66	U/L	(33)	^&l1O^(8U^(sØp16.66h8.5vØs-3bØT

Cartridge 92286C

Courier	P	12.00	Fixed 10	U/B	(29)	^&lØO^(ØU^(sØp1Øh12vØs3b3T
Courier	P	12.00	Fixed 10	U/B	(9)	^&lØO^(ØG^(sØp1Øh12vØs3b3T
Courier	P	12.00	Fixed 10	U/B	(23)	^&lØO^(1S^(sØp1Øh12vØs3b3T
Courier	P	12.00	Fixed 10	U/B	(22)	^&lØO^(Øs^(sØp1Øh12vØs3b3T
Courier	P	12.00	Fixed 10	U/B	(12)	^&lØO^(ØI^(sØp1Øh12vØs3b3T
Courier	P	12.00	Fixed 10	U/B	(7)	^&lØO^(ØF^(sØp1Øh12vØs3b3T
Courier	P	12.00	Fixed 10	U/B	(6)	^&lØO^(1E^(sØp1Øh12vØs3b3T
Courier	P	12.00	Fixed 10	U/B	(3)	^&lØO^(ØD^(sØp1Øh12vØs3b3T
Courier	P	12.00	Fixed 10	U/B	(33)	^&lØO^(8U^(sØp1Øh12vØs3b3T
Courier	P	12.00	Fixed 10	U/B	(5)	^&lØO^(ØE^(sØp1Øh12vØs3b3T
Courier	P	12.00	Fixed 10	U/M	(29)	^&lØO^(ØU^(sØp1Øh12vØsØb3T
Courier	P	12.00	Fixed 10	I/M	(29)	^&lØO^(ØU^(sØp1Øh12v1sØb3T
Courier	P	12.00	Fixed 10	U/M	(9)	^&lØO^(ØG^(sØp1Øh12vØsØb3T
Courier	P	12.00	Fixed 10	I/M	(9)	^&lØO^(ØG^(sØp1Øh12v1sØb3T
Courier	P	12.00	Fixed 10	U/M	(23)	^&lØO^(1S^(sØp1Øh12vØsØb3T
Courier	P	12.00	Fixed 10	I/M	(23)	^&lØO^(1S^(sØp1Øh12v1sØb3T

Courier	P	12.00	Fixed 10	U/M	(22)	^&lØO^(Øs^(sØp1Øh12vØsØb3T
Courier	P	12.00	Fixed 10	I/M	(22)	^&lØO^(Øs^(sØp1Øh12v1sØb3T
Courier	P	12.00	Fixed 10	U/M	(12)	^&lØO^(Øl^(sØp1Øh12vØsØb3T
Courier	P	12.00	Fixed 10	I/M	(12)	^&lØO^(Øl^(sØp1Øh12v1sØb3T
Courier	P	12.00	Fixed 10	U/M	(7)	^&lØO^(ØF^(sØp1Øh12vØsØb3T
Courier	P	12.00	Fixed 10	I/M	(7)	^&lØO^(ØF^(sØp1Øh12v1sØb3T
Courier	P	12.00	Fixed 10	U/M	(6)	^&lØO^(1E^(sØp1Øh12vØsØb3T
Courier	P	12.00	Fixed 10	I/M	(6)	^&lØO^(1E^(sØp1Øh12v1sØb3T
Courier	P	12.00	Fixed 10	U/M	(3)	^&lØO^(ØD^(sØp1Øh12vØsØb3T
Courier	P	12.00	Fixed 10	I/M	(3)	^&lØO^(ØD^(sØp1Øh12v1sØb3T
Courier	P	12.00	Fixed 10	U/M	(33)	^&lØO^(8U^(sØp1Øh12vØsØb3T
Courier	P	12.00	Fixed 10	I/M	(33)	^&lØO^(8U^(sØp1Øh12v1sØb3T
Courier	P	12.00	Fixed 10	U/M	(5)	^&lØO^(ØE^(sØp1Øh12vØsØb3T
Courier	P	12.00	Fixed 10	I/M	(5)	^&lØO^(ØE^(sØp1Øh12v1sØb3T
Line Printer	L	8.50	Fixed 16.66	U/L	(29)	^&l1O^(ØU^(sØp16.66h8.5vØs-3bØT
Line Printer	L	8.50	Fixed 16.66	U/L	(9)	^&l1O^(ØG^(sØp16.66h8.5vØs-3bØT
Line Printer	L	8.50	Fixed 16.66	U/L	(23)	^&l1O^(1S^(sØp16.66h8.5vØs-3bØT
Line Printer	L	8.50	Fixed 16.66	U/L	(22)	^&l1O^(Øs^(sØp16.66h8.5vØs-3bØT
Line Printer	L	8.50	Fixed 16.66	U/L	(12)	^&l1O^(Øl^(sØp16.66h8.5vØs-3bØT
Line Printer	L	8.50	Fixed 16.66	U/L	(7)	^&l1O^(ØF^(sØp16.66h8.5vØs-3bØT
Line Printer	L	8.50	Fixed 16.66	U/L	(6)	^&l1O^(1E^(sØp16.66h8.5vØs-3bØT
Line Printer	L	8.50	Fixed 16.66	U/L	(3)	^&l1O^(ØD^(sØp16.66h8.5vØs-3bØT
Line Printer	L	8.50	Fixed 16.66	U/L	(33)	^&l1O^(8U^(sØp16.66h8.5vØs-3bØT
Line Printer	L	8.50	Fixed 16.66	U/L	(5)	^&l1O^(ØE^(sØp16.66h8.5vØs-3bØT
Line Printer	P	8.50	Fixed 16.66	U/L	(29)	^&lØO^(ØU^(sØp16.66h8.5vØs-3bØT
Line Printer	P	8.50	Fixed 16.66	U/L	(9)	^&lØO^(ØG^(sØp16.66h8.5vØs-3bØT
Line Printer	P	8.50	Fixed 16.66	U/L	(23)	^&lØO^(1S^(sØp16.66h8.5vØs-3bØT
Line Printer	P	8.50	Fixed 16.66	U/L	(22)	^&lØO^(Øs^(sØp16.66h8.5vØs-3bØT
Line Printer	P	8.50	Fixed 16.66	U/L	(12)	^&lØO^(Øl^(sØp16.66h8.5vØs-3bØT
Line Printer	P	8.50	Fixed 16.66	U/L	(7)	^&lØO^(ØF^(sØp16.66h8.5vØs-3bØT
Line Printer	P	8.50	Fixed 16.66	U/L	(6)	^&lØO^(1E^(sØp16.66h8.5vØs-3bØT
Line Printer	P	8.50	Fixed 16.66	U/L	(3)	^&lØO^(ØD^(sØp16.66h8.5vØs-3bØT
Line Printer	P	8.50	Fixed 16.66	U/L	(33)	^&lØO^(8U^(sØp16.66h8.5vØs-3bØT

Line Printer	P	8.50	Fixed 16.66	U/L	(5)	^&lØO^(ØE^(sØp16.66h8.5vØs-3bØT

Cartridge 92286D

Prestige	P	10.00	Fixed 12	U/B	(29)	^&lØO^(ØU^(sØp12h1ØvØs3b8T
Prestige	P	10.00	Fixed 12	U/B	(33)	^&lØO^(8U^(sØp12h1ØvØs3b8T
Prestige	P	10.00	Fixed 12	U/B	(5)	^&lØO^(ØE^(sØp12h1ØvØs3b8T
Prestige	P	10.00	Fixed 12	U/M	(29)	^&lØO^(ØU^(sØp12h1ØvØsØb8T
Prestige	P	10.00	Fixed 12	I/M	(29)	^&lØO^(ØU^(sØp12h1Øv1sØb8T
Prestige	P	10.00	Fixed 12	U/M	(33)	^&lØO^(8U^(sØp12h1ØvØsØb8T
Prestige	P	10.00	Fixed 12	I/M	(33)	^&lØO^(8U^(sØp12h1Øv1sØb8T
Prestige	P	10.00	Fixed 12	U/M	(5)	^&lØO^(ØE^(sØp12h1ØvØsØb8T
Prestige	P	10.00	Fixed 12	I/M	(5)	^&lØO^(ØE^(sØp12h1Øv1sØb8T

Cartridge 92286E

Letter Gothic	P	12.00	Fixed 12	U/B	(29)	^&lØO^(ØU^(sØp12h12vØs3b6T
Letter Gothic	P	12.00	Fixed 12	U/B	(33)	^&lØO^(8U^(sØp12h12vØs3b6T
Letter Gothic	P	12.00	Fixed 12	U/B	(5)	^&lØO^(ØE^(sØp12h12vØs3b6T
Letter Gothic	P	12.00	Fixed 12	U/M	(29)	^&lØO^(ØU^(sØp12h12vØsØb6T
Letter Gothic	P	12.00	Fixed 12	I/M	(29)	^&lØO^(ØU^(sØp12h12v1sØb6T
Letter Gothic	P	12.00	Fixed 12	U/M	(33)	^&lØO^(8U^(sØp12h12vØsØb6T
Letter Gothic	P	12.00	Fixed 12	I/M	(33)	^&lØO^(8U^(sØp12h12v1sØb6T
Letter Gothic	P	12.00	Fixed 12	U/M	(5)	^&lØO^(ØE^(sØp12h12vØsØb6T
Letter Gothic	P	12.00	Fixed 12	I/M	(5)	^&lØO^(ØE^(sØp12h12v1sØb6T

Cartridge 92286F

Helv	P	14.40	Prop	U/B	(29)	^&lØO^(ØU^(s1p14.4vØs3b4T
Helv	P	14.40	Prop	U/B	(33)	^&lØO^(8U^(s1p14.4vØs3b4T
Helv	P	14.40	Prop	U/B	(5)	^&lØO^(ØE^(s1p14.4vØs3b4T
Tms Rmn	P	10.00	Prop	U/B	(29)	^&lØO^(ØU^(s1p1ØvØs3b5T
Tms Rmn	P	10.00	Prop	U/B	(33)	^&lØO^(8U^(s1p1ØvØs3b5T

Tms Rmn	P	10.00	Prop	U/B	(5)	^&lØO^(ØE^(s1p1Øv0s3b5T
Tms Rmn	P	8.00	Prop	U/L	(29)	^&lØO^(ØU^(s1p8vØs-3b5T
Tms Rmn	P	8.00	Prop	U/L	(33)	^&lØO^(8U^(s1p8vØs-3b5T
Tms Rmn	P	8.00	Prop	U/L	(5)	^&lØO^(ØE^(s1p8vØs-3b5T
Tms Rmn	P	10.00	Prop	U/M	(29)	^&lØO^(ØU^(s1p1ØvØsØb5T
Tms Rmn	P	10.00	Prop	I/M	(29)	^&lØO^(ØU^(s1p1Øv1sØb5T
Tms Rmn	P	10.00	Prop	U/M	(33)	^&lØO^(8U^(s1p1ØvØsØb5T
Tms Rmn	P	10.00	Prop	I/M	(33)	^&lØO^(8U^(s1p1Øv1sØb5T
Tms Rmn	P	10.00	Prop	U/M	(5)	^&lØO^(ØE^(s1p1ØvØsØb5T
Tms Rmn	P	10.00	Prop	I/M	(5)	^&lØO^(ØE^(s1p1Øv1sØb5T
Line Printer	P	8.50	Fixed 16.66	U/L	(29)	^&lØO^(ØU^(sØp16.66h8.5vØs-3bØT
Line Printer	P	8.50	Fixed 16.66	U/L	(33)	^&lØO^(8U^(sØp16.66h8.5vØs-3bØT
Line Printer	P	8.50	Fixed 16.66	U/L	(5)	^&lØO^(ØE^(sØp16.66h8.5vØs-3bØT

Cartridge 92286G

Prestige	P	10.00	Fixed 12	U/B	(29)	^&lØO^(ØU^(sØp12h1ØvØs3b8T
Prestige	P	10.00	Fixed 12	U/B	(30)	^&lØO^(1U^(sØp12h1ØvØs3b8T
Line Printer	P	12.00	Fixed 12	U/M	(2)	^&lØO^(Øb^(sØp12h12vØsØbØT
Prestige	P	10.00	Fixed 12	U/M	(29)	^&lØO^(ØU^(sØp12h1ØvØsØb8T
Prestige	P	10.00	Fixed 12	I/M	(29)	^&lØO^(ØU^(sØp12h1Øv1sØb8T
Prestige	P	10.00	Fixed 12	U/M	(30)	^&lØO^(1U^(sØp12h1ØvØsØb8T
Prestige	P	10.00	Fixed 12	I/M	(30)	^&lØO^(1U^(sØp12h1Øv1sØb8T
Prestige	L	7.00	Fixed 16.66	U/M	(29)	^&l1O^(ØU^(sØp16.66h7vØsØb8T
Prestige	L	7.00	Fixed 16.66	U/M	(30)	^&l1O^(1U^(sØp16.66h7vØsØb8T
Prestige	P	7.00	Fixed 16.66	U/M	(29)	^&lØO^(ØU^(sØp16.66h7vØsØb8T
Prestige	P	7.00	Fixed 16.66	U/M	(30)	^&lØO^(1U^(sØp16.66h7vØsØb8T

Cartridge 92286H

Courier	P	12.00	Fixed 10	U/B	(29)	^&lØO^(ØU^(sØp1Øh12vØs3b3T
Courier	P	12.00	Fixed 10	U/B	(30)	^&lØO^(1U^(sØp1Øh12vØs3b3T
Courier	P	12.00	Fixed 10	U/B	(33)	^&lØO^(8U^(sØp1Øh12vØs3b3T

Courier	P	12.00	Fixed 10	U/M	(29)	^&lØO^(ØU^(sØp1Øh12vØsØb3T
Courier	P	12.00	Fixed 10	I/M	(29)	^&lØO^(ØU^(sØp1Øh12v1sØb3T
Courier	P	12.00	Fixed 10	U/M	(30)	^&lØO^(1U^(sØp1Øh12vØsØb3T
Courier	P	12.00	Fixed 10	I/M	(30)	^&lØO^(1U^(sØp1Øh12v1sØb3T
Courier	P	12.00	Fixed 10	U/M	(33)	^&lØO^(8U^(sØp1Øh12vØsØb3T
Courier	P	12.00	Fixed 10	I/M	(33)	^&lØO^(8U^(sØp1Øh12v1sØb3T
Line Printer	P	12.00	Fixed 10	U/M	(2)	^&lØO^(Øb^(sØp1Øh12vØsØbØT
Prestige	L	7.00	Fixed 16.66	U/M	(29)	^&l1O^(ØU^(sØp16.66h7vØsØb8T
Prestige	L	7.00	Fixed 16.66	U/M	(30)	^&l1O^(1U^(sØp16.66h7vØsØb8T
Prestige	P	7.00	Fixed 16.66	U/M	(29)	^&lØO^(ØU^(sØp16.66h7vØsØb8T
Prestige	P	7.00	Fixed 16.66	U/M	(30)	^&lØO^(1U^(sØp16.66h7vØsØb8T

Cartridge 92286J

Prestige	P	10.00	Fixed 12	U/B	(29)	^&lØO^(ØU^(sØp12h1ØvØs3b8T
Prestige	P	10.00	Fixed 12	U/B	(33)	^&lØO^(8U^(sØp12h1ØvØs3b8T
Prestige	P	10.00	Fixed 12	U/B	(5)	^&lØO^(ØE^(sØp12h1ØvØs3b8T
Prestige	P	10.00	Fixed 12	U/M	(29)	^&lØO^(ØU^(sØp12h1ØvØsØb8T
Prestige	P	10.00	Fixed 12	I/M	(29)	^&lØO^(ØU^(sØp12h1Øv1sØb8T
Prestige	P	10.00	Fixed 12	U/M	(37)	^&lØO^(ØQ^(sØp12h1ØvØsØb8T
Prestige	P	10.00	Fixed 12	U/M	(38)	^&lØO^(1Q^(sØp12h1ØvØsØb8T
Prestige	P	10.00	Fixed 12	U/M	(16)	^&lØO^(ØA^(sØp12h1ØvØsØb8T
Prestige	P	10.00	Fixed 12	U/M	(18)	^&lØO^(8M^(sØp12h1ØvØsØb8T
Prestige	P	10.00	Fixed 12	U/M	(36)	^&lØO^(15U^(sØp12h1ØvØsØb8T
Prestige	P	10.00	Fixed 12	U/M	(36)	^&lØO^(2Q^(sØp12h1ØvØsØb8T
Prestige	P	10.00	Fixed 12	U/M	(33)	^&lØO^(8U^(sØp12h1ØvØsØb8T
Prestige	P	10.00	Fixed 12	I/M	(33)	^&lØO^(8U^(sØp12h1Øv1sØb8T
Prestige	P	10.00	Fixed 12	U/M	(5)	^&lØO^(ØE^(sØp12h1ØvØsØb8T
Prestige	P	10.00	Fixed 12	I/M	(5)	^&lØO^(ØE^(sØp12h1Øv1sØb8T
Prestige	P	7.00	Fixed 16.66	U/M	(29)	^&lØO^(ØU^(sØp16.66h7vØsØb8T
Prestige	P	7.00	Fixed 16.66	U/M	(37)	^&lØO^(ØQ^(sØp16.66h7vØsØb8T
Prestige	P	7.00	Fixed 16.66	U/M	(38)	^&lØO^(1Q^(sØp16.66h7vØsØb8T
Prestige	P	7.00	Fixed 16.66	U/M	(18)	^&lØO^(8M^(sØp16.66h7vØsØb8T

Prestige	P	7.00	Fixed 16.66	U/M	(33)	^&lØO^(8U^(sØp16.66h7vØsØb8T
Prestige	P	7.00	Fixed 16.66	U/M	(5)	^&lØO^(ØE^(sØp16.66h7vØsØb8T

Cartridge 92286K

Tms Rmn	P	10.00	Prop	U/B	(29)	^&lØO^(ØU^(s1p1Øv0s3b5T
Tms Rmn	P	10.00	Prop	U/B	(33)	^&lØO^(8U^(s1p1ØvØs3b5T
Tms Rmn	P	10.00	Prop	U/B	(5)	^&lØO^(ØE^(s1p1ØvØs3b5T
Tms Rmn	P	10.00	Prop	U/M	(29)	^&lØO^(ØU^(s1p1ØvØsØb5T
Tms Rmn	P	10.00	Prop	I/M	(29)	^&lØO^(ØU^(s1p1Øv1sØb5T
Tms Rmn	P	8.00	Prop	U/M	(29)	^&lØO^(ØU^(s1p8vØsØb5T
Tms Rmn	P	10.00	Prop	U/M	(33)	^&lØO^(8U^(s1p1ØvØsØb5T
Tms Rmn	P	10.00	Prop	I/M	(33)	^&lØO^(8U^(s1p1Øv1sØb5T
Tms Rmn	P	8.00	Prop	U/M	(33)	^&lØO^(8U^(s1p8vØsØb5T
Tms Rmn	P	10.00	Prop	U/M	(5)	^&lØO^(ØE^(s1p1ØvØsØb5T
Tms Rmn	P	10.00	Prop	I/M	(5)	^&lØO^(ØE^(s1p1Øv1sØb5T
Tms Rmn	P	8.00	Prop	U/M	(5)	^&lØO^(ØE^(s1p8vØsØb5T

Cartridge 92286L

Courier	L	12.00	Fixed 10	U/B	(33)	^&l1O^(8U^(sØp1Øh12vØs3b3T
Courier	P	12.00	Fixed 10	U/B	(33)	^&lØO^(8U^(sØp1Øh12vØs3b3T
Courier	L	12.00	Fixed 10	U/M	(33)	^&l1O^(8U^(sØp1Øh12vØsØb3T
Courier	L	12.00	Fixed 10	I/M	(33)	^&l1O^(8U^(sØp1Øh12v1sØb3T
Courier	P	12.00	Fixed 10	U/M	(33)	^&lØO^(8U^(sØp1Øh12vØsØb3T
Courier	P	12.00	Fixed 10	I/M	(33)	^&lØO^(8U^(sØp1Øh12v1sØb3T
Line Printer	L	8.50	Fixed 16.66	U/L	(33)	^&l1O^(8U^(sØp16.66h8.5vØs-3bØT
Line Printer	P	8.50	Fixed 16.66	U/L	(33)	^&lØO^(8U^(sØp16.66h8.5vØs-3bØT

Cartridge 92286M

Prestige	L	10.00	Fixed 12	U/B	(29)	^&l1O^(ØU^(sØp12h1ØvØs3b8T
Prestige	L	10.00	Fixed 12	U/B	(33)	^&l1O^(8U^(sØp12h1ØvØs3b8T

Prestige	L	10.00	Fixed 12	U/B	(5)	^&/1O^(ØE^(sØp12h1ØvØs3b8T
Prestige	P	10.00	Fixed 12	U/B	(29)	^&/ØO^(ØU^(sØp12h1ØvØs3b8T
Prestige	P	10.00	Fixed 12	U/B	(33)	^&/ØO^(8U^(sØp12h1ØvØs3b8T
Prestige	P	10.00	Fixed 12	U/B	(5)	^&/ØO^(ØE^(sØp12h1ØvØs3b8T
Prestige	L	10.00	Fixed 12	U/M	(29)	^&/1O^(ØU^(sØp12h1ØvØsØb8T
Prestige	L	10.00	Fixed 12	I/M	(29)	^&/1O^(ØU^(sØp12h1Øv1sØb8T
Prestige	L	10.00	Fixed 12	U/M	(33)	^&/1O^(8U^(sØp12h1ØvØsØb8T
Prestige	L	10.00	Fixed 12	I/M	(33)	^&/1O^(8U^(sØp12h1Øv1sØb8T
Prestige	L	10.00	Fixed 12	U/M	(5)	^&/1O^(ØE^(sØp12h1ØvØsØb8T
Prestige	L	10.00	Fixed 12	I/M	(5)	^&/1O^(ØE^(sØp12h1Øv1sØb8T
Prestige	P	10.00	Fixed 12	U/M	(29)	^&/ØO^(ØU^(sØp12h1ØvØsØb8T
Prestige	P	10.00	Fixed 12	I/M	(29)	^&/ØO^(ØU^(sØp12h1Øv1sØb8T
Prestige	P	10.00	Fixed 12	U/M	(33)	^&/ØO^(8U^(sØp12h1ØvØsØb8T
Prestige	P	10.00	Fixed 12	I/M	(33)	^&/ØO^(8U^(sØp12h1Øv1sØb8T
Prestige	P	10.00	Fixed 12	U/M	(5)	^&/ØO^(ØE^(sØp12h1ØvØsØb8T
Prestige	P	10.00	Fixed 12	I/M	(5)	^&/ØO^(ØE^(sØp12h1Øv1sØb8T

Cartridge 92286N

Letter Gothic	L	12.00	Fixed 12	U/B	(33)	^&/1O^(8U^(sØp12h12vØs3b6T
Letter Gothic	P	12.00	Fixed 12	U/B	(33)	^&/ØO^(8U^(sØp12h12vØs3b6T
Letter Gothic	L	12.00	Fixed 12	U/M	(33)	^&/1O^(8U^(sØp12h12vØsØb6T
Letter Gothic	L	12.00	Fixed 12	I/M	(33)	^&/1O^(8U^(sØp12h12v1sØb6T
Letter Gothic	P	12.00	Fixed 12	U/M	(33)	^&/ØO^(8U^(sØp12h12vØsØb6T
Letter Gothic	P	12.00	Fixed 12	I/M	(33)	^&/ØO^(8U^(sØp12h12v1sØb6T

Cartridge 92286P

Tms Rmn	L	10.00	Prop	U/B	(33)	^&/1O^(8U^(s1p1ØvØs3b5T
Tms Rmn	P	10.00	Prop	U/B	(33)	^&/ØO^(8U^(s1p1ØvØs3b5T
Tms Rmn	L	10.00	Prop	U/M	(33)	^&/1O^(8U^(s1p1ØvØsØb5T
Tms Rmn	L	10.00	Prop	I/M	(33)	^&/1O^(8U^(s1p1Øv1sØb5T
Tms Rmn	P	10.00	Prop	U/M	(33)	^&/ØO^(8U^(s1p1ØvØsØb5T

Tms Rmn	P	10.00	Prop	I/M	(33)	^&lØO^(8U^(s1p1Øv1sØb5T

Cartridge 92286Q

Courier	L	12.00	Fixed 10	U/B	(33)	^&l1O^(8U^(sØp1Øh12vØs3b3T
Courier	P	12.00	Fixed 10	U/B	(33)	^&lØO^(8U^(sØp1Øh12vØs3b3T
Courier	L	12.00	Fixed 10	U/M	(33)	^&l1O^(8U^(sØp1Øh12vØsØb3T
Courier	L	12.00	Fixed 10	I/M	(33)	^&l1O^(8U^(sØp1Øh12v1sØb3T
Courier	P	12.00	Fixed 10	U/M	(33)	^&lØO^(8U^(sØp1Øh12vØsØb3T
Courier	P	12.00	Fixed 10	I/M	(33)	^&lØO^(8U^(sØp1Øh12v1sØb3T
Letter Gothic	P	12.00	Fixed 12	U/B	(33)	^&lØO^(8U^(sØp12h12vØs3b6T
Letter Gothic	P	12.00	Fixed 12	U/M	(33)	^&lØO^(8U^(sØp12h12vØsØb6T

Cartridge 92286R

Presentations	L	18.00	Fixed 6.5	U/B	(29)	^&l1O^(ØU^(sØp6.5h18vØs3b1T
Presentations	L	18.00	Fixed 6.5	U/B	(30)	^&l1O^(1U^(sØp6.5h18vØs3b1T
Presentations	P	18.00	Fixed 6.5	U/B	(29)	^&lØO^(ØU^(sØp6.5h18vØs3b1T
Presentations	P	18.00	Fixed 6.5	U/B	(30)	^&lØO^(1U^(sØp6.5h18vØs3b1T
Presentations	L	16.00	Fixed 8.1	U/B	(29)	^&l1O^(ØU^(sØp8.1h16vØs3b1T
Presentations	L	16.00	Fixed 8.1	U/B	(30)	^&l1O^(1U^(sØp8.1h16vØs3b1T
Presentations	P	16.00	Fixed 8.1	U/B	(29)	^&lØO^(ØU^(sØp8.1h16vØs3b1T
Presentations	P	16.00	Fixed 8.1	U/B	(30)	^&lØO^(1U^(sØp8.1h16vØs3b1T
Line Printer	L	14.00	Fixed 10	U/B	(39)	^&l1O^(4Q^(sØp1Øh14vØs3bØT
Line Printer	P	14.00	Fixed 10	U/B	(39)	^&lØO^(4Q^(sØp1Øh14vØs3bØT
Presentations	L	14.00	Fixed 10	U/B	(29)	^&l1O^(ØU^(sØp1Øh14vØs3b1T
Presentations	L	14.00	Fixed 10	U/B	(30)	^&l1O^(1U^(sØp1Øh14vØs3b1T
Presentations	P	14.00	Fixed 10	U/B	(29)	^&lØO^(ØU^(sØp1Øh14vØs3b1T
Presentations	P	14.00	Fixed 10	U/B	(30)	^&lØO^(1U^(sØp1Øh14vØs3b1T
Letter Gothic	L	14.00	Fixed 10	U/M	(29)	^&l1O^(ØU^(sØp1Øh14vØsØb6T
Letter Gothic	L	14.00	Fixed 10	U/M	(30)	^&l1O^(1U^(sØp1Øh14vØsØb6T
Letter Gothic	P	14.00	Fixed 10	U/M	(29)	^&lØO^(ØU^(sØp1Øh14vØsØb6T
Letter Gothic	P	14.00	Fixed 10	U/M	(30)	^&lØO^(1U^(sØp1Øh14vØsØb6T

Line Printer	L	14.00	Fixed 10	U/M	(2)	^&l1O^(Øb^(sØp1Øh14vØsØbØT
Line Printer	P	14.00	Fixed 10	U/M	(2)	^&lØO^(Øb^(sØp1Øh14vØsØbØT

Cartridge 92290S1

Courier	L	12.00	Fixed 10	I/M	(19)	^&l1O^(ØN^(sØp1Øh12v1sØb3T
Courier	L	12.00	Fixed 10	I/M	(34)	^&l1O^(1ØU^(sØp1Øh12v1sØb3T
Courier	L	12.00	Fixed 10	I/M	(35)	^&l1O^(11U^(sØp1Øh12v1sØb3T
Courier	L	12.00	Fixed 10	I/M	(33)	^&l1O^(8U^(sØp1Øh12v1sØb3T
Courier	P	12.00	Fixed 10	I/M	(19)	^&lØO^(ØN^(sØp1Øh12v1sØb3T
Courier	P	12.00	Fixed 10	I/M	(34)	^&lØO^(1ØU^(sØp1Øh12v1sØb3T
Courier	P	12.00	Fixed 10	I/M	(35)	^&lØO^(11U^(sØp1Øh12v1sØb3T
Courier	P	12.00	Fixed 10	I/M	(33)	^&lØO^(8U^(sØp1Øh12v1sØb3T
Courier	L	10.00	Fixed 12	U/B	(19)	^&l1O^(ØN^(sØp12h1ØvØs3b3T
Courier	L	10.00	Fixed 12	U/B	(34)	^&l1O^(1ØU^(sØp12h1ØvØs3b3T
Courier	L	10.00	Fixed 12	U/B	(35)	^&l1O^(11U^(sØp12h1ØvØs3b3T
Courier	L	10.00	Fixed 12	U/B	(33)	^&l1O^(8U^(sØp12h1ØvØs3b3T
Courier	P	10.00	Fixed 12	U/B	(19)	^&lØO^(ØN^(sØp12h1ØvØs3b3T
Courier	P	10.00	Fixed 12	U/B	(34)	^&lØO^(1ØU^(sØp12h1ØvØs3b3T
Courier	P	10.00	Fixed 12	U/B	(35)	^&lØO^(11U^(sØp12h1ØvØs3b3T
Courier	P	10.00	Fixed 12	U/B	(33)	^&lØO^(8U^(sØp12h1ØvØs3b3T
Courier	L	10.00	Fixed 12	I/M	(19)	^&l1O^(ØN^(sØp12h1Øv1sØb3T
Courier	L	10.00	Fixed 12	U/M	(19)	^&l1O^(ØN^(sØp12h1ØvØsØb3T
Courier	L	10.00	Fixed 12	I/M	(34)	^&l1O^(1ØU^(sØp12h1Øv1sØb3T
Courier	L	10.00	Fixed 12	U/M	(34)	^&l1O^(1ØU^(sØp12h1ØvØsØb3T
Courier	L	10.00	Fixed 12	I/M	(35)	^&l1O^(11U^(sØp12h1Øv1sØb3T
Courier	L	10.00	Fixed 12	U/M	(35)	^&l1O^(11U^(sØp12h1ØvØsØb3T
Courier	L	10.00	Fixed 12	I/M	(33)	^&l1O^(8U^(sØp12h1Øv1sØb3T
Courier	L	10.00	Fixed 12	U/M	(33)	^&l1O^(8U^(sØp12h1ØvØsØb3T
Courier	P	10.00	Fixed 12	I/M	(19)	^&lØO^(ØN^(sØp12h1Øv1sØb3T
Courier	P	10.00	Fixed 12	U/M	(19)	^&lØO^(ØN^(sØp12h1ØvØsØb3T
Courier	P	10.00	Fixed 12	I/M	(34)	^&lØO^(1ØU^(sØp12h1Øv1sØb3T
Courier	P	10.00	Fixed 12	U/M	(34)	^&lØO^(1ØU^(sØp12h1ØvØsØb3T

Courier	P	10.00	Fixed 12	I/M	(35)	^&lØO^(11U^(sØp12h1Øv1sØb3T
Courier	P	10.00	Fixed 12	U/M	(35)	^&lØO^(11U^(sØp12h1ØvØsØb3T
Courier	P	10.00	Fixed 12	I/M	(33)	^&lØO^(8U^(sØp12h1Øv1sØb3T
Courier	P	10.00	Fixed 12	U/M	(33)	^&lØO^(8U^(sØp12h1ØvØsØb3T

Cartridge 92290S2

Helv	L	14.00	Prop	U/B	(19)	^&l1O^(ØN^(s1p14vØs3b4T
Helv	L	14.00	Prop	U/B	(34)	^&l1O^(1ØU^(s1p14vØs3b4T
Helv	L	14.00	Prop	U/B	(35)	^&l1O^(11U^(s1p14vØs3b4T
Helv	L	14.00	Prop	U/B	(33)	^&l1O^(8U^(s1p14vØs3b4T
Helv	P	14.00	Prop	U/B	(19)	^&lØO^(ØN^(s1p14vØs3b4T
Helv	P	14.00	Prop	U/B	(34)	^&lØO^(1ØU^(s1p14vØs3b4T
Helv	P	14.00	Prop	U/B	(35)	^&lØO^(11U^(s1p14vØs3b4T
Helv	P	14.00	Prop	U/B	(33)	^&lØO^(8U^(s1p14vØs3b4T
Tms Rmn	L	12.00	Prop	U/B	(19)	^&l1O^(ØN^(s1p12vØs3b5T
Tms Rmn	L	12.00	Prop	U/B	(34)	^&l1O^(1ØU^(s1p12vØs3b5T
Tms Rmn	L	12.00	Prop	U/B	(35)	^&l1O^(11U^(s1p12vØs3b5T
Tms Rmn	L	12.00	Prop	U/B	(33)	^&l1O^(8U^(s1p12vØs3b5T
Tms Rmn	P	12.00	Prop	U/B	(19)	^&lØO^(ØN^(s1p12vØs3b5T
Tms Rmn	P	12.00	Prop	U/B	(34)	^&lØO^(1ØU^(s1p12vØs3b5T
Tms Rmn	P	12.00	Prop	U/B	(35)	^&lØO^(11U^(s1p12vØs3b5T
Tms Rmn	P	12.00	Prop	U/B	(33)	^&lØO^(8U^(s1p12vØs3b5T
Tms Rmn	L	8.00	Prop	U/M	(19)	^&l1O^(ØN^(s1p8vØsØb5T
Tms Rmn	L	12.00	Prop	I/M	(19)	^&l1O^(ØN^(s1p12v1sØb5T
Tms Rmn	L	12.00	Prop	U/M	(19)	^&l1O^(ØN^(s1p12vØsØb5T
Tms Rmn	L	8.00	Prop	U/M	(34)	^&l1O^(1ØU^(s1p8vØsØb5T
Tms Rmn	L	12.00	Prop	I/M	(34)	^&l1O^(1ØU^(s1p12v1sØb5T
Tms Rmn	L	12.00	Prop	U/M	(34)	^&l1O^(1ØU^(s1p12vØsØb5T
Tms Rmn	L	8.00	Prop	U/M	(35)	^&l1O^(11U^(s1p8vØsØb5T
Tms Rmn	L	12.00	Prop	I/M	(35)	^&l1O^(11U^(s1p12v1sØb5T
Tms Rmn	L	12.00	Prop	U/M	(35)	^&l1O^(11U^(s1p12vØsØb5T
Tms Rmn	L	8.00	Prop	U/M	(33)	^&l1O^(8U^(s1p8vØsØb5T

Tms Rmn	L	12.00	Prop	I/M	(33)	^&l1O^(8U^(s1p12v1sØb5T
Tms Rmn	L	12.00	Prop	U/M	(33)	^&l1O^(8U^(s1p12vØsØb5T
Tms Rmn	P	8.00	Prop	U/M	(19)	^&lØO^(ØN^(s1p8vØsØb5T
Tms Rmn	P	12.00	Prop	I/M	(19)	^&lØO^(ØN^(s1p12v1sØb5T
Tms Rmn	P	12.00	Prop	U/M	(19)	^&lØO^(ØN^(s1p12vØsØb5T
Tms Rmn	P	8.00	Prop	U/M	(34)	^&lØO^(1ØU^(s1p8vØsØb5T
Tms Rmn	P	12.00	Prop	I/M	(34)	^&lØO^(1ØU^(s1p12v1sØb5T
Tms Rmn	P	12.00	Prop	U/M	(34)	^&lØO^(1ØU^(s1p12vØsØb5T
Tms Rmn	P	8.00	Prop	U/M	(35)	^&lØO^(11U^(s1p8vØsØb5T
Tms Rmn	P	12.00	Prop	I/M	(35)	^&lØO^(11U^(s1p12v1sØb5T
Tms Rmn	P	12.00	Prop	U/M	(35)	^&lØO^(11U^(s1p12vØsØb5T
Tms Rmn	P	8.00	Prop	U/M	(33)	^&lØO^(8U^(s1p8vØsØb5T
Tms Rmn	P	12.00	Prop	I/M	(33)	^&lØO^(8U^(s1p12v1sØb5T
Tms Rmn	P	12.00	Prop	U/M	(33)	^&lØO^(8U^(s1p12vØsØb5T

Cartridge 92286T

Helv	P	14.00	Prop	U/B	(29)	^&lØO^(ØU^(s1p14vØs3b4T
Helv	P	12.00	Prop	U/B	(29)	^&lØO^(ØU^(s1p12vØs3b4T
Helv	P	10.00	Prop	U/B	(29)	^&lØO^(ØU^(s1p1ØvØs3b4T
Helv	P	8.00	Prop	U/B	(29)	^&lØO^(ØU^(s1p8vØs3b4T
Helv	P	8.00	Prop	U/B	(29)	^&lØO^(ØU^(s1p8vØs3b4T
Helv	P	6.00	Prop	U/B	(29)	^&lØO^(ØU^(s1p6vØs3b4T
Line Printer	P	12.00	Fixed 10	U/B	(2)	^&lØO^(Øb^(sØp1Øh12vØs3bØT

Cartridge 92286U

Helv	P	14.00	Prop	U/B	(33)	^&lØO^(8U^(s1p14vØs3b4T
Helv	P	12.00	Prop	U/B	(33)	^&lØO^(8U^(s1p12vØs3b4T
Helv	P	10.00	Prop	U/B	(33)	^&lØO^(8U^(s1p1ØvØs3b4T
Helv	P	14.00	Prop	U/B	(5)	^&lØO^(ØE^(s1p14vØs3b4T
Helv	P	12.00	Prop	U/B	(5)	^&lØO^(ØE^(s1p12vØs3b4T
Helv	P	10.00	Prop	U/B	(5)	^&lØO^(ØE^(s1p1ØvØs3b4T

Helv	P	8.00	Prop	U/M	(33)	^&lØO^(8U^(s1p8vØsØb4T
Helv	P	6.00	Prop	U/M	(33)	^&lØO^(8U^(s1p6vØsØb4T
Helv	P	8.00	Prop	U/M	(5)	^&lØO^(ØE^(s1p8vØsØb4T
Helv	P	6.00	Prop	U/M	(5)	^&lØO^(ØE^(s1p6vØsØb4T
Line Printer	P	12.00	Fixed 10	U/B	(2)	^&lØO^(Øb^(sØp1Øh12vØs3bØT
Letter Gothic	P	9.50	Fixed 16.66	U/M	(33)	^&lØO^(8U^(sØp16.66h9.5vØsØb6T
Letter Gothic	P	9.50	Fixed 16.66	U/M	(5)	^&lØO^(ØE^(sØp16.66h9.5vØsØb6T

Cartridge 92286V

Helv	L	14.00	Prop	U/B	(33)	^&l1O^(8U^(s1p14vØs3b4T
Helv	L	12.00	Prop	U/B	(33)	^&l1O^(8U^(s1p12vØs3b4T
Helv	L	10.00	Prop	U/B	(33)	^&l1O^(8U^(s1p1ØvØs3b4T
Helv	L	14.00	Prop	U/B	(5)	^&l1O^(ØE^(s1p14vØs3b4T
Helv	L	12.00	Prop	U/B	(5)	^&l1O^(ØE^(s1p12vØs3b4T
Helv	L	10.00	Prop	U/B	(5)	^&l1O^(ØE^(s1p1ØvØs3b4T
Helv	L	8.00	Prop	U/M	(33)	^&l1O^(8U^(s1p8vØsØb4T
Helv	L	6.00	Prop	U/M	(33)	^&l1O^(8U^(s1p6vØsØb4T
Helv	L	8.00	Prop	U/M	(5)	^&l1O^(ØE^(s1p8vØsØb4T
Helv	L	6.00	Prop	U/M	(5)	^&l1O^(ØE^(s1p6vØsØb4T
Line Printer	L	12.00	Fixed 10	U/B	(2)	^&l1O^(Øb^(sØp1Øh12vØs3bØT
Letter Gothic	L	9.50	Fixed 16.66	U/M	(33)	^&l1O^(8U^(sØp16.66h9.5vØsØb6T
Letter Gothic	L	9.50	Fixed 16.66	U/M	(5)	^&l1O^(ØE^(sØp16.66h9.5vØsØb6T

Cartridge 92286W1

Line Printer	P	12.00	Fixed 4.6	U/M	(40)	^&lØO^(ØY^(sØp4.6h12vØsØbØT
Line Printer	P	12.00	Fixed 8.1	U/M	(40)	^&lØO^(ØY^(sØp8.1h12vØsØbØT
Letter Gothic	P	14.00	Fixed 10	U/M	(29)	^&lØO^(ØU^(sØp1Øh14vØsØb6T
Letter Gothic	P	14.00	Fixed 10	U/M	(33)	^&lØO^(8U^(sØp1Øh14vØsØb6T
Letter Gothic	P	14.00	Fixed 10	U/M	(5)	^&lØO^(ØE^(sØp1Øh14vØsØb6T
Line Printer	P	12.00	Fixed 10	U/M	(2)	^&lØO^(Øb^(sØp1Øh12vØsØbØT
Line Printer	P	12.00	Fixed 10	U/M	(20)	^&lØO^(ØO^(sØp1Øh12vØsØbØT

Letter Gothic	P	9.50	Fixed 16.66	U/M	(29)	^&lØO^(ØU^(sØp16.66h9.5vØsØb6T
Letter Gothic	P	9.50	Fixed 16.66	U/M	(33)	^&lØO^(8U^(sØp16.66h9.5vØsØb6T
Letter Gothic	P	9.50	Fixed 16.66	U/M	(5)	^&lØO^(ØE^(sØp16.66h9.5vØsØb6T

Cartridge 92286X

Letter Gothic	P	14.00	Fixed 10	U/M	(29)	^&lØO^(ØU^(sØp1Øh14vØsØb6T
Letter Gothic	P	14.00	Fixed 10	U/M	(33)	^&lØO^(8U^(sØp1Øh14vØsØb6T
Letter Gothic	P	14.00	Fixed 10	U/M	(5)	^&lØO^(ØE^(sØp1Øh14vØsØb6T
Line Printer	P	12.00	Fixed 10	U/M	(2)	^&lØO^(Øb^(sØp1Øh12vØsØbØT
Line Printer	P	12.00	Fixed 10	U/M	(21)	^&lØO^(1O^(sØp1Øh12vØsØbØT
Line Printer	P	12.00	Fixed 10	U/M	(41)	^&lØO^(3Q^(sØp1Øh12vØsØbØT
Letter Gothic	P	9.50	Fixed 16.66	U/M	(29)	^&lØO^(ØU^(sØp16.66h9.5vØsØb6T
Letter Gothic	P	9.50	Fixed 16.66	U/M	(33)	^&lØO^(8U^(sØp16.66h9.5vØsØb6T
Letter Gothic	P	9.50	Fixed 16.66	U/M	(5)	^&lØO^(ØE^(sØp16.66h9.5vØsØb6T

Cartridge 92286Y

Courier	P	12.00	Fixed 10	U/B	(42)	^&lØO^(9Q^(sØp1Øh12vØs3b3T
Courier	P	12.00	Fixed 10	U/B	(43)	^&lØO^(8Q^(sØp1Øh12vØs3b3T
Courier	P	12.00	Fixed 10	U/M	(42)	^&lØO^(9Q^(sØp1Øh12vØsØb3T
Courier	P	12.00	Fixed 10	I/M	(42)	^&lØO^(9Q^(sØp1Øh12v1sØb3T
Courier	P	12.00	Fixed 10	U/M	(43)	^&lØO^(8Q^(sØp1Øh12vØsØb3T
Courier	P	12.00	Fixed 10	I/M	(43)	^&lØO^(8Q^(sØp1Øh12v1sØb3T
Line Printer	L	8.50	Fixed 16.66	U/M	(42)	^&l1O^(9Q^(sØp16.66h8.5vØsØbØT
Line Printer	L	8.50	Fixed 16.66	U/M	(43)	^&l1O^(8Q^(sØp16.66h8.5vØsØbØT
Line Printer	P	8.50	Fixed 16.66	U/M	(42)	^&lØO^(9Q^(sØp16.66h8.5vØsØbØT
Line Printer	P	8.50	Fixed 16.66	U/M	(43)	^&lØO^(8Q^(sØp16.66h8.5vØsØbØT

Cartridge 92286Z

Helv	P	10.00	Prop	U/B	(29)	^&lØO^(ØU^(s1p1ØvØs3b4T
Helv	P	12.00	Prop	U/B	(29)	^&lØO^(ØU^(s1p12vØs3b4T

Helv	P	14.00	Prop	U/B	(29)	^&lØO^(ØU^(s1p14vØs3b4T
Helv	P	10.00	Prop	U/B	(19)	^&lØO^(11Q^(s1p1ØvØs3b4T
Helv	P	12.00	Prop	U/B	(19)	^&lØO^(11Q^(s1p12vØs3b4T
Helv	P	14.00	Prop	U/B	(19)	^&lØO^(11Q^(s1p14vØs3b4T
Tms Rmn	P	10.00	Prop	U/B	(29)	^&lØO^(ØU^(s1p1ØvØs3b5T
Tms Rmn	P	12.00	Prop	U/B	(29)	^&lØO^(ØU^(s1p12vØs3b5T
Tms Rmn	P	14.00	Prop	U/B	(29)	^&lØO^(ØU^(s1p14vØs3b5T
Tms Rmn	P	10.00	Prop	U/B	(19)	^&lØO^(11Q^(s1p1ØvØs3b5T
Tms Rmn	P	12.00	Prop	U/B	(19)	^&lØO^(11Q^(s1p12vØs3b5T
Tms Rmn	P	14.00	Prop	U/B	(19)	^&lØO^(11Q^(s1p14vØs3b5T
Helv	P	8.00	Prop	U/M	(29)	^&lØO^(ØU^(s1p8vØsØb4T
Helv	P	10.00	Prop	U/M	(29)	^&lØO^(ØU^(s1p1ØvØsØb4T
Helv	P	10.00	Prop	I/M	(29)	^&lØO^(ØU^(s1p1Øv1sØb4T
Helv	P	12.00	Prop	U/M	(29)	^&lØO^(ØU^(s1p12vØsØb4T
Helv	P	12.00	Prop	I/M	(29)	^&lØO^(ØU^(s1p12v1sØb4T
Helv	P	8.00	Prop	U/M	(19)	^&lØO^(11Q^(s1p8vØsØb4T
Helv	P	10.00	Prop	U/M	(19)	^&lØO^(11Q^(s1p1ØvØsØb4T
Helv	P	10.00	Prop	I/M	(19)	^&lØO^(11Q^(s1p1Øv1sØb4T
Helv	P	12.00	Prop	U/M	(19)	^&lØO^(11Q^(s1p12vØsØb4T
Helv	P	12.00	Prop	I/M	(19)	^&lØO^(11Q^(s1p12v1sØb4T
Tms Rmn	P	8.00	Prop	U/M	(29)	^&lØO^(ØU^(s1p8vØsØb5T
Tms Rmn	P	10.00	Prop	U/M	(29)	^&lØO^(ØU^(s1p1ØvØsØb5T
Tms Rmn	P	10.00	Prop	I/M	(29)	^&lØO^(ØU^(s1p1Øv1sØb5T
Tms Rmn	P	12.00	Prop	U/M	(29)	^&lØO^(ØU^(s1p12vØsØb5T
Tms Rmn	P	12.00	Prop	I/M	(29)	^&lØO^(ØU^(s1p12v1sØb5T
Tms Rmn	P	8.00	Prop	U/M	(19)	^&lØO^(11Q^(s1p8vØsØb5T
Tms Rmn	P	10.00	Prop	U/M	(19)	^&lØO^(11Q^(s1p1ØvØsØb5T
Tms Rmn	P	10.00	Prop	I/M	(19)	^&lØO^(11Q^(s1p1Øv1sØb5T
Tms Rmn	P	12.00	Prop	U/M	(19)	^&lØO^(11Q^(s1p12vØsØb5T
Tms Rmn	P	12.00	Prop	I/M	(19)	^&lØO^(11Q^(s1p12v1sØb5T

APPENDIX D

Table of PCL Commands

Function	Esc	Parameter
Job Control		
Soft Reset	^E	
Number of Copies	^&l#X	# is number of copies (1 to 99)
Page Control		
Paper Source	^&l#H	# is 0 to eject page, 1 to feed from tray, 2 for manual feed, 3 for manual envelope feed
Paper Size	^&l#A	# is 1 for Executive, 2 for Letter, 3 for Legal, 26 for A4, 80 for Monarch, 81 for Commercial, 90 for International DL, 91 for International C5
Page Length	^&l#P	# is number of lines
Orientation	^&l#O	# is 0 for portrait, 1 for landscape
Left Margin	^&a#L	# is column number
Right Margin	^&a#M	# is column number
L & R Margin Reset	^9	
Top Margin	^&l#E	# is number of lines
Text Length	^&l#F	# is number of lines
Perforation Skip	^&#L	# is 0 to disable perforation skip, 1to activate perforation skip
Horizontal Motion Index (HMI)	^&k#H	# is number of 1/20 inch increments per column
Vertical Motion Index (VMI)	^&l#C	# is number of 1/48 inch increments per line
Lines per inch	^&#D	# is lines per inch

Function	**Esc**	**Parameter**
Cursor Positioning		
Horizontal Position (columns)	^&a#C	# is column number
Horizontal Position (decipoints)	^&a#H	# is number of decipoints
Horizontal Position (dots)	^*p#X	# is number of dots
Vertical Position (lines)	^&a#R	# is row number
Vertical Position (decipoints)	^&a#V	# is number of decipoints
Vertical Position (dots)	^*p#Y	# is number of dots
Half-Line Feed	^=	
Push/Pop	^&f#S	# is 0 to push, 1 to pop
Line Termination	^&k#G	# is 0 to set carriage return = carriage return, line feed = line feed, and form feed = form feed; 1 to set CR=CR+LF, LF=LF, and FF=FF; 2 to set CR=CR, LF=CR+LF, and FF=CR+FF; 3 to set CR=CR+LF, LF=CR+LF, and FF=CR+FF (See Chapter 18, "Selecting Fonts with PCL" for an explanation.)
Primary Font Selection		
Orientation	^&l#O	# is 0 for portrait, 1 for landscape
Character Set	^(#	# is character set code. (See Table 1 in Chapter 18, "Selecting Fonts with PCL.")
Spacing	^(s#P	# is 1 for proportional, 0 for fixed
Pitch	^(s#H	# is number of characters per inch
Point Size	^(s#V	# is number of points
Style	^(s#S	# is 0 for upright, 1 for italic
Stroke Weight	^(s#B	# ranges from -3 for light to 3 for bold
Typeface	^(s#T	# is typeface code (See Table 2 in Chapter 18, "Selecting Fonts with PCL.")
Select Default	^(3@	
Select by ID	^(#X	# is ID number
Secondary Font Selection		
Orientation	^&l#O	# is 0 for portrait, 1 for landscape
Character Set	^)#	# is character set code. (See Table 1 in Chapter 18, "Selecting Fonts with PCL.")
Spacing	^)s#P	# is 1 for proportional, 0 for fixed
Pitch	^)s#H	# is number of characters per inch
Point Size	^)s#V	# is number of points
Style	^)s#S	# is 0 for upright, 1 for italic
Stroke Weight	^)s#B	# ranges from -3 for light to 3 for bold
Typeface	^)s#T	# is typeface code. (See Table 2 in Chapter 18, "Selecting Fonts with PCL.")
Select Default	^)3@	

Function	Esc	Parameter
Select by ID	^)#X	# is ID number
Other Font Selection		
Pitch (for both primary and secondary)	^&k#S	# is 0 for 10.00 pitch, 2 for 16.66 pitch
Enable Underlining	^&d#D	# is 0 for fixed underlining, 3 for floating
Disable Underlining	^&d@	
Font Management		
Assign Font ID	^*c#D	# is font ID number
Delete Fonts	^*c#F	# is 0 to delete all fonts, 1 to delete all temporary fonts, 2 to delete the last font ID specified
Make Font Permanent	^*c5F	
Make Font Temporary	^*c4F	
Font Creation		
Create Font (Font Header)	^)s#W[Data]	# is number of bytes
Download Character	^(s#W[Data]	# is number of bytes
Character Code	^*c#E	# is ASCII code number, expressed in decimal
Raster Graphics		
Resolution	^*t#R	# is 75 for 75 dpi, 100 for 100 dpi, 150 for 150 dpi, 300 for 300 dpi
Location to Start	^*r#A	# is 0 for left graphics margin, 1 for current cursor position
Transfer	^*b#W [Data]	# is number of rows
End Graphics	^*rB	
Rectangle Graphics		
Width of Rectangle in Dots	^*c#A	# is number of dots
Width of Rectangle in Decipoints	^*c#H	# is number of decipoints
Height of Rectangle in Dots	^*c#B	# is number of dots
Height of Rectangle in Decipoints	^*c#V	# is number of decipoints
Fill Rectangle	^*c#P	# is 0 for solid rule, 2 for gray shade, 3 for HP pattern
Shade	^*c#G	# designates percentage black, where 0 is white and 100 is solid black. Any number between 0 and 100 is permitted, but shades are discrete at 2 (1-2 percent

Function	Esc	Parameter
		requested), 10 (3-10 percent requested), 15 (11-20 percent requested), 30 (21 to 35 percent requested), 45 (36-55 percent requested), 70 (56-80 percent requested), 90 (81-99 percent requested), and 100 (100 percent requested).
Pattern	^*c#G	# is 1 for horizontal lines, 2 for vertical lines, 3 for upward-sloping diagonal lines, 4 for downward-sloping diagonal lines, 5 for square grid, 6 for diagonal grid
Macros		
Macro ID	^&f#Y	# is macro ID
Macro Control	^&f#X	# is 0 to start macro definition, 1 to end macro definition, 2 to execute macro, 3 to call macro, 4 to enable overlay, 5 to disable overlay, 6 to delete all macros, 7 to delete all temporary macros, 8 to delete macro ID, 9 to make macro temporary, 10 to make macro permanent
Programming Aids		
Display Functions-On	^Y	
Display Functions-Off	^Z	
Transparent Print Data	^&p#X[Data]	
End-of-Line Wrap	^&s#C	# is 0 to enable, 1 to disable

APPENDIX E

Font Directory

This appendix is intended as a shopper's guide to LaserJet fonts. It was compiled by Los Angeles font maven Dr. Katherine Pfeiffer. Most of the fonts shown are downloadable soft fonts; however, the directory also includes cartridge fonts manufactured by Computer Peripherals Inc., Hewlett-Packard, and IQ Engineering.

—TN & MG

Bitstream, Inc.

Address Athenaeum House, 215 First Street
Cambridge, MA 02142
(800) 522-3668; (617) 497-7514

Product Fontware

Typefaces ITC Avant Garde Gothic Book; Baskerville; ITC Bookman Light; Century Schoolbook; Bitstream Charter; Bitstream Cooper Light; Courier (10 pitch); Dutch (Times Roman); Futura; ITC Galliard; ITC Garamond; Goudy Old Style; Bitstream Cooper Black; University Roman; Cloister Black; Broadway; Brush Script; Blippo Black; Hobo; Windsor; Swiss (Helvetica); Exotic (Peignot); ITC Zapf Chancery; Coronet Bold; Clarendon; ITC Korinna; Letter Gothic (12 pitch); News Gothic; Prestige (12 Pitch); Serifa; ITC Souvenir; Zapf Calligraphic (Palatino); Zapf Humanist (Optima).

Point Sizes Outline fonts in user-defined sizes (limited only by printer)

Character Sets Ventura Publisher International; Ventura Publisher US; PostScript

Notes Installation kits for installing Fontware fonts with a variety of popular applications are available from Bitstream or directly from the application vendor. See Chapter 14, "Font Generators," and "Profile: Fontware."

Compugraphic Corporation

Address 200 Ballardvale Street
Wilmington, MA 01887
(800) 822-5524; (617) 658-5600

Notes Compugraphic is one of the largest suppliers of type designs for all types of printing. It supplies bitmapped fonts to many soft-font vendors. Type Director is a PC Utility program that uses Compugraphic's Intellifont technology to create bitmapped fonts for displays and Laserjet printers. It runs under DOS, Windows, and GEM.

Computer Editype Systems

Address 509 Cathedral Parkway #10A
New York, NY 10025
(212) 222-8148

Product Magic Font, Soft Font Library

Typefaces Magic Roman (Times Roman); Magic Delite (Optima); Magic Symbol (symbols)

Point Sizes Vary with family, 8 to 72

Character Sets Standard ASCII

Computer Peripherals, Inc.

Address 667 Rancho Conejo Blvd.
Newbury Park, CA 91320
(800) 854-7600

Products JetFont cartridges: JetFont 123, JetFont 4-in-1, JetFont B, JetFont F, and JetFont Z

Typefaces Line Printer, TmsRmn, Helv, Courier, Prestige Elite, Letter Gothic, Lotica

Point Sizes 8 to 14.4

Notes JetFont 123 comes with drivers for 1-2-3, Symphony, and dBASE III plus. JetFont 4-in-1 comes with drivers for Microsoft Word, WordPerfect, IBM DisplayWrite 4, MultiMate Advantage II, and WordStar 2000. The B, F, and Z cartridges match the HP cartridges. Lotica is specially designed for fitting the maximum number of characters on a spreadsheet page. The smallest size fits 30 characters per horizontal inch.

Conographic Corporation

Address 16802 Aston
Irvine, CA 92714
(714) 474-1188

Products Conofonts, CG Times (Times Roman)

Typefaces Triumvirate (Helvetica); ITC Souvenir; Borders; ITC Dingbats (Zapf Dingbats); CG Dingbats; Miscellaneous Dingbats; Old English (Engraver's Old English); Uncial; Raphael; Commercial Script; Trade Bold Condensed; CG Palacio (Palatino); Zapf Chancery; ITC LSC Manhattan; ITC Benguiat; Uncle Sam Open; American Classic Bold; Dom Casual; Globe Gothic Outline

Point Sizes Vary with face, 6 to 30

Character Sets Vary with font; Conographic; special Math and Greek

Notes Conofonts include a variety of Compugraphic bitmapped fonts and a unique collection of tradtional typographic borders and dingbats.

Font Center

Address 509 Marin Street #227
Thousand Oaks, CA 91360
(805) 373-1919

Product Font Center Fonts

Typefaces AG (Alternate Gothic); CR (Courier); PR (Prestige Elite); LG (Letter Gothic); LP (Line Printer); SC (Brother Print Wheel script); ZA (Key Tops); ZB (Code 39 Bar Code); FG (Franklin Gothic); ZC (CRT Display); MT (Metro); VG (Vogue); ANSI MICR; CMC7; Dunhill.

Point Sizes Vary with face, 6 to 15

Character Sets Vary with font; standard ASCII; Special; Bar Code

Notes The Font Center provides a select collection of carefully designed, small-point-size, bitmapped fonts. Included with the fonts is a free downloading utility.

The Font Factory

Address P.O. Box 5429
Kingwood, TX 77339
(713) 358-6954

Products Office Series Typefaces; Professional Series Typefaces; Fontmaker for Windows

Typefaces (See Qume)

Notes Font Factory fonts are distributed by Qume.

GNU Business Information Systems

Address 100 Hilltop Rd.
Ramsey, NJ 07446
(201) 825-1222

Products Custom Font Cartridges

Typefaces (See Bitstream)

Notes GNU offers to create a font cartridge to your specifications using any of the typefaces in the Bitstream Fontware library. The first four fonts are $199; additional fonts are $45 each.

Gradco/CTI

Address 7 Morgan
Irvine, CA 92718
(714) 770-1223

Products GPA Soft Font Generator

Typefaces Herald (Times Roman); Lucerne (Helvetica); Courier; GPA Symbol (symbols). (To these will soon be added the remainder of the standard 35 PostScript-width-compatible fonts.)

Point Sizes User-defined, from 4 points and up (limited only by printer)

Character Sets Adobe Character Set and Roman 8

Notes GPA (Geometric Primitive Algorithm) is a completely new method of generating printer and screen fonts in real time, invented by Ron Mintle of CTI (Composition Technology International). According to Gradco, it produces screen and printer fonts four times to hundreds of times faster than outline methods. Fonts can be created in any size, weight, slant, fill, etc.

Hewlett-Packard

Address Boise Division
P.O Box 15
Boise, ID 83707
(208) 323-6000

Products Soft Fonts: AC, AD, AE, AF, AG, DA, EA, RA, RB, SA, SB, TA, TB, UA, UB
Cartridge Fonts: A (Courier 1), B (TMS Proportional 1), C (International 1), D (Prestige Elite), E (Letter Gothic), F (TMS Proportional 2), G (Legal Elite), H (Legal Courier), J (Math Elite), K (Math TMS), L (Courier P&L); M (Prestige Elite P&L); N (Letter Gothic P&L), P (Tms Rmn P&L), Q (Memo 1), S1 (Courier Document 1), S2 (TmsRmn/Helv Report 1), T (Tax 1), U/V (Forms Portrait/Landscape), W1 (Bar Code 3-of-9/OCR-A), X (EAN/UPC), Y (PC Courier 1), Z (Microsoft 1A)

Typefaces (soft fonts) TmsRmn; Helv Condensed; Helv Outline; Serifa Black; Letter Gothic; Presentation; Prestige Elite; Line Printer; LineDraw;

PC Line; ITC Garamond; Century Schoolbook; Zapf Humanist (Optima); Bauer Bodoni; Broadway; Cooper Black; Coronet; University Roman

Point Sizes Vary with face, 6 to 30 points; the Helv Headlines (33412AG) comes in six sizes, 14 to 48.

Character Sets ASCII, Roman-8,

Typefaces (cartridge fonts) Courier; Prestige Elite; Letter Gothic; TmnsRmn (Times Roman); Helv (Helvetica); Presentation (Letter Gothic); Barcode; OCR-B

Point Sizes Vary with font, 6 to 30

Character Sets ASCII (Roman-8); French; German; Italian; Spanish; Swe/Fin; Dan/Nor; U.K.; Legal; Line Draw; Tax Line Draw; Math-7; Math-8a; Math-8b; Pi Font-a; OCR-A; Bar 3-0f-9; Bar Ean/upc; OCR-B; OCR-B Ext.; PC Line

Notes Hewlett-Packard offers a variety of re-edited Bitstream bitmapped fonts in sets, some containing complementary sets of faces and some containing a single face in many point sizes. Soft fonts come with FontLoad, a downloading utility. The AG soft font set includes a utility for expanding the compressed font files.

IQ Engineering

Address P.O. Box 60955
Sunnyvale, CA 94086
(408) 733-1161

Products Super Cartridge 1

Typefaces TmsRmn, Helv, Courier, OCR-A, Presentation, Letter Gothic, Prestige Elite, Line Printer, Line Draw, PC Line Draw

Character Sets USASCII; OCR-A; PC Line; Linedraw; some sizes of Prestige Elite and Letter Gothic also available in a 7-bit version of Roman-8; Prestige Elite also available in the Legal symbol set

Notes Super Cartridge 1 provides 55 fonts designed to match and supplement those on Hewlett-Packard's font cartridges. Although the designs and widths generally match those of the HP cartridges, there are numerous minor differences, so a careful reading of the IQ's excellent manual is recommended.

Information System Consultants

Address 3830 W. Irving Park Rd.
Chicago, IL 60618
312/539-0039

Products Big Foot Fonts, Bali Fonts

Typefaces Serif (Times Roman); Sans Serif (Helvetica)

Point Sizes Big Foot Fonts: 32, 34, 36; Bali Fonts: 6 to 3

Notes I.S.C. now sells what were previously the Harvey Software and Janus Associates font products.

Janus Associates

Address 991 Massachusettes Ave.
Cambridge, MA 02138
(617) 354-1999

Notes See Harvey, Big Foot Fonts.

LaserMaster Corporation

Address 7156 Shady Oak Road
Eden Prairie, MN 55344
(800) 562-7568, (612) 944-6069

Products CAP/Card

Typefaces Bitstream Fontware (see Bitstream).

Character Sets Same as Bitstream (see Bitstream).

Notes Besides dramatically enhancing the printing capabilities of the LaserJet, in certain product configurations the LaserMaster CAP/Card provides Bitstream Fontware products for "on the fly" font production. The fonts are width-compatible with the 35 PostScript fonts that are resident in the LaserWriter Plus and other PostScript printers. LaserMaster's selection includes Zapf Dingbats, which is not otherwise available from Bitstream.

LeBaugh Software Corporation

Address 10824 Old Mill, Suite 6
Omaha, Nebraska 68154
(800) 532-2844, (402) 334-4820

Typefaces LePrint Times Roman; Helvetica; Clarendon; LCD; Old English (Cloister Black); Park Avenue; Pica 10; Courier; Prestige Elite; Letter Gothic 12; Symbols

Point Sizes User-defined (limited only by printer). Le Print makes graphics files, not soft fonts.

Character Sets LePrint Extended ASCII; Greek; Math Symbols; Special Symbols; PC Style.

Notes LePrint's fonts are not in standard LaserJet soft font format, so they cannot be used by other programs. They are intended for use with Le Baugh's own self-contained typesetting system. However, files from Le Print can be exported in various graphics formats including PCX, PCC, GEM, IMG, and PCQ. Thus, large headlines generated within Le Print can be imported into PageMaker and Ventura as graphics.

Lexisoft

Address Box 1950
Davis, CA 95617
(916) 758-3630

Product SDP Font Library

Typefaces Souvenir, Times, Triumvirate (Helvetica), Triumvirate Condensed, Commercial Script, Uncle Sam Open, American Classic, Dom Casual, Uncial, Raphael, Olde English, Globe Gothic Outline, Palacio (Palatino), Zapf Chancery, Benguiat, Manhattan

Point Sizes 6 to 30

Notes Repackaged Conographic fonts.

Menar Tech International

Address 1630 Oakland Road, Suite A-215
San Jose, CA 95131
(408) 947-1515

Typefaces Barrani Noskh and Koofy (Kufic)

Point Sizes 12 only

Notes Used with Arabwriter (a word processor).

Metro Software

Address 2509 N. Campbell #214
Tucson, AZ 85719
(800) 621-1137, (602) 299-7313

Product FontPac

Typefaces New Swiss (Helvetica); Modlike (Baskerville); Bookman; Showtime (Broadway Engraved); Courier; Elite (Prestige Elite); Times (Times Roman); Old Brit (Cloister Black); Pinch; Push; Stacks; Gothic1 (News Gothic); Condo Script (Palace Script); Unic1 (American Uncial); Advantage (Avant Garde Gothic Book)

Point Sizes All fonts user defined, 4 to 48 points

Character Sets Twenty predefined character mappings available for all fonts. Custom character mappings can be created by the user as well.

Notes FontPac is a font-generating program. Each disk comes with one typeface master. The user then defines the point size, degree of slant and boldness, spacing, regular, outline or shadow, etc.

Office Automation Systems

Address 9940 Barns Canyon Road
San Diego, CA 92121

Notes Soft fonts available only through dealers.

Prosoft

Address 7248 Bellaire Ave., Box 560
North Hollywood, CA 91603-0560
(818) 765-4444

Products Fontasy, Font Converter

Typefaces HPrmn (Roman); HPss (Sans Serif); Brush Calligraphy; ITC Souvenir

Point Sizes Vary with family, 5 to 44

Character Sets Vary with font

Notes Fontasy was developed primarily for use with dot matrix printers. Prosoft offers a few fonts designed specifically for the LaserJet and Font Convertor, a program that converts Fontasy fonts into soft fonts.

Qume Corporation

Address 500 Yosemite Drive
Milpitas, CA 95035
(800) 543-6687

Products Office Series Typefaces; Professional Series Typefaces; Fontmaker for Windows

Typefaces *Office Series:* Courier; Helv (Helvetica); Line Printer; TmsRmn (Times Roman); Prestige Elite; Letter Gothic; Presentation; OCR-A; OCR-B
Professional Series: CG Times (Times Roman); CG Triumvirate (Helvetica); Antique Olive; ITC Avant Garde Gothic Book; Baskerville II; Brush Script; Century Textbook; Century Light II; Futura; Garamond Antiqua; Gill Sans; CG Omega (Optima); Rockwell; ITC Souvenir; Univers; CG Palacio (Palatino)

Fontmaker for Windows: To be announced

Point sizes *Office Series:* Varies with font, 6 to 18 points.
Professional Series: 6 to 36 for all fonts
Fontmaker for Windows: Varies with font

Character Sets *Office Series:* emulates Hewlett-Packard cartridge series (see Hewlett-Packard)
Professional Series: Ventura Publisher International; Ventura Publisher US

Notes Qume is the sole distributor of Font Factory font products. Most of the original font maps and outlines come from Compugraphic. Fontmaker for Windows, recently announced, will use Compugraphic outline fonts to produce bitmapped printer fonts and real-time screen fonts.

SoftCraft, Inc.

Address 16 N. Carroll Street, Suite 500
Madison, WI 53703
(800) 257-2300

Products Typefoundry Series; Standard Series

Typefaces *Typefoundry Series:* (See complete Bitstream listing)
Standard Series: Roman (Century Schoolbook); Fixed Width (ITC American Typewriter); Classic (Times New Roman); Sans Serif; Tall; Olde English (Engraver's Old English, a.k.a. Linotext); Olde English Hollow; Formal (Coronet Bold); Script (Commercial Script); Script Hollow; Calligrapher; Twist (Arnold Bocklin); Computer; Math Symbols; Copyright and Symbols; Chess; Accents & Ligatures; Cyrillic; International Phonetic Alphabet; Indic; Indic Italic; Proto-Indoeuropean; Greek; Hebrew; Hebrew Sans Serif; Nouveau; Nouveau Bold; Manual Alphabet; Modern (Broadway Engraved); Block Outline; Bar Code/OCR; Dots/Vertical Borders; LCD; Elegant

Script (Kaufmann Script); Orbit; Optical; Keys; Oriental; Persian; Borders; Music Font; Caribbean (Calypso); Lfonzo.

Point Sizes *Typefoundry Series:* Outline fonts, 4 points and up
Standard Series: Vary with face, 6 to 72

Character Sets *Typefoundry Series:* Same as Bitstream Fontware
Standard Series: Varies with font; among the special sets available are Standard ASCII, French, and Spanish, and German

Notes SoftCraft offers the widest variety of fonts available from any one source. From the full Bitstream Fontware collection on the high-quality, high-priced end, to user-contributed fonts of unusual foreign alphabets and symbols, to fonts from the Hershey database, to modestly priced fonts designed by SoftCraft itself.

Specific Solutions

Address 1898 Anthony Court
Mountain View, CA 94040
(415) 941-3941

Products Specific Fonts

Typefaces Rocky (Rockwell); Hi Tech; Rockout (Rockwell Outline); SwissOut (Helvetica Outline); Compac; CompOut; BigFoot; Shady; Typist; Collage; Greek and Symbol Library.

Point Sizes Vary with face, 7 to 36 points

Character Sets Vary with fonts; ASCII and European

Notes Specific Solutions offers three sets of fonts for GEM applicatons (screen and printer fonts in each set) and the LaserJet

Straightforward

Address 3901 Vio Oro Avenue
Long Beach, CA 90810
(213) 830-8773 or 830-8774
(800) 553-3332 USA

Products Z-Font Series; Compugraphic/ITC Series

Typefaces Orator; Artisan; Century; Courier; Delegate; Prestige Elite; Helvetica; Letter Gothic; Optima; Palatino; Pica; ITC Tiffany; Times (Times Roman); Old English (Engraver's Old English); Bodoni; Baskerville; Titan; Terminal; Dom Casual; Park Ave; Script (Typewriter Script); Times Roman; Palelo (Palatino); Optimal (Optima); OCR-A; OCR-B; Bar Code

Point Sizes Vary with face, 6 to 16

Character Sets ASCII; Roman 8; International (e.g., French, German, Spanish, Italian); PC with Line Draw; Math/Symbols Sets; ANSI 1.30

Notes Straightforward offers a wide variety of in-house (Z-Font Series) and Compugraphic/ITC bitmapped fonts and is among the very few companies licensed to sell Linotype registered fonts such as Palatino, Optima, and Helvetica. Straightforward specializes in careful tuning of bitmaps to optimize font appearance for specific printers.

SWFTE International

Address P.O. Box 219
Rockland, DE 19732
(800) 237-9383
(302) 658-1123

Product Glyphix

Typefaces Roman (Times Roman); Helvette (Helvetica); Rockland (Rockwell); Chancelor (Zapf Chancery); Amertype (American Typewriter); Big City (Broadway); Optimis (Optima); Coop (Cooper Black); Abber (Cloister Black); Beget (Benguiat); Garamont (Garamond); Basque (Baskerville); Centrum (Century Schoolbook); Palatine (Palatino); Orna.

Point Sizes All fonts, 6 to 60 points

Character Sets Standard ASCII and PC Extended with Line Draw for all fonts

Notes Glyphix is a font-generating program that allows the user to produce a family of fonts from a single master font. The fonts produced can be any size, slant, or weight, and condensed, expanded, patterned, or shaded, etc. All fonts become standard soft fonts. Glyphix comes with four basic fonts; others can be purchased separately.

VS Software (Division of VideoSoft, Inc.

Address PO Box 6158
Little Rock, AR 72216
(501) 376-2083

Products VS Library, CG Library, Executive Headlines, Designer Collection, Executive Type Classics, Times/Triumvirate Combo

Typefaces *VS Library:* VS Bookman; VS Century; VS Helv (Helvetica); VS BHS (Bauhaus); Old English Cloistered; Park Avenue; Broadway; Broadway Engraved; Tall Man; VS Prestige Elite
Compugraphic and ITC Library: Antique Olive; ITC Avant Garde Gothic Book; Baskerville II; Century II; Century Textbook; Brush; Courier; Elite (Prestige Elite); Futura; Garamond Antiqua; Gill Sans; Modern Gothic (Letter Gothic); CG Omega (Optima); ITC Souvenir; CG Times (Times Roman); CG Triumvirate (Helvetica); Rockwell; Univers

Point Sizes *VS Library:* Vary with font, 6 to 30 points
Compugraphic and ITC Libary: All proportional fonts, 6 to 30; fixed-width fonts vary with family

Character Sets *VS Library:* VS International Extended Set
Compugraphic and ITC Library: Compugraphic/ITC Proportional Set or Compugraphic/ITC Fixed Space Set (note: a few symbols not available in the 30-point Compugraphic Proportional fonts)

Notes VS Software offers a full range of fonts, from the VS Library of in-house designs to the Compugraphic/ITC Font Library. Fonts are packaged in family sets. VS provides, to anyone who requests it, the most complete and useful font catalog of any developer.

Weaver Graphics

Address Fox Pavilion Box 1132
Jenkintown, PA 19046
(215) 884-9286

Products LJ Fonts

Typefaces AGB (Avant Garde Gothic Book); AT (American Typewriter); BG (Benguiat); BK (Bookman); BV (Baskerville); CS (New Century); FQ (Fritz Quadrata); GD (Goudy Old Style); GM (Garamond); HL (Helvetica); KR (Korinna); LG (Lubalin Graph); ML (Melior); OP (Optima); PT (Palatino); SV (Souvenir); TR (Times Roman); CR (Courier); LT (Letter Gothic); PE (Prestige Elite); LP (Line Printer); CH (Zapf Chancery); PK (Park Ave); HVB-O (Helvetica Outline); OPB-O (Optima Outline); TB-O (Times Outline); HVB-R (Helvetica Reverse); MC (Machine); DB (Zapf Dingbats); SYM (Symbol); Bar39 (Bar Code 3 of 9).

Point Sizes Most fonts, 6 to 72

Notes Bitmapped font families in an exceptionally wide point size range (6 to 72). Among the unusual fonts are those similar to Benguiat in normal weight, Fritz Quadrata, Melior, and 16 different faces of the Helvetica family. Weaver does its own bitmaps.

Wilkes Publishing Corporation

Address 25251 Paseo de Alicia #200
Laguna Hills, CA 92653
(714) 855-0730

Product Alphabets

Typefaces Vanilla (Helvetica); Herald (Times Roman); Pretty (Courier); Etienne (Century Schoolbook); Dechaus (Bauhaus); Memento (Optima); Benson (Benquiat); Swash (IBM Script typewriter element); Swirl

Point Sizes Comes with Ventura set already generated for 6 to 30 point sizes; otherwise scalable, user-defined.

Character Sets All Fonts: Standard ASCII and Ventura Publisher International

Notes Alphabets is a font-generating program that makes an infinite number of fonts from master fonts. It not only makes all sizes, weights, and degrees of slant, but it can create fancy variations: outlines, stripes, fills, etc. Four fonts come with the Alphabets font editor; others may be purchased separately.

APPENDIX F

Product Directory

1040 Solution
Creative Solutions, Inc.
230 Collingwood, Suite 250
Ann Arbor, MI 48103
313/995-8811
Price: $1,495
Description: Tax preparation package; requires T cartridge.

4Print
Korenthal Associates
230 West 13th St.
New York, NY 10011
Price: $25 registration fee
Description: A formatting utility. (See Chapter 26, "LaserJet Shareware.")

Alphabets
Wilkes Publishing Company
25251 Paseo de Alicia #229
Laguna Hills, CA 92653
714/855-0730
Price: $195
Description: Includes four master typefaces; allows customization of character sets, orientation, slope, and other special characters; includes a font editor and a library of special symbols.

A-PlusTax 1040
Arthur Anderson & Co.
630 South Orange Ave.
Sarasota, FL 33577
800/872-1040
Price: $1495 to $1995
Description: Works with the L and T cartridges.

Arabic Fonts
Menar Tech International
1630 (old) Oakland Rd., Suite A215
San Jose, CA 95131
408/947-1515
Price: $290
Description: Includes Barrani Noskh style and Koofy style in 12-point sizes. Different sizes also available

Arts & Letters
Computer Support Corporation

15926 Midway Road
Dallas, TX 75244
214/661-8960
Price: $395
Description: A clip art manipulation program that runs under Windows. See "Profile: Arts & Letters."

AutoCAD
AutoSketch
AutoDesk
2320 Marinship Way
Sausalito, CA 94965
(415) 332-2344
Price: $300 to $2,850 AutoCAD, $79 AutoSketch without math coprocessor support, $99 AutoSketch with math co-processor support
Description: High-end and low-end design programs. (See "Profile: AutoSketch.")

B

ByLine
Ashton-Tate
20101 Hamilton Ave.
Torrance, CA 90502
213/329-8000
Price: $295
Description: A hybrid word processing program and desktop publishing program. Allows database and spreadsheet files to be easily imported for formatting.

C

CAPCard
LaserMaster Corp.
7156 Shady Oak Rd.
Eden Prairie, MN 55344
612/944-6069
Description: An accelerator controller board. (See "Profile: LaserMaster CAPCard.")

Collaser
AVN, Inc.
P.O. Box 1036
1036 E. 820 N.
Provo, UT 84603-2202
801/375-8533
Price: $34.50
Description: A paper catcher for the original LaserJet and the LaserJet Plus. Puts documents in the correct order by allowing pages to flip over as they exit the printer.

Computer Linguist
Cochrane & Associates
P.O. Box 70742
Eugene, OR 97401
503/345-1494
Price: $195
Description: A WYSIWYG utility that works in conjunction with WordStar to let you print in Russian, Hebrew, Greek, and other languages.

Conofonts Manager
Conographic Corp.
16802 Aston St.

Irvine Business Complex
Irvine, CA 92714
714/474-1188
Price: $70
Description: Downloads fonts and generates drivers for MultiMate Advantage II, WordPerfect, Microsoft Word, and WordStar 2000.

D

DBL Software Drivers
DLB Software
12808 Woodbend Court
Dallas, TX 75243
214/238-5945
Price: $75 to $125
Description: A utility designed to assist printing with IBM DisplayWrite.

Designer
See Windows Designer

Diagraph Arts & Letters
see Arts & Letters

Download Font Converter
Prosoft
7248 Bellaire Ave.
N. Hollywood, CA 91605
818/765-4444
Price: $49.95
Description: Converts Fontasy fonts to LaserJet format.

Drawing Gallery
Hewlett-Packard Company
Business Computing Systems
10520 Ridgeview Court.
Cupertino, CA 95014
800/367-4772
Price: $395
Description: Clip art and drawing program. (See "Profile: HP Graphics Gallery.")

DWLaser
Koch Software Industries
11 W. College Dr., Bldg. G
Arlington Heights, IL 60004
312/398-5440
Price: $195
Description: A utility designed to assist printing with IBM DisplayWrite.

E

Easy Laser
Acorn Plus, Inc.
4219 West Olive Ave. #2011
Burbank, CA 91505
213/876-5237
Price: $99.95
Description: A memory-resident utility for formatting documents.

EnvLJ
Steven Stern
JMB Realty Corp.
900 N. Michigan Ave.
Chicago, IL 60611

Price: $35 registration fee
Description: An envelope printing utility. (See Chapter 25, "LaserJet Shareware.")

EPAW
Network Technology Corp.
6825 Lamp Post Lane
Alexandria, VA 22306
703/765-4506
Price: $1,295
Description: Page layout program.

ERMASoft Laser Envelopes
ERMAssociates
P.O. Box 1032
Agoura Hills, CA 91301-1032
818/707-3818
Price: $39.95
Description: A utility for printing envelopes.

EROFF
Elan Computer Group, Inc.
410 Cambridge Ave., Suite A
Palo Alto, CA 94306
415/322-2450
Price: $795 to $4,995
Description: Page layout program.

Exact
Technical Support Software
72 Kent St. #110
Brookline, MA 02146
617/734-4130
Price: $475
Description: A code-base program designed for technical documents.

EZ-Laser
JRM Software Ltd.
P.O. Box 2847
2035 Lakewinds Dr.
Reston, VA 22091
703/860-3085
Price: $99.95
Description: Text-formatting program.

E-Z-Set
Orbit Enterprises, Inc.
799 Roosevelt Rd., Bldg. 6, Suite 1
Glen Ellyn, IL 60137
312/469-3405
Price: $49.95
Description: A setup utility. (See "Profile: E-Z-Set.")

Fancy Font
Fancy Word
SoftCraft, Inc.
16 N. Carroll St. #500
Madison, WI 53703
800/351-0500
608/257-3300
Price: Fancy Font $180, Fancy Word $140
Description: Text formatting-programs that work in conjunction with word processors.

First Impression
Megahaus Corp.
6215 Ferris Square
San Diego, CA 92121
619/450-1230
Price: $895

Description: A WYSIWYG page layout program.

Floppy Fonts Office Series
Floppy Fonts Professional Series
The Font Factory
P.O. Box 5429
Kingwood, TX 77339
713/358-6954
Price: $99.85 to $149.95
Description: Soft fonts.

Fontastic
Koch Software Industries
11 W. College Dr., Bldg G
Arlington Heights, IL 60004
312/398-5440
Price: $120
Description: A text-formatting utility.

Fontasy
ProSoft
7248 Bellaire Ave.
Box 560
North Hollywood, CA 91603
800/824-7888 operator 577 (orders only)
818/765-4444
Price: $49.95 including 28 fonts; $24.95 each additional disk of 8 to 12 typefaces; discounts for three or more font disks
Description: A simple page creation program that handles text and graphics. Does not work with LaserJet soft fonts.

Font Effects
SoftCraft, Inc.
16 N. Carroll St. #500
Madison, WI 53703
800/351-0500
608/257-3300
Price: $95
Description: Enhances soft fonts with patterns, outlines, shadows, etc.

FontGen IV+
VS Software
P.O. Box 6158
2101 South Broadway
Little Rock, AR 72206
501/376-2083
Price: $250
Description: Font-editing program.

FontLoad
Hewlett-Packard Company
Boise Division
11311 Chinden Blvd.
Boise, ID 83707
800/538-8787
408/738-4133 in California
Price: $20
HP part number 33407B
Description: A font-downloading utility

FontMaster
Cooperative Office Systems
207 Holly Rd.
Edgewater, MD 21037
301/261-7570
Price: $150
Description: A font-editing program.

Fontpac
Metro Software
2509 N. Campbell #214
Tucson, AZ 85719
800/621-1137
Price: $150
Description: One of the distinctive features of this font generator is that you can construct your character set entirely to your own taste from a library of over 300 symbols. Point sizes range from 4 to

48. In addition to size, you can specify the orientation, spacing, and boldness of the font you want to create, and produce outline and shadow fonts.

Fontrix
Data Transforms
616 Washington
Denver, CO 80203
303/832-1501
Price: $155
Description: A WYSIWYG graphics and layout program that provides its own fonts.

Fontware
Bitstream, Inc.
215 First St.
Cambridge, MA 02142
617/497-6222
Price: $95 for installation program, $195 for each additional font package.
Description: A font-generating program. Separate installation kits are available for individual software packages, such as WordPerfect, Microsoft Word, GEM, Xerox Ventura Publisher, PageMaker, and Manuscript.

FormEasy
Graphics Development International
20 C Pimentel Court #4
Novato, CA 94947
415/382-6600
Price: $495
Description: More or less WYSIWYG (doesn't require a graphics monitor) form-generation program. Supports data merging. (See Chapter 11, "Form and Tax Preparation Software.")

FormMaker II
FormMaker Software Inc.
57 S. Schillinger Rd.
Mobile, AL 36608
205/633-3676
Price: $495
Description: A menu-driven, WYSIWYG, form-generation program that supports data merging. (See Chapter 11, "Form and Tax Preparation Software.")

FormsManager DB
Software Concepts, Inc.
45 Church St.
Stanford, CT 06906
203/357-0522
Price: $399
Description: A form-generation program. (See Chapter 11, "Form and Tax Preparation Software.")

Form Set
Orbit Enterprises, Inc.
799 Roosevelt Rd., Bldg. 6, Suite 1
Glen Ellyn, IL 60137
312/469-3405
Price: $189.95
Description: A form-generation program. (See Chapter 11, "Form and Tax Preparation Software.")

Forms Flipper
BDT Products, Inc.
17152 Armstrong Ave.
Irvine, CA 92417
714/660-1386
Price: $140
Description: An output tray for the LaserJet and LaserJet Plus that holds 500 sheets and puts pages in correct order.

Form Tool
Bloc Development Corp.
1301 Dade Blvd.
Miami Beach, FL 33139
305/531-5486
Price: $95
Description: A form-generation program. (See Chapter 11, "Form and Tax Preparation Software.")

Formworx
Formworx Corp.
1365 Massachusetts Ave.
Arlington, MA 02174
617/641-0400
Price: $95
Description: A form-generation program. (See Chapter 11, "Form and Tax Preparation Software.")

Front Page Personal Publisher
Haba/Arrays, Inc.
6711 Valjean Ave.
Van Nuys, CA 91406
818/994-1899
Price: $199
Description: Page layout program.

G

GEM Desktop Publisher
Digital Research, Inc.
60 Garden Court, Box DRI
Monterey, CA 93942
408/649-3896
Price: $395
Description: A menu-driven desktop publishing program similar to Xerox Ventura Publisher, but scaled down in features.

GEM Draw Plus
Digital Research Inc.
60 Garden Court, Box DRI
Monterey, CA 93942
800/443-4200
Price: $299
Description: A drawing program. (See "Profile: GEM Draw Plus.")

Glowstx Tax Processing System
Orion Microsystems, Inc.
Lafayette Bldg. #910
5th & Chestnut St.
Philadelphia, PA 19106
215/928-1119
Price: $1295 to $1995
Description: Multi-user accounting and tax preparation system; works with T cartridge.

Glyphix Basics, Glyphix Basics II, Glyphix Book Faces, Glyphix Sans Serif Faces, Glyphix Decorative Faces, Glyphix Fixed Faces, Glyphix WordPerfect Font Manager, Glyphix MS Word Font Manager, Glyphix Pop 'n' Print
SWFTE International
Box 5773
Wilmington, DE 19808
800/237-9383
302/733-0956
Price: $79.95 WordPerfect Font Manager, $79.95 MS Word Font Manager, all others $99.95

Description: Font generator, font outlines, and installation kit for word processing programs.

GNU Cartridge Fonts
GNU Business Information Systems
100 Hilltop Road
Ramsey, NJ 07446
201/825-1222
Price: first four fonts $199; each additional font $45
Description: GNU Business Systems sells font cartridges loaded with your own customized selection of fonts from the Bitstream type library. Provided you stick to sizes of 14 points or less, you can have about nine fonts on a cartridge. A typical GNU cartridge might hold ITC Galliard in 6-, 8-, 10-, and 12-point roman; 10- and 12-point italic; and 10-, 12-, and 14-point bold.

GPA Soft Font Generator
Gradco Systems, Inc.
7 Morgan
Irvine, CA 92718
714/770-1223
Price: $495
Description: A font generator that creates fonts automatically based on the following user-controlled parameters: pont size, outline or solid, regular weight or bold, roman or italic, and rotation.

GrabPlus
Paul Mayer
ZPAY Payroll Systems
3516 Roby St.
Franklin Park, IL 60131
Price: $15 registration fee
Description: A memory-resident envelope-printing utility. (See Chapter 26, "LaserJet Shareware.")

GrafPlus
Jewell Technologies, Inc.
4740 44th Ave. SW #203
Seattle, WA 98116
206/937-1081
Price: $49.95
Description: A screen-capture utility. (See "Profile: GrafPlus.")

Graphics Gallery 2.0
Hewlett-Packard Personal Software Division
3410 Central Expressway
Santa Clara, CA 95051
(408) 749-9500
Price: $395 (Drawing Gallery), $495 Drawing Gallery & Charting Gallery, $95 (Additional graphics packages)
Description: A collection of draw and chart programs with clip art. (See "Profile: HP Graphics Gallery.")

The Graphics Link
PC Quik Art
394 Milledge Ave.
Athens, GA, 30606
800/523-1796
Price: $99
Description: A program for converting pictures from one graphics format to another. (See Chapter 9, "Graphics Conversion Programs.")

H

Halo DPE (Desktop Publishing Editor)

Media Cybernetics
8484 Georgia Ave. Suite 200
Silver Spring, MD 20910
800/446-HALO
Price: $195
Description: A paint program with scanner support. (See "Profile: Halo DPE.")

HiJaak

Inset Systems
12 Mill Plain Road
Danbury, CT 06811
(203) 794-0396
Price: $89
Description: A utility for capturing files or screens and converting pictures from one graphics format to another. (See Chapter 9, "Graphics Conversion Programs.")

HotShot Grab
HotShot Graphics

SymSoft
444 First Street
Los Altos, CA 94022
415/941-1552
Price: $99 HotShot Grab, $249 HotShot Graphics.
Description: HotShot Grab is a simple screen capture utility. HotShot Graphics adds a painting program for enhancing captured screens. (See "Profile: HotShot Graphics.")

HP Laser Program

New Image Technology, Inc.
10300 Greenbelt Rd. #104
Seabrook, MD 20706
301/464-3100
Price: $39.95
Description: Lets you print MacPaint files on a LaserJet.

I

Inset

Inset Systems, Inc.
12 Mill Plain Rd.
Danbury, CT 06811
203/794-0396
Price: $99
Description: A utility for capturing graphics and merging them into word processed documents. (See "Profile: Inset.")

IPrint and IMerge: The Laser Office

Indigo Software Ltd.
1568 Carling Ave.
Ottawa, Ontario
Canada K1Z 7M5
613/728-0016
Also available from Hewlett-Packard direct 800/538-8787
Price: IPrint $349.95, IMerge $249.95 - $2500
Hewlett-Packard part number 351288D
Description: Form generation software. (See "Profile: IPrint.")

J

JetNET/4+1

Qubit Corporation
544 Weddell Dr. #2
Sunnyvale, CA 94089-2123
408/747-0740
Price: $495
Description: A plug-in board for the LaserJet II that allows up to five computers to share the printer simultaneously. Includes a 256Kb buffer that can be expanded to 1.25MB.

JetScript

Hewlett-Packard Company
Boise Division
11311 Chinden Blvd.
Boise, ID 83714
208/323-2551
Price: $2,795
Description: A PostScript controller for the LaserJet II. (See "Profile: JetScript.")

Jet-Set

Probe Software
23 Rumbrook Rd.
Elmsford, NY 10523
201/285-1500
Price: $129
Description: A setup utility.

JetSet 1.2

Intex Solutions
568 Washington St.
Wellesley, MA 02181
617/431-1063
Price: $79.95
Description: An add-in utility for Lotus 1-2-3 that provides control over margins and fonts from the 1-2-3 menu.

JetSet II

DataMate Company
4135 S. 100th East Ave. #128
Tulsa, OK 74146
800/262-7276
Price: $99
Description: A setup utility and text-formatting program.

JLaserPlus

Tall Tree Systems
2585 E. Bayshore Rd.
Palo Alto, CA 94303
415/964-1980
Description: A controller board that bypasses the LaserJet's own controller; provides 2MB of memory. Bundled with Bitstream Fontware.

L

Lacerte Tax Preparation Software 1040

Lacerte Software Corporation
3447 Atlantic Ave.
Long Beach, CA 90807
800/331-8614
213/595-0901
Price: $2,000
Description: Requires the T cartridge.

Laser Bat
Sumsion Enterprises
P.O. Box 102
Springfield, UT 84663
801/798-8434
Price: $25
Description: A setup utility.

LaserConnection ESI-1312 (Extended Systems)
Extended Systems
P.O. Box 4937
6062 Morris Hill
Boise, ID 83711
208/322-7163
Price: $895
Description: A utility designed to assist printing with IBM DisplayWrite.

LaserControl
Insight Development Corp.
1024 Country Club Dr.
Moraga, CA 94556
415/376-9451
Also available from Hewlett-Packard Direct: 800/538-8787
Price: $150
HP part number 35190J
Description: A setup utility. (See "Profile: LaserControl.")

Laser Fonts
Keller Software
1825 Westcliffe Dr.
Newport Beach, CA 92660
714/854-8211
Price: $49
Description: A memory-resident utility for embedding font codes in documents.

Laser Fonts
SoftCraft, Inc.
16 N. Carroll St. #500
Madison, WS 53703
800/351-0500
608/257-3300
Price: $180
Description: Downloads fonts and creates drivers for word processing programs. (See "Profile: Laser Fonts.")

Laserific
Computerific, Inc.
316 Fifth Ave.
New York, NY 10001
212/695-2100
Price: $149
Description: A memory-resident setup and formatting utility.

LaserPlotter SW
Insight Development Corp.
1024 Country Club Dr.
Moraga, CA 94556
415/376-9451
Also available from Hewlett-Packard Direct: 800/538-8787
Price: $150
HP part number 35186A
Description: A software utility that allows the LaserJet to emulate various HP plotters.

Laser Press
Award Software, Inc.
130 Knowles Dr.
Los Gatos, CA 95030
408/370-7979
Price: $198
Description: A low-end code-based program.

Laser Print Plus
Janus Associates
94 Chestnut St.
Boston, MA 02108
617/720-5085
Price: $395
Description: A text-formatting program.

LaserScript
Command Technology Corp.
1900 Mountain Blvd.
Oakland, CA 94611
415/339-3530
Price: $695
Description: A code-based formatting program designed especially for very long, highly structured documents.

Laser-Set
Laser Technologies Int'l, Inc.
15403 E. Alondra Blvd.
La Mirada, CA 90638
714/739-2478
Price: $199.95
Description: A text-formatting program.

Lasersoft/PC
Business Systems International, Inc.
20942 Osborne St.
Canoga Park, CA 91304
Phone: 818/998-7227
Price: $995
Description: The Lasersoft system comprises two separately sold programs. Lasersoft/PC, which sells for $295, lets you create forms using a code-based system. Lasersoft/Data Entry ($295) can be used to enter data, which is then automatically merged with forms created using Lasersoft/PC. There is also a version of Lasersoft for the HP 3000. (See "Profile: Lasersoft/PC.")

Laser Stacker
BairnWare Industries
23 Braddock Way
Asheville, NC 28801
704/252-4491
Price: $29.95
Description: A correct-order output bin for the LaserJet and LaserJet Plus.

Laserstart
Phoenix Technologies
7192 Kalanianaole Hwy. #205
Honolulu, HI 96825
800/367-5600
Price: $95
HP part number 35179M with cable; HP part number 35178M without cable
Description: A utility that allows a Macintosh to print on the LaserJet.

Laser Tax Form Software
Nelco Tax Forms
P.O. Box 10208
3130 South Ridge Rd.
Green Bay, WI 54307-0208
414/337-1000
Price: $100 to $400
Description: Works in conjunction with other tax packages; generates tax forms using the T cartridge.

Lasertex Virtual Fonts
Lasertex Electronic Forms Tools
Network Technology Corp.
6825 Lamp Post Lane
Alexandria, VA 22306
703/765-4506
Price: Lasertex Virtual Fonts $35 and up, Lasertex Electronic Forms Tools $295
Description: Virtual Fonts is a library of specialized fonts, such as chemical sym-

bols and bar codes. Electronic Forms Tools is a forms-generation program.

LaserTORQ
LaserTools Corporation
3025 Buena Vista Way
Berkeley, CA 94708
800/346-1353
415/843-2234
Price: $99
Description: An intelligent spooler that can use extended memory, expanded memory, or the hard disk to buffer data on the way to the printer. Allows full-page, 300-dpi graphics to be printed on a 512K LaserJet. See "Profile: LaserTORQ."

LaserType
Reon Technology
Box 191
Cochiti Lake, NM 87041
505/465-2990
Price: $400
Description: A text-formatting program.

Laserware
SWFTE International
Box 5773
Wilmington, DE 19808
800/237-9383
302/733-0956
Price: $99.95
Description: A RAM-resident formatting program.

LaserWord
Bonnie Blue Software
P.O. Box 536
4395 Princess Path
Liverpool, NY 13090
315/652-1304
Price: $299
Description: A word processor designed for laser printer output.

Laser Word Processor Tool Kit
VS Software
P.O. Box 6158
2101 South Broadway
Little Rock, AR 72206
501/376-2083
Price: $50
Description: A utility that downloads fonts and creates drivers for word processing programs.

LePrint
LePrint Headliner
LeBaugh Software
10824 Old Mill Rd. #6
Omaha, NE 68154-9979
800/532-2844
402/334-4820
Price: LePrint $175 to $325, LePrint Headliner $100 (includes program and five type styles) plus additional typeface packages at $60 each
Description: LePrint is a page layout program that does not work with soft fonts. LePrint Headliner lets you create words in very large type and save them in PCX format for merging into Ventura or PageMaker. Allows creation of letters ranging in size from 4 points to full pages.

LJBook
139 White Oak Circle
Petaluma, CA 94952
Price: $15 registration fee
Description: A utility for printing text files. (See Chapter 25, "LaserJet Shareware.")

M

MacScan Page Scanning System
Magic

New Image Technology, Inc.
10300 Greenbelt Rd. #104
Seabrook, MD 20706
301/464-3100
Price: MacScan $1,547, Magic $399 to $549
Description: MacScan is a scanning system for the Macintosh and IBM PC. Magic is a Macintosh program that lets you print images captured by a video camera.

MagicSeries: MagicFont
MagicSeries: MagicPrint

Computer Editype Systems
509 Cathedral Parkway, 10-A
New York, NY 10025
800/251-2223
212/222-8148
Price: MagicFont $59, MagicPrint $99 to $149
Description: MagicFont is a font generation program. MagicPrint is a text formatter.

Manuscript

Lotus Development Corp.
55 Cambridge Pkwy.
Cambridge, MA 02142
800/343-5414
617/577-8500
Price: $495
Description: A technical word processing program with good equation-generating capabilities.

Master Tax

CPAID
1061 Fraternity Circle
Kent, OH 44240
216/678-9015
Price: $1,795
Description: Tax preparation program that works with the T cartridge and generates actual federal forms.

Micrografx Windows Designer

See Windows Designer.

Micrografx Windows Draw

See Windows Draw.

Microsoft Windows

Microsoft Corporation
P.O. Box 97017
16011 N.E. 36th Way
Redmond, WA 98073-9717
206/882-8080
Price: $99
Description: An applications environment that provides a standard interface between programs and devices such as the LaserJet. See Chapter 23, "Microsoft Windows."

Microsoft Word 4.0

Microsoft Corporation
P.O. Box 97017
16011 N.E. 36th Way
Redmond, WA 98073-9717
206/882-8080
Price: $450
Description: A word processing program quite well suited to use with the LaserJet. Extensive support for both cartridge and soft fonts. See "Profile: Microsoft Word."

MicroTex
Addison-Wesley Publishing Co.
EMS Division
6 Jacob Way
Reading, MA 01867
617/944-6795
Price: $495
Description: A code-based text formatting program. Noted mainly for its good typographic capabilities and equation generating.

MP-XL
Micro Print-X, Inc.
P.O. Box 581
119 North 8th St.
Ballinger, TX 76821
915/365-2343
Price: $395
Description: A text-formatting program.

MultiMate Advantage II
Ashton-Tate
52 Oakland Ave.
E. Hartford, CT 06108
203/247-3447
Price: $595
Description: A word-processing program. See "Profile: MultiMate Advantage."

N

News Master
Unison World
2150 Shattuck Ave. #902
Berkeley, CA 94704
415/848-6670
Price: $99.95
Description: A low-end desktop publishing program. Not recommended for professional use.

The Newsroom Pro
Springboard
7808 Creekridge Circle
Minneapolis, MN 55435
612/944-3912
Price: $129
Description: A WYSIWYG program intended only for casual use.

O

Office Publisher
Laser Friendly, Inc.
930 Benecia Ave.
Sunnyvale, CA 94086
408/730-1921
Price: $995
Description: A menu-driven, feature-laden desktop publishing program. Much less popular than its faster rival, Xerox Ventura Publisher.

P

PageMaker

Aldus Corp.
411 First Ave. S. #200
Seattle, WA 98104
206/622-5500
206/628-2375
Price: $795
Description: One of the two leading desktop publishing programs. Uses a menu-driven, WYSIWYG interface. Runs under Microsoft Windows. (See "Profile: PageMaker.")

Page Perfect

IMSI
1299 Fourth St.
San Rafael, CA 94901
415/454-7101
Price: $495
Description: A low-end desktop publishing program

PageView

Microsoft Corporation
16011 N.E. 36th Way
Redmond, WA 98073-9717
206/882-8080
Price: $50
Description: A Windows-based formatting and graphics merging utility for Microsoft Word.

PageWriter

The Computer Group
1717 W. Beltline Hwy.
Madison, WI 53713
608/273-1803
Price: $495
Description: A text-formatting program.

Pamphlet

Martin Beattie
9190 Rolling Tree Lane
Fair Oaks, CA 95628
Price: $25 registration fee
Description: A utility for printing text files. See Chapter 25, LaserJet Shareware."

PC Em-U-Print

Koch Software Industries
11 W. College Dr., Bldg. G
Arlington Heights, IL 60004
312/398-5440
Price: $95
Description: A utility that makes the LaserJet emulate an IBM Graphics Printer.

PC Paintbrush Plus, Publisher's Paintbrush

ZSoft
450 Franklin Road #100
Marietta, GA 30067
(404) 428-0008
Price: PC Paintbrush $95, PC Paintbrush Plus $149, PC Paintbrush for Windows $84, Publisher's Paintbrush $285
Description: Paint programs. (See "Profile: PC Paintbrush & Family.")

PCLPak

Hewlett-Packard Company
Boise Division
11311 Chinden Blvd.

Boise, ID 83714
800/538-8787 Direct Marketing Line
Price: $79
HP part number 33406B
Description: A utility for downloading fonts and creating simple graphics.

PC/Professional Tax Partner
Best Programs, Inc.
2700 S. Quincy Rd.
Arlington, VA 22206
800/368-2405
Price: $995
Description: Prepares state and federal individual returns; uses T cartridge.

PC Quik Art
PC Quik-Art, Inc.
394 S. Milledge Ave. #200
Athens, GA 30606
800/523-1796
Description: See Chapter 8, "Clip Art."

PPC Tex
Personal Tex, Inc.
12 Madrona
Mill Valley, CA 94941
415/388-8853
Price: $249
Description: A code-based text formatting program. Noted mainly for its good typographic capabilities and equation generating.

PC-Write
QuickSoft, Inc.
219 First North #224
Seattle, WA 98109
206/282-0452
Price: $89
Description: Word processing program with excellent LaserJet support.

PFS: First Publisher
Software Publishing
1901 Landings Dr.
P.O. Box 7210
Mountain View, CA 94039
415/962-8910
Price: $99
Description: A page layout program.

Pizazz Plus
Application Techniques, Inc.
10 Lomar Park Dr.
Pepperell, MA 01463
617/433-5201
Price: $149
Description: Screen capture utility.

Polaris Forms, Labelmaker, RAM-Resident PrintMerge, Symbol Sheet, Setup Utility, PrintMerge, Font Control, Crunch
Polaris Software
613 West Valley Parkway #323
Escondido, CA 92025
800/338-5943
619/743-7800
800/231-3531 in California
Price: $149 Forms, $124 Labelmaker, $149 RAM-Resident PrintMerge, $49.95 Symbol Sheet, $25 Setup Utility, $124 PrintMerge, $99 Font Control, $49.95 Crunch
Description: Forms, Labelmaker, and PrintMerge all use a code-based formatting method. (See Chapter 11, "Form and Tax Preparation Software"; and Chapter 22, "Label Sheets.") PrintMerge is specifically for printing with WordStar. Symbol Sheet is a collection of symbols that can be merged into documents. RAM-Resident PrintMerge is a code-based formatting and graphics merge program for use

with any word processor. (See "Profile: Polaris RAM-Resident PrintMerge." Font Control assists with downloading. Crunch is a utility that compresses large graphics files.

PowerText Formatter
Beaman Porter, Inc.
417 Halstead Ave.
Harrison, NY 10528
800/431-0007
914/835-3156
Price: $149.95
Description: A text-formatting program.

Printer Marshall
Client Marketing Systems
2582 N. Santiago Blvd.
Orange, CA 92667
714/921-1768
Price: $19.95
Description: A memory-resident font selection utility.

Printer Optimizer
Applied Creative Technology
10529 Olympic Dr. #101
Dallas, TX 75220
800/433-5373
Price: $428
Description: A programmable print buffer with expandable memory.

Printility
Metro Software
2509 N. Campbell #214
Tucson, AZ 85719
800/621-1137
Price: $179
Description: A RAM-resident setup utility.

Printrix
Data Transforms
616 Washington
Denver, CO 80203
303/832-1501
Price: $165
Description: A page-layout program.

PrintStar
Echelon, Inc.
885 N. San Antonio Rd.
Los Altos, CA 94022
415/948-3820
Price: $120
Description: A utility program for printing with WordStar.

Printworks for the Mac/Laser Version
Printworks for PC/Laser Version
Phoenix Technologies (formerly SoftStyle)
7192 Kalanianaole Hwy. #205
Honolulu, HI 96825
800/367-5600
Also available from Hewlett-Packard Direct 800/538-8787
Price: Printworks for the Mac $145, Printworks for PC $125
Mac: HP part number 35179P
PC: HP part number 35184C
Description: Setup utilities. (See "Profile: Printworks for PC/Laser" and "Chapter 24, "Using theLaserJet with the Macintosh.")

Profont Editing System
FontCenter
509 Marin St., #227
Thousand Oaks, CA 91360
805/373-1919
Price: $400

Description: A font editor.

PS Jet Plus
The Laser Connection, Inc.
P.O. Box 850296
Mobile, AL 36689
205/633-7223
Description: A replacement top for the LaserJet or the LaserJet Plus that provides PostScript capability. (See "Profile: PS Jet.")

Publisher's Paintbrush
See PC Paintbrush.

Publisher's PicturePaks
Marketing Graphics Incorporated
401 E. Main St.
Richmond, VA 23219
804/788-8844
Price: $99.95 per edition, or three editions for $250
Description: Clip art in PCX and CGM format, suitable for loading into Ventura or PageMaker. Three editions are available: Executive and Management, Finance and Administration, and Sales and Marketing. Each contains approximately 200 pictures.

Publisher's Type Foundry
ZSoft
450 Franklin Road, Suite 100
Marietta, CA 30067
(404) 428-0008
Price: $495
Description: A font-editing program. See "Profile: Publisher's Type Foundry."

Q

Q&A
Symantec Software
10201 Torre Ave.
Cupertino, CA 95014
408/252-5700
Price: $349
Description: File manager and word processor with excellent LaserJet support. Works in conjunction with Lotus 1-2-3.

S

ScenicWriter
Scenicsoft, Inc.
100 Second Ave. S.
Edmonds, WA 98020
800/422-2994
Price: $695
Description: A code-based text formatting program.

scLaserPlus
Pursang Corp.
Software Channels Division
1320 Yonge St. #301
Toronto, Ontario
Canada M4T 1X2
416/967-4290
Price: $495

Description: A code-based desktop publishing program.

SDP Font Library

Lexisoft, Inc.
P.O. Box 1950
Davis, CA 95617
916/758-3630
Price: $125
Description: Soft fonts.

SLed

VS Software
P.O. Box 6158
Little Rock, AR 72216
501/ 376-2083
Price: $149.95 or $295
Description: A paint program that stores images as unique fonts. (See "Profile: SLed.")

SoftCraft Font Editor

SoftCraft, Inc.
16 N. Carroll St. #500
Madison, WS 53703
800/351-0500
608/257-3300
Price: $290
Description: A font editing program.

Soft Font Disks

Computer Editype Systems
509 Cathedral Parkway, 10-A
New York City, NY 10025
800/251-2223
212/222-8148
Price: $50
Description: Soft fonts containing special symbols.

SoftJet

Theta Systems Corp.
307-2150 W. Broadway
Vancouver, B.C.
Canada V6K 4L9
604/732-4323
Price: $120
Description: A utility that lets you preview a document onscreen exactly as it would appear if it were printed on the LaserJet.

Spellbinder Desktop Publisher

Lexisoft, Inc.
P.O. Box 1950
Davis, CA 95617
916/758-3630
Price: $695
Description: A code-based word processing and page layout program that includes a WYSIWYG preview mode.

T

Tabin

Corel Systems Corporation
Corel Bldg.
1600 Carling Ave.
Ottawa, Ontario
Canada K1Z 7M4
613/728-8200
Price: $99
Description: A utility for merging spreadsheets into Ventura Publisher.

Tax Refund System
UFS Good-Year, Inc.
534 Burmont Rd.
Drexel Hill, PA 19026
215/623-6140
Price: $399.95
Description: Tax preparation package; works with T cartridge.

Tax Resources 1120
Tax Resources Ten40
Tax Resources, Inc.
1111 North Loop West #920
Houston, TX 77008
713/868-2937
Price: $495
Description: Tax Resources 1120 prepares federal corporate income tax returns; Tax Resources Ten40 prepares over 50 federal forms. Both work with the T cartridge.

TurboFonts
Image Processing Software, Inc.
P.O. Box 5016
4414 Regent St.
Madison, WI 53705
608/233-5033
Price: $175
Description: Lets you see scientific and foreign characters on the screen from your word processing program.

Ventura Publisher
See Xerox Ventura Publisher

Visual Forms
Deeresoft, Inc.
P.O. Box 1360
Melbourne, FL 32902
305/768-2477
Price: $89.95
Description: A form-generation program. (See Chapter 11, "Form and Tax Preparation Software.")

VP/Base, VP/Fonts, VP/Saddle, XVP/Tabs
Laser Edge
360 - 17th St. #203
Oakland, CA 94612
415/835-1581
Price: $99 XVP/Tabs, $89 VP/Base, $79 VP/Fonts, $79 VP/Saddle
Description: Four utilities for Ventura Publisher. VP/Tabs assists with merging spreadsheets into Ventura, VP/Base assists with merging database information, VP/Fonts adds new HP soft fonts to the Ventura menu, and VP/Saddle prints two-up and other formats with a PostScript printer.

Volts Tax Preparation & Planning
Hanson Software Systems
1344 E. Katella Ave.
Anaheim, CA 92805
714/385-1556
Price: $975
Description: Tax program; separate modules for individual, professional, partnership, and corporate taxes. Works with the T cartridge.

VS Library of Fonts
VS Software
P.O. Box 6158
2101 South Broadway

Little Rock, AR 72206
501/376-2083
Price: $39.95 to $179.95
Description: Soft fonts.

Windows
See Microsoft Windows.

Windows Designer
Windows Draw
Micrografx, Inc.
1820 N. Greenville Ave.
Richardson, TX 75081
212/234-1769
Price: $695 Windows Designer, $299 Windows Draw
Description: Drawing programs. (See "Profile: Windows Designer" and "Profile: Windows Draw.")

Word
see Microsoft Word.

WordPerfect 5.0
WordPerfect Corporation
288 West Center
Orem, UT 84057
800/321-5906
801/225-5000
Price: $495
Description: Release 5.0 of this popular word processing program features superb support for LaserJet fonts and imported graphics. Provides a WYSIWYG preview mode. See "Profile: WordPerfect."

WordStar 3.3 and 4.0
MicroPro International Corp.
33 San Pablo Ave.
San Rafael, CA 94903
800/227-5609
415/499-8320
Price: $350
Description: Word processing program See "Profile: WordStar."

WordStar 2000 Plus
MicroPro International Corp.
33 San Pablo Ave.
San Rafael, CA 94903
800/227-5609
415/499-8320
Price: $495
Description: Word processing program with excellent LaserJet support. See "Profile: WordStar 2000."

WYSIfonts!
SoftCraft, Inc.
16 N. Carroll St. #500
Madison, WS 53703
800/351-0500
608/257-3300
Price: $95
Description: A utility that creates screen fonts from printer fonts and installs fonts for Windows and PageMaker or for Ventura Publisher. See "Profile: WYSIfonts!"

Xerox Ventura Publisher

Xerox Corporation
101 Continental Blvd.
El Segundo, CA 90245
800/822-8221
Price: $890
Description: One of the two leading desktop publishing programs. Uses a menu-driven, WYSIWYG interface. See "Profile: Ventura Publisher."

XVP/Tabs

See VP/Tabs.

Z

Z Director

Straightforward
15000 Halldale Ave. #115
Gardena, CA 90247
818/762-8150
Price: $200 to $400
Description: A typesetting program that includes bit-tuned soft fonts.

APPENDIX F

Glossary

ascender The part of a lowercase letter that extends above the body of the letter (as in b or d).

ASCII American Standard Code for Information Interchange. It refers to a type of file that contains only the characters of a standard computer keyboard.

baseline The invisible line on which type rests and below which descenders hang.

bitmap A representation of a character or a graphic image in which each printed dot is stored as a digital bit.

character set The set of characters that makes up a font. Usually includes the letters of the alphabet, standard punctuation marks, and a variety of special symbols. Same as symbol set.

clip art Collections of commercial illustrations.

control code A string of characters that directs the operations of the laser printer.

Control Panel The font status panel and buttons on the LaserJet.

controller The on-board computer that directs the physical mechanisms of the laser printer.

descender The part of a lowercase letter that extends below the baseline (as in p and q.) The size of a font is measured from ascenders to descenders.

dithering In computer graphics, using dot patterns to simulate gradations of gray.

download To transfer font files from the computer into the LaserJet's RAM memory.

driver A software module that translates the output of an application into the format required by a particular printer, monitor, or other device.

EP cartridge Electrophotographic cartridge. The replaceable plastic unit that contains toner, developer, and a light-sensitive drum.

escape sequence An alternative way of referring to LaserJet control codes, because such codes always begin with the escape character, ASCII 27.

extension The three letters to the right of the period in a file name. Indicates the type of file.

font The complete set of characters, including punctuation symbols, for a typeface. In traditional typography this meant the actual metal type. With the advent of computer "fonts," it refers files stored on disks or on ROM cartridges.

font cartridge A plastic unit that inserts into the front of the LaserJet. Contains fonts stored in ROM.

font editor A program used to create fonts from scratch or alter the appearance of an existing font.

font generator A program that creates soft fonts from master font outlines.

font ID A number used to access a font.

grid The design "skeleton" on which a document is built; includes design standards for columns and frames, margins, leading and tracking, justification, headers and footers, and graphics.

header A design element repeated at the top of each page of straight text; can include chapter titles, book title, and/or page numbers.

italic Slanted style of a given typeface, used for emphasis, for instance to offset book titles from the main text.

justified type A line of type that is precisely spaced so that it rests flush against both margins of the column.

kerning Moving two letters closer together or farther apart to give them a better fit.

landscape Refers to printing a page so that when positioned for reading, the page is wider than it is long.

leader characters Characters (usually periods) used to fill up the space between tabs. Frequently used in tables of contents.

leading The space, in points, between lines of type and measured from baseline to baseline. For example, a 10/12 specification for type means 10-point type on 12 points of leading (6 lines to the inch).

letter spacing Adjusting the space within words to assist line justification.

macro A string of commands stored under a single name.

object graphics Graphics that are stored and transmitted as geometrical descriptions. Also called object-oriented graphics.

outline font A type of font in which the shape of each character is stored as a geometric description rather than as a bitmap.

parallel communications A method of data communications in which a group of digital bits is transmitted simultaneously. Faster than serial communications.

PCL Printer Command Language. The set of commands that direct the operations of the LaserJet and control the appearance of text and graphics on the page.

permanent font A soft font that is not erased when the LaserJet receives a soft reset, ${}^{E}{}_{c}$E.

pica Typographic unit of measurement equal to 12 points or 1/6 inch.

pixel The smallest unit of a digitized picture, either on the screen or printed.

point Typographic unit of measurement equal to 1/12 pica or 1/72 inch. The "point size" of a font is measured from the bottom of the descenders to the top of the ascenders.

port A place to connect a communications cable.

portrait Refers to printing a page so that when positioned for reading, the page is longer than it is wide.

PostScript A computer programming language created by Adobe Systems specifically for controlling laser printers.

primary font A font designation that allows selection via a very short escape code. (Compare with secondary font.)

proportional spacing The method of setting type in which wide letters, such as W, receive more space and thin letters, such as i, receive less space.

ragged justification Unjustified type, that is, centered or flush to one side but not to the other.

RAM Random access memory. Dynamic memory that is erased when power is turned off.

RAM-resident software Programs that are loading into the computer's RAM and remain accessible at all times. Generally, such programs can be activated by pressing a particular key combination.

raster graphics A type of image in which each dot is stored and transmitted as a digital bit.

resident font A font that is permanently stored in the LaserJet.

RIP Raster image processor. A laser printer controller board.

ROM Read-only memory. Permanent memory that is not erased when power is turned off.

RS232C The standard mode of serial communication in the personal computer industry.

rule A line used as a design element on the page.

sans serif A typeface designed without serifs, such as Helvetica.

scaling Enlarging or reducing a picture.

screen snapshot A printed picture of the contents of computer display. Also called a screen dump, screen shot, or screen capture.

secondary font A font designation that allows selection via a very short control code.

serial communications A method of data communications in which each digital bit is transmitted sequentially. Slower than parallel communications.

serifs Small counter strokes that "finish off" the ends of the body strokes of a letter; also, typefaces that incorporate such strokes. In theory, serifs help the eye recognize the shapes of different letters, thus aiding readability.

setup utilities Programs that configure the parameters of the LaserJet, select fonts, and in some cases allow the LaserJet to emulate other printers.

soft font A font stored on a floppy disk or on the computer's hard disk.

symbol set The set of characters that make up a font. Usually includes the letters of the alphabet, standard punctuation marks, and a variety of special symbols. Same as character set.

temporary font A soft font that is erased when the LaserJet receives a soft reset, $^{E}{}_{C}$E.

thin space A space the width of a period.

toner Fine plastic particles that act as the "ink" for the laser printer.

tracking The spacing of the letters throughout a passage of text. Typically loosened or made tighter to accommodate justification or enhance readability, while still maintaining an overall effect of uniformity.

typeface A particular type design, such as Palatino or Goudy.

WYSIWYG "What You See Is What You Get"; a description of layout programs in which the picture on the screen is an accurate representation of the page that is ultimately printed.

Index

1-2-3
  See Lotus 1-2-3
1040 Solution, 465
1181 WP Terminal, 361
4Print, 366, 465

A

A-Plus Tax 1040, 465
Accelerator boards, 13, 222
Accessories, 406
ACX-PM Printer Manager, 362
Adobe Illustrator, 129
Allied Corporation, 233
Alphabets, 464, 465
Amiga graphics format, 150
ANSI character set, 240
Apricot Laser, 351
Arabic Fonts, 465
The Art of Desktop Publishing, 154
Arts & Letters, 145, 146, 465
  compared with HP Graphics Gallery, 145
Arts and Letters, 142
Artware Graphics Library, 142
Ascender, 489
ASCII, 489
  definition, 243
ASCII character set, 295
  lack of typographical characters, 243
Auto-continue, 20, 23, 24
Auto-T Switch Series, 390
AutoCAD, 106, 107, 466
  use with PageMaker, 185
AutoCAD DXF graphics format
  See DXF graphics format
AUTOEXEC.BAT file, 6, 271
AutoSketch, 111-113, 466
  compared with Windows Draw and GEM Draw Plus, 113
Avery labels, 346

B

B cartridge
  trouble accessing fonts, 410
B cartridge versus F cartridge, 426
Bali Fonts, 454
Ballot box symbol
  adding to a font, 279
Baseline, 237, 489
BASIC, 417
  embedding the escape character, 306
BASIC graphics format, 149
Batch files, 5
  downloading fonts with, 270
Bauer Bodoni Black typeface selection code, 296
BFG4MD, 390
Big Foot Fonts, 454
Bit, 28
Bitmap, 239, 489
Bitmapped graphics, 28, 29
Bitstream Cooper, 255

Bitstream Corporation
  first digital type foundry, 251
Bitstream fonts, 447
Bitstream Fontware. *See* Fontware
Blank pages ejecting, 404
Brainerd, Paul, 153, 183
Broadway, 255
Broadway typeface selection code, 296
BufferPlus, 388
buffers, 386, 388
Burroughs, 360
Buttonware, 363
Byline, 161, 162, 466
  generating forms with, 215
Byte, 28

C

C language, 417
C-Write, 363
Cable extenders, 387, 389
Cables, 4
CAD. *See* computer-aided design
Canon LBP-CX engine, 6, 381
  upgrading with PS Jet Plus, 379
Canon LBP-SX engine, 6, 10, 381
CAPCard, 13, 178, 179, 222, 249, 371, 373, 381, 383, 466
  compared with JLaser, 373
  using with Fontware, 247
Carbon copies, 426
Cartridge fonts, 239
  advantages versus soft fonts, 410
  difference between B and F cartridges, 426
  troubleshooting, 409
Caution
  EP cartridges, 425
  font cartridges, 425
  moving the printer, 425
  transparencies, 425
Centronics parallel interface
  advantages over serial interface, 407
Century Schoolbook, 243, 255
Century Schoolbook typeface selection code, 296
CGA, 324, 329, 333
  screen snapshots, 324
CGM graphics format, 132, 143, 145
Character set, 242, 244, 245, 256, 293, 295, 427, 428, 489
  ASCII, 243
  how to select from the Control Panel, 244
  IBM, 243
  miscellaneous, 245
  of resident fonts, 240
  Roman-8, 243
  seven-bit and eight-bit, 242
  Ventura, 243
Chart Interpreter, 124
Charter, 255
Charting Gallery, 147
Chinese character set, 295
ClickArt Portfolio Series, 142
Clip art, 139-143, 489
  directory of, 142, 143
  included with Windows Designer, 132
Clip Art (Stephens & Associates), 142
Cloister Black, 255
Co-Optic Parallel Sub-LAN Link, 389
Co-Optic Power Share, 390
COBOL, 417
Collaser, 389, 466
Collators, 385, 389
Color Graphics Adapter. *See* CGA
Color separations, 133

Compressed print, 410
Compugraphic Corporation, 247, 248
Compugraphic fonts, 448
CompuServe GIF graphics format, 150
Computer Editype fonts, 448
Computer Linguist, 466
Computer-aided design, 107, 111
Conodesk 6000, 373
Conofonts, 449
Conofonts Manager, 466
CONTINUE/RESET key, 15, 17, 18
Control code, 489
Control Panel, 12, 15-26, 33, 489
  changing to the IBM character set, 322
  selecting character sets, 244
  selecting manual feed, 348
Controller, 489
Convergent Technologies Workstation, 359
Converting graphics files, 331
Cooper Black typeface selection code, 296
Copies, number printed, 19, 22
Coronet Bold typeface selection code, 296
Courier, 255, 277
Courier typeface code, 296
CP/M, 360
CPT, 362
Crooked printout, 405
Crosspoint 8 Group Data Switch, 390

D

Danish, 240, 257, 258
Data Manager I and II Mega Buffer, 390
dBASE, 201-214
  CHR( ) function, 203
  CREATE REPORT command, 206, 207
  embedding the escape character, 306
  label-printing program, 211-214
  label sheets, 210
  memory variables, 204
  output commands, 205
  printing labels, 208, 211
  program for printing labels, 350
  reports, 206
  sample PCL program, 314
  sending the escape character, 203
dBASE II, 203
dBASE III, 203
dBASE IV, 201, 202
  CREATE LABEL command, 209
DBL Software Drivers, 53, 54, 467
DEC VAX, 360
Decorative typefaces, 234
Default font
  changing, 413
  how to change, 19
Descender, 489
Designer, 467. *See* Windows Designer
Designer Clip Art, 142
Desktop Art, 142
Desktop publishing, 153–162
  books, 154
  bulletin boards, 156
  code-based versus WYSIWYG, 159
  magazines, 154
  newsletters, 155
  organizations, 156
Desktop Publishing Dialog, 350
Desktop Publishing With Style, 155
Diablo emulation, 33, 192, 403
Diagraph Arts & Letters, 467
Digitizers, *See* scanners
Dingbats, 234, 280
Dinter, Heintz, 350
Display typefaces, 234

DisplayWrite, *See* IBM DisplayWrite
Dithering, 489
Doctor pin, 416
DOS batch files
  sending the escape character, 306
Download Font Converter, 467
Downloading fonts, 242, 263-268, 489. *See also* fonts, downloading
  speeding with LaserTORQ, 399
  with batch files, 267, 270
Draw programs, 105, 106
Drawing Gallery, 147, 148, 467
Driver, 31, 32, 264, 301, 489
Dutch, 255, 276, 277
DWLaser, 53, 467
DXF graphics format, 113, 132, 137

E

E-Z-Set, 34, 35, 39, 468
Easy Laser, 35, 467
ECMA character set, 256
ECMA-94 character set, 240, 295
EEPROMs, 17
EGA, 275, 324, 329, 333
  screen snapshots, 324
EGA Paint, 149
Eight-bit character sets, 242
Embedded commands, 302
Embedding the escape character, 306
Emulation, 33
  Diablo 630, 43
  Epson, 43, 47, 49
  IBM Graphics Printer, 43
  NEC 3550, 43
  NEC 5510, 43
  NEC 7710, 43
  Qume Sprint V, 43
Emulazer, 361
Encapsulated PostScript, *See* EPS
Enhanced Graphics Adapter, *See* EGA
ENTER key, 21
Envelope printing, 8, 337-343, 406, 411
  jamming, 420
  printing with WordStar 2000, 90
  Shareware utilities, 364
  with MultiMate Advantage, 68
EnvLJ, 341, 364, 366, 467
EP cartridge, 6, 415, 490
  avoiding strong light, 425
  extending life, 415
  life expectancy, 8, 11, 416
  shelf life, 416
  troubleshooting, 415
  when to replace, 423
EPAW, 162, 468
EPS graphics format, 145, 150, 331
Epson emulation, 33, 192, 200, 403
ERMASoft Laser Envelopes, 341, 343, 468
EROFF, 162, 163, 468
Error messages
  Error-40, 413
  Error-50, 77, 414
  Error-54, 413
  PC B5, 77
  PC Load Exec, 77
Escape character, 196, 292, 302
  embedding in an application, 417
  sending from applications, 306
  sending from DOS, 306
  sending to the LaserJet with dBASE, 203
Escape sequences, 30, 203, 302, 427, 490
  compressing, 295, 296
  font selection, 294
ESI-2646 LaserConnection, 361

European character set, 244
Exact, 162, 468
Excel
  merging charts with PageView, 98
Extended type, 235
Extension, 490
EZ-Laser, 35, 468
EZQueue, 386, 391

F

F font cartridge
  support by Ventura, 187
Fancy Font, 468
Fancy Word, 468
Feeder Guide, 415
Fill pattern
  PCL commands, 310
Finnish, 257, 258
First Impression, 162, 468
Floppy Fonts Office Series, 469
Floppy Fonts Professional Series, 469
Fluegelman, Andrew, 363
Font, 490
  changing the default, 19, 413
  Control Panel ID's versus PCL ID's, 25
  default font, 22
  definition, 233
  how to select from the Control Panel, 24
  ID number, 22
  primary versus secondary, 291, 294
Font cartridge escape sequences, 427
Font cartridges, 8, 490
  advantages and drawbacks of, 241
  don't remove when printer is on line, 425
  life expectancy, 424
  maximizing life, 241
  using with PageMaker, 187
  Y cartridge, 322, 323
Font Center fonts, 450
Font Converter, 458
Font downloading. *See also* Downloading
  automatic with Word and Ventura, 242
Font editing
  Publisher's Type Foundry, 283
Font editors, 279, 280, 281, 490
Font Effects, 281, 282, 287-289, 469
font enhancers, 281
Font Factory fonts, 451
Font file naming conventions, 245
Font file, contents of, 239
Font generators, 247-249, 490
Font ID numbers, 412, 490
  troubleshooting, 413
Font versus typeface, 233
Fontastic, 35, 469
Fontasy, 458, 469
FontControl, 265
FontGen IV+, 264, 266, 282, 469
FontLoad, 265, 269, 270, 271, 469
Fontmaker for Windows, 458
FontMaster, 282, 469
Fontpac, 248, 457, 469
Fontrix, 470
Fonts, *See also* Downloading fonts
  Adobe PostScript format, 133
  bit map versus outline, 283
  cartridge, 239
  classifying, 233
  downloadable, 9
  downloading, 242, 263, 264
  downloading with Microsoft Word, 64
  effect of CONTINUE/RESET, 409
  how to select from the Control Panel, 24
  LaserJet II capabilities, 12

  - management codes in PCL, 305
  - maximum number per page, 411
  - measurement of, 235
  - measuring height, 293
  - orientation, 293
  - PCL font creation codes, 310
  - permanent, 18, 19, 20, 21
  - portrait versus landscape orientation, 293
  - primary 291, 294, 427, 491
  - printing reversed type with SLed, 128
  - resident, 17, 239
  - sample printout, 17, 18
  - secondary 291, 294, 427, 491
  - selecting with PCL, 291
  - serif and sans serif, 234
  - size limits in the LaserJet and LaserJet Plus, 12
  - storage locations, 239
  - storage requirements, 256
  - style, 293
  - trademarks, 233
  - using Halo DPE for headlines, 120
  - weight, 293
- Fonts on the Fly, 248, 249
- Fontware, 116, 179, 247-258, 263, 447, 470
  - font size limits, 256
  - generating PostScript fonts, 253
  - LaserMaster CAPCard compiler, 383
  - screen fonts, 252, 276
  - selecting a character set, 256, 258
  - using with PageMaker, 187
  - using with WordPerfect, 76
- Foreign character sets, 90, 240, 242, 257, 258, 295, 428
- FORM FEED key, 19, 21, 403
- Form Length, 22
- Form Set, 470
- Form Tool, 216, 471
- FormEasy, 216, 470
- FormMaker II, 216, 470
- Forms, 215-220
- Forms Flipper, 389, 470
- Forms Library Disks, 217
- Forms Manager DB, 216, 470
- FormScan, 216
- Formworx, 216, 471
- FORTRAN, 417
- Four Channel Buffer, 391
- FreeWare, 363
- French, 240, 244, 257, 258, 295
- Front Page Personal Publisher, 162, 471
- Futura Book, 255
- Futura Light, 255
- Futura Medium, 255

- Garamond, 243, *See also* ITC Garamond
- GBT printer interfaces, 361
- GEM, 115, 116
- GEM Desktop Publisher, 162, 471
- GEM Draw
  - Business Library, 117
  - compared with Windows Draw, 135
  - generating forms with, 215
  - using with Ventura Publisher, 117
- GEM Draw graphics format, 132, 137
- GEM Draw Plus, 115, 116, 117, 140, 471
  - compared with HP Drawing Gallery, 116
  - compared with Windows Draw, 115-117
  - using with Ventura Publisher, 116
- GEM graphics environment, 170
  - compared with Microsoft Windows, 183
  - using with Fontware, 247
- GEM graphics format, See GEM Draw or GEM IMG graphics format

GEM IMG graphics file format, 127, 149, 331
GEM Paint graphics format
  See GEM IMG graphics format
Gender changers, 5
GEnie network, 156
German, 244, 257, 258, 295
Glowstx Tax Processing System, 471
Glyphix, 248, 259-262, 461, 471
Glyphix Font Manager for Microsoft Word, 265
Glyphix Font Manager for WordPerfect, 265
Glyphix Pop 'n Print, 248
GNU custom font cartridges, 241, 472
GPA Soft Font Generator, 248, 451, 472
GrabPlus, 341, 364-366, 472
Gradco/CTI fonts, 451
GrafPlus, 324, 333, 334, 472
  memory requirements, 327
Graphics
  as text, 32
  bitmapped, 28, 29
  maximum size, 9
  memory requirements for full page, 408
  memory requirements of, 107
  object-oriented, 28, 30
  PCL commands, 313
Graphics conversion programs, 132, 149, 150
Graphics Gallery, 142, 147, 148, 472
The Graphics Link, 149, 150, 472
Graphics software, 105
  draw programs, 105-107
  memory requirements of, 107
  paint programs, 105
Greek character sets, 295

H

Halo DPE, 119-121, 473
  compared with PC Paintbrush, 119
  compared with Publisher's Paintbrush, 119
  GRAB graphics capture utility, 120
  using with scanners, 120
Halo DPE graphics format, 149
Header, 490
Headline Typefaces, 243
Helv, 243
Helv typeface code, 296
Helvetica, 235, 255, 277
Hercules Graphics Card, 324, 329, 333
  screen snapshots, 324
Hewlett-Packard
  Direct Marketing Division, 406
  FontLoad, 265
  font naming convention, 246
  fonts, 452
  ScanJet, 108
High Resolution Image Libraries, 142
High-bit characters, 243
HiJaak, 150, 324, 327, 473
  memory requirements, 327
Horizontal Motion Index (HMI), 304
Horizontal spacing, 427
Hotshot Grab, 324, 329, 331, 473
  memory requirements, 327
Hotshot Graphics, 149, 324, 325, 329, 332, 473
Hotshot's WINGRAB utility
  memory requirements, 327
HP Laser Program, 473
HPGL emulation, 380
HPGL graphics format
  compatibility with PageMaker, 185

I

I.S.C. fonts, 454
IBM 370, 362
IBM character set, 240, 243, 244, 257, 258
  selecting with the Control Panel, 322
IBM Color Graphics Adapter
  See CGA
IBM DisplayWrite, 53
  merging graphics with text, 101
IBM DisplayWriter, 361
IBM Enhanced Graphics Adapter
  See EGA
IBM line-drawing character set, 408
IBM mainframes, 361
IBM PC character set, 240, 243, 244, 257, 258
IBM Systems 34/36/38, 361
IBM Video Graphics Adapter, *See* VGA
IMG graphics format, *See* GEM IMB graphics format
In*A*Vision, 185
Input paper tray, 8
Input/output, 23
Inset, 88, 95, 96, 327, 328, 473
Intellifont, 247, 448
Interface, how to change, 20
Interlynx/5251, 362
IPrint, 217, 225-227
IQ Engineering, 241
IRMAPrint, 362
IRV character set, 295
ISO foreign language character sets, 295
Italian, 244, 257, 258, 295
Italic, 490
ITC Avant Garde, 255
ITC Galliard, 255
ITC Garamond, 243, 255
ITC Garamond typeface selection code, 296
ITC Korinna, 255
ITC Souvenir, 255

J

James River Corporation labels, 346
Janus Associates fonts, 454
Jet-Set, 36, 474
JetFeed I and III, 394
JetFont 123, 241
JetNET/4+1, 386, 391, 474
JetScript, 14, 129, 179, 253, 371, 373, 375-377, 474
JetSet, 474
JetSet II, 36, 41, 474
JetSpool, 388
JIS ASCII character set, 295
JLaser Plus, 179, 371, 372, 373, 474
  compared with CAPCard, 372
  using with Fontware, 247
Job offset, 412
The Juggler, 391
Justification, 236, 490

K

Katakana character set, 295
Kerning, 236, 490
Kyocera F-1010, 351

L

Label sheets, 345-350
  manual versus automatic feeding, 347
  printing with dBASE, 208, 350
  sample program, 209-214
Lacerte Tax Preparation Software 1040, 474
Landscape orientation, 293
  printing compressed type, 410
  problems printing a graphic, 409
  trouble selecting, 423
  versus portrait orientation, 426
Lanier, 362
Laser Bat, 36, 475
Laser Connection ESI-1312, 54, 475
Laser Fonts, 37, 76, 265, 273, 475
Laser Graphics, 274
Laser Helper, 359
Laser Optimizer, 360
Laser Press, 162, 475
Laser Print Plus, 164, 476
Laser printers
  similarity to personal computers, 371
Laser Word Processor Tool Kit, 266, 477
Laser-Set, 164
LaserBoard, 386, 391
LaserConnection ESI-1312, 54, 475
LaserControl, 34, 36, 43-45, 192, 200, 475
LaserFeeder, 394
LaserFile Plus, 359
Laserific, 37, 475
LaserJet
  activating defaults, 24, 25
  bit-mapped graphics mode, 29
  configuring the printer, 4, 5, 6
  controller, 30
  doctor pin, 416
  Feeder Guide, 415
  introduction of, 7
  life expectancy, 6
  macros, 222
  manuals, 4
  maximum fonts per page, 411
  memory, 8, 108
  memory upgrades, 8, 408
  moving, 425
  paper recommendations, 414
  ports, 8
  print quality, 8, 414
  printing slower than 8 pages per minute, 406
  raster graphics, 29
  ROM, 239
  setting page parameters, 33
  speeding up, 425
  supplies, 406
  switching interfaces, 407
  text mode, 28
  unprintable area, 406
  using with other computers, 359
  weight of, 8
LaserJet (original model)
  features of, 8
  resident fonts, 240
  unable to use soft fonts, 241
LaserJet 2000, 7
LaserJet 500 Plus, 7, 9, 412
  accessing second paper tray, 412
  job offset, 412
LaserJet enhancements
  buffers and spoolers, 386, 388
  cable extenders, 387, 389
  collators, 385, 389
  output bins, 389
  paper feeders, 385
  printer-sharing devices, 386, 390
  sheet feeders, 394
LaserJet family

features comparison, 8
LaserJet II, 7, 9, 412
accessing the two menu levels, 413
amount of memory available for fonts, 268
design accomodates expansion, 371
features of, 8, 9, 10
fonts, 12
I/O slot, 386
memory upgrades, 12
overcoming memory limitations with LaserTORQ, 399
paper handling, 11
resident fonts, 17, 240, 412
resident foreign language characters, 242
warmup speed, 11
LaserJet Plus, 7, 9
features of, 8
font size limit, 12, 256, 268
memory, 7, 9
memory available for fonts, 268
overcoming memory limitations with LaserTORQ, 399
printing envelopes, 343
resident fonts, 240
LaserJet Printer Specifications Guide, 345
LaserJet Printer Technical Reference Manual, 318
LaserJet series II, *See* LaserJet II
LaserMaster CAPCard, *See* CAPCard
LaserMaster fonts, 455
LaserMate 500, 362
LaserNet-A, 359
LaserPlotter, 409, 475
LaserScript, 159, 164, 165, 476
Lasersoft/PC, 217, 229, 230
Laserstart, 356, 357
Lasertex Electronic Forms Tools, 217
LaserTORQ, 376, 387, 397-399
LaserType, 164, 477
Laserware, 477
LaserWord, 477
Last page, how to print, 21
LBI, 362
Leader characters, 490
Leading, 236, 491
LeBaugh Software fonts, 455
Left justification, 236
Legal character set, 245, 257, 258
Legal paper, 91
LePrint, 477
LePrint fonts, 455
Letter Gothic, 255
Letter Gothic typeface code, 296
LETTer spacing, 491
Lexitron, 362
Line Draw font, 245
Line Printer typeface code, 296
Lines per page
how to change, 20
LJBook, 365, 366, 477
The Logical Connection, 392
Logos On-Line, 142
Long-Link Parallel Extension 7,000 Feet, 390
Looking Good in Print, 155
Loose lines, 236
Lotica, 241
Lotus 1-2-3, 191-199
embedding formatting codes, 193
embedding the escape character, 307
enhancing graphics with Chart Interpreter, 124
fixing wobbly columns, 196
graphics limitations, 44, 50
Phoenix drivers, 198
printer setup strings, 194, 195
PrintGraph, 50, 198, 200
printing the last page of a spreadsheet, 193
using with PageMaker, 185
using with Ventura Publisher, 196

Lotus Manuscript, *See* Manuscript
Lotus WKS files, *See* WKS files, 196

M

Mac PICT graphics format, 132
MacGraphics 2.0 (for the PC), 142
Macintosh, 355-357
  lack of LaserJet drivers, 355
  printing graphics on the LaserJet, 355
  printing text on the LaserJet, 356
MacMemories Series, 143
MacPaint graphics format, 149, 150
Macros, 9, 222, 317, 491
  Printer Command Language, 311
MacScan Page Scanning System, 478
Magic, 478
Magic Font, 448
MagicSeries, 164, 282, 478
Manual feed, 8, 22, 405
  selecting with the Control Panel, 348
  turning off and on, 19
Manuals, 4
Manuscript, 164, 167, 478
  using with Fontware, 247
Margin creep, 404
Master Tax, 478
MasterLink, 392
Math character sets, 295
Math8 character set, 245
MCS Group Printer Driver, 360
Mechanical switch boxes, 425
Mega-Link, 392
Memomaker, 417
Memory, 7, 9, 13
Memory upgrades, 8, 12, 408
Memory-resident programs, 34
Menar Tech International fonts, 456
MENU key, 19, 22, 23
Merging text and graphics, 48, 93, 94
Metro Software fonts, 457
Micom, 362
Micro Image Printing System, 360
Micrografx Windows Designer, *See* Windows Designer
Micrografx Windows Draw, *See* Windows Draw
Microsoft Windows, 145, 146, 158, 183, 277, 351-353, 478
  Clipboard, 98, 129
  installing LaserJet, 351
  installing soft fonts, 352, 353
  PageView, 97
  PC Paintbrush Windows version, 124
  screen fonts, 275
  screen snapshots, 325
  speeding up printing with LaserTORQ, 399
  using the Clipboard for screen snapshots, 324
  using with cartridge fonts, 352
  WIN.INI, 353
Microsoft Word, 55-57, 60, 157, 264
  automatic font downloading, 242
  creating new drivers, 62
  DAT files, 62
  drivers, 264
  generating forms with, 215
  Glyphix MS Word Font Manager, 248, 259
  LaserJet drivers, 63
  MERGEPRD, 62
  merging graphics with Laser Graphics, 274
  merging graphics with text, 101
  PRD files, 62
  printing envelopes, 340
  style sheets not working, 421
  turning off auto-downloading, 64
  using with FontControl, 265

using with FontLoad, 265
using with Fontware, 247
using with Glyphix MS Word font manager, 248
using with Laser Fonts, 273
using with Laser Word Processor Tool Kit, 266
using with LaserMaster Fonts-on-the-Fly, 249
using with PageView, 97, 325
using with SLed, 127
using with Ventura Publisher, 173
MicroTex, 159, 161, 164, 479
MODE command, 5, 6
not working, 421
Moniterm monitors
using with Fontware, 247
Monospacing versus proportional spacing, 235
Motorola 68000 microprocessor, 371
Moving the LaserJet, 425
MP-XL, 164
MS-DOS 3.2 problems, 407
MultiFeeder, 394
MultiMate Advantage II, 67, 69, 479
embedding the escape character, 307
merging graphics with text, 101
printing envelopes, 340
using with Ventura Publisher, 173
Multiplan
embedding the escape character, 308

N

NADTP Journal, 156
NADTP RoundTable, 156
National Association of Desktop Publishers, 156
NBI, 361
News Master, 164, 479
The Newsroom Pro, 166, 479
Norwegian, 240, 257, 258, 295
Novell Network, 266

Object graphics, 28, 30, 491
Obliqued type, 235
OCR character sets, 295
Office Automation Systems fonts, 457
Office Publisher, 166, 479
generating forms with, 215
Office Series Typefaces, 458
OfficePower Integrated Office System, 360
ON LINE key, 17, 18, 244
Optima typeface selection code, 296
Orientation, 293, 427
Outline font, 491
Output paper tray, 8

P

Page Perfect, 166, 480
PageMaker, 146, 153, 157-161, 166, 183-187, 253, 480
compared with Ventura Publisher, 158
creating graphics with Windows Designer, 131
drawing tools, 186, 187
formatting text, 185
generating forms with, 215
importing graphics, 185
importing text, 185
Soft Font Installer, 183, 188
special features, 187
using with font cartridges, 187

using with Fontware, 187, 247
using with WYSIfonts!, 277
PageMaker
screen fonts, 277
PagePerfect
using with Fontware, 247
PageView, 97, 98, 99, 480
PageWriter, 166, 480
paint programs, 105, 108
Pamphlet, 365, 366, 480
Paper, 414
recommended type, 415
using same pages twice, 424
Paper Feeders, 385
Paper handling, 11
Paper jams, 419, 420
Paper sizes, 405
Paper tray
accessing second tray in LaserJet 500 Plus, 412
PaperJet 400, 395
Parallel interface, 4, 491
advantage over serial interface, 407
switching to serial interface, 407
Pascal, 417
PC B5, 77
PC Em-U-Print, 480
PC Load Exec, 77
PC Paint Plus graphics format, 149
PC Paintbrush, 123-126, 325
compared with Halo DPE, 119
compared with SLed, 128
converting PCX graphics files, 150
editing screen snapshots, 325
PC Paintbrush
Frieze screen snapshot utility, 324
PC Paintbrush Designer Series, 124
PC Paintbrush Plus, 124, 480
PC Publisher Kit, 373
PC Quik-Art, 141, 143, 149, 481
PC Tex, 159, 161, 166
PC World, 363
PC-8 character set, 295
PC-File, 363
PC-Write, 481
PC/Professional Tax Partner, 481
PCL, See Printer Command Language
PCLPak, 480
PCS Director, 360
PCX graphics format, 123, 124, 127, 139, 143, 149, 325, 331
Perforation Skip, 304
Peripheral Sharing Device, 392
Permanent fonts, 18-21, 491
versus temporary fonts, 267
Personal Publishing magazine, 154
PFS: First Publisher, 161, 166, 481
PFS:Write
embedding the escape character, 308
Pi Font character set, 245, 295
Pi Fonts, 234
PIC graphics format, 124, 132
Pica, 235, 491
Pitch
changing from 10 pitch to 12 pitch, 411
Pixel, 491
Pizazz Plus, 324, 325, 327, 481
Point (defined), 491
Point sizes, 235
Polaris Crunch, 101, 481
Polaris Font Control, 481
Polaris Forms, 217, 481
Polaris LabelMaker, 349, 481
Polaris PrintMerge, 81, 481
Polaris RAM-Resident PrintMerge, 54, 93, 101, 102, 481
Polaris Setup Utility, 481
Polaris Symbol Sheet, 349, 481
Port, 491

Portrait orientation, 293, 491
Portrait versus landscape mode, 426
Portuguese character set, 240, 295
PostScript, 108, 129, 135, 253, 491
  adding to LaserJet, 371
  clone boards, 372
  compared with PCL, 372
  JetScript, 375, 380
  proofing with CAPCard, 383
  PS Jet Plus, 379
  speed tips, 376
Power 5/32, 360
PowerText Formatter, 166, 482
PPC Tex, 481
Presentations typeface selection code, 296
Prestige, 255
Prestige typeface selection code, 296
Previewing documents, 97, 157
Primary font, 291, 294, 427, 491
Prime Computer, 359
Print buffers, 386
PRINT FONTS key, 18
Print Master Printer Controllers, 393
Print quality, 11, 414
Print screen. *See* screen snapshots
Print Spoolers. *See* spoolers
Printdirector MS-1 and MS-10, 392
Printer buffer, 403
Printer Command Language, 15, 30, 108, 196, 301
  categories of commands, 303
  compared with PostScript, 372
  cursor positioning commands, 304
  debugging, 311
  font creation codes, 310
  font management commands, 305
  font selection, 305
  graphics commands, 310, 313
  horizontal cursor positioning, 304
  job control commands, 303
  limitations for graphics, 108
  line termination options, 304
  macros, 222, 311, 317
  page control commands, 303
  push/pop cursor, 305
  selecting fonts, 291-297
  vertical cursor positioning, 305
Printer Driver for Wang PC, 360
Printer engine, 8
Printer Marshall, 37, 482
Printer Optimizer,392, 482
Printer-sharing devices, 386, 390
Printer-Sharing Hardware CA-4 Family, 393
PrintGraph, *See* Lotus 1-2-3
Printility, 37, 482
PrintMaster graphics format, 150
PrintQ, 388
Printrix, 168, 482
PrintStar, 360, 482
Printworks for the Mac/Laser Version, 356, 357, 482
Printworks for the PC/Laser Version, 34, 37, 47, 48, 343, 482
Pro-Tech labels, 346
Problems, *See* Troubleshooting
Professional Series Typefaces, 458
Profont Editing System, 282, 482
Proportional spacing, 235, 491
Prosoft fonts, 458
PS Jet Plus, 129, 371, 373, 379, 380, 483
PS Portfolio, 143
Publish! magazine, 154
Publisher's Paintbrush, 107, 125, 126, 480
  compared with Halo DPE, 119
  Frieze screen snapshot utility, 324
Publisher's PicturePaks, 143, 483
Publisher's Type Foundry, 279, 281, 283-286, 483

compared with SoftCraft Font Editor, 281
using fonts with Publisher's Paintbrush, 126
Publishing From the Desktop, 155

Q

Q&A, 483
QMS JetScript, *See* JetScript
QROFF, 360
QuadLaser, 351
Questions
see troubleshooting, 404
QuickSoft, 363
Qume Corporation fonts, 458
Quotation marks
adding true typographic quote marks to a font, 279

R

Ragged justification, 491
RAM, 492
RAM-Resident Printmerge, 481
RAM-resident software, 492
Rapid, 361
Raster, 27
Raster graphics, 310, 316, 492
Raytheon, 362
Read only memory. *See* ROM, 239
ReadyPort, 393
Rectangles
PCL codes, 310
RESET key, 17
RESET MENU key, 22
Resident fonts, 240, 492. *See also* Fonts, resident
Resolution of the printer
changing with PCL, 316
Right justification, 236
Rightray, 389
RIP, 492
Robox Print Extenders, 390
ROM, 239, 492
Roman Extension character set, 244, 258, 295
Roman type, definition of, 235
Roman-8 character set, 243, 257, 258, 295
Rotating graphics
in Windows Designer, 131
Rounded type, 235
RS232C communications, 5
Rule, 492
Runoff, 41, 42

S

Sans serif fonts, 234, 492
preference in Europe for, 234
Scaling, 492
ScanJet, 108
Scanned images
tracing in Windows Designer, 131
Scanners, 108
SLed, 128
using with Halo DPE, 120
using with Publisher's Paintbrush, 126
using with Windows Designer, 129
ScenicWriter, 168, 483
scLaserPlus, 168, 483
Screen fonts, 252, 275, 276
generating with Fontware, 253

relation to printer fonts, 243
Screen snapshots, 45, 321, 408, 492
controlling parameters, 325
file formats, 325
GrafPlus, 333
Hotshot Graphics, 329
memory requirements, 327
text screens, 321, 322
utilities, 324
with Orbit Font 10, 324
with Y cartridge, 323
SDP Font Library, 484
Secondary font, 291, 294, 427, 492
Serial Automatic Scanner, 393
Serial interface, 4, 5, 492
switching to parallel interface, 407
Serif fonts, 234, 492
preference in the United States for, 234
Service dealers, 406
SetLaser, 41
Setup commands, 302
versus embedded commands, 301, 302
Setup utilities, 33, 34, 35, 492
Seven-bit character sets, 242
The Seybold Report on Desktop Publishing, 155
Shading
PCL command, 310
ShareSpool, 386, 393
Shareware, 363-367
Sheet feeders, 394
SideKick
embedding the escape character, 308
printing envelopes, 338
SLD graphics file format, 113
SLed, 127, 128, 149, 484
compared with PC Paintbrush, 128
Soft Font Disks, 484
Soft fonts, 241, 245, 246, 492. *See also* Fonts, downloading
advantages and disadvantages of, 241
automatic downloading of, 242
Hewlett-Packard sets, 243
naming conventions, 246
versus cartridge fonts, 410
Soft reset (Escape E)
sending with the Control Panel, 267
SoftCraft character set, 257, 258
SoftCraft Font Editor, 279-282, 484
compared with Publisher's Type Foundry, 281
SoftCraft font naming convention, 246
SoftCraft fonts, 459
Spacing, 293
Spanish, 240, 244, 257, 258, 295
Specific Solutions fonts, 460
Speeding up the printer, 425
Spellbinder Art Library, 143
Spellbinder Desktop Publisher, 168, 266, 484
Spoolers, 386, 388
LaserTORQ, 397
Status panel, 8
Straightforward fonts, 461
Style sheet
Microsoft Word, 61
Style sheet formatting, 157
Super Cartridge, 241
SuperPage, 168
SuperPrint, 168
SW2-HP1/SW3-HP1, 393
Swedish, 240, 257, 258, 295
SWFTE International fonts, 461
Swiss, 255, 276, 277
Swiss Light, 255
Switchboxes, 390
danger of using mechanical switchboxes, 414, 425
Symbol font, 245
Symbol set, 23, 242, 492
how to change the default, 20

of resident fonts, 240
Symbol typeface, 277
Symphony, 198
enhancing charts with Chart Interpreter, 124
graphics limitations, 44
Systematic Printer-Sharing System, 394
Systemizer Printer-Sharing System, 394

T

Tabin, 197, 484
Tagged Image File Format. *See* TIFF graphics format
Tax preparation software, 220-223
directory, 222
Tax Refund System, 485
Tax Resources 1120, 485
Tax Resources Ten40, 485
Temporary fonts, 492
versus permanent fonts, 267
TEST key, 21
Text as graphics, 32
Thin space, 492
TIFF graphics format, 149, 150, 331
compatibility with PageMaker, 185
Tiling, 187
Times Roman, 235, 255, 277
Tms Rmn typeface selection code, 296
TmsRmn, 243
Toner, 492
darkness of, 8, 11
Toner cartridges
See EP cartridges
Toner intensity, 8, 11
Tracking, 493
Trademark symbols
adding to a font, 279
Transparencies, 425
Transparent print, 305
Troubleshooting
accessing fonts from the Control Panel, 412
blank pages ejecting, 404
blank pages printing, 421
breaking a graphic between pages, 409
cartridge font not working, 409
changing the default font, 413
control codes not working, 421
creeping margin, 404
crooked printout, 405
dark vertical smear, 414
envelopes, 406
envelopes jamming, 420
EP cartridges, 415
Error 40, 413
Error 50, 414
Error 54, 413
escape sequence not working, 417
first line not printing, 420
font ID numbers, 413
landscape mode not working, 423
last page of document missing, 423
Word style sheets not working, 421
missing text at edge of sheet, 406
MODE commands not working, 421
MS-DOS 3.2, 407
nothing happending, 419
nothing printing, 404
only a few lines printing on each page, 423
pages breaking in the wrong place, 420
parts of control codes being printed, 423
positioning graphics, 421
print fading from left to right, 416
printer freezes when computer reboots, 422
printer ignores control codes, 423
printer won't switch to bold, 422

printing bold with Memomaker, 417
problem accessing fonts, 410
problem printing envelopes, 411
problem selecting fonts with Control Panel, 412
problem switching from italics to bold, 410
problem with landscape graphics, 409
problem with right margin alignment, 411
problems with fonts, 409
problems with graphics, 408
recurring paper jam, 419
service dealers, 406
vertical smears, 414
vertical streaks, 420
weird symbols, 422
white blanks or black stripes, 420
white stripes or faint areas, 420
wrong line spacing, 422
TSR. *See* Memory-resident programs
TurboFonts, 485
Type. *See* Fonts, Typefaces
Type Director, 247, 248, 448
Type family, 235
Type Weights, 235
Typeface, 427, 493
decorative, 234
definition, 233
display, 234
groups, 234
selection codes, 296
specifying with PCL, 293
versus font, 233
Typography, 233-236
justification, 236
kerning, 236
leading, 236
loose lines, 236
measurement units, 235
monospacing versus proportional spacing, 235
pitch, 236
type families, 235
word and character spacing, 235

United Kingdom character set, 240, 257, 258, 295
Universal Printer Buffer, 389
University Roman, 255, 296
Unlocking the LaserJet with Lotus 1-2-3, 198
Unprintable area, 348, 406
USASCII character set, 256

VAX, 360
Vector graphics, 409
Ventura character set, 243, 244
Ventura Publisher, 158, 159, 161, 168-180, 253
adding new fonts, 179
automatic font downloading, 242
compared with PageMaker, 158
drivers, 264
frames, 172
generating forms with, 215
graphics capabilities, 175, 176
high-speed driver for CAPCard, 383
importing graphics from Windows Draw, 137
LaserMaster Fonts-on-the-Fly, 249
pagination and typography, 176
performance on AT versus XT, 170
preparing graphics with Windows Designer, 131
screen fonts, 275, 277
symbol font, 245

using with GEM Draw Plus, 116, 117
using with JetScript, 179
using with Lotus 1-2-3, 196
using with the LaserJet, 178
using with the LaserMaster CAPCard, 178
using with upgraded LaserJets, 179
using with WYSIfonts!, 277
WID files, 264
word processor compatibility, 173
Ventura Tips and Tricks, 169
Vertical Motion Index (VMI), 304
VGA, 275, 324, 329
screen snapshots, 324
Video Graphics Adapter. *See* VGA
Visual Forms, 217, 485
VM/SP operating system, 361
VMI, 304
Volkswriter
embedding the escape character, 308
merging graphics with text, 101
Volts Tax Preparation & Planning, 485
VP International character set, 256
VP US character set, 256
VP/Base, 485
VP/Fonts, 181, 485
VP/Saddle, 485
VP/Tabs, 197
VP220 Printer Buffer, 394
VPMail, 349, 350
VS Library of Fonts, 485
VS Software, 264
VS Software fonts, 462
VS Ventura Supplemental FontPak, 180, 181

Wang, 359, 360
Wang PC Word Processing, 360
Weaver Graphics fonts, 463
WID files, 264
WIN.INI file, 353
Windows. *See* Microsoft Windows
Windows Convert, 137
Windows Designer, 129-133, 486
compared with Windows Draw, 129, 135
Windows Draw, 135, 137, 478, 486
compared with GEM Draw, 135
compared with Designer, 129, 135
generating forms with, 215
importing into Ventura, 137
using with PageMaker, 185
Windows Paint, 149
using with PageMaker, 185
WINGRAB, 331
WKS files, 196
Word. *See* Microsoft Word
Word Processor Tool Kit, 264
WordPerfect, 71-77, 157, 161, 264
desktop publishing with, 159
drivers, 264
embedding the escape character, 308
generating forms with, 215
Glyphix WordPerfect Font Manager, 259
making screen shots using GRAB, 326
memory requirements of GRAB, 327
merging graphics with Laser Graphics, 274
merging graphics with text, 93, 101
printing envelopes, 340
screen snapshot utility, 324
using with FontLoad, 265
using with Fontware, 247

using with Glyphix WordPerfect Font Manager, 248
using with Laser Fonts, 273
using with Laser Word Processor Tool Kit, 266
using with SLed, 127
using with Ventura Publisher, 173
WordPerfect 5: Desktop Publishing in Style, 74
WordStar, 80
embedding the escape character, 309
merging graphics with text, 101
patching WordStar 3.3, 81
using with Ventura Publisher, 173
WordStar 2000, 85, 87, 325
comparison with Microsoft Word, 87
drivers, 264
foreign characters, 90
formatting columns, 88
hyphenation in, 89
merging graphics with text, 93, 101
printing envelopes, 90
screen snapshot utility, 324
using with FontControl, 265
WordStar 2000 Plus, 486
Wyse 700, 329
WYSIfonts!, 180, 276, 277, 278, 486
quality of screen fonts, 278
WYSIWYG, 157, 159, 275, 493

Xerox Ventura Publisher. *See* Ventura Publisher
Xerox Writer
using with Ventura Publisher, 173
XVP/Tabs, 197, 485
XyWrite
embedding the escape character, 309
merging graphics with text, 101

Y font cartridge, 322, 327, 408

Z

Z Director, 487
Z-Font Series, 461
Z-System, 360
Zapf Calligraphic, 255
Zapf Humanist, 255

More from Peachpit Press . . .

Ventura Tips and Tricks

by Ted Nace

Unlike most computer books, *Ventura Tips and Tricks* does not attempt to recapitulate the manual. Instead, it's a fresh approach to the challenge of giving people mastery of a hard-to-learn piece of software. The book contains something for everyone: simple tutorials for the novice, and a wealth of fantastic hints, tricks, and shortcuts for intermediate and advanced users.

Looking Good in Print

by Roger Parker (Ventana Press)

If you're like most desktop publishers, you want to produce better-looking documents without becoming a professional graphic artist. *Looking Good in Print* shows you how to apply proven design techniques to create appealing, persuasive printed material. The book uses "before" and "after" examples to teach the elements of good design.

WordPerfect 5: Desktop Publishing in Style

by Daniel Will-Harris

The most popular word processing program in the world, WordPerfect has recently been upgraded with font and graphics capabilities that bring it into direct competition with page layout programs like Ventura Publisher, PageMaker, and ByLine. *WordPerfect 5: Desktop Publishing in Style* tells how to use the new features of WordPerfect to create illustrated documents like financial reports, presentations, flyers, catalogs, invitations, forms, and label sheets. Numerous humorous examples make the book fun to read, but the author also provides a wealth of technical information not found anywhere else.

IBM AT Clone Buyer's Guide and Handbook

by Edwin Rutsch (Modular Information Systems)

For AT clone owners and people who wish to take advantage of this dollar-saving alternative to the IBM AT, this book is both a buyer's guide and a computer owner's reference. It gives comprehensive information on clone computers in the $800 to $2000 price range. Also included are instructions for upgrading an existing XT to an AT.

IBM 386 Computer Buyer's Guide and Handbook

by Edwin Rutsch (Modular Information Systems)

Like the *AT Clone Buyer's Guide*, this book tells you how to save money purchasing a computer with the Intel 80386 advanced microprocessor. Includes instructions for upgrading an existing computer.

Order Form:

Mail to Peachpit Press or call 415/527-8555 to order direct.
Dealers: please ask for quantity discount schedule.

Quantity	Item	Unit Price	Total
	LaserJet Unlimited, Edition II	$24.95	
	Ventura Tips and Tricks	18.95	
	Looking Good in Print	23.95	
	WordPerfect 5: Desktop Publishing in Style	19.95	
	IBM AT Clone Buyer's Guide and Handbook	24.95	
	386 Computer Buyer's Guide and Handbook	29.95	

Tax of 6.5% applies to California residents only.
U.S. shipping (UPS): $3.50 first item, $.50 each additional. UPS 2nd day is $7.00 first item, $1 each additional.
Canadian shipping (air mail): $5.00 first item, $1.00 each additional.
Overseas shipping (air mail): $10.00 each item.

Subtotal	
Tax	
Shipping/handling	
Total	

Name	
Company	
Address	
City	
State	Zip

Check ____ Visa ____ MasterCard ____ COD ____

Card Number	
Card Holder	
Expiration Date	Phone Number

PEACHPIT PRESS
1085 Keith Ave.
Berkeley, CA 94708
415/527-8555